Nicolai N. Petro
The Tragedy of Ukraine

De Gruyter Contemporary Social Sciences

Volume 9

Nicolai N. Petro

The Tragedy of Ukraine

What Classical Greek Tragedy Can Teach Us About
Conflict Resolution

DE GRUYTER

ISBN 978-3-11-074324-1
e-ISBN (PDF) 978-3-11-074337-1
e-ISBN (EPUB) 978-3-11-074347-0
ISSN 2747-5689

Library of Congress Control Number: 2022944100

Bibliographic information published by the Deutsche Nationalbibliothek
The Deutsche Nationalbibliothek lists this publication in the Deutsche Nationalbibliografie;
detailed bibliographic data are available on the internet at http://dnb.dnb.de.

© 2023 Walter de Gruyter GmbH, Berlin/Boston
Cover image: maxsyd / iStock / Getty Images Plus
Printing and binding: CPI books GmbH, Leck

www.degruyter.com

—

Justice tilts the scale to give learning to those who suffer.

Aeschylus, *Agamemnon*, 250.

Contents

List of Figures and Tables —— IX

Acknowledgements —— XI

Introduction —— XIII

A Note on Transliteration —— XVII

Chapter One
What Does Athens Have to Do with Kiev? —— 1
1.1   The *Dionysia:* Classical Greek Theater as a Political Institution —— 3
1.2   How Tragedy Created Better Citizens —— 5
1.3   How Modern Politics Lost Sight of Tragedy —— 11
1.4   Tragedy and the Limits of Modern Political Realism —— 16
1.5   What Tragedy Has to Offer Modern Politics —— 21
1.6   Applying Tragedy's Untapped Potential to Ukraine —— 31

Chapter Two
Two Nations in One State —— 36
2.1   Debating the Origins of Rus —— 37
2.2   How Ukraine Joined the Russian Empire —— 40
2.3   Maloross Ukraine under Russian Rule: Shulgin vs. Hrushevsky —— 44
2.4   Galician Ukraine under Austro-Hungarian Rule: The Political
        Debate —— 48
2.5   Maloross and Galician Responses to the Collapse of Empire —— 51
2.6   1991: A Flawed Independence —— 70

Chapter Three
The Fatal Attraction of the Far Right —— 90
3.1   The Parliamentary Far Right: Svoboda (Freedom Party) —— 91
3.2   The Extra-Parliamentary Far Right: The Right Sector —— 94
3.3   The Maidan in Power: Mainstreaming the Far Right —— 106
3.4   Searching for a Better Nationalism —— 120

Chapter Four
The Mental Habits of Nationalism —— 124
4.1   Patriotism versus Nationalism —— 129
4.2   The Nationalist Struggle to Vaccinate Ukraine —— 136
4.3   The Consequences of Economic Nationalism —— 142
4.4   Jacob and Esau in Ukraine: Culture and Religion as Sources of Social
         Disunity —— 163

Chapter Five
The Tragedies of Crimea and Donbass —— 174
5.1   Crimea's Quest for Autonomy —— 178
5.2   The Donbass Difference —— 201
5.3   Is There No Escape from Tragedy? —— 220

Chapter Six
A Flawed Peace —— 223
6.1   From Geneva to Minsk: Why Peace Failed —— 224
6.2   Domestic Peace Proposals —— 235
6.3   How Cleft Societies Can Be Made Whole —— 247
6.4   Truth and Reconciliation: A Model for Ukraine? —— 253
6.5   Afterword: The Lessons of Tragedy —— 265

Index —— 275

List of Figures and Tables

Map 2.1:   Electoral Divisions in Ukraine (1994–2019).
Figure 4.1: Private Transfers to Ukraine Compared to FDI in Billions of USD (2012–2017).
Figure 5.1: Regions Asked "What is Your Homeland?" (January 2013).
Table 2.1: Percentage of the Electorate Approving the 1991 "Act of Independence."
Table 2.2: How Important for Ukraine Is the Problem of Developing the Ukrainian Language? (September 2020).
Table 3.1: President Petro Poroshenko on the Ukrainian Fifth Column.
Table 3.2: Ukrainian Officials on the Treasonous Nature of Maloross Ukrainians.
Table 4.1: The Cycle of Tragedy and Healing.
Table 4.2: Ukraine's Projected Debt Repayment Schedule (2019).
Table 4.3: Number of Ukrainians Receiving Russian Citizenship (2017–2020).
Table 4.4: What Language Do Ukrainians Ages 14–29 Speak at Home? (2018).
Table 5.1: Donetsk Referendum and Lugansk Opinion Poll of March 27, 1994.
Table 5.2: Donetsk and Lugansk Referenda of May 11, 2014.

https://doi.org/10.1515/9783110743371-001

Acknowledgements

Over the decade that it has taken me to write this book, I have received generous assistance from many different sources. My debt begins with the Ukrainian Academy of Sciences and Ukrainian Forum, which first invited me to visit Kiev in 2008. Two years later, Vladimir Karazin National University in Kharkov arranged for me to give a series of talks there. The US Fulbright Commission sponsored me on a Fulbright to Ilya Mechnikov National University in Odessa, Ukraine for the academic year 2013–2014, where then Rector Igor N. Koval, Dean Viktor Glebov, and Professor Volodymyr Dubovyk graciously organized several lectures for me.

The Universities of Pisa and Bologna in Italy not only offered me opportunities to speak, but also invited me to participate in the supervision of three graduate theses dealing with Ukraine. This culminated, in 2021, in a Visiting Fellowship at the Institute for Advanced Studies of the University of Bologna, where I first presented three lectures that later became the foundation for this book. Subsequent speaking engagements at Brown, Johns Hopkins, the Monterey Summer Symposium on Russia, Fairfield University, the Austrian International Institute for Peace, and the Research Center of Post-Soviet Countries in Moscow, all helped me to further refine my arguments.

Unsparing financial assistance was provided by the University of Rhode Island, which not only funded two year-long sabbatical leaves, most of which were spent in Ukraine, but also helped defray the costs of copyediting and indexing through competitive awards from the URI Center for Humanities and the URI Provost's Office. Special thanks go to Michaela Goebels, De Gruyter's Book Content Editor, for shepherding this book through to publication.

Finally, no words can ever adequately express my debt to my wife, Allison, who patiently endured my many weekends writing, media interviews at all hours of the day, and long stays overseas, often in less than ideal circumstances. Having been married to her for nearly forty years, I can honestly say that this is *our* book.

https://doi.org/10.1515/9783110743371-002

Introduction

I have been following events in Ukraine since 2008, when I was invited to give a talk by the National Academy of Sciences of Ukraine, and participated in a panel chaired by former Ukrainian President Leonid Kuchma.[1] Since then, my wife and I have visited Ukraine almost every year. While there we traveled widely, fascinated by the country's rich history and regional diversity. In 2013 I was awarded a Fulbright research award to go to Ukraine for the entire academic year. It proved to be a fateful year, with the Maidan protests beginning just three months after our arrival. My original research agenda, which was to explore the role of the Russian Orthodox Church in Ukraine, quickly fell by the wayside as I struggled to understand what was taking place around me.

The most popular view then, as now, is that the country's post-Maidan crisis is entirely the result of Russian aggression. What makes this explanation less than complete, however, is that Ukraine's historical and cultural divisions are well established, and have been a prominent theme in scholarly writing about the country. It is hard to imagine how they could suddenly be divorced from current events. I therefore agree with Mykola Riabchuk (with whom I agree on little else) that, "the problem remains to find the essence of the Ukrainian discord that cannot be exclusively attributed to Russian subversion or even invasion."[2] To my mind, this means paying more, not less, attention to Ukraine's historical and cultural diversity.

I had no satisfactory framework for explaining the intensity and persistence of the country's internal discord, however, until I stumbled upon Richard Ned Lebow's book, *The Tragic Vision of Politics*.[3] In it, I recognized processes comparable to those I had witnessed in Ukraine – passionate nationalism and revolutionary zeal, followed by the repudiation of sound policy options and the rise of social tensions. Lebow's classic work focuses on international relations, but I felt confident that approaching Ukrainian society through the lens of classical Greek tragedy would reveal many of the same underlying social pathologies.

Further study of classical Greek tragedy led me to the conclusion that a tragic political cycle can manifest itself in a number of different ways. Social decline,

---

1 "Security and Development Strategies in 21st Century," November 13–14, 2008 in Kiev, Ukraine, sponsored by the Ukrainian Forum and the National Academy of Sciences of Ukraine.
2 Mykola Riabchuk, "'Two Ukraines' Reconsidered: The End of Ukrainian Ambivalence?," *Studies in Ethnicity and Nationalism*, April 22, 2015, https://doi.org/10.1111/sena.12120.
3 Richard Ned Lebow, *The Tragic Vision of Politics* (Cambridge: Cambridge University Press, 2003).

https://doi.org/10.1515/9783110743371-003

for example, is often foreshadowed by the increasing shrillness of domestic political discourse and the demonization of one's domestic opponents. Another prominent feature is the rise of nationalism, which can itself become a form of collective psychosis. But despite classical Greek tragedy's value for gaining insight into the emotional roots of conflict, modern political science seems to have entirely forgotten that its most important function was to heal society and to reconcile former enemies; in other words to assist in conflict resolution.

This provided me with the missing piece of the puzzle. The essence of the Ukrainian discord, to use Riabchuk's felicitous phrase, lay in the state's reluctance to recognize the Other Ukraine – the third of the population that regards its own Russian cultural identity as compatible with a Ukrainian civic identity – as a legitimate part of the Ukrainian nation. Today's tragic events thus form part of a much larger tragic cycle that has befuddled Ukrainian political elites for over a century. This cycle is fed by the destructive narratives that one side tells about the other, which then legitimize conflict in the name of achieving justice. Trapped by their insistence on correcting the injustices of the past *before* engaging in dialogue, both sides have unwittingly contributed to the perpetuation of their mutual tragedy.

My discussion of the role that tragedy has played in Ukraine's social discord, and the role that it can play in its healing, proceeds as follows. Chapter One reminds readers of the unique social and therapeutic impact of tragedy during the heyday of Athenian democracy – the fifth century BCE. After describing how tragedy sought to transform Athenians into better and more compassionate citizens, it explores why modern political science abandoned tragedy, and concludes by suggesting that a tragic vision of politics has untapped potential for healing Ukraine.

Chapter Two delves deeply into the recurring cycle of Ukrainian tragedy, showing how it is linked to nationalism. It describes several key historical narratives that divide eastern and western Ukraine, and how they are still being used today to manipulate political and social discourse in Ukraine.

Chapter Three explores the appeal of Far Right nationalism in Ukraine, which rests on its claim that only nationalism can guarantee national unity. I describe how the mainstreaming of the Far Right after 2014 has instead intensified the social conflict between eastern and western Ukraine, and suggest that republican patriotism, which has its origins in a very different sense of community from nationalism, might be more effective for achieving national unity.

Chapter Four describes the concrete damage that nationalism has done in such areas of national policy as healthcare, economics, culture, and religion, while Chapter Five looks at the impact that nationalism has had on Ukraine's geopolitical and security interests. I argue that, while the territorial loss of Crimea and parts of Donbass were due to Russia's military intervention, its psychological origins can be traced to three decades of nationalist policies that alienated the local population.

In the final chapter I review efforts to bring peace to Ukraine. These fall into two broad categories: external efforts, like the Minsk Accords, and internal efforts, like the National Platform for Reconciliation and Unity. Both failed to achieve peace because they did not include any mechanisms for fostering social healing among Ukrainians themselves. I suggest that a Ukrainian Truth and Reconciliation Commission could provide such mechanisms.

Russia's 2022 invasion began just as I was putting the finishing touches on the final chapter. It confirmed some parts of my analysis, while forcing me to re-evaluate others. Most importantly, it confirmed my view of politics as a tragic cycle propelled by mutual fear and the loss of the ability to communicate. This suggests to me that no matter how the military conflict is resolved, it will not bring an end to Ukraine's tragic cycle unless the country's elites also recognize how their own actions are contributing to its perpetuation.

Recurring conflict is as much a problem of the heart, as it is of institutions, and the enduring value of classical Greek tragedy is that it seeks to induce a change of heart, a *catharsis*. Oedipus was blinded by his anger long before he laid hands upon himself, and only began to see truly when he lost his outward sight, and was forced to look inward. It is my hope that by drawing attention to the tragic cycle that entangles them, more Ukrainians will be encouraged to look inward. That is where they will find the compassion and forgiveness needed for reconciliation.

Kingston, Rhode Island   Nicolai N. Petro
Odessa, Ukraine

A Note on Transliteration

The transliteration system used in this book is a simplified version of the one used for Russian and Ukrainian by the American Library Association and Library of Congress (ALA-LC), with the following exceptions. Both hard and soft signs have been omitted. When a soft sign appears in the middle of a word preceded by a vowel, it has been replaced by a "y." The letters "ю" and "я" are transliterated as "yu" and "ya." The letter "й" is transliterated as "i" in Russian, but "y" in Ukrainian (as in "Andrei" and "Andriy").

In the transliteration of proper names, I have tried to use the form that currently predominates in English usage, as determined by the frequency of internet usage. I have therefore transliterated "ий" as "y" in Russian, but "ій" as "iy" in Ukrainian (as in "Volodymyr Zelensky" and "Andriy Parubiy"). For place names, I have given preference to the predominant local language. Thus Lviv, rather than Lwow or Lvov; Lugansk, rather than Luhansk; Odessa, rather than Odesa, and Kiev, rather than Kyiv.

When citing translations and quoting from them, I have preserved the original transliteration. My multilingual graduate assistant, Ekaterina Sylvester, was an invaluable help in checking my translations, transliterations, and references throughout the book. Any mistakes that remain are entirely my own.

https://doi.org/10.1515/9783110743371-004

Chapter One
What Does Athens Have to Do with Kiev?

Tragedy is born at the moment when myth starts to be seen from the viewpoint of the citizen and in relation to law and the city.
Simon Critchley, professor of philosophy[1]

This is not a "crisis." This is something else, something much deeper and more fatal ... we are witnessing a drama of destruction; even worse of self-destruction. External factors, Russian and global, play only a minimal role. This is the national elite and, if truth be told, a large portion of the populace, determining its fate.
Dmitry Vydrin, advisor to four Ukrainian presidents, Rada MP (2006–2007)[2]

Since 2014, Ukraine has been in the news mostly because of its conflicts with Russia. Many in the West assume that these conflicts began in 2014, with the "Revolution of Dignity," which led first to Russia's annexation of Crimea, and then to the conflict in the Donbass region of Eastern Ukraine. The Ukrainian government responded to these events by launching an "anti-terrorist operation" (ATO) in April 2014. Four year later, it became a full-fledged military operation against Russia, designated "the aggressor-nation."[3]

In fact, however, the current conflict is merely the latest in a series of conflicts that have bedeviled this area of the world for more than a century. These include: the great power rivalry between Russia and the West; the conflict between Russia and Ukraine; and finally, the conflict within Ukraine itself over its national identity, its relationship to Russia, and its role in the world. It is, in sum, a conflict about who gets to define Ukrainian identity.

For many in Western Ukraine, inspired by the historical example of Galicia, being Ukrainian means rejecting all things Russian – language, religion, trade, resources, science, music, books – everything. Only after Ukraine has thus "decolonized" itself, will the true Ukraine be able to emerge. During the 2014 Maidan this was referred to as a "civilizational choice."

For many in Eastern, or Maloross Ukraine, however, being Ukrainian means having a regional identity that acknowledges the country's historical and cultural ties to Russia. Most people in this Russophile half of Ukraine, therefore, saw

---

1 Simon Critchley, *Tragedy, the Greeks, and Us* (New York: Vintage Books, 2020), 40.
2 Konstantin Kevorkyan, "Vydrin: Vlast – eto kogda stranoi pravyat idei," [Vydrin: Power Is When Ideas Rule the State] *Ukraina.ru*, February 3, 2020, https://ukraina.ru/interview/20200203/1026505926.html.
3 "ATO zavershilas," [The ATO is Over] *TSN.ua*, April 30, 2018, https://tsn.ua/ru/ato/ato-zavershilas-poroshenko-obyavil-nachalo-operacii-obedinennyh-sil-1147884.html.

https://doi.org/10.1515/9783110743371-005

the call for a civilizational choice as unnecessary, divisive, and demeaning. This conflict of visions regarding Ukraine's past and future has erupted into armed conflict within Ukraine at least four times – during World War I, during World War II, after the 2014 Maidan, and now again in 2022.

Why does it persist? How did this bountiful country, whose political leaders promised that after independence it would quickly rival France in its standard of living, instead wind up declining by a third in population, and becoming the poorest country in Europe?[4] The answer to this question, which has bedeviled political analysts, is rooted in the long and difficult struggle to establish an independent Ukrainian nation. This struggle has given rise to civic engagement based on a common identity, but also to social pathologies that pit Ukrainians against one another. To understand the persistence of these pathologies requires an analytical approach that appreciates how deep-seated fears can still be evoked today by events that took place decades or even centuries ago.

The study of the classical Greek tragedy offers such an analytical approach. In contrast to modern political science, which treats all social actors as profit-maximizers, tragedy focuses particular attention on emotions such as rage, hatred, or love. An approach that combines the politics and classical Greek tragedy therefore allows us to better understand Ukrainian nationalism, and why it has been able to exert such extraordinary influence over the thinking of generations of Ukrainians.

The reason is that classical Greek tragedy played a key role in shaping the thinking of Athenian society on contemporary political events. It promoted social harmony and helped to foster peace with Athens's most bitter enemies. It can thus offer modern societies a form of conflict resolution that is particularly well suited to deeply divided societies, which can sometimes become so obsessed by fear that their own institutions fail them.

Before tackling the specific aspects of Ukraine's tragedy, therefore, it is important to recall tragedy's political significance and civic function in ancient Athens. I will then look at why, despite such a distinguished pedigree, modern political science turned its back on tragedy as an analytical tool, and conclude by arguing that a tragic approach to politics can be especially valuable for understanding and healing contemporary Ukraine.

---

4 Andrei Anoshin, "Skarshevksy: 27 let Ukrainy – put is pustyni v boloto," [Skarshevsky: 27 years of Ukraine – From the Desert to the Swamp] *Ukraina.ru*, August 24, 2018, https://ukraina.ru/exclusive/20180824/1020917780.html.

1.1 The *Dionysia:* Classical Greek Theater as a Political Institution

As a theatrical genre, tragedy has been with us for more than 2,500 years. In this span of time it has taken on a variety of forms: from pure theater, to philosophy, psychology (both individual and social), social protest, even burlesque.[5] This very richness has led some to conclude that "no definition of tragedy more elaborate than 'very sad' has ever worked."[6] But this is an exaggeration. We know, for example, that in ancient Athens the performance of tragedy was an essential part of civic education, an institution of governance that taught citizens how to grapple with the political and social crises of the day. It was the beating heart of Athenian democracy on public display.

It is commonly assumed that tragedy emerged from the religious rituals performed in honor of the Greek god Dionysus. These were the main attraction at the *Dionysia,* the annual city festival of Athens. Each year, during these festivals, four plays were performed – three tragedies and one comedy or farce.[7] A special fund subsidized tickets for the poor, and even provided expensive meats to attract the masses – the *hoi polloi.* The largest arena, the theater of Dionysus on the south slope of the Acropolis, can hold as many as 18,000 people, leading some scholars to conclude that the majority of Athenian citizens attended.[8]

Some idea of the importance of the *Dionysia* can be gleaned from the time and expense that went into these productions.[9] Preparations took more than half the year, and could involve over a thousand performers. Wealthy citizens often vied with each other to support the large choruses – as many as fifty singers – who were exempted from military service, even during the long and exhausting war with Sparta. Actors and writers were paid out of the city's coffers,

---

5 Mary-Kay Gamel, "The Postclassical Reception of Greek Tragedy," in Mary Lefkowitz and James Romm, eds., *The Greek Plays* (New York: Modern Library, 2016), 816.

6 Terry Eagleton, *Sweet Violence: The Idea of the Tragic* (Oxford: Blackwell, 2003), 3.

7 Daniel Mendelsohn, "'Saving the City,' Tragedy in Its Civic Context," in Lefkowitz and Romm, *The Greek Plays,* 793; Simon Goldhill, "The Audience of Athenian Tragedy," in P.E. Easterling, ed., *The Cambridge Companion to Greek Tragedy* (Cambridge, UK: Cambridge University Press, 1997), 54–68.

8 Rush Rehm, *Understanding Greek Tragic Theater* (New York: Routledge, 2017), 19, 31; John Ferguson, *A Companion to Greek Tragedy* (Austin and London: University of Texas Press, 1972), 13.

9 Jacob Burckhardt speaks of the "quite incalculable wealth and variety of festivals." Christian Meier, *The Political Art of Tragedy* (Baltimore: Johns Hopkins University Press, 1993), 44–45, 52–56.

and productions so meticulously supervised, that Plato once contemptuously referred to Athens as a *theatrokratia*, a city ruled by its theater.[10]

The very word for theater in Greek, *theaomai*, refers to a place where all issues and all people are visible and exposed.[11] Performances often dealt with controversial topics and could serve as a safety valve for those outside the political process – women, slaves, and resident foreigners. In the theater they had a voice that Athenian citizens were forced to listen to. We should think of classical Greek theater performances not as the silent places of detached observation we are familiar with today, but rather as having the rambunctious atmosphere of a political convention. "Politics for this audience," writes John Ferguson, "was not a remote professionalism, but their breath of life, and we are right to seek the political context of any play, whether tragedy or comedy."[12]

It seems that the performance of tragedy was first adapted for political use at the cusp of the sixth and fifth centuries BCE. At that time Athens was flush with pride at its victory over Persia, but also in turmoil because of Cleisthenes's democratic reforms. Plato complained that the laws were shifting so rapidly that anyone who had been away from the city for three months would not be able to find their way around.[13]

Tragedy provided an anchor in this storm in three ways. First, it offered a venue for political discussion. Euripides's *The Trojan Women*, for example, is a heart-rending account of the fate of women captured in war, produced a year after the Athenians had themselves voted to enslave the women and children of Melos. In *The Suppliants*, Aeschylus has the chorus comment on the injustice of this.

Second, tragedy brought up controversial issues that could not be addressed in other civic venues. In *Phoenician Women*, Euripides's characters discuss the circumstances under which one might betray and even attack one's own country.[14] In *Antigone*, the central dilemma is whether a citizen's responsibility should be to the family, the *polis*, or the gods. Such moral conflicts were com-

---

10 Simon Critchley, *Tragedy, the Greeks, and Us*, 42.
11 Silvia Zappulla, "Reading *Antigone* through Hannah Arendt's Political Philosophy," prepared for the 5th Mediterranean Congress of Aesthetics, 2011. https://www.um.es/vmca/proceedings/docs/11.Silvia-Zappulla.pdf.
12 John Ferguson, *A Companion to Greek Tragedy*, 12.
13 Christian Meier, *The Political Art of Greek Tragedy*, 10, 34.
14 Simon Goldhill, "Greek Drama and Political Theory," in Christopher Rowe and Malcolm Schofield, eds., *The Cambridge History of Greek and Roman Political Thought* (Cambridge, UK: Cambridge University Press, 2005), 74.

monly debated in classical Greek tragedy, where they could be set in the distant past, and the gods used to restore proper social order.

Finally, it provided a model of proper social behavior. Thus, in *The Persians*, Aeschylus provides both a political and a theological explanation for the Greek victory over the Persians. In Homer's *Iliad*, Sarpedon and Glaucus reason that a country should honor warriors not for their military skill, but for choosing to sacrifice their lives for the good of the *polis*.[15] In *Ajax*, Sophocles suggests that even kings must be subject to divine justice. When Agamemnon rejects this, he pays a heavy price for his defiance.[16]

More realism on the stage meant more political realism as well. According to Simon Goldhill, the tragic playwright is always trying to persuade the audience of the correct civic and moral stance to take, be it on the nature of citizenship, the treatment of enemies, or the justness of war.[17] Through such interaction Athenians were taught to recognize situations they might have to confront as citizens, and how to respond to them.

Of course, Athenian democracy was far from perfect. In fact, neither democracy nor classical tragedy survived the century. Nevertheless, over the course of this remarkable century, the theater became an essential institution of Athenian democracy, and attending plays was regarded as much a civic duty as attending the assembly, or serving on a jury.

1.2 How Tragedy Created Better Citizens

Athenians believed that their volatile democracy could be managed better with the help of the evocative narratives of the theater, a place where dissonant voices could be molded into something resembling a civic culture. Aristophanes says quite explicitly, in his depiction of the competition between Aeschylus and Euripides in Hades, that the better writer must be considered the one who can make "people into better citizens."[18]

These plays conveyed the precise meaning of good citizenship by reiterating a consistent social message. Since just 3 percent of plays have survived to this day, we may never know if they reflected the whole tragic corpus. Nevertheless,

---

15 Emily Katz Anhalt, *Enraged: Why Violent Times Need Ancient Greek Myths* (New Haven, CT: Yale University Press, 2017) 74.
16 Christian Meier, *The Political Art of Greek Tragedy*, 172, 166.
17 Terry Eagleton, *Sweet Violence*, 144.
18 Christian Meier, *The Political Art of Greek Tragedy*, 160.

even this remnant displays an astonishing consistency of themes, in plays as diverse as *Prometheus Bound*, *Ajax*, *Antigone*, and the *Oresteia* trilogy.[19]

1.2.1 *Prometheus Bound:* Pity Leads to Wisdom

In *Prometheus Bound* (457 BCE), Aeschylus shows us that victory over one's adversary is not sufficient, in and of itself, to end the cycle of tragedy. Justice demands reconciliation with the defeated, and even Zeus himself must learn this lesson.

Aeschylus portrays Zeus as a tyrant, someone who thinks that absolute power will allow him to get away with anything. Along the way, however, Zeus is forced to learn that the proper order of the universe demands moderation and reconciliation. It is Zeus's half-human son, Herakles, who reveals this to him by freeing Prometheus against his father's wishes.

In Aeschylus's retelling of this ancient Greek myth, Prometheus's greatest gift to humanity is not fire, but his own Christ-like suffering, through which mankind learns pity. Moved by Prometheus's example, Zeus's arrogance gives way to pity, and he is able to mature from a tyrant into a wise leader.

1.2.2 *Ajax:* Compassion Is Needed to End the Cycle of Tragedy

In *Ajax* (442 BCE), Sophocles takes up another familiar theme: the danger of arrogance and conceit in victory. The play revolves around the conflict between duty to state and duty to family, which is expressed in the family's desire to honor someone who, from the state's perspective, died dishonorably. The conflict is resolved when Odysseus insists that there is a higher obligation than loyalty to the state – loyalty to the Greek community as a whole.

Odysseus, Ajax's mortal enemy in life, insists that after death all enmity must cease; the common frailty that binds mankind (death) must be above po-

---

19 John Ferguson, *A Companion to Greek Tragedy*, 238, 244, 243, 463. Euripides too fits this pattern, although I have not included any of his plays. While some have argued that Euripides was more interested in theater for theater's sake, Ferguson sees in his plays a determined pacifism, hatred for the subjugation of women, and anti-imperialism. He highlights the connections between the thinking of Euripides and Thucydides, and points to a tradition that says that Thucydides wrote the poet's epitaph.

litical expediency.[20] By transcending his personal enmity, and becoming Ajax's spokesman in death, Odysseus removes any motive for future revenge, and prevents the tragic cycle from being repeated. Odysseus's "true wisdom" (*sophein skopein*) has given him insight into the divine laws that set out the proper conduct for mankind.[21]

Sophocles gives added poignancy to his message by showing that, when Agamemnon reluctantly yields to Odysseus's argument, he does so for the wrong reasons. Unlike Odysseus, who places the common good above personal advantage, Agamemnon seeks to create an obligation on Odysseus's part, for which he can extract future payment. He has not learned the meaning of true justice, and is therefore destined to suffer further tragedy – he is later murdered by his wife, Clytemnestra.

1.2.3 *Antigone:* True Justice Requires the Triumph of the Whole

Antigone (442 BCE) is likewise steeped in politics. The play was staged at the time of Pericles's decree elevating allegiance to Athens above all other allegiances, even those to one's own family. This becomes the very issue at the heart of *Antigone*, which Sophocles sets in the rival city of Thebes. The local tyrant, Creon, insists that Antigone's brother, Polyneices, who attacked Thebes to resolve a dynastic dispute, cannot be buried with honor because "once an enemy, never a friend, not even after death!"[22]

Antigone disobeys this decree, so Creon has her walled up alive for defying his authority. Creon's defense is that he is only pursuing the best interests of the *polis*. His absolute devotion to *raison d'etat*, however, prevents him from seeing that true justice is about the triumph of the whole, rather than the triumph of his own, partial, view of justice. This leads to his downfall.

Sophocles's genius lies in showing that Antigone herself suffers from the same tragic flaw. No less than Creon, she too is trying to manipulate justice for the fulfillment of her own wishes, misleading officials about who actually buried Polyneices. Creon is wrong for disobeying the laws of the gods, but Antigone is wrong for acting as if she were as "a law [un]to herself" (Sophocles, *Antigone*, line 875). The obstinate refusal to see any other point of view but one's

---

20 Christian Meier, *The Political Art of Greek Tragedy*, 177. As Meier notes, the words that Sophocles uses are the same ones that Athens used when referring to its vassal-states, making the political implications crystal clear to his audience.
21 Christian Meier, *The Political Art of Greek Tragedy*, 183.
22 Christian Meier, *The Political Art of Greek Tragedy*, 190.

own leads each one, in his own way, to stand in opposition to the *polis*, a condition that Sophocles refers to as madness (*dysboulian*).[23]

The ability to sacrifice personal gain for the common good is the very foundation upon which the wellbeing of the *polis* rests. Creon's demand for total authority in order to maintain order and save the city – a typical "national security" argument – fails because no lasting order can be achieved without constant dialogue. In Thebes there is no shared space (tyranny annihilates it), and no shared community (people are isolated from each other). It can therefore no longer be considered a true *polis*.[24]

1.2.4 *Oresteia:* Compassion Leads to True Justice and Prosperity

Aeschylus's *Oresteia* trilogy (458 BCE) deserves special mention because it is the only complete trilogy that has survived to our times. Its plot illuminates the dilemmas of injustice and inequality, of conflicting loyalties and civil strife, that followed the destruction of Troy. It teaches that crimes that remain unforgiven will always spawn new crimes, to the eternal misery of mankind.

In the first play, *Agamemnon*, Clytemnestra, Agamemnon's wife, murders her husband after his triumphant return from Troy, for having sacrificed their daughter Iphigenia in order to obtain his victory. In the sequel, *The Libation Bearers*, this blood curse passes to their offspring, Orestes and Elektra. As Orestes vows to kill his mother to avenge his father, he refers to himself as "wearing the stain of victory," as Agamemnon did for sanctioning the killing of Iphigenia.[25]

Finally, in *The Kindly Ones* (*Eumenides*), the goddess Athena herself intervenes. When Orestes is charged with his mother's murder, she convenes a jury to hear both sides. When the jury acquits Orestes, the Furies, the spirits of righteousness, are at first outraged, but when Athena offers them a place of honor in exchange for showing compassion to Orestes, they are transformed.

Because true justice has triumphed over vengeance, rich blessings are conferred upon Athens: blight shall not infect bud and blossom, women shall find husbands, children shall prosper, civil war fade, and concord reign.[26] The conclusion of the trilogy thus fulfills the promise made by Zeus in *Agamemnon*

---

23 Silvia Zappulla, "Reading *Antigone* through Hannah Arendt's Political Philosophy."
24 Silvia Zappulla, "Reading *Antigone* through Hannah Arendt's Political Philosophy."
25 Rush Rehm, *Understanding Greek Tragic Theatre*, 112.
26 John Ferguson, *A Companion to Greek Tragedy*, 106.

that the ultimate victory will go to those who promote reconciliation and restore proper order to the *polis*.[27]

From this brief summary of six plays (out of a total of thirty-three extant) we see that they shared a common purpose: to teach the citizenry how to end chaos and restore order. To this end, tragedies promulgated a consistent set of values. Pride and vengeance were values to be avoided at all costs. Pride led to disaster because men, and sometimes even gods, often failed to grasp the full scope of true justice, and thus sought vengeance instead. William Arrowsmith paints this bleak picture of Apollo's vengeance on Argos for Orestes's crime: "the burning palace, the dead girl, the screaming mob, and the degenerate heirs dying in the arson of their own hatred."[28] Each new cycle of tragedy is watered by the blood of those seeking revenge for past offenses.

But Zeus has revealed another path, which can lead to wisdom, if men choose to take it. By witnessing onstage the horrors that result from the unyielding pursuit of vengeance, audiences can choose *catharsis*, a purging of emotions so powerful that it allows new emotions, such as pity (*eleos*) and compassion (*oiktos*), to enter the soul and take the place of rage. Our pity tends to be reserved for those whom we know well, but tragedy evokes pity for those whom we know not at all, in order to achieve a deeper and more lasting *catharsis*. Euripides uses this technique in *Andromache* by initially focusing only on Sparta's wickedness, but then gradually expanding his attention to all of Greece.[29] Pity and compassion allow us to forge the bonds of identity that sustain community. "Uneducated men are pitiless," Orestes tells his sister Elektra, "but we who are educated pity much" (Euripides, *Elektra*, 295).

By combining the performance of plays with public debate, the Dionysian festivals promoted a novel form of civic engagement – direct democracy. Tragedies assisted in the formation of a citizenry prepared to rule by setting up an artificial contest, or *agon*, that mimicked the conflicts in society. As the play unfolds the hero must explain the reasoning behind his or her actions to the audience, as if speaking to an assembly of jurors. After that, the opposing party responds, thus establishing a dialogue for the audience to evaluate. Sometimes, as in Aeschylus's *Eumenides*, Euripides's *Suppliant Women*, and Sophocles's *Oedipus at Colonus*, trials were made a part of the actual plot.

Achieving compassion for one's enemy was an essential part of the civics lesson, for without it the tragic cycle could never be broken. In *Women of*

---

27 Christian Meier, *The Political Art of Greek Tragedy*, 135.
28 John Ferguson, *A Companion to Greek Tragedy*, 566.
29 John Ferguson, *A Companion to Greek Tragedy*, 333.

Troy, Euripides allows that justice was on the side of the Greeks, not the Trojans, but he is more concerned with drawing tears from his audience, so that Athenians would see in their victory "not glory at all, but shame, and blindness, and a world swallowed up in night."[30] Classical Greek tragedy was not just about suffering; it was a civic celebration of suffering.[31] According to J. Peter Euben, citizens were expected to "undergo a transformation of character such that their anger toward others becomes gentleness and a self-directed sense of shame."[32]

Onstage behavior that was prudent and selfless was self-evidently noble (*arete*), and classical Greek playwrights took great care to show how such behavior benefited society as a whole. *Hubris* and *hamartia* (the word that the Septuagint often uses for "sin") were not so much moral flaws, but category errors that could endanger the *polis*. Overconfidence, or blind hatred caused leaders to take unnecessary risks, whereas tragedy trained citizens to recognize and avoid policies that could lead to disaster. The citizenry was to be systematically led away from *hubris* toward compassion and *catharsis*, which Aristotle describes as the introduction of order into "otherwise disorderly or incoherent souls."[33] By replacing irrational emotions with proper reasoning, *catharsis* could liberate individuals and societies from the endless repetition of a tragic script.

One of the most enduring tragic scripts, in ancient as well as modern times, is the presumed imperative for war. In Euripides's *The Suppliant Women*, the herald deflates Theseus's pompous call to arms by sardonically remarking, "If death stood before our eyes as we gave our votes, Greece would not now be perishing of war-madness."[34]

It didn't always work. Athens's appetite for empire and conquest was ultimately its undoing. That some Athenians understood this is shown in Thucydides's account of the speech the Athenian envoys gave to the Spartan assembly on their reasons for declaring war: "And at last, when almost all hated us, when some had already revolted and had been subdued, when you had ceased to be the friends that you once were, and had become objects of suspicion and dislike,

---

30 John Ferguson, *A Companion to Greek Tragedy*, 48, 336.

31 "Greek tragedy is a celebration of the willingness and ability of the citizens of Athens to share each other's pain. Pericles transforms pain-sharing into an act of civic virtue." C. Fred Alford, "Greek Tragedy and Civilization: The Cultivation of Pity," *Political Science Quarterly* 46, no. 2 (June 1993): 266.

32 J. Peter Euben, ed., *Greek Tragedy and Political Theory* (Berkeley: University of California Press, 1986), 282–283.

33 J. Peter Euben, *Greek Tragedy and Political Theory*, 283–284, 287.

34 John Ferguson, *A Companion to Greek Tragedy*, 312.

it appeared no longer safe to give up our empire; especially as all who left us would fall to you."[35]

But before we dismiss the civic use of tragedy as a failure for not eradicating baser human instincts, we should consider its success in inculcating pity and compassion during the remarkable century in which it thrived. According to Herodotus, theater audiences burst into tears during the performance of Phrynichus's *Capture of Miletus*. At one point, the play was banned because it reminded people too intensely of their suffering.[36] Athenian prisoners of war returning from the Sicilian expedition reported being released because they could recite the plays of Euripides.[37] It is therefore quite possible, as Emily Anhalt Katz suggests, that the tragic plays that focused on the conflict between civic and moral obligations caused Athenians to have second thoughts about the trade-offs between democracy and empire, and to be a bit less arrogant about their capacity to shape human events.[38]

It has also been suggested that audiences brought lessons from the theater into their deliberations in the assembly or the law courts. There is, for example, an account of the priestess Theano disobeying a public decree requiring all priests to publicly curse the Athenian general Alcibiades. In her famous refusal she makes the same case as Antigone, saying that her function in the *polis* is not to curse, but to pray.[39]

1.3 How Modern Politics Lost Sight of Tragedy

In the centuries since the fall of Athens, Greek tragedy has continued to be a source of inspiration for theater, philosophy, psychology, literature, art, indeed all the humanities, but its most important function – that of sparking dialogue among citizens on civic values and behavior – has been all but forgotten.

There are many reasons for this. The most obvious is the passage of time, which has left us with less than 3 percent of the texts of the classical Greek tragedies, and perhaps 10 percent of the titles.[40] Another is the downfall of Athenian democracy. Having been a major part of democracy's rise, it should come as no

---

35 Richard Ned Lebow, *The Tragic Vision of Politics* (Cambridge: Cambridge University Press, 2003), 269.

36 Christian Meier, *The Political Art of Greek Tragedy*, 61–63, 219.

37 John Ferguson, *A Companion to Greek Tragedy*, 245, 163.

38 Emily Katz Anhalt, *Enraged*, Introduction.

39 Christian Meier, *The Political Art of Greek Tragedy*, 201.

40 Rush Rehm, *Understanding Greek Tragic Theater*, 26.

surprise that tragedy's social influence declined with democracy's demise. By the time modern democracies emerged, most audiences either no longer grasped tragedy's social significance, or simply found cathartic introspection too burdensome.[41] Some scholars have argued that tragedy is especially unappealing to Americans because of their tendency to view their own political culture as "almost innocent of irony and tragedy."[42]

But, we have Plato to thank most of all for the current rift between tragedy and politics. His arguments against tragedy align closely with his influential critique of democracy in *The Republic*. Democracy's greatest flaw, as Plato saw it, was that it empowered the lowly and the ignorant. This encouraged "a dangerous, wild and lawless form of desire" that inevitably led to chaos, civil war, and tyranny. Censoring public functions that aroused excess passions, like tragedy, was therefore essential to preventing civil war within the soul.[43]

In modern times, calls to restrain public passions to avoid chaos sound positively undemocratic. Indeed, it is sometimes suggested that in authoritarian societies a certain amount of chaos ought to be welcomed as a harbinger of democracy.[44] Such a complete role reversal has led some to conclude that any political wisdom that tragedy might once have had clearly no longer applies today. With the attention of modern social science firmly fixed on data-gathering and modeling, fate has become something that good social planning should be able to avoid. The belief in scientific progress has thus effectively erased tragedy from our social awareness, and along with it any understanding of how it once shaped our political behavior. In this context, the idea that the study of tragedy could be a valuable part of the democratic process, a bulwark against chaos, seems quaint.

In truth, however, we need tragedy today as much as ever, for the same reasons the Greeks did. First, because, like the ancient Greeks, we continue to search for meaning and order in a world engulfed by chaos. One vital function of tragedy was to set down deep anchors, rooted in history and tradition, that societies in turmoil could rely on to restore order.[45] Second, because tragedy re-

---

41 George Steiner, "'Tragedy,' Reconsidered," in Rita Felski, ed., *Rethinking Tragedy* (Baltimore: Johns Hopkins University Press, 2008), 29 – 44.
42 Harvey Mansfield, "The Tragedy of Weber," *Washington Examiner*, December 9, 1996, https://perma.cc/7SYG-A2LV.
43 Derek W.M. Barker and David W. McIvor, "Tragedy and Politics," *The Encyclopedia of Political Thought* (Wiley Online Library), July 18, 2014, https://doi.org/10.1002/9781118474396.wbept1009.
44 Anne Applebaum, "Nationalism Is Exactly What Ukraine Needs," *The New Republic*, May 13, 2014, https://newrepublic.com/article/117505/ukraines-only-hope-nationalism.
45 Raymond Williams, *Modern Tragedy* (Stanford, CA: Stanford University Press, 1966), 29, 46.

lies on storytelling, a most effective mechanism for giving meaning and structure to the world. "The idea of fate," as Terry Eagleton puts it, is "the idea of a narrative which adds up."[46] There is no reason to think that if tragic stories were told today they could not serve the same purpose they served two thousand years ago – to force us to confront directly the sources of our discontent.

It is sometimes said, in rebuttal, that tragedy can hardly be expected to play such a socially significant role today because the underlying assumptions of modernity are "non-tragic." Raymond Williams, however, stands this argument on its head. He suggests that modern ideologies, which depict mankind as torn asunder by internal contradictions, are actually cries for help to escape quintessentially tragic circumstances. If tragedy stems from contradictions that are inherent in the human condition, then perhaps modernity itself, he suggests, is a classical tragedy?[47]

The horrific cruelty, loss of life, and cataclysmic upheavals of the twentieth century led many political thinkers to conclude that something vital had been lost in the quest for modernity. Appalled at how easily politicians lost sight of order, meaning, and values in political discourse, they turned to classical Greek tragedy for remedies, spawning an approach to politics known as political realism. Notable proponents of political realism, like Hannah Arendt, Hans J. Morgenthau, Reinhold Niebuhr, and Richard Ned Lebow, relied so heavily on classical Greek tragedy, that they might well be called modern tragic realists. In the final analysis, however, I believe that their appreciation for the role of tragedy in politics did not go far enough.

1.3.1 Hannah Arendt: The Importance of Tragic Narratives

According to her biographer, Robert C. Pirro, Arendt considered Greek tragedy "the political art par excellence," because it enabled "the cultivation of citizen's capacity to see things from the points of view of their fellow citizens."[48] Most evil in the world, she concluded, is done by people who never make up their minds to do good. Such people need an intellectual basis for resisting evil, an internal

---

46 Terry Eagleton, *Sweet Violence*, 129.
47 Raymond Williams, *Modern Tragedy*, 189.
48 Robert C. Pirro, *Hannah Arendt and the Politics of Tragedy* (DeKalb: Northern Illinois University Press, 2001), 139.

dialogue that could spur their conscience.[49] Tragic performances, she suggested, could turn this internal dialogue into an external one.

Arendt agreed with Aristotle that actions on the stage could provoke a sense of personal recognition in the audience, and create in them a capacity for reconciliation. As an example, she cites a scene from the *Iliad* where Odysseus, incognito, listens to the story of his own life, his personal "reconciliation with reality" coming through tears of remembrance.[50] By fostering both individual and collective reflection, tragedy, she hoped, could foster public dialogue.

1.3.2 Hans J. Morgenthau: The Tragedy of Nationalism

If for Arendt tragedy was a story that needed to be told from multiple perspectives, for Morgenthau it was a terminal condition. Humanity's tragedy is that it is trapped between a spiritual destiny which it cannot fulfill, and an animal nature to which it cannot return. The frustration this evokes is multiplied by the fact that any political action that an individual might take to resolve this contradiction involves doing some harm.[51] Under these circumstances, the best that an individual can do is to "minimize the intrinsic immorality of the political act" by choosing the lesser evil.[52]

Because of this rather dismal assessment of the human condition, the "Father of Realpolitik" is often accused of amorality. His supporters, however, argue that Morgenthau never saw the ubiquity of evil as meaning that ethics should be disregarded, but rather that, when considering the alternatives, political wisdom meant adopting the lesser evil. Morgenthau argues that it is precisely the absence of such political wisdom that led to the tragedy of twentieth-century nationalism, which projects humankind's lust for power onto the nation and glorifies it.

---

49 Hannah Arendt, "Some Questions of Moral Philosophy," in *Arendt and Morgenthau on Responsibility, Evil and Political Ethics* (New York: Schocken Books, 2003), 96; Hannah Arendt, "Thinking," in *Arendt and Morgenthau on Responsibility, Evil and Political Ethics* (New York: Harcourt Brace & Co., 1978), 179–193.
50 Robert C. Pirro, *Hannah Arendt and the Politics of Tragedy*, 135.
51 Hans J. Morgenthau, *Scientific Man vs. Power Politics* (Chicago: University of Chicago Press, 1946), 221.
52 Sean Molloy, "Aristotle, Epicurus, Morgenthau and the Political Ethics of Lesser Evil," *Journal of International Political Theory* 5, no. 1 (2009): 99.

Nationalism is a totalitarian evil because it transforms the nation into "the only moral space in an amoral world."[53] Because it is a political religion, it deprives leaders of the detachment needed to accurately assess the world around them and leads them to overestimate their own resources and skill (he considered Nazi Germany to be a prime example of this). Its deleterious effects, however, can be reversed by cultivating prudence, compassion, and wisdom among political leaders. While Morgenthau's critics complain that this is little more than a statement of *noblesse oblige*, he proposes two further steps that should be taken to combat nationalism.

One is the conscious pursuit of the balance of power for the preservation of peace. Preserving a balance of power, he says, will force international actors to recommit to "the underlying values and sense of community that bound together the actors in the system."[54] It is important to point out that Morgenthau is *not* talking about exporting values, like democracy or human rights, in order to achieve such a community. On the contrary, he stresses "the frailty of human reason, carried on the waves of passion and unequal to the rich complexities of experience. In that frailty all men share; Greeks and Persians, Americans and Russians. Beholding them as brothers in blindness, we can be just to them."[55]

His second step, likewise borrowed from Greek tragedy, involves direct tutelage of statesmen.[56] At the height of the Vietnam War, Morgenthau seemed to believe, rather naively, that more intellectuals in the White House might help president Lyndon Johnson become such a statesman: "What the President needs, then, is an intellectual father-confessor, who dares to remind him of the brittleness of power, of its arrogance and blindness, of its limits and pitfalls; who tells him how empires rise, decline, and fall, how power turns to folly, empires to ashes. He ought to listen to that voice and tremble."[57]

53 Konstantinos Kostagiannis, "Hans Morgenthau and the Tragedy of the Nation-State," *The International History Review* 36, no. 3 (May 27, 2014): 517, https://doi.org/10.1080/07075332.2013.828639.
54 Richard Ned Lebow, *The Tragic Vision of Politics*, 228.
55 Hans J. Morgenthau, *Truth and Power: Essays of a Decade, 1960–70* (New York: Praeger, 1970), 82.
56 Richard Ned Lebow, *The Tragic Vision of Politics*, 225.
57 Hans J. Morgenthau, *Truth and Power*, 14.

1.3.3 Richard Ned Lebow: The Tragic Vision of Politics

One of Morgenthau's students at the University of Chicago, Lebow carries forward his mentor's political realism, also drawing explicitly on its classical Greek heritage. Lebow emphasizes the importance of justice for providing a framework within which to formulate interests. When policy becomes divorced from justice, its aims become unlimited, with tragic consequences.[58]

These tragic consequences are described in Thucydides's *Peloponnesian War*. According to Lebow, Thucydides saw the war as the result of a series of bad judgments by Greece's political leaders, which can be traced back to the collapse of the institutions and conventions (*nomos*) that sustained their shared civilization. Simply put, war erupted because the Greeks felt that they no longer shared ideas, identity, and values that bound them to one another. Unable to distinguish friend from foe on the basis of shared values, Athenians set out to gain whatever advantages they could for themselves, and wound up making the whole world their enemy.[59]

For Thucydides, although tragic heroes tend to make bad choices, they also have the power to correct them. So do societies. To restore order and balance, the speech (*logoi*) and deeds (*erga*) that resulted in strife (*stasis*) must be replaced with speech and deeds that reinforce peace and rest (*hesuchia*). Thucydides wrote *The Peloponnesian War* to help restore harmony and balance to Greek civilization, thereby becoming, in Lebow's words, "the last of the tragedians."[60]

1.4 Tragedy and the Limits of Modern Political Realism

This brief synopsis of the impact of classical Greek tragedy on the thinking of modern political realists could be much longer. There are similar references in the writings of Reinhold Niebuhr, E.H. Carr, Sir Herbert Butterfield, George F. Kennan, Jr., and my own university mentors, Kenneth W. Thompson and J.H. Adam Watson. One would think that this alone would guarantee classical Greek tragedy a central place in the political science canon. To understand why this is not the case, we must understand the modern critique of political realism.

---

58 Richard Ned Lebow, *The Tragic Vision of Politics*, xii.
59 Richard Ned Lebow, *The Tragic Vision of Politics*, 89, 119, 127.
60 Richard Ned Lebow, *The Tragic Vision of Politics*, 20, 117–118, 148–149.

Many social scientists reject political realism, and its tragic underpinnings, on the grounds that: (1) it leads to resignation and passivity; (2) it relativizes evil and is morally repugnant; and (3) it is unscientific because it offers no testable alternatives. Each of these criticisms, however, stems from a flawed understanding of classical Greek tragedy.

The notion that political realism's tragic view of human nature leads to resignation and passivity in the face of evil has been a persistent criticism. Hannah Arendt uses it to criticize Morgenthau's "lesser evil" standard for political behavior. The trouble with this standard, she says, is that it could be used to legitimize evil-doing.[61] For Arendt, political understanding should allow us to comprehend the nature of evil, so that we may resist it.[62]

But if Morgenthau can be criticized for relativizing evil, Arendt can be criticized (just as inaccurately) for arguing that different kinds of evil merit different treatment. In contrast to Morgenthau, for example, she refused to approach the Holocaust from the standpoint of tragedy, saying that it demanded a total reappraisal of the boundaries between collective and individual responsibility, not a retreat into personal grief and tragic remembrance.[63]

Ultimately, Arendt relied on the law to mete out both moral accountability and practical justice. Morgenthau, however, felt that the law would be too weak to stand against raw power, and urged statesmen not to indulge in such fantasies. Although Morgenthau is often criticized for failing to confront the moral challenges posed by evil, ultimately, I suspect that both he and Arendt would have agreed that choosing the proper action to take against evil would depend on the circumstances.[64]

Political realists, and Morgenthau in particular, also stand accused of giving political actors a marvelously elastic rationale for breaking any law in the service of their preferred policy goals; something that Michael Ignatieff derides as moral narcissism.[65] This is deemed insufferably elitist since it "lures us into the exalt-

---

61 Robert C. Pirro, *Hannah Arendt and the Politics of Tragedy*, 143.
62 Douglas Klusmeyer, "Beyond Tragedy: Hannah Arendt and Hans Morgenthau on Responsibility, Evil and Political Ethics," *International Studies Review* 11, no. 2 (2009): 335. It is interesting to consider the lessons that Arendt draws from Aeschylus's *Oresteia*. She argues that Orestes did the right thing in slaying his mother and lover to avenge their murder of his father, Agamemnon, but that he is still guilty of a heinous crime. Athena's creative solution to this conundrum is to create a tribunal to maintain right order, while at the same time lifting the curse. Arendt thus sees the law as sufficient to resolve the tragic conflicts of both individuals and political communities.
63 Robert C. Pirro, *Hannah Arendt and the Politics of Tragedy*, 143.
64 Douglas Klusmeyer, "Beyond Tragedy," 335.
65 Douglas Klusmeyer, "Beyond Tragedy," 344.

ing realm of grandeur, and thus, despite all clear-eyed honesty, its obscures the truth. Tragedy becomes the privilege of the exalted few – all others must be content to be wiped out indifferently in disaster."[66]

Finally, there are critics who argue that the so-called universal truths expressed in tragedy are so nebulous that they make tragedy inappropriate for the study of politics. "Human life is not 'tragic,'" Michael Oakeshott writes, "either in part or in whole: tragedy belongs to art, not to life. ... To children and to romantic women, but to no one else, it may appear 'tragic' that we cannot have Spring without Winter, eternal youth or passion always at the height of its beginning."[67] Tragedy is of no value whatsoever for political analysis, says international relations theorist Mervyn Frost, because the "tragic hero" is stuck in the past and always obliged to make a choice with negative consequences.[68]

But Frost's criticism focuses too much on the outcome of the tragic play, and too little on the learning process that is taking place as the audience is watching it. Frost is right to point out that Greeks considered perfection to be impossible, but he is wrong to imply that this meant ethical paralysis. There is always a preferred moral outcome in the play, which the hero should strive to attain. Moreover, his description of *agon* as nothing more than an internal ethical conflict misses the social implications of this conflict. The *agon* did not, as Frost suggests, simply move the tragedy along aimlessly; it moved it toward the restitution of social order. The plot forces the hero to make conscious moral choices, and the very point of the performance is to illustrate the consequences that flow from these choices.[69]

It is thus precisely *not* the point of tragedy to show up protagonists "as hapless social scientists."[70] On the contrary, the protagonist's failure is typically not one of oversight or omission, but of recklessness. To suggest, as Frost does, that a Greek hero would have felt ethically bound to commit atrocities under any circumstances confuses fate with agency. In fact, as Rita Felski points out, it is precisely the unraveling of this distinction that distinguishes classical Greek tragedy.[71]

---

66 Douglas Klusmeyer, "Beyond Tragedy," 344.
67 Nicholas Rengger, "Tragedy or Scepticism? Defending the Anti-Pelagian Mind in World Politics," *International Relations* 19 (2005): 47.
68 Mervyn Frost, "Tragedy, Ethics and International Relations," *International Relations* 17, no. 4 (2003): 477–495.
69 J. Peter Euben, *Greek Tragedy and Political Theory*, 12.
70 Mervyn Frost, "Tragedy, Ethics and International Relations," 485.
71 Rita Felski, *Rethinking Tragedy*, 11.

It is noteworthy that all these criticisms tend to ascribe the flaws of modern political realism to the influence of classical Greek tragedy. This presumed flaw is then compounded by the fact that the natural heirs of the classical Greek tradition, political realists themselves, often fail to appreciate tragedy's therapeutic social function.

A telling example is Reinhold Niebuhr who, like many political realists, wrote poignantly about the insights that Greek tragedies provided into humanity's tragic condition.[72] For Niebuhr that tragedy lay in the attempt to avoid what is inescapable: humanity's propensity for self-destruction. This propensity goes hand-in-hand with the realists' skepticism about modern democracy which, they feared, has neither the stamina nor the social and cultural cohesion that Athens once had. Niebuhr, Kennan, Morgenthau, and more recently Brands and Edel, therefore see the main lesson of tragedy as one of fear, rather than hope.[73]

The Greek view of tragedy, however, was far from fearful. While modern realists see tragedy as a reminder that politics can never result in anything but imperfect compromises, the Greeks saw tragedy as having a much more ambitious agenda – to shape the character of Athenian citizens by demonstrating the proper content of a noble soul, and the type of actions that such a soul could undertake. It was incumbent upon the tragic playwright to point out how to do so, so that tragedy could fulfill its therapeutic calling. Modern realists, by contrast, have no need for this therapeutic aspect of tragedy, because they deem tragedy to be part of the human condition, which is irredeemably flawed.

Another fundamental difference between classical tragedy and modern realism is the latter's assumption that there is an insurmountable chasm between personal and collective morality. This creates a moral dilemma for realists, who tend to define collective action in the national interest as being, by definition, moral, but also recognize that it can descend into barbarism.[74]

Many modern realists have grappled with how to bridge the gap between individual and collective morality, but they typically ignore how the ancient Greeks

---

72 Reinhold Niebuhr, "Greek Tragedy and Modern Politics," *The Nation* 146, no. 1 (January 1938): 740.

73 Hal Brands and Charles N. Edel, *The Lessons of Tragedy: Statecraft and World Order* (New Haven, CT: Yale University Press, 2019).

74 In *The Irony of American History* (New York: Charles Scribner's Sons, 1962), Niebuhr sharply criticized George Kennan's suggestion that the "national interest" should serve as the moral touchstone of American diplomacy, saying that this would vacate foreign policy goals of their moral content. It must be possible, he wrote, to conduct a foreign policy in the national interest, while preserving a "decent respect for the opinions of mankind" (p. 148).

solved this dilemma – by treating moderation and prudence not as gifts bestowed upon a select few, but as skills (*tekne*) accessible to all. Within the *polis* collective and individual morality were inseparable because of the extensive social obligations of citizenship.[75]

Finally, modern realists generally pay too little attention to the social component of *hamartia* and as a result rarely mention *catharsis*. Typical in this regard are Hal Brands and Charles Edel, who assert that Greek tragedy was meant to teach the audience a muscular and militaristic form of heroism, designed explicitly for the defense of the nation (by which they mean the *polis*). *Catharsis*, in their telling, merely serves to show that disastrous outcomes were "eminently avoidable."[76] I believe, by contrast, that *catharsis* is meant to evoke compassion, and thereby transform the soul of both the individual and the *polis*.

In his own brand of Christian realism, Niebuhr depicted compassion as an antidote to individual *hubris*, but still could not imagine it as an instrument for social transformation. The latter, for Niebuhr, required God's salvific, eschatological intervention in human affairs. For Niebuhr, such divine intervention marks the end of human history and the dawn of a new age. For the Greeks, however, divine intervention was just another learning opportunity in the ongoing cycle of human history.

We should therefore distinguish between the two very different ways in which modern political realists use the term "tragic." One describes as tragic our limited knowledge of the nature of human existence. By making us more aware of this limitation, the study of tragedy can teach us to be more sensitive to ethical dilemmas, and more restrained in our ambitions. Morgenthau, Lebow, and Niebuhr all fit comfortably into this category.

Another approach, by contrast, sees tragedy itself as the limitation because it is incompatible with social progress. Douglas Klusmeyer thinks of tragedy as irretrievably backward looking and pessimistic; Nicholas Rengger describes it as nothing more than a romanticization of life's vicissitudes; while Rita Felski argues that the entire genre ought to be condemned as reactionary.[77]

The ancient Greeks typically had more in common with the former view than the latter. They regarded tragic knowledge as teachable, in much the same way

---

75 John Ferguson, *A Companion to Greek Tragedy*, 210.
76 Hal Brands and Charles N. Edel, *The Lessons of Tragedy*, 2–3.
77 Douglas Klusmeyer, "Beyond Tragedy"; Nicholas Rengger, "Tragedy or Scepticism?," 327; Rita Felski, *Rethinking Tragedy*, Introduction.

that knowledge of law or politics can be taught.[78] It is truly unfortunate that undergraduates studying political science today are not required to cover the topic of political tragedy; doubly so since tragic narratives were explicitly designed to bring political and moral dilemmas to life for debate and evaluation.

In later chapters we will attempt to reconnect tragedy and politics by identifying those elements of the former that remain analytically and practically useful, but first we must ask ourselves what tragedy can offer to politics today?

1.5 What Tragedy Has to Offer Modern Politics

Finding the proper balance between theory and practice was always a central concern of classical Greek thought. As Critchley points out, the ancient Greek word for "spectator" was *theoros*, from which we derive the word theory. The verb *theorein*, "to see," and the Greek word for theater (*theatron*) derive from the same root. *Praxis*, or action, is that which can be viewed in the theater, demonstrated from a theoretical perspective.[79]

Among other things, tragedy alerted Athenians to the manipulations of politicians.[80] Among the favorite targets of tragic playwrights were the justifications given for war. Regardless of what political leaders may say, Euripides reminds us that war is always fought over an illusion: "You who win honor in war at the point of your sturdy spears, ignorantly trying to halt the trouble of the world – you're all mad. If bloodshed is to settle the issue, violence will never abandon the cities of men."[81]

The only real antidote to war-madness is compassion, a quality that could be taught. Euripides shows how in his play *Hecabe*. Staged in the midst of the long and bloody war against Sparta, he presents his Athenian audience with this heart-rending scene:

Yes, and by Eurotas's splendid stream
some Spartan woman sits at home in tears
and a grey-haired mother
whose children have died

---

78 Richard Ned Lebow, *The Tragic Vision of Politics*, 59–60. Tekne is the mastery of crafted knowledge, rather than primary knowledge [*episteme*]. When *episteme* and *tekne* are combined, it results in *sophia*, which is an understanding of life that goes beyond discrete knowledge to integrate life's deeper meaning.
79 Simon Critchley, *Tragedy, the Greeks, and Us*, 5.
80 Richard Ned Lebow, *The Tragic Vision of Politics*, 378.
81 John Ferguson, *A Companion to Greek Tragedy*, 413, 423.

beats her head and tears her cheeks,
rends till her nails drip with blood.[82]

According to the founding myth of Greek civilization, civilization itself arose out of compassion. As the story is told, the first humans banded together for protection against wild animals, but then treated each other so badly, that they retreated for safety into their individual caves. Zeus took pity on them and sent Hermes to teach them *aidos* (respect, reverence) and *dike* (justice), so that they could live together in harmony. *Aidos* enforced justice through shame, while *dike* obliged them to see things from the other's point of view. Together they created the bonds of affection that brought order to chaos.[83]

Classical Greek tragedy therefore remains relevant today because it forces us to reflect on the importance of mutual affection for the social order, and how to apply it to improve the moral character of the citizenry. Albert Hirschman once famously argued that human progress relies on the transformation of passions (pleasure, domination, and gain) into interests. He felt that the best hope for transforming such passions into socially benevolent behavior would be to pit them against each other through commercialization.[84] The Greek approach of countering uncivilized passions with a moral education in the civilized passions was deemed theology, not politics, with the net result, as C. Fred Alford points out, of squeezing *both* the civilized and the uncivilized passions out of politics.[85]

It is therefore not at all surprising that the post-Maidan regime in Ukraine has sought to dehumanize its opponents and to portray its opposition to Russia as a clash of civilizations. This is exactly what Agamemnon did to Ajax, and what Creon did to Antigone. Classical Greek tragedy condemns this not only on moral grounds, but also on the practical grounds that it prevents conflict resolution – the same practical grounds on which political realists criticize nationalism.

But this is as far as most modern political realists will go when discussing the value of tragedy for contemporary politics. Even those sympathetic to the tragic view of politics, like J. Peter Euben, insist that it should not be used as "an ingredient in a recipe."[86] Not as an ingredient, perhaps, but why not as the recipe itself? A recipe for social healing that begins with ingredients like ca-

82 John Ferguson, *A Companion to Greek Tragedy*, 301.
83 Richard Ned Lebow, *The Tragic Vision of Politics*, 276.
84 Albert Hirschman, *The Passions and the Interests* (Princeton, NJ: Princeton University Press, 1977).
85 C. Fred Alford, "Greek Tragedy and Civilization," 261.
86 J. Peter Euben, "The Tragedy of Tragedy," *International Relations* 21, no. 1 (2007): 15.

tharsis and dialogue, and then proceeds to institutionalize them to create a more just social order.

1.5.1 Tragedy as Social Therapy

The Greeks considered tragedy to be a form of therapy, both for the soul of the individual, and for the soul of society. As Critchley puts it, it is "the just city that lives in the soul."[87]

To this end, classical Greek tragedies drew particular attention to actions that were in conflict with justice; that is, contrary to the will of the gods and the proper order. The tragic spectacle being enacted on stage served as a model for resolving conflicts and healing the community. The hero's *agon* (struggle) had to be demonstrated vividly and publicly, so that it could lead to *catharsis* (cleansing) and healing. Until the prot/agonist (literally the first to persevere in the struggle) reaches *catharsis* and shows others the path to compassion, future generations are condemned to repeat the cycle of tragedy.

This laborious process involves *peripeteia* (wanderings), *agon*, *agnorisis* (recognition), *catharsis*, and finally *metanoia* (transformation). As the hero learns compassion, he is also healing the *polis*. That is why so many of the terms used in Greek drama, like *mimesis* and *pharmakos*, are medicinal.[88]

In classical Greek tragedies, the narrative moves from disorder to order. First, the loss of order must be recognized by all (*anagnorisis*). Such recognition is essential, because proper order cannot be restored through the hero's efforts alone; it must be the work of the entire community. If the tragedy involves the death of the hero, that death *per se* is not the point. The point is to show how social propriety can be restored, even after death, by "some gratuitous act of foregoing and forgiveness" on the part of the community.[89]

Classical Greek tragedy is thus, quintessentially, an interlocking set of dialogues: between the characters themselves, and between the audience and the play. These dialogues lead the audience to *ekstasis*, the experience of being outside of oneself and seeing, perhaps for the first time, the point of view of the enemy Other.[90] Dialogue can lead to *catharsis* – a purging of the soul that restores healthy balance by removing toxic emotions and ambitions. Catharsis

---

87 Simon Critchley, *Tragedy, the Greeks, and Us*, 160, 185.
88 Simon Critchley, *Tragedy, the Greeks, and Us*, 33–34, 138–139, 204.
89 Raymond Williams, *Modern Tragedy*, 58; Terry Eagleton, *Sweet Violence*, 151.
90 Richard Ned Lebow, *The Tragic Vision of Politics*, 358; J. Peter Euben, "The Tragedy of Tragedy," 22.

heals through "participation in the disorder, as a way of ending it."[91] The Greeks believed the impact of *catharsis* to be so profound that it had the power to liberate both individuals and societies from their scripts, and to transform them into agents of change.[92]

To a social scientist, *catharsis* sounds a lot like revolution, but there is one crucial difference. *Catharsis* is based on compassion – the ability to see the enemy, the Other, as a co-sufferer. Revolution, on the other hand, is typically a settling of accounts with that enemy. Most modern revolutionaries are averse to the lessons of tragedy because they are seeking to overturn the status quo, not restore order to society. They are unable to comprehend how their own actions are actually perpetuating disorder, and hence cannot see that the real solution lies in what Williams calls a "quite different peacemaking that would attempt to resolve rather than to cover the determining tragic disorder. Any such resolution would mean changing ourselves, in fundamental ways."[93]

We are shown how this entire process unfolds in the only complete trilogy that we have – the *Oresteia*.

1.5.2 The Political Lessons of the *Oresteia*

Is a just social order the result of retribution or forgiveness? This is the question that Aeschylus poses in his last major work, the *Oresteia*, which won First Prize at the Athenian *Dionysia* in 458 BCE, just two years before his death. The three plays that comprise it – *Agamemnon*, *The Libation Bearers* (*Cheophori*), and *The Kindly Ones* (*Eumenides*) – were to be viewed in one sitting, thus forming a single, multigenerational narrative.[94]

The first play introduces us to the tragic cycle that has been darkening the House of Atreus for generations. Clytemnestra perpetuates this cycle by murdering her husband, Agamemnon. In the second play their children, Orestes and Elektra, avenge their father's murder. In the final play all conflicts are resolved by the goddess Athena. I view this final play, *The Kindly Ones*, as a profound contribution to what today would be called conflict resolution. By changing the def-

---

91 Raymond Williams, *Modern Tragedy*, 81; Richard Ned Lebow, *The Tragic Vision of Politics*, 151.
92 Stephen G. Salkever, "Tragedy and the Education of the Demos," in J. Peter Euben, ed., *Greek Tragedy and Political Theory* (Berkeley: University of California Press, 1986), 284.
93 Raymond Williams, *Modern Tragedy*, 64, 80 – 81.
94 Mary Lefkowitz and James Romm, *The Greek Plays*, 45.

inition of justice from vengeance to compassion, it argues that a new social contract was created between the citizens of Athens and their gods.

Here is how the tragedy unfolds.

1.5.2.1 *Agamemnon:* Vengeance Is the Reason for Tragedy

After ten long years, Agamemnon's ship has returned home from the Trojan War. A festive welcome is prepared by his wife, Clytemnestra, but there are signs of trouble in the songs of the chorus and of the seer, Cassandra, who has returned as Agamemnon's slave and concubine. Indeed, soon after giving him a warm welcome, Clytemnestra murders Agamemnon and installs her lover, Aegisthus, as tyrant of Argos.

Clytemnestra explains that her actions are in retribution for the killing of their daughter, Iphigenia, who was sacrificed to the gods by Agamemnon so that the Greek fleet could set sail for Troy. From the chorus, however, we learn that the curse upon the House of Atreus began much earlier. Most recently there was the crime of Atreus, who murdered the children of his brother Thyestes and served them up to him as a meal at what was supposed to be a feast of reconciliation. Thyestes's son, the aforementioned Aegisthus, is therefore exacting his own revenge by seducing Clytemnestra and plotting Agamemnon's death.

After his return, Agamemnon vowed to heal the wounds of war, both at home and abroad. Clytemnestra too says that her actions are designed to "do away with the frenzy of killing back and forth in this palace" (Aeschylus, *Agamemnon*, 1570 – 1575). Their efforts are doomed, however, because what they truly seek is not justice, but vengeance.

1.5.2.2 *The Libation Bearers:* Does Justice Call Out for Blood?

Years pass. As the second play begins, Clytemnestra and Aegisthus still rule in Argos, but their reign is anything but peaceful and just. The heavens are in turmoil, and the god Apollo commands Agamemnon's exiled son, Orestes, now of age to claim the throne, to return home and avenge his father.

Orestes seems reluctant to do so. On his way home, he stops at his father's graveside to ask for blessing. There he happens to meet his sister, Elektra, who is praying for a savior to avenge her father's murder. Their doubts assuaged by this improbable encounter, together they conspire to kill Clytemnestra and Aegisthus.

After the murder, Orestes wonders whether his actions were truly just, but it is now too late. He is a murderer tainted with *miasma*, a pollution so foul than none may touch or even speak to him. As *The Libation Bearers* ends, Orestes flees the city hounded by the Furies, the divine tormentors of those who have spilled kindred blood. The chorus laments: "When will all this cease? When will murder, its fury spent, rest at last in sleep?" (Aeschylus, *The Libation Bearers*, 1075).

No one can say. The situation seems utterly hopeless, not just for the House of Atreus, which seems bent on self-destruction, but for mankind as a whole. Throughout these first two plays vengeance is still equated with justice. The chorus actually eggs Orestes on, urging him to strike swiftly and give no heed to Clytemnestra's pleas for mercy. After the deed is done, however, the chorus is full of dread at the new wave of killings that is bound to follow, and is eager to see Orestes go. How are we to understand the chorus's willingness to abandon to such a dismal fate someone they so recently hailed as the city's savior?

I believe that Aeschylus is preparing his audience for a tectonic shift in the very definition of justice. While the chorus, which represents the *polis*, still argues that the sins of the past must be expiated through blood ("as taught by the gloriously deep-thinking Furies" – Aeschylus, *The Libation Bearers*, 651), it is beginning to realize that vengeance can only lead to more of the same. In their lust for vengeance, Clytemnestra, Aegisthus, Elektra, and Orestes are all alike – they are described as "monsters nursed by the earth ... which makes all men akin to brute beasts" (Aeschylus, *The Libation Bearers*, 585, 601).

But there is a path to healing. At its heart lies a new wisdom that is obtainable only through compassion:

> Zeus who has set men the route
> to good sense, set firm this sovereign rule,
> that wisdom is the child of pain.
> Displacing sleep before the heart there drips
> the constant memory of grief, and wisdom comes,
> like it or not, upon men.
> (Aeschylus, *Agamemnon*, 175 – 181)

The memory of grief can bring compassion and forgiveness, but the chorus is not yet ready to embrace this path. It is still under the illusion that good fortune can be restored simply by removing the current tyrant. The chorus regrets the need for Orestes to be sacrificed, but insists that the wellbeing of the city must come first. Clytemnestra's murder is therefore celebrated because it frees the city from tyranny, not because it will bring about an end to the cycle of vengeance. The chorus understands perfectly well that it will not.

Besides, it argues, there is still hope that Orestes will be held blameless, since he was commanded to do this awful deed by the god Apollo himself. At the end of the second play, therefore, we see the chorus dispatching Orestes to the Oracle of Apollo at Delphi, the only one who can now save him.

1.5.2.3 *The Kindly Ones:* Justice Is "a Song Proper to a Common Victory"

With the exception of Orestes and his sister, all the murderers have now been murdered, yet justice remains as distant as ever. Even when violence is done for a righteous cause – to liberate Argos from the tyranny of Aegisthus – it fails to obtain justice. But if blood-for-blood vengeance is what tradition and the laws command, why does the cycle of tragedy continue? The answer, Aeschylus suggests, is that vengeance is not the same as justice.

Orestes flees, pursued by the Furies. After months wandering the Greek hillsides, he finally arrives at Delphi and appeals to Apollo. Apollo casts a sleeping spell on the Furies, and magically whisks Orestes away to Athens to be judged by Athena herself. Apprised of the issues of the case, Athena decides that the matter is too complex for her to judge alone, and she orders that Orestes stand trial before a new institution – a jury of the best citizens of Athens.

Athena introduces the jury as a fundamental innovation in Athenian life. The audience of course knows that there have long been juries in Athens, but this one will be invested with the unique responsibility of adjudicating murder cases. This is significant because the authority to punish homicide was viewed by the Greeks as the first step in humanity's transition from a beastly to a communitarian existence. The *polis* owes its very existence to this distinction. The creation of a new jury therefore implies that the gods now recognize that human wisdom and autonomy rivals their own. The relationship, while certainly not one of equals, is becoming one of co-dependence.[95]

A point in favor of this interpretation is that, as the jury's foreman, Athena feels that she needs to explain her vote, thus placing herself on a par with the other jurors. The jury votes six to five to condemn Orestes, but Athena's final vote ties the ballot, and Orestes is acquitted. Athena's intervention changes the outcome but, more importantly, it does so in order to establish a new standard of justice. From the trajectory of the three plays we sense that this new standard involves forgetting, rather than remembering, past slights.

The ability to forget, and hence to forgive, now becomes a crucial requirement for justice and social harmony. There are hints throughout the trilogy that rest, forgetfulness, and sleep help to overcome thoughts of revenge.[96]

---

95 K.J. Dover, "The Political Aspect of Aeschylus's Eumenides," *The Journal of Hellenic Studies* 77, part 2 (1957): 232.

96 Fear is contrasted to sleep by the watchman in the opening scene of *Agamemnon* (lines 13–15); anger is contrasted to sleep by Clytemnestra (*Agamemnon*, 345–347); sleep is likened to healing by Cassandra in *Agamemnon* (1247–1248), and contrasted to the voice of fear in *The Libation Bearers* (line 35); Clytemnestra's ghost upbraids the Furies for letting sleep dim their deadly anger and forget her torment in *The Kindly Ones* (95–135).

Zeus's justice is described as coming "in sleep against the heart grief of memory" (Aeschylus, *Agamemnon*, 179 – 180). At the beginning of *The Kindly Ones*, Apollo puts the Furies to sleep, so that Orestes can escape to Athens and seek justice there (Aeschylus, *The Kindly Ones*, 60 – 70). At the end of the *Libation Bearers*, the chorus asks: "When will murder, its fury spent, rest at last in sleep?" (Aeschylus, *The Libation Bearers*, 833). Finally, Athena enjoins the Furies to "put to sleep the bitter strength in the black wave and live with me and share my pride of worship"; or, if not, to "at least let the feud sleep" (Aeschylus, *The Kindly Ones*, 888 – 889).

Having made his point, Aeschylus must now "sell" this idea to a skeptical Athenian audience, most of whom will no doubt be on the side of the jury that voted to condemn Orestes. He must radically alter their traditional view of justice as blood vengeance. In order for them to undergo *catharsis*, he must have the Furies themselves, the very spirits of vengeance, undergo such a *catharsis* first.

At first, the Furies are quite angered by the verdict, which they say makes a mockery of the oaths they hold most sacred. Athena tries to appease them by pointing out that the majority of the jury voted in their favor. When that does not work, she offers them a place of honor "on shining thrones" in Athens, if they will but stay their wrath. The Furies reject this as a cunning deception, and insist on their vengeance.

Athena then redoubles her efforts. She reminds them, as if in passing, that she holds the keys to Zeus's thunderbolts, but then immediately shifts away from the implied threat by praising the wisdom of the Furies. If, in their wisdom, they choose to bless Athens, then they will become co-proprietors of the land, honored forevermore. The Furies remain skeptical and ask Athena to describe what benefits their blessing would bring. Athena lays out for them a vision of a new social compact, described in terms of musical harmony:

> *Chorus:* What magic do you bid me place in song upon this land?
> *Athena:* A song that is proper to this time of common victory:
> a song from the earth and the depths of the sea,
> from the sky, like a breeze full of sunlight,
> light and bright airs that descend, caressing the land;
> a song to ensure the abundance of fruit in the land,
> never failing, and a wealth of fine beasts for the folk,
> ensuring the safety and health of their mortal seed.
> (Aeschylus, *The Kindly Ones*, 902 – 909)

This new song of civility and justice will endure forever because Athena intends to transfer her oversight over Athens to the Furies. While the Furies invoke blessings upon the Athenians, Athena will bring them victory in war and glories that "all mankind can see." Moreover, she warns the Athenians that should they offend the Furies they will now have her wrath to contend with as well (Aeschylus, *The Kindly Ones*, 914, 932).

Finding this final assurance credible, the Furies agree to view the outcome of the trial not as a defeat, but as a common victory, under the terms of a new system of True Justice of which they are now a foundational part. Athena's compassion for them has allowed them to achieve *catharsis*, and has in turn unlocked their compassion for the Athenians. The Furies, now transformed, become the Kindly Ones (*Eumenides*). Compassion has prevailed, and the final antistrophe rejoices in this "pact for peace [that] will live for all time!" (Aeschylus, *The Kindly Ones*, 1044).

1.5.3 Athena's Strategy for Social Harmony

In his final play of the trilogy, Aeschylus lays out a comprehensive strategy for social healing. First, the aggrieved parties appeal to someone they consider to be an impartial adjudicator – Athena. Some do so eagerly, others reluctantly, but they all expect their interests to be heard fairly and respectfully.

Athena quickly realizes that no judgment she can render will satisfy all parties, so she "passes the buck." She creates a new institution – the jury – that places the burden of judgment upon the entire *polis*. By doing so, she also redefines her own role. She is no longer a judge who renders a verdict, but a statesman who proposes a framework for conflict resolution. This latter role requires a broader definition of justice, which will in turn form the basis of a new and all-inclusive social order.

That is why, when the jury acquits Orestes, Athena's first step is to defend the institution as part of a new order that was ordained by Zeus himself (Aeschylus, *Eumenides*, 970 – 975). But then she goes further. She suggests to the Furies that they could become the pillars of this new order, if they are willing to undergo *catharsis* and learn compassion, for it is compassion, not vengeance, which is to be the foundation of this new social order.

The new social order that emerges thus has three co-founders, all of whom have a vital stake in the prosperity of Athens: the Jury, which pledges to rule justly; the Furies, who pledge to safeguard the wellbeing of Athens; and Athena herself, who pledges to spread the fame and glory of Athens. Working side-by-side, they deepen the social cohesion and stability of the *polis*.

Aeschylus wants the audience to see that creating a harmonious social order requires former enemies to become stakeholders in society. The process of moving society from tragedy to reconciliation goes through the following stages:

1) *Anagnorisis*, which entails raising the public's awareness that the restoration of social harmony will require the combined efforts of the whole community;

2) *Catharsis*, which involves purging the soul of hatred, so that confrontation can give way to true dialogue;

3) *Dialogue*, which evokes both compassion and forgiveness. Its true objective is a self-transformation that allows for the formation of a new relationship with the Other. Classical Greek tragedy is, quintessentially, a series of dialogues in which we are encouraged to expose our own tragic flaws to ourselves, since only when the participants grasp how their own actions have stoked the hatred of others, can they choose a different path.

Anagnorisis, catharsis, and dialogue lead, ultimately, to true justice, which is rooted in compassion rather than vengeance. When compassion replaces vengeance on a sufficiently wide scale in society, it allows for the creation of a new social compact. That social compact will be secure when former enemies become stakeholders and active participants in the social order.

Some scholars are skeptical that Aeschylus had anything so grandiose in mind when he wrote *Oresteia*. The esteemed classicist Richard Livingstone believes that he was probably more concerned with getting Athenians to think about the costs of reforming the Areopagus, particularly since Ephialtes, the author of those reforms, had recently been assassinated.[97]

But there is much more going on here than an argument about the merits of the new Areopagus. Throughout the play, Aeschylus carefully weaves a middle road between detractors and supporters of reform, at times extoling the Areopagus as the guardian of revered Athenian traditions, at other times suggesting that its social base is too narrow. I believe this hints at the approach to politics that Aeschylus himself favors, which he places on the lips of the Goddess of Wisdom herself: "The god has ever granted power to moderates, although the objects of

---

97 R.W. Livingstone, "The Problem of the Eumenides of Aeschylus," *The Journal of Hellenic Studies* 45, no. 1 (1925): 124, https://doi.org/10.2307/624909; "Ephialtes," accessed October 21, 2021, https://www.stoa.org/demos/article_ephialtes@page=all&greekEncoding=UnicodeC.html. The previous decade had seen Themistocles (524–460 BCE) ostracized, tried, and sentenced to death; Themistocles's protégé Ephialtes then taking revenge on his predecessor Cimon by gutting the power of the Areopagus and having Cimon banished for ten years; and, finally, Ephialtes himself assassinated, some suspect, by his own protégé, Pericles (495–429 BCE).

his choice may change. Moderation is the creed I preach" (Aeschylus, *The Kindly Ones*, 529–531).

Kenneth Dover seems to me to be more on the mark when he suggests that Aeschylus's message needs to be read more broadly, as a warning against sudden political change.[98] This also fits with Robin Bond's modern translation of Aeschylus, in which he renders Athena's famous passage about there being a time and a place for terror, even in a democracy, as follows: "the inborn dread of citizens, that quells injustice, shall, both day and kindly night alike, prevent the citizens from introducing laws that foster revolution" (Aeschylus, *The Kindly Ones*, 517–521).

In sum, while classical Greek tragedy was never just about politics, it was always relevant to politics. The plays asked the audience to participate in a thought experiment: to consider the social consequences of the actions being demonstrated on stage. Sometimes these consequences proved quite calamitous, while at other times they led to a resolution of the conflict. In either case, the catalyst turns out to be the hero's willingness, or unwillingness, to undergo *catharsis*.

The Greeks also had the advantage of a collective understanding of the social good. Any individual who considered himself or herself to be the sole font of wisdom was either guilty of *hubris*, or an *idiotes*, someone to be shunned because they lived outside the norms of society.[99] Tragedies were the vehicle by which one's personal morality could be measured against the collective morality and social norms. It is hard to think of a better definition of civic education.

1.6 Applying Tragedy's Untapped Potential to Ukraine

It should now be readily apparent why I view the crisis in Ukraine as a tragedy reminiscent of the Peloponnesian War, which Simon Critchley aptly describes as a "long suicide" of the Athenian city-state.[100] Raymond Williams captures its essence when he writes: "Tragedy rests not in the individual destiny ... but in the general condition, of a people reducing or destroying itself because it is not conscious of its true condition."[101] Tragedy can thus be defined, most simply, as an outcome made inescapable by the fact that the actors do not see how their own actions are leading to the very outcome they are trying to avoid. This, of course,

---

98 K.J. Dover, "The Political Aspect of Aeschylus's Eumenides," 232–233.
99 Silvia Zappulla, "Reading *Antigone* through Hannah Arendt's Political Philosophy."
100 Simon Critchley, *Tragedy, the Greeks, and Us*, 45.
101 Raymond Williams, *Modern Tragedy*, 162.

implies that if the actors could recognize this connection, and change their behavior, the tragic cycle could be broken.

Perhaps by combining social analysis with tragedy we can shed light on two questions that have long troubled analysts: Why do the reform efforts announced by every Ukrainian government since 1990 so quickly run out of steam? And, why, despite every effort to forge national unity, do political conflicts replicate themselves so tenaciously along the country's traditional cultural divide? Ukraine's failure to achieve social consolidation, despite large amounts of financial, diplomatic, and technical assistance is so obvious that it has even been given its own diagnosis – "Ukraine fatigue."[102]

The answer to these questions is rooted in the tragic nature of Ukraine's internal crisis, which replicates itself in every aspect of Ukrainian society. This does not mean that other factors, and I am referring here specifically to Russian intervention before 2022, are irrelevant. It does, however, mean that focusing on external factors to the exclusion of these recurring indigenous factors, will not help to either understand or solve Ukraine's deep dysfunctions. Approaches that focus on single issues – corruption, oligarchical infighting, Russian intervention, Western external administration – treat the symptoms of the disease rather than its underlying causes. The advantage of tragedy is that it was designed to reveal, and then to heal, the root causes of social conflict.

Introspection and self-correction, however, are never popular solutions. Aeschylus was keenly aware of this, and therefore wrote the conclusion of the *Oresteia* like a doctor prescribing a medication. According to R.W. Livingstone: "he made them up in a pill. Pills do not deceive us; but their rounded and agreeable surface enables us to take drugs which in their naked state we should refuse."[103]

Some Ukrainians, in search of a quicker remedy for Ukraine's chronic lack of unity, have turned to nationalism. The difficulty with nationalism, however, is that it greatly aggravates the problem of achieving social harmony. That is because nationalists tend to believe that Ukrainian history, and Ukrainian identity, first must be thoroughly cleansed of Russian cultural influences before the population can be allowed to participate in nation-building. Such efforts to lobotomize Ukraine's national consciousness, by erasing all positive memories of Russia, has sparked resistance among the 40 percent of Ukrainians (two-thirds in the east), who as late as 2021 still regarded the two as one people.[104]

---

102 Steven Pifer, "Curing 'Ukraine Fatigue,'" *Brookings* (blog), November 30, 2001, https://www.brookings.edu/opinions/curing-ukraine-fatigue/.
103 R.W. Livingstone, "The Problem of the Eumenides of Aeschylus," 130 – 131.
104 In July 2021, the Ukrainian polling agency *Rating* asked Ukrainians whether they agreed with President Putin's statement that "Russians and Ukrainians are one people, who belong

An alternative approach, like Athena's strategy for reconciliation in *The Kindly Ones*, would require both new institutions, and a new and more compassionate social consciousness. One will not work without the other, and of the two, transforming social consciousness will be more difficult. It starts with the transformation of individual attitudes toward the enemy Other, and must eventually be linked to new institutions that make the Other Ukraine an integral part of society.

Before moving on to specifics in the next chapters, it is important to address some potential criticisms of my approach. One is that focusing exclusively on tragedy's applicability to politics artificially narrows the concept and allows it to be manipulated to obtain whatever results one desires. Acknowledging, as I do, the richness and complexity of classical Greek tragedy, however, does not imply that it did not also seek to teach wisdom and its practical application. As Euben notes, "Every *tekne*, including the tragic, aims at some good or at some need or deficiency it intends to fill."[105] To suggest otherwise is to divorce *theoria* from *praxis*, and *sophia* from *tekne*, which runs counter to Greek thinking.[106]

I reaffirm this connection by suggesting that tragic actions take place not only on the theater stage, but in real life as well. The political consequences of such actions can be objectively defined as tragic, if they are observed in recurring patterns of behavior that undermine the sense of civic community. This loss can be measured through traditional social science instruments, such as surveys and sociological data. Such research can reveal the impact that tragedy has had on a society, trace its impact in specific policies, and test the hypothesis that countering this impact can help to break the tragic cycle.

Although my approach derives its inspiration from classical Greek tragedy, it is actually not that different from the way that political scientists traditionally determine a critical variable. As the late Harry Eckstein pointed out, such variables are determined by creating a model of reality against which to test their hypothesis.[107] Classical Greek tragedy would call this a *mimesis* of reality. In both

---

to one historical and spiritual space." Nationwide 41 percent said they did. "Suspilno-politychni nastroi naselennya (23–25 lypnia 2021) – Ukraina – Doslidzhennya – Sotsiolohichna hrupa Reitynh," [Socio-Political Sentiments of the Population (July 23–25, 2021) – Ukraine – Research – Sociological Group Rating] http://ratinggroup.ua/research/ukraine/obschestvenno-politicheskie_nastroeniya_naseleniya_23–25_iyulya_2021.html, 21.

105 J. Peter Euben, *Greek Tragedy and Political Theory*, 292.

106 Richard Ned Lebow, *The Tragic Vision of Politics*, 59–60.

107 Harry Eckstein, "Case Study and Theory in Political Science," in Fred I. Greenstein and Nelson W. Polsby, eds., *Strategies of Inquiry: Handbook of Political Science* 7 (Reading, MA: Addison-

instances, the purpose is the same, to highlight the contradictions between the hypothesis, and what is happening in real life. From a social science perspective, therefore, in the following chapters I will be testing the hypothesis that Ukrainian politics is following a typical tragic pattern by comparing it to actual recent events.

Another likely criticism is that there was no internal strife in Ukraine, and hence no tragic cycle, before Russia intervened militarily in 2014. This is the Ukrainian government's position. As Greek tragedians are quick to point out, however, appeals to righteousness miss the problem entirely. It is not differences of interpretation that lead to cyclical conflict, but rather the attempt to derive justice for one's own group at the expense of justice for the Other. For social harmony to be restored, society must embrace a definition of justice that is acceptable to all parties. This means involving the Other in the construction of a society in which all will have a stake.

This is precisely what the Ukrainian government has failed to do. Rather than acting like the Kindly Ones in *Oresteia*, they have acted like the Furies, driven by a sense of righteous vengeance, both against Russia and against their own Russophile citizens, who are frequently cast as a "fifth column" for Russia inside Ukraine.[108] This demonization sets up a perpetual confrontation between Western Ukrainians, who are deemed to be "true Ukrainians," and Russian-speaking Eastern and Southern Ukrainians, who are not.[109] While such policies are under-

---

Wesley, 1975). Case studies, Eckstein argues, permit an intensive analysis of multiple variables, increasing the likelihood that critical variables and relations will be found.

108 Aleksandr Belous, "Poroshenko rasskazal o 'Pyatoi Kolonne' i atamanshchine," [Poroshenko Spoke of the "Fifth Column" and Atamanshchina] *Zerkalo nedeli*, January 22, 2018, https://zn.ua/POLITICS/poroshenko-rasskazal-o-pyatoy-kolonne-i-atamanschine-272799_.html; Vitalii Plakhotnii, "Na lbu ne napisano," [Not Written on a Forehead] *Fakti.com*, March 26, 2018, https://fakty.com.ua/ru/ukraine/20180326-na-lobi-ne-napysano-poroshenko-zayavyv-pro-p-yatu-kolonu-v-ukrayini/; "Poroshenko: Nam khvatit uma i sil, chtoby 'Pyataya Kolonna' i ne dumala podnyat golovu," [Poroshenko: We Have Enough Presence of Mind and Strength to Prevent the "Fifth Column" from Even Thinking about Raising Its Head] *Gordon.ua*, August 24, 2017, https://gordonua.com/news/politics/poroshenko-nam-hvatit-uma-i-sil-chtoby-pyataya-kolonna-i-ne-dumala-podnyat-golovu-203989.html.

109 "Crimean Peninsula Could Be the Next South Ossetia," *The Independent*, October 22, 2011, https://www.independent.co.uk/news/world/europe/crimean-peninsula-could-be-the-next-south-ossetia-910769.html; Taras Kuzio, *The Crimea: Europe's Next Flashpoint?* (Washington, DC: The Jamestown Foundation), http://www.taraskuzio.com/Nation%20and%20State%20Building_files/CrimeaFlashpoint.pdf. The term "Fifth Column" was also used in the Ukrainian emigration to describe Russian-speaking regions like Crimea. Eleanor Knott, "Identity in Crimea before Annexation: A Bottom-Up Perspective," in Pål Kolstø and Helge Blakkisrud, eds., *Russia*

taken in the name of national unity and justice, they are in fact laying the seeds for future vengeance and retribution – the next round of the tragic cycle.

The fear among supporters of the 2014 Maidan is that any compromise that grants legitimacy to the Other Ukraine will only increase Russia's cultural and political influence in Ukraine. As a result, any attempt to end the tragic cycle by addressing the concerns of Russian-speaking Ukrainians, quickly winds up being labeled as treason by the most ardent Ukrainian nationalists. Surveys, however, suggest that the vast majority of Russian speakers are loyal Ukrainians willing to defend their country from any undue Russian influence. Treating them as potential traitors, therefore, is not only unlikely to lead to national unity, but is actively destructive of it.

Fortunately, there is another path. Policies and rhetoric that promote hatred and vengeance can be replaced with ones that promote compassion and reconciliation. To achieve this, however, Ukrainians will have to recognize that the country's disharmony and sense of malaise are being fed by efforts to obtain partial justice for one group, rather than a true justice that can be shared by all.

The rest of this book is organized around specific issues of contention, highlighting the tragic flaw that runs through them like a red skein – the lack of meaningful dialogue between Galicia and Donbass – the cultural heartlands, respectively, of Ukrainian-speaking and Russian-speaking Ukraine. It is my hope that a deeper understanding of these will provide what Thucydides once called, "a grammar to aid in the reconstruction of the language of politics."[110]

before and after Crimea: Nationalism and Identity, 2010–17 (Edinburgh: Edinburgh University Press, 2018), 286.
110 Richard Ned Lebow, *The Tragic Vision of Politics*, 299.

Chapter Two
Two Nations in One State

> Ukrainian history should only be read after taking a bromide. Before that, it is one of the most unhappy, senseless, and helpless histories ... a series of endless and uninterrupted uprisings, wars, fires, famines, raids, military coups, intrigues, quarrels, and sabotage. And isn't the same thing happening now?
> Volodymyr Vynnychenko, Chairman of Ukrainian Directorate (1918–1919)[1]

> The entire history of Ukraine is a struggle of two different Ukraines summed up in the phrases "Away from Moscow!" on one side, and "Together Forever" on the other. This "away" unites Mazepa, various independence activists, and the followers of Bandera. In both 1917 and 1990 the ideologists of Ukrainianism were united in trying not to mention their ultimate goal out loud for as long as possible.
> Vladimir Kornilov, Donbass historian[2]

> Ukraine contains three little Ukraine: the Southeast, Center, and West. Different historical roots, different mentalities, different historical memories.
> Leonid Kravchuk, President of Ukraine (1991–1994)[3]

One cannot understand the persistent political divisions that plague Ukraine without first understanding that they derive from very different stories about the same country: about its origins, about its aspirations, and about who is to blame for the fact that these aspirations were so frequently thwarted. This chapter looks at this contested history through the narratives of two distinct Ukrainian identities – Galician and Maloross.

The competition between these two mutually exclusive versions of Ukrainian identity plays a central role in Ukrainian history. During much of the twentieth century, these two identities struggled to coexist and find common ground. The achievement of independence in 1991 seemed to offer hope for success, but the shattering impact of the Maidan revolts of 2004 and 2014 renewed their mutual wariness. Such historical and cultural fragmentation is not unusual for nations that were once parts of competing empires. What is unusual is the degree to which these debates are still being used today to blame the other side for the ongoing failure to achieve a united and successful Ukrainian state.

---

1 "12 tsytat vid Volodymyra Vynnychenka," [12 Quotes by Volodymyr Vynnychenko] *Istorychna pravda*, July 27, 2021, https://www.istpravda.com.ua/articles/2020/07/27/157869/.
2 Alexander Chalenko, "100 let pervoi nezavisimosti," [100 Years since First Independence] *Ukraina.ru*, January 22, 2018, https://ukraina.ru/exclusive/20180122/1019802575.html.
3 "Kravchuk posporil s Savchenko o trekh raznykh Ukrainakh," [Kravchuk Argued with Savchenko about Three Different Ukraines] *RIA Novosti*, January 3, 2020, https://ria.ru/20200103/1563095636.html.

https://doi.org/10.1515/9783110743371-006

This pattern of blaming the Other can be traced back to the contentious debates on the eve of World War I over how to assess Bohdan Khmelnitsky's decision in 1654 to join the Russian Empire; to the debates over why Ukraine failed to achieve nationhood after that war; to the renewed failure to achieve nationhood after World War II; all the way to the current debate over why, after more than thirty years of independence, the country is still, in the words of former President Viktor Yushchenko, a "quasi-nation."[4]

2.1 Debating the Origins of Rus

The view that Ukraine contains two distinct nations has a long pedigree. It was widely shared by publicists, scholars, and statesmen at the turn of the twentieth century, when the issue of Ukrainian independence took on new urgency in relations between the Russian and Austro-Hungarian empires. It was cited by Tsar Nichols II's Interior Minister, Peter N. Durnovo, as a major reason not to yield to the temptation to annex Galicia, which was then part of the Austro-Hungarian Empire.[5] In modern times this distinction is such an obvious truism that every Ukrainian president since 1991 has made reference to it, while Western observers have routinely warned that the persistence of this division would end in the fragmentation of Ukraine.[6]

---

4 "Byvshiy prezident Ukrainy Viktor Yushchenko nazval zhitelei strany 'kvazinatsiei,'" [Former President of Ukraine Viktor Yushchenko Called the Citizens of the Country a "Quasination"] *Argumeny nedeli*, August 28, 2021, https://argumenti-ru.turbopages.org/argumenti.ru/s/world/2021/08/736023; "Kuchma nazvav odnu z naibilsh boliuchykh nevyrishenykh problem Ukrainy," [Kuchma Named One of the Most Painful Unresolved Problems of Ukraine] *112ua.tv*, February 21, 2019, https://ua.112ua.tv/polityka/kuchma-nazvav-odnu-z-naibilsh-boliuchykh-nevyrishenykh-problem-ukrainy-481460.html.

5 Stanislav Smagin, "Tragediya ukraintsa-rusofila," [The Tragedy of a Ukrainian-Russophile] *Ukraina.ru*, July 27, 2020, https://ukraina.ru/history/20200727/1028344214.html. Durnovo wrote: "It is clearly unprofitable for us, in the name of the idea of national sentimentalism, to annex to our fatherland a region that has lost any living connection with it ... The so-called Ukrainian or Mazepa movement is not scary in our country now, but we should not let it grow, increasing the number of restless Ukrainian elements, since in this movement there is an undoubted embryo of an extremely dangerous Maloross (Little Russian) separatism." Ostensibly recovered among the tsar's papers some years after his execution, some scholars consider this document apocryphal.

6 "Ukrainians in 2018," *David R. Marples*, January 11, 2018, https://davidrmarples.wordpress.com/2018/01/11/ukrainians-in-2018-where-do-they-stand/; Samuel Huntington, *The Clash of Civilizations and Remaking of World Order* (New York: Simon & Schuster, 2007), 138; "Kissinger's Flawed and Offensive Analysis of Ukraine," *The Washington Times*, March 10, 2014, https://

Since 2014, however, analysts and politicians are more likely to say that such a division of Ukraine into East and West is too simplistic, or even an invention of Russian propaganda.[7] It is my contention, however, that since many of the issues raised by the current conflict go back to divisions that were apparent long before Ukraine achieved independence, they are likely to continue until those divisions are resolved.

At its heart this is a debate about power – the power to define Ukrainian identity. In this power struggle both sides appeal to history, which since 2014 has become a minefield that must be navigated very carefully. The issue of whether to interpret a millennia of common history with Russia – as a colonial imposition to be rejected, or an imperial heritage to be proud of – has often been used to keep the conflict between these two competing Ukrainian national identities burning.

A good example of this is the debate over the origins of Rus – or Rus-Ukraina as nationalist Ukrainian historians prefer to call it – the Eastern Slavic proto-state from which, according to the twelfth-century *Tale of Bygone Years*, "the Russian Land came to be."[8] According to the traditional view, the three main branches of the Eastern Slavic peoples – Great Russians in the north, Little Russians in the south, and White Russians in the west – were once part of a single ethnos that gradually evolved into the Russian, Ukrainian, and Belarusian nations of today.

This thesis was imbued with political significance by the First Abbot of the Kievan Monastery of the Caves, Innocent (Gizel), in his *Kievan Synopsis* (1674). Innocent drew a sharp distinction between the geopolitical role played in the Ukrainian borderlands by the Orthodox Christian kingdom of Russia, and the Cath-

---

www.washingtontimes.com/news/2014/mar/10/carnes-kissingers-flawed-and-offensive-analysis-uk/; George Beebe, "Groupthink Resurgent," *The National Interest*, December 22, 2019, https://nationalinterest.org/feature/groupthink-resurgent-106951; John E. Herbst, "Think Again," *Atlantic Council* (blog), January 16, 2020, https://www.atlanticcouncil.org/blogs/ukrainealert/think-again/; Olha Ostriitchouk, *Les Ukrainiens face à leur passé* [Ukrainians Face Their Past] (Brussels: Peter Lang, 2013).

7 Anne Applebaum, Peter Pomerantsev, et al., "From 'Memory Wars' to a Common Future: Overcoming Polarisation in Ukraine," *Arena Program at LSE. The Institute for Global Affairs at LSE* (July 2020), 23, https://www.lse.ac.uk/iga/assets/documents/Arena-LSE-From-Memory-Wars-to-a-Common-Future-Overcoming-Polarisation-in-Ukraine.pdf. This rather typical report, asserts that "the latest sociology in Ukraine points out that the simplistic east-west dichotomy is less clear-cut than we are led to believe by Russian propaganda and the divisive campaigns of some Ukrainian political actors."

8 "Otkuda est poshla Russkaya zemlya," [Where Did the Russian Land Come From] accessed October 22, 2021, https://cyberleninka.ru/article/n/otkuda-est-poshla-russkaya-zemlya-1/viewer.

olic kingdom of Poland – a thesis that fit the expansionist ambitions of the Russian tsars, who made this work one of the most widely disseminated in seventeenth-century Russia.[9]

Abbot Innocent supported his thesis that the three populations are one people with four main points. The first is territorial unity. Here he cites monastic chronicles from both northern and southern Russia that refer to cities from the north to the south as "cities of the Rus."

His second point is the rapid establishment of confessional unity. Just two centuries after the schism between the Catholic and Eastern Orthodox churches, Orthodoxy was well established throughout Rus, and was increasingly cited as a rationale for political unity.

His third point is dynastic unity. All of Rus's ruling princes descend from the line of Ryurik, says Father Innocent, and the earliest chroniclers routinely extolled princes who sought to preserve political harmony among their brethren.

His final point is linguistic unity. Ancient chronicles, literary works, and popular fables, were shared throughout Rus, from north to south, with no need for translation. This, according to Father Innocent, points to the existence a single literary tradition, with its seat in Kiev. This makes Kiev the cradle of the Russian nation – "the mother of the cities of Rus," as Nestor the Chronicler famously put it. Although it was eventually succeeded by Moscow as the seat of imperial power, this makes all the subsequent accomplishments of the Russian Empire the common inheritance of Ukrainians, Russians, and Belarusians.

The most famous critic of this view was Kievan university professor Mikhailo Hrushevsky (a.k.a. Mikhail Grushevsky) (1866–1934). Hrushevsky was also an active member of the Ukrainian national movement. He briefly led the Central Rada, Ukraine's parliament, from March 1917 to April 1918. After the Bolshevik Revolution he emigrated to Prague, but after Lenin's death he returned to Kiev and became a prominent cultural figure in Soviet Ukraine.

Hrushevsky argued that the emergence of "Ukraina-Rus" on the territory of modern Ukraine could be traced further back, to the steppe cultures of Scythia. Its distinct ethnic and cultural origins led to divergent patterns of development in Ukraine and Russia, including a distinct line of statehood for "Kievan Rus" that survived in the Principality of Galicia-Volhynia, and later in the Zaporozhian Sich, before it was finally incorporated into the Russian Empire by Catherine the Great.

---

9 Evgenii Konstantinov, "Drevnerusskaya narodnost," [The Ancient Russian Nationality] *Ukraina.ru*, July 23, 2020, https://ukraina.ru/history/20200723/1028331967.html.

Hrushevsky's writings remain the bedrock of contemporary Ukrainian nationalist historiography, although subsequent Ukrainian historians have added some new elements to his arguments. One, is that the vast territory of Rus was never uniformly Orthodox. They therefore emphasize the lingering confessional dissimilarities, rather than confessional similarities to Russia. Another is that the territories of northwestern Rus were settled later than Kiev and primarily by Finno-Ugric peoples. For some Ukrainian historians, this suggests that the north was never more than a colony of Kievan Rus.[10]

For the most part, however, the Ukrainian nationalist version of history does not reject the argument of common origins, but instead reverses its polarity. Thus, instead of Moscow's rise being a response to the Mongol razing of Kiev in 1240, it is seen as something poisonous and alien that prevented Kiev from establishing its rightful place under the sun.

The key point for nationalist historians is that "Rus" should never be confused with "Russia." The appropriate term for the latter, they argue, is "Muscovy." This makes post-Soviet Ukraine the sole cultural descendant of Kievan Rus. The constant confusion of Rus and Russian, by contrast, only serves to mask the colonial suppression of Ukrainian identity, culture, and statehood, first in the Russian Empire and later in the USSR.[11]

2.2 How Ukraine Joined the Russian Empire

Another historical episode that continues to cast a long political shadow is the decision by Hetman (Cossack leader) Bohdan Khmelnitsky and the Zaporozhian Cossack Assembly of 1654 to join the Russian Empire. Generations of Ukrainians have debated about how to characterize this act, and what tone it set for relations between Ukrainians and Russians.

---

10 Today this confrontation is being played out online. For contemporary nationalist interpretations see https://www.istpravda.com.ua/. For the traditionalist interpretations see https://ukraina.ru/history/.

11 Vladimir Shevchuk, "Konets Rossii," [The End of Russia] *Apostrophe*, December 28, 2021, https://apostrophe.ua/article/politics/foreign-policy/2021–12–28/konets-rossii-kak-deputatyi-reshili-poizdevatsya-nad-agressorom/43664; Konstantin Kevorkyan, "Kompleks nepolnotsennosti Ukrainy," [Ukraine's Inferiority Complex] *Ukraina.ru*, January 6, 2022, https://ukraina.ru/opinion/20220106/1033023733.html; Ivan Gladilin, "Russkie – vragi ukraintsev," [Russians Are Enemies of Ukrainians] *KM.ru*, February 13, 2013, https://www.km.ru/v-rossii/2013/02/13/istoricheskoe-edinstvo-rossii-i-ukrainy/703952-russkie-vragi-ukraintsev-potomu-c.

The dynastic struggles of the sixteenth century between the Polish-Lithuani-an Kingdom and Russia left much of the territory of upper Left-Bank Ukraine in the hands of the Polish nobility, while the lower portion, "beyond the rapids" (*za porog*), was overseen by the Ottoman Empire and the Crimea Khanate. The Christians who settled in these lands, later known as Cossacks, organized militarily around forts (*sich*), hence the name Zaporozhian Sich.

During the early seventeenth century, popular resentment against the Polish landlords had led to multiple peasant uprisings, with many people fleeing from Polish domains to the Zaporozhian Sich. But, as is often the case, the spark that set off the "Great Revolt" against the Poles was a very personal slight. A local Polish official named Daniel Czapliński, decided to plunder the estate of another nobleman, Bohdan Khmelnitsky, in the process killing his ten-year-old son and kidnapping the woman he loved. When Khmelnitsky, as a Polish nobleman, sought redress from the Polish courts, he was told that he had no documents that proved his title to the estate. His appeal to the Polish king was also denied, and he was thrown in jail. Freed by his friends, he headed to the Sich, looking for others similarly inclined to wreak vengeance on the Poles.

Elected Hetman of the Sich in January 1648, he launched a military cam-paign against the Poles, but after a few months asked the Polish king, Vladislav IV, for forgiveness and offered to submit himself to the king's judgment. As fate would have it, however, Vladislav died before Khmelnitsky's letter arrived and the war party at the Polish court had gained the upper hand. Seeing no prospect of reconciling with the Poles, Khmelnitsky changed tack, and in June 1648 sent a letter to Russia's Tsar Alexei Romanov, then just nineteen years old, imploring him to join in attacking the Poles. The Cossack army, he vowed, stood ready to assist in fulfilling God's "familiar prophecy of ancient times" to raise up an Orthodox tsar to defend all true Christian believers.[12]

Russia's highest deliberative body, the Council of the Gentry (*Zemsky Sobor*), however, felt that Russia was not ready for war with Poland. It offered financial assistance, but delayed taking any direct action until the military and political situation had settled. This, as it turns out, took five years.

When Khmelnitsky renewed his appeal for protection in October 1653, the *Zemsky Sobor* agreed "to take the hetman Bohdan Khmelnitsky and all the Cos-sack Host, with cities and lands, under the protection of the Tsar." The exact terms of this protection were to be determined by a diplomatic mission to the Za-porozhian Sich. It arrived on December 19, 1653, and on January 8, 1654 Khmel-

---

12 "Vosstanie Khmelnitskogo," [Khmelnytsky's Uprising] *Wikipedia*, September 14, 2021, https://ru.wikipedia.org/w/index.php?title=Vosstanie_Khmel'nitskogo.

nitsky convened a General Assembly (*Rada*) of the Cossack Host in the town of Pereyaslavl.

Khmelnitsky told the assembly that six years without a sovereign's protection had laid waste to Cossack lands, and proposed that the assembly choose among four candidates vying for their allegiance – the Turkish Sultan, the Khan of Crimean Tatars, the King of Poland, and the Tsar of Russia. After arguing in favor of the latter on the basis of religious affinity, Khmelnitsky put the issue to a vote, which overwhelmingly favored the tsar. The Russian delegation then visited 117 villages and towns to determine their allegiances.[13] Although the Pereyaslavl Rada's decision was met with occasional resistance, both Russian and Ukrainian chroniclers describe the overall decision to swear allegiance to the tsar as meeting with overwhelming approval.[14]

Since there is not much disagreement on this point, debate has instead raged over how to interpret the terms under which the Cossack Host joined the Russian Empire. In March 1654 the tsar's new Cossack subjects made eleven requests, now known as the Articles of March. By the time their delegation arrived in Moscow, the number of requests had doubled.

The original requests deal mostly with the entire military host, some 60,000 men, being added to the state payroll (art. 9). One point deals with foreign relations, and asks the tsar to allow the Cossack Host to retain the right to receive foreign emissaries, excepting those from the Turkish Sultan and the King of Poland (art. 5). The added demands include a list of the privileges and remunerations to be granted to Khmelmitsky himself, and to the upper ranks of the Cossack Host. There are also the customary acknowledgments of the ancient privileges of local government (art. 3, 7), religious liberty (13, 16, 17), local legal authority (1, 16), and the collection of local taxes, under the tsar's supervision (art 4, 15).

The tsar agreed to provision the Sich with supplies and weaponry (art, 12), but declined to pay for the entire army, saying that Khmelnitsky had promised not to ask for provisions that would be burdensome to the crown. The final agreement retains the restrictions on the Cossack Host's dealings with foreign emissaries, adding only that any emissaries "with ill-intent" should be detained by the Cossacks until they received further instructions from Moscow (art. 14).[15]

---

13 Orest Subtelny, *Ukraine: A History* (Toronto: University of Toronto Press, 2000), 135.
14 Y.I. Dzyr, *Litopys Samovydtsya* [Chronicle of an Eyewitness] (Kiev: Naukova Dumka, 1971), 67, http://izbornyk.org.ua/samovyd/sam.html.
15 "Martovskie statyi," [March Articles] *Wikipedia*, April 18, 2021, https://ru.wikipedia.org/w/index.php?title=Martovskie_stat'i.

This agreement did not satisfy all leaders of the Cossack Host. Khmelnitsky's death, just three years later, therefore led to efforts to get an even better deal from Poland. After Russia defeated Poland, however, it also re-negotiated the terms agreed to in 1654, imposing additional restrictions on the autonomy of the Cossack Sich, and making the election of any new Cossack hetman subject to confirmation by the tsar.[16]

Historians have traditionally described Khmelnitsky's accession as made under the duress of military misfortune, but also note that it met with wide popular acceptance. Indeed, with the notable exception of Hetman Ivan Mazepa (1639–1709) who switched his allegiance from Peter the Great to Swedish King Charles XII on the eve of the Battle of Poltava, there seems to have been little effort among the Cossacks to set up a distinct Ukrainian political entity until the early twentieth century. When, in 1775, Empress Catherine the Great extended her personal rule over the Cossack Sich, and ended its special privileges, the Cossacks offered no resistance.

Ukrainian nationalist historians, however, tell a very different story. Khmelnitsky's covenant with the tsar, they say, was purely a marriage of convenience, which the tsar then abused in order to extend his rule over Cossack lands. This injustice led to subsequent rebellions, which became increasingly bloody and repressive. The absence of any Ukrainian national movement until modern times is explained by centuries of heavy-handed tsarist oppression, and Mazepa is mythologized as a national hero who sought to restore Cossack (read Ukrainian) independence.[17] For this reason, Mazepa, and his scribe Philip Orlyk, are often touted by Ukrainian nationalists as being much worthier ancestors than Khmelnitsky.[18]

---

16 Aleksandr Vasilyev, "Byla li Pereyaslavskaya rada vossoedineniem Ukrainy s Rossiei," [Was the Pereyaslavskaya Rada a Reunification of Ukraine and Russia?] *Ukraina.ru*, January 21, 2019, https://ukraina.ru/history/20190121/1022370094.html.

17 Serhii Plokhy, *The Cossack Myth: History and Nationhood in the Age of Empires* (Cambridge: Cambridge University Press, 2012).

18 "Stanovlenie Kazatsko-Getmanskogo Gosudarstva" [The Formation of the Cossack-Hetman State] *Onlain Biblioteka*, accessed October 22, 2021, https://banauka.ru/2210.html. Mazepa died soon after his defeat at Poltava, but his scribe P(h)ilip Orlyk (1672–1742), continued to make the case for the continuity of Cossack statehood in his "Pact and Constitution of Laws and Freedoms of the Zaporozhian Host," often called the Orlyk Constitution and in his "Conclusion on the Rights of Ukraine," which argued that Ukraine should be considered an independent kingdom because Khmelnitsky had entered into a voluntary agreement with the Russian tsar in 1654. Since the tsar violated this accord by later imposing restrictions on Ukrainian sovereignty, that agreement, according to Orlyk, was no longer valid.

2.3 Maloross Ukraine under Russian Rule: Shulgin vs. Hrushevsky

Dynastic ambitions, exacerbated by the efforts of the Catholic and Orthodox clergy to influence dynastic succession, ensured that the borderlands of Poland, Russia, and Austro-Hungary became a civilizational battleground. After the third partition of Poland in 1795, the Russian Empire was given most of Right-Bank Ukraine, while the Habsburg Monarchy (later the Austro-Hungarian Empire) was rewarded with the regions of Galicia and Bukovina.

According to the traditional interpretation, over the course of three centuries of Russian rule, Ukraine (then commonly known as "Little Russia" or even simply Southern Russia) forged close ties with Russia while maintaining the distinct local cultural identity and language immortalized in the writings of Nikolai Gogol, Ivan Kotlyarevski, Anton Chekhov, Taras Shevchenko, and others.[19]

---

19 Luigi De Biase, "L'Ucraina, piccola Rus," [Ukraine, Little Rus] *Il Foglio*, April 14, 2014, https://www.ilfoglio.it/articoli/2014/04/14/news/lucraina-piccola-rus-50579/; Oleg Rostovtsev, "Gogol obyedinyaet dazhe v razdiraemoi na kuski Ukraine," [Gogol Unites Even in a Ukraine Torn to Pieces] *Nezavisimaya Gazeta*, May 18, 2017, http://www.ng.ru/kartblansh/2017–05–18/100_gogolukr.html; Andrei Vidishenko, "Oles Buzina byl prodolzhatelem dukhovnykh traditsii Gogolya i Bulgakova," [Oles Buzina Was the Successor of the Spiritual Traditions of Gogol and Bulgakov] *Ukraina.ru*, April 16, 2020, https://ukraina.ru/sn/20200416/1027429152.html; V. V. Rozanov, "Golos malorossa o neomalorossakh," [A Maloross Voice about the Neo-Maloross] *Novoe Vremya*, January 19, 1914, 13598 edition, http://dugward.ru/library/rozanov/rozanov_golos_malorossa.html; Maksim Minin, "Vse merzavtsy," [Everyone is a Bastard] *Strana.ua*, May 15, 2021, https://strana.one/news/333426-mikhail-bulhakov-130-let-nazad-rodilsja-avtor-mastera-i-marharity-chto-on-hovoril-ob-ukraine.html; Bogdan Chervak, "'Formalnyi' i 'realnyi' natsionalizm Franko," [Franko's "Formal" and "Real" Nationalism] *Den*, August 28, 2009, https://day.kyiv.ua/ru/article/kultura/formalnyy-i-realnyy-nacionalizm-franko-ili-uroki-odnoy-polemiki; Oleg Khavich, "Den v istorii. 4 oktyabrya: vo Lvove sozdana russko-ukrainskaya partiya," [A Day in History. 4 October: Russian-Ukrainian Party Established in Lviv] *Ukraina.ru*, October 4, 2020, https://ukraina.ru/history/20201004/1029121815.html; Oleg Izmailov, "Istoriya gimna po-ukrainski: sovmestnoe tvorchestvo rusofobov pripisali levaku s khoroshimi svyazyami," [The History of the Anthem in Ukrainian: The Joint Work of Russophobes Was Attributed to a Well-Connected Leftist] *Ukraina.ru*, January 27, 2019, https://ukraina.ru/exclusive/20190127/1022461479.html; Anton Chemakin, "'My dolzhny reshitelno skazat: my – russkie, i Kiev – nash,'" ["We Must Confidently Say: We Are Russians, and Kiev Is Ours"] *Ukraina.ru*, February 14, 2019, https://ukraina.ru/history/20190214/1022667672.html; Fyodor Gaida, "Zrada na million griven," [Betrayal for a Million Hryvnias] *Ukraina.ru*, November 19, 2019, https://ukraina.ru/history/20191119/1025712466.html. As Gogol put it, "I myself do not know whether my soul is Ukrainian (*khokhlatskaia*) or Russian. I know only that on no account would I give priority to the Maloross before the Russian, or to the Russian before the Maloross. Both natures are too richly endowed by God, and, as if by design, each of them separately contains within itself what

Kiev was its administrative and religious center; Kharkov its primary university and a prominent center of Ukrainian literature, philology, and intellectual life; while Odessa, the port city created by Catherine the Great, became Russia's largest commercial gateway and "Third Capital."[20]

In this vast territory, roughly the size of France, Russian predominated in the cities, while Ukrainian predominated in the countryside. Tsarist officials tried to eradicate this discrepancy through a series of decrees that mandated the use of Russian throughout Ukraine. This was explained at the time as an effort to improve the integration of rural populations into the mainstream of the empire, a process common throughout Europe at the time.[21] Today, however, many historians view it as an attempt to suppress the emergence of a distinct Ukrainian national culture and identity.

The first notable Ukrainian national movement was the Brotherhood of Saints Cyril and Methodius, which was established in Kiev in 1845 and shut down just two years later. It included such luminaries as the writer Taras Shevchenko and historian Nikolai Kostomarov. Its goal was not Ukrainian independence, but the transformation the Russian Empire into a confederation, in which Ukraine would be one of six historical Russian nationalities.[22]

The effort to achieve greater autonomy for Ukraine, while avoiding a complete separation from Russia, would become *the* leitmotif of Maloross Ukrainian politics. Its advocates saw the Ukrainian ethnos as a distinct part of the larger Russian cultural family, and many assumed that this distinctiveness would some day lead to self-government.[23] That is why, on the eve of World War I,

---

the other lacks – a sure sign that they complement one another," quoted in Andrew Wilson, *The Ukrainians: Unexpected Nation* (New Haven, CT: Yale University Press, 2002), 88 – 89. The list of Russophile Ukrainians even includes several luminaries now enrolled in the pantheon of Ukrainian nationalists, such as Ivan Franko, Mikhail Drahomanov, Pavel Chubinsky, the author of the Ukrainian national anthem, Igor Sikorsky, and Vladimir Vernadsky.

20 Felix Kamenetsky, "Odessa ... – reshitelno tretya stolitsa Rossii ..." [Odessa ... Definitely the Third Capital of Russia] *Porto-Franco*, no. 23 (819), June 16, 2006, https://perma.cc/QK78-WREZ.
21 Eugen Weber, *Peasants into Frenchmen: The Modernization of Rural France: 1870 – 1914* (Stanford, CA: Stanford University Press, 2007).
22 Ivan Lappo, "Proiskhozhdenie ukrainskoi ideologii noveishego vremeni," [The Origin of the Ukrainian Ideology of Modern Times] *Imperskoe Vozrozhdenie*, no. 7 (2007): 101.
23 "V.V. Shulgin – Ukrainstuyushchie i my!," [V.V. Shulgin – The Ukrainianizers and Us!] accessed October 22, 2021, https://www.angelfire.com/nt/oboguev/images/shulgin1.htm. As Shulgin put it: "We will advocate for everything that would make it easier for the population of southern Russia to succeed on its material and mental cultural path, which is distinct from northern Russia ... when the time comes, we will seek all sorts of 'autonomies,' both administrative and in the form of broad self-government. But one thing needs to be remembered firmly: *we will not relinquish the unity of the Russian people to anyone at anytime.*"

when it seemed that world events might provide Ukrainians an opportunity for a different future than the one chosen by Khmelnitsky two-and-a-half centuries earlier, a fierce debate arose in the Ukrainian press over that choice.

Up to this time Khmelnitsky had been seen by most Ukrainians as a unifying figure. He was viewed positively both by those who saw Ukraine as a southern branch of the Russian nation, and by those who favored the idea of a confederation between Ukraine and Russia.[24] Indeed, when the idea arose to establish a monument to Khmelnitsky in the very heart of Kiev (where it still stands today), it was supported by all the leading Ukrainian historians of the day, including Nikolai Kostomarov and Vladimir Antonovich, Mikhailo Hrushevsky's teacher and mentor. By the early twentieth century, however, the debate over Khmelnitsky's legacy had become a marker identifying one's political aspirations for Ukraine.

The traditional view of Khmelnitsky as unifying the nation was defended by Vasily Shulgin, the editor of the monarchist newspaper *Kievlyanin* (The Kievan). As Shulgin put it, "There are two kinds of Ukrainophiles ... some defend the idea of the unity of the Russian people, its cultural, national, and, consequently, political unity. These are the Bohdanovite-Ukrainophiles. Others stand for the cultural, national and, consequently, political independence (*samostiinost*) of Malorossiya. Those who insist on the independence of the Ukrainian people, however, are not Ukrainophiles, but Mazepovites." It should be apparent to all, he said, that "Moscow without Kiev would not be Russia, but merely Muscovy; while Kiev without Moscow would no longer be Rus, but merely an extension of Austria."[25]

This characterization was immediately challenged by Hrushevsky, who insisted that Khmelnitsky's ambitions reached far beyond autonomy and were, in fact, "a conscious embodiment of the idea of Ukrainian statehood." According to Hrushevsky, Khmelnitsky sought to counterbalance Muscovite autocracy by making other alliances. He even agreed to a joint campaign with the Swedes against the Poles in 1657. Shortly before his death, according to Hrushevsky, he was considering a formal union with Sweden, a goal that was eventually realized by Mazepa. Hrushevsky's rebuttal helped to crystallize the view in nation-

---

24 Oles Buzina, "Ukraina – ne Galichina," [Ukraine Is Not Galicia] *Buzina.org*, January 10, 2012, https://buzina.org/publications/2129-ukraina-ne-galichina-7.html.
25 Evgenii Antonyuk, "Den v istorii. 11 avgusta: rodilsya deyatel, kotorogo nazyvayut pervym ukrainskim ministrom inostrannykh del," [A Day in History. August 11: A Figure Is Born Who Is Called the First Ukrainian Minister of Foreign Affairs] *Ukraina.ru*, August 11, 2020, https://ukraina.ru/history/20200811/1028479197.html. Interestingly, many of Shulgin's relatives advocated for Ukrainian independence. Simon Petlyura even appointed his second cousin, Alexander Shulgin, to be the foreign minister of the UNR.

alist circles that Ukraine had been struggling for independence from Muscovy for centuries. This view appealed very much to Simon Petlyura, later president of the brief-lived Ukrainian People's Republic, who re-published it in his journal *Ukrainian Life*, under the title "The New Nationalist Banner."[26]

In his reply, Shulgin acknowledged that Khmelnitsky had sought new allies, but insisted that his goal in doing so was not to liberate Malorossiya from Muscovy, but to liberate it from Poland. In pursuit of this goal, Khmelnitsky would have forged an alliance with the devil himself, says Shulgin, but he would never call into question the unity of Russian lands or their allegiance to the Orthodox faith. That is why, says Shulgin, the agreement reached at Pereyaslavl never mentions the words "Ukraine" or "Ukrainian," but speaks only of "Malorossiya," "the Russian people," and of actions taken "in the name of Russia."[27]

Shulgin argued that Khmelnitsky's ambitious geopolitical project was to bind Ukraine to Russia in perpetuity. This put him at odds with the Muscovite establishment of the time, which preferred to have Ukraine as a buffer zone with the Poles and the Ottomans, rather than as a part of the Russian Empire.[28] In Shulgin's version of history, Khmelnitsky emerges as a Russian nationalist for refusing to let the Muscovite tsar forget that the true origins of his kingdom, Rus, lay in Kiev.

This conflict of visions, so eloquently articulated by two of the leading intellectuals of their day, continued to echo well beyond the World Wars I and II. Hrushevsky became a prominent figure in the new government of the Ukrainian People's Republic (1917–1921), and is today revered as one of the Founding Fathers of Ukrainian independences. Shulgin, by contrast, sided with General Anton Denikin's Volunteer Army of Southern Russia (the Whites), and wrote the manifesto that Denikin's troops distributed upon their entry into Kiev. In an odd twist of fate, after fleeing the Bolshevik regime, both men eventually wound up back in the Soviet Union as supporters of the communist regime.

It is perhaps worth stressing that, despite its emotional intensity, this was a debate among people who acknowledged each other's patriotism. It would never have occurred to either Shulgin or Hrushevsky to torture, jail, or otherwise deprive his opponent of the right to voice his opinion. They were competitors in

---

26 Anton Chemakin, "'Russky natsionalist' ili 'ukrainsky avtonomist'?" ["Russian Nationalist" or "Ukrainian Autonomist?"] *Ukraina.ru*, February 25, 2019, https://ukraina.ru/history/20190225/1022806360.html.

27 Anton Chemakin, "'Russky natsionalist' ili 'ukrainsky avtonomist'?"

28 Alexander Pronin, "'Volim pod tsarya vostochnogo, pravoslavnogo!'," [We Want To Be Under the Orthodox Tsar of the East!] *Stoletie*, January 13, 2014, http://www.stoletie.ru/territoriya_istorii/volim_pod_cara_vostochnogo_pravoslavnogo__383.htm.

the cause of Ukraine, rather than enemies, because the only Ukraine that either of them could imagine was multiethnic, multilingual, and religiously pluralistic. But with each successive failure to attain the object of their heart's desire – an independent and prosperous Ukraine – such tolerance would be in increasingly short supply.

2.4 Galician Ukraine under Austro-Hungarian Rule: The Political Debate

The Ukrainian lands of the Austro-Hungarian Empire formally included the kingdoms of Galicia, Lodomeria, Bukovina, and Transcarpathia. Although its rural population referred to itself as Rusyn (anglicized as Ruthenians), or "sons of Russia," political influence in this region was hotly contested with the Poles, who were seeking to re-establish their own state, lost at the end of the eighteenth century.[29] Polish influence was especially strong in urban centers like Lviv (Lwow).

To offset Polish dominance, in 1860 the Viennese court expanded Galician self-rule. This led, in 1890, to the formation in Lviv of the Russian-Ukrainian Radical Party, considered the first Ukrainian political party. Organized by such noted Ukrainian intellectuals as Mikhail Dragomanov, Ivan Franko and Mikhail Pavlyk, its stated goal was the "political autonomy [*samostoyatelnost*] of the Ukrainian people."[30] It was succeeded by the Ukrainian People's Democratic Party, which combined both nationalist and socialist aspirations, and included Franko, Hrushevsky, and Evhen Petrushevich, who later became president of the short-lived Western Ukrainian National Republic.[31]

According to modern-day Ukrainian nationalist historians, the Austro-Hungarian Empire was more politically and culturally advanced than the Russian Empire, which gave Galicians the chance to forge a distinct political identity

---

29 Anton Chemakin, "'Russky natsionalist' ili 'ukrainsky avtonomist'?" According to Chemakin, Ukrainian socialists often criticized the efforts of Galicians to invent a "Ukrainian particularism," pointing out that they had been calling themselves Rusyn for centuries.
30 Andrei Teslya, "Federalizm M.P. Dragomanova," [M.P. Dragomanov's Federalism] *Filosofiya. Zhurnal Vysshei shkoly ekonomiki* 1, no. 1 (March 31, 2017): 72–90, https://doi.org/10.17323/2587–8719–2017-I-1–72–90; Oleg Khavich, "Den v istorii. 4 oktyabrya: vo Lvove sozdana russko-ukrainskaya partiya"; "Mikhail Dragomanov," *Onlain Biblioteka*, accessed November 4, 2021, https://banauka.ru/2216.html.
31 Vasilii Azarevich, "Galitskoe ukrainstvo," [Galician Ukrainianness] *Ukraina.ru*, February 20, 2019, https://ukraina.ru/history/20190220/1022757181.html.

and become, in Hrushevsky's words, "the Piedmont of Ukraine" – a conscious reference to the leadership role played by the Piedmont region in the unification of Italy. Hrushevksy felt that Galicia might serve as the cultural and intellectual magnet for Ukraine, Eastern Maloross Ukraine as its economic and industrial magnet, and Kiev as its political center. This stereotypical division survives to this day.[32]

Into this mix, however, must be added Galicia's now largely forgotten Russophilia.[33] Historically, Galicia's primary antagonists were Poland and Catholicism, and regional antipathy toward them far outweighed regional antipathy toward Moscow. This helps explain the Galician army's decision to join first with the Whites, then with the Reds, against the forces of Ukrainian Central Rada, after the latter sided with the Poles during the Bolshevik Revolution.[34]

Austro-Hungary's "Eastern Policy" had long sought to counteract Russophilia in the empire's eastern provinces by funding political organizations, like the Union for the Liberation of Ukraine, which advocated for an independent Ukraine that would defend Europe against Russia and "free the Slavic world

---

32 Oleg Khavich, "Den v istorii. 11 iyulya: ukrainskie natsionalisty provozglasili sebya 'demokratami,'" [A Day in History. July 11: Ukrainian Nationalists Declare Themselves "Democrats"] *Rambler,* July 10, 2020, https://news.rambler.ru/ukraine/44488434-den-v-istorii-11-iyulya-ukrainskie-natsionalisty-provozglasili-sebya-demokratami/.

33 Vyacheslav Korotin, "Pochemu zhiteli Galitsii ne lyubyat russkikh," [Why Galicians Do Not Like Russians] *Russkaya semerka*, May 14, 2020, https://russian7.ru/post/pochemu-zhiteli-galicii-ne-lyubyat-russki/. The most prominent Russophile Galician politician was no doubt Dmitry Andreevich Markov, who twice won in electoral campaigns to the Austro-Hungarian parliament against the future president of ZUNR, Evhen Petrushevich. Markov, who insisted on calling himself a Maloross, spoke out regularly in support of what he called "our Little Russian dialect," but at the same time he considered "Ukrainophilism in its present, so-called exclusively Galician edition, dangerous." He was one of an estimated 2,000 leading Galician Russophiles pre-emptively arrested on the eve of World War I. They were later joined by some 80,000 others in the Austro-Hungarian concentration camps of Thalerhof and Teresien, where roughly a third died.

34 Dimitry V. Lehovich, *White against Red: The Life of General Anton Denikin* (New York: Norton, 1974); Evgenii Antonyuk, "Petlyura u vlasti," [Petlyura in Power] *Ukraina.ru*, May 25, 2020, https://ukraina.ru/history/20200525/1027795002.html; Dmitry Gubin, "Kiev vozvrashchaetsya v sostav edinoi i nedelimoi Rossii," [Kiev Returns to United and Indivisible Russia] *Ukraina.ru*, August 31, 2019, https://ukraina.ru/history/20190831/1024802006.html; Anton Chemakin, "Psikhoz otorvannosti ot vsego mira," [The Psychosis of Isolation from the Whole World] *Ukraina.ru*, April 11, 2019, https://ukraina.ru/history/20190411/1023248067.html. When Petlyura complained about his commanders wanting to forge a federation with Russia, he cited "first and foremost the Galicians," and when he tried to rally them to join with the Poles against Moscow, they were his fiercest opponents. The UNR Minister of Internal Affairs, Isaak Mazepa, recalls being told by Galician army commanders that Galician soldiers would not fight for Kiev until they had first taken back Lviv from the Poles.

from the deleterious influence of pan-Muscovitism."[35] It forbade the import of Russian language books into Galicia after 1822, as well as the teaching of Russian in local schools which, as the governor (*Statthalter*) of Galicia, Count Agenor Romuald Gołuchowski, put it, would only "strengthen the population's orientation toward Russia."[36] It also actively encouraged the development of a Ukrainian language distinct from Russian by introducing German, Yiddish, and Polish words to replace the Russian words in more common use, a policy that modern Ukrainian governments have continued.[37]

Thus, on the eve of World War I, within the four predominantly Ukrainian regions of the empire – Lviv, Volyn, Ternopil, and Stanislavov (now Ivano-Frankivsk) – a narrative had emerged that looked to Galicia as the seat of Ukrainian identity, and the best hope for Ukrainian nationhood. According to this narrative, Galicia's historical separation from the rest of Ukraine, while unfortunate, was also in some ways fortuitous, since it had led the formation of a distinctive language, a distinctive political culture, and an exposure to Catholicism. And since the struggle to establish an independent Ukraine had emerged within the context of the struggle for Galician identity, its ultimate success had become associated with the cultural and political supremacy of Galician norms within Ukraine.

By contrast, the Maloross Ukrainian identity of Left-Bank Ukraine, with its major urban centers Kiev, Kharkov, Odessa, Dnipro, and Donetsk, saw itself as distinct from, but still complementary to Russian culture. It rejected the view that Ukraine must chose between Europe and Russia, preferring instead a partnership with both. If the modern Galician ideal is a Ukraine that can serve as

---

35 Gearóid Barry, Enrico Dal Lago, and Róisín Healy, eds., *Small Nations and Colonial Peripheries in World War I* (Leiden and Boston: Brill, 2016); Charles Kellar Burns, "The Balkan Policy of Count Gyula Andrassy" (Thesis, Rice University, 1980), https://scholarship.rice.edu/handle/1911/15533; Evgenii Antonyuk, "Den v istorii. 4 avgusta: emigranty iz Rossii sozdali soyuz za otdelenie Ukrainy," [A Day in History. August 4: Emigrants from Russia Form an Alliance for the Secession of Ukraine] *Ukraina.ru*, August 4, 2020, https://ukraina.ru/history/20200804/1028429702.html.
36 Vyacheslav Korotin, "Pochemu zhiteli Galitsii ne lyubyat russkikh."
37 "Neveroyatno, No Fakt: Ukraintsy Na Ukraine Ne Ponimayut 'novoukrainskogo' Yazyka," [Unbelievable but Fact: Ukrainians in Ukraine Don't Understand the "New Ukrainian" Language] accessed October 27, 2021, https://www.youtube.com/watch?v=TD9s5gVPNLE; Elena Murzina, "Chakhlyk i Khmarochos," [Shaman and Skyscraper] *Ukraina.ru*, February 13, 2021, https://ukraina.ru/exclusive/20210213/1030493658.html; Natalya Zalevskaya, "Nemaya Ukraina," [Mute Ukraine] *Novorossiya*, February 10, 2021, https://novorosinform.org/nemaya-ukrainaya-kak-v-sssr-ukrainskij-literaturnyj-yazyk-sozdavali-13516.html. After 1991, the Ukrainian government continued this strategy of introducing Galician particularisms into standard Ukrainian, in an effort to widen its distinction from Russian. Two Nations in One State 49.

Europe's bulwark against Russia, the Malorossiyan ideal is that Ukraine can serve as a bridge between Europe and Russia.

The contrast between these two visions of Ukraine is now so stark that it suffuses nearly every political and cultural debate in Ukraine. One telling indication of how each region's distinctive historical consciousness has survived to this day, is a survey taken on the three-hundredth anniversary of the Battle of Poltava, in 2009. In the western regions of Ukraine, 41 percent said they would have sided with Mazepa against Peter the Great, whereas in the east and south, only 7.1 percent would have made this choice.[38]

2.5 Maloross and Galician Responses to the Collapse of Empire

With the collapse of the Russian and Austro-Hungarian empires, these palpable divisions very quickly erupted into violence. Two distinct political entities, each one originally calling itself the Ukrainian People's Republic, emerged from their now cracked imperial shells, one in Kiev and one in Lviv. Although both spoke of wanting a united Ukraine, they referred to each other as Greater and Lesser Ukraine, or sometimes as Dniepr-based Ukraine (*naddniprianska Ukraina*) and Galicia.[39]

After the fall of the Russian monarchy, democrats and socialists in Kiev decided to establish their own parliament, or Central Rada. At first this Rada did not request independence, but rather called upon the Provisional Government in Petrograd to create a Ukrainian territorial administration out of the twelve southern provinces of the Russian Empire with a predominantly ethnic Ukrainian population. It also called for a Ukrainian army, and for autonomy within a democratic Russia.[40]

---

38 "300 letie Poltavskoi bitvy: geroi i predateli," [300th Anniversary of the Battle of Poltava: Heroes and Traitors] *Research & Branding Group*, April 1– 9, 2009, https://www.slideshare.net/ RB_Group/300 – 87851172.
39 "Velikaya i Malaya Rus," [Great and Little Russia] *Russkaya semerka*, September 28, 2021, https://russian7.ru/post/velikaya-i-malaya-rus-kakie-zemli-tak-na/; M. Smolin, "Niskhozhdenie Ukrainskogo separatizma," [The Descent of Ukrainian Separatism,] *Maloros.ru*, accessed November 4, 2021, https://malorus.ru/ukrstor/smolin_nishozhdenije.htm. According to Smolin, the terms "Greater" and "Lesser" Rus arose from the practice of the Patriarch of Constantinople to so address the two parts of its bishopric, the northern and the southwestern, which had become administratively severed as a result of the Mongol invasion.
40 Evgenii Antonyuk, "Den v istorii. 11 fevralya: V Kharkove poyavilas pervaya ukrainskaya politicheskaya partiya," [A Day in History. February 11: The First Ukrainian Political Party Appeared

After the Provisional Government rejected this proposal, the Central Rada declared Ukrainian sovereignty, albeit still within the Russian Empire. A delegation from the Russian Duma was then sent to Kiev in June 1917 to negotiate an agreement whereby the Rada would submit its proposals to the All-Russian Constituent Assembly. But after city council elections throughout Ukraine showed that the parties that favored outright Ukrainian independence had gotten less than a fifth of the votes, the Duma delegates withdrew.[41]

In was only in its Third Universal, adopted on November 22, 1917, that the Central Rada declared Ukraine's independence over a territory encompassing nine regions (*gubernii*): Kiev, Chernigov, Kharkov, Kherson, Podolsk, Poltava, Volyn, Yekaterinoslav, and Tavriya (not including the Crimean peninsula).[42] Curiously, the Central Rada did not claim the territories of the Don Cossack Host (*Oblast Voisko Donskogo*) for the new Ukraine, although it left open the possibility of adding other districts in the future.[43]

Even this self-proclaimed independence, however, was heavily qualified. Its authors consistently reiterated that they aspired to

> the protection of rights and revolution not only in our own lands, but in all of Russia, with the newly formed "Ukrainian People's Republic" as a part of the Russian republic … [W]ithout separating from the Russian Republic, and preserving its unity, we will stand firmly on our land and with our forces help all of Russia, so that the entire Russian Republic becomes a federation of equal and free peoples.[44]

---

in Kharkov] *Ukraina.ru*, February 11, 2019, https://ukraina.ru/history/20190211/1022631526.html. This call for federation with Russia is in keeping with the tradition of most Greater Ukrainian political parties, starting with the prototypical "Revolutionary Ukrainian Party" established on February 11, 1900, which rejected calls for separation from Russia as too extreme. Although it invited the noted Ukrainian nationalist journalist Mykola Mikhnovsky to write its political platform, it later publicly disavowed his manifesto for being unrepresentative of the aspirations of the party and the Ukrainian people.

41 Richard Pipes, *The Formation of the Soviet Union: Communism and Nationalism, 1917–1923*, rev. ed, Russian Research Center Studies 13 (Cambridge, MA: Harvard University Press, 1964), 53–61.

42 "III Universal ukrainskoi tsentralnoi Rady," [III Universal of the Ukrainian Central Rada] *Likbez*, accessed October 27, 2021, http://likbez.org.ua/iii-decree-ukrainian-central-rada.html.

43 "Ideologiya organizatsii ukrainskikh natsionalistov," [Ideology of the Organization of Ukrainian Nationalists] *Wikipedia*, June 21, 2021, https://ru.wikipedia.org/w/index.php?title=Ideologiia_Organizatsii_ukrainskikh_natsionalistov; M.I. Mikhnovsky, *Samostiina Ukraina* [Independent Ukraine] (Kiev: Diokor, 2002), https://refdb.ru/look/2177265-pall.html.

44 Aleksandr Vasilyev, "Den v istorii. 20 noyabrya: vo imya spaseniya Rossii provozglashena Ukrainskaya Narodnaya Respublika," [A Day in History. November 20: The Ukrainian People's Republic Is Proclaimed in the Name of Saving Russia] *Ukraina.ru*, November 20, 2018, https://ukraina.ru/history/20181120/1021803240.html.

For its part, the besieged Bolsheviks offered to recognize the Central Rada as its local representative in five of these nine regions, excluding Novorossiya in the south, and Slobozhanshchina in the northeast.

To sum up, the first three of the four Universals issued by the Central Rada all envisioned some form of federal relationship between a socialist Ukraine and a socialist Russia, with considerable local autonomy. It was not until the Fourth Universal, issued on January 9 (22), 1918, that the Kievan Rada declared the Ukrainian People's Republic to be a fully sovereign and independent state of the Ukrainian people.

Facing imminent defeat, the Habsburg Monarchy of Austro-Hungary had also decided to form a new confederation. Seizing the moment, on September 22, 1918 the Ukrainian deputies of the Austro-Hungarian parliament established the Ukrainian National Council, and declared their intention to create a Ukrainian national state in the kingdoms of Galicia, Lodomeria, and Bukovina. The delegates from Bukovina, however, refused this offer, and to this day Transcarpathians vote very differently from their Galician neighbors, and occasionally express separatist sentiments.[45]

The Austro-Hungarian monarchy, however, had already granted these same regions, known in Polish as *Malopolska* or Little Poland, to the Polish members of the Austro-Hungarian parliament as part of a newly formed Polish state. To pre-empt this transfer, the Ukrainian National Council seized control of Lviv and, on November 1, 1918, established the Western Ukrainian People's Republic (ZUNR in Ukrainian), setting up a direct conflict between Western Ukraine and the newly formed Polish state.

---

45 Fyodor Koloskov, "Zakarpatye – novyi ukrainsky 'Donbass'?," [Transcarpathia – the New Ukrainian Donbas?] *Ritm Eurasia*, December 16, 2020, https://www.ritmeurasia.org/news–2020–12–16–zakarpate-novyj-ukrainskij-donbass-52393; Natalya Bratus, "Deputaty ot Partii Vengrov ustroili demarsh na pervom zasedanii Zakarpatskogo Oblsoveta," [Deputies from the Hungarian Party Staged a Demarche at the First Meeting of the Transcarpathian Regional Council] *Zerkalo nedeli*, December 7, 2020, https://zn.ua/UKRAINE/deputaty-ot-partii-venhrov-ustroili-demarsh-na-pervom-zasedanii-zakarpatskoho-oblsoveta.html; Sergei Rakhmanin and Vladimir Kravchenko, "Het vid Kieva?," [Away from Kiev?] *Zerkalo nedeli*, June 8, 2019, https://zn.ua/internal/get-vid-kiyeva-320129_.html; Yuri Kondratyev, "Lider rusinov," [The Leader of the Ruthenians] *Pravda.ru*, July 23, 2019, https://www.pravda.ru/world/1422193-tjasko/; Katerina Tyshchenko, "Lyshe chvert zakarpattsiv khochut zhyty v unitarnii tsentralizovanii Ukraini," [Only a Quarter of Transcarpathians Want to Live in a Unitary Centralized Ukraine] *Ukrainska pravda*, June 8, 2019, http://www.pravda.com.ua/news/2019/06/8/7217536/; Vasilii Azarevich, "Russkie bez Rossii," [Russians without Russia] *Ukraina.ru*, October 30, 2018, https://ukraina.ru/history/20181030/1021599648.html.

Like the Austro-Hungarian Empire of which it had been a part, ZUNR aspired to be a multiethnic commonwealth. About the size of Ireland, its six million people were 71% Ukrainian, 14% Pole, and 13% Jewish; 62% were Greek-Catholics, 18% Roman Catholics, 13% Jews, and just 6% Orthodox Christians. Its leaders promised self-determination, social justice, and equality for minorities. Although the Ukrainian language was given primacy, all national minorities were given the right to study in their own languages, and to use their languages in all official institutions. "In the Ukrainian State," ZUNR leaders declared, "all citizens without reference to language, faith, ancestry, inheritance or sex, will be truly free before the law, manifest in a transparent democratic system."[46]

The ZUNR government then sent a delegation to Hetman Pavel Skoropadsky, newly installed by the German forces who were at the time occupying Kiev, to appeal for military assistance against the Poles. By the time they arrived, however, ZUNR had lost control of Lviv to the Poles, and in Kiev Skoropadsky had been ousted by a new government known as the Directorate. The Directorate was headed by political patriarch Volodymyr Vinnichenko, together with increasingly influential journalist, Simon Petlyura, who held the curious title of "Head of Ukrainian [Russian] Republican Troops."[47]

This historic encounter between two Ukrainian national projects, one from Galicia and the other from Malorossiya, resulted in the Act of Unification (*Akt Zluki*) of January 22, 1919, which is celebrated in modern Ukraine as the first united Ukrainian state. In reality, it was only a declaration of intent to set up a federal system in which the western regions of the Ukrainian People's Republic would retain cultural, political, and legislative self-rule, the details of which were to be worked out at a later date. Meanwhile, the two governments agreed to continue to act separately, and even sent separate delegations to the Paris Peace Conference of 1919.[48]

---

46 "Use pro respubliku zakhidnykh ukraintsiv," [All About the Republic of Western Ukrainians] *Istorychna pravda*, accessed November 4, 2021, https://www.istpravda.com.ua/articles/2018/11/13/153262/. On November 20, 1919 the League of Nations awarded Poland a twenty-five-year mandate to rule over Eastern Galicia, but on March 15, 1923, the territory was simply given to Poland by the Council of Ambassadors of the Entente.
47 "Predvstupitelnyi dogovor," [Pre-Accession Agreement] accessed November 4, 2021, https://prostopravo.com.ua/klub_yuristov/zakonodatelstvo/istoriko_pravovye_dokumenty/predvstupitelnyy_dogovor_01_12_1918.
48 Evgenii Norin, "Strashnee velikogo i strashnogo," [More Terrible than the Great and Terrible] *Ukraina.ru*, January 17, 2019, https://ukraina.ru/history/20190117/1022370061.html; Dmitry Zaborin, "Globus Ukrainy," [Globe of Ukraine] *Ukraina.ru*, January 23, 2020, https://ukraina.ru/history/20200123/1026429521.html. ZUNR sought an independent Galician state under a League of Na-

As it turned out, however, none of this would make any difference. In February 1919, Kiev was taken by the Red Army, and the Directorate was never able to send troops to assist western Ukraine. By June all of western Ukraine was absorbed into either Poland, Romania, Hungary, or Czechoslovakia.

Historians continue to debate whether the Act of Unification was a *bona fide* attempt to constitute a united Ukrainian state, or merely a means to gain leverage in subsequent negotiations. The public rhetoric at the time suggests that national unity had considerable popular appeal, although, even at this early stage, Galicians and Maloross tended to regard only themselves as the true standard-bearers of Ukrainian identity. Each side was therefore interested first and foremost in the survival of its own version of Ukraine, if necessary, at the expense of the other.

This is precisely what happened. The Act of Unification was denounced by ZUNR after it was discovered that Petlyura had agreed to cede all of western Ukraine to Poland, in exchange for Polish support against the Red Army. It is therefore quite ironic that, in 2016, the Ukrainian Rada adopted a resolution honoring Petlyura, who effectively orchestrated Ukraine's disintegration.[49] Greater and Lesser Ukraine would not be re-united for another three decades, until the 1939 Molotov-Ribbentrop Pact.

Another telling piece of this complicated jigsaw puzzle is what was happening at the time in eastern and southern Ukraine, and in the neighboring regions of Kuban and Don at the time. Regional identity in the latter tended to be Cossack, but loyal to a Great Russian rather than Maloross identity. Many supported General Denikin, who sought a united Russia that included Ukraine, while others supported a united Russia under the banners of the Red Army. In January 1919 the Red Army took Kharkov and declared the Ukrainian Soviet Republic.[50]

---

tions protectorate, while the Central Rada in Kiev sought recognition for an independent Ukraine.

49 "Za chto nash zemlyak ubil Simona Petlyuru," [Why Our Fellow Countryman Killed Simon Petlyura] *Timer-Odessa*, accessed November 4, 2021, https://perma.cc/RS54-VNCB.

50 "Den Sobornosti," [Unity Day] accessed November 4, 2021, http://novorossy.ru/history-lessons/news_post/den-sobornosti-epokhalnaya-peremoga-ili-godovshchina-istoricheskogo-anekdota; Dmitry Gubin, "Kiev vozvrashchaetsya v sostav edinoi i nedelimoi Rossii"; Aleksandr Vasilyev, "24 sentyabrya. Ukraina obyavila voinu Rossii," [September 24th. Ukraine Declared War on Russia] *Ukraina.ru*, September 24, 2018, https://ukraina.ru/history/20180924/1021217159.html. It is worth noting that Denikin's appeal of August 25, 1919 "To the Population of Malorossiya," written by Shulgin, included both an emotional appeal "to ancient Kiev, the Mother of Russian cities," and a pledge to create a new order based on "the principles of self-government and decentralization with absolute respect for the specifics of local life," including the free use of the Ukrainian language in the press and in all public institutions and schools.

Oddly enough, the Reds' victory satisfied many Ukrainians outside of Galicia. Socialists, political reformers, and even monarchists could justify supporting the Reds because they saw them as offering certain continuities with the Russian Empire. Monarchists appreciated that the Bolsheviks sought to gather Russian territory back into the new USSR; socialists appreciated the ideological objectives they fought for; while national reformers appreciated that the Bolsheviks promoted the use of Ukrainian in society, a process later known as *korenizatiia*.

As a result, many leading Ukrainians who had initially supported the Ukrainian People's Republic and fled after the Bolshevik victory, later returned to the USSR, or supported it from abroad. This includes Hrushevsky, the first head of the Rada, and his successor Volodymyr Vinnichenko, who even served briefly as deputy chairman of the Council of People's Deputies of the Ukrainian SSR.[51] Even Shulgin, who served as foreign minister of the White government of Southern Russia, was favorably impressed by Lenin's New Economic Policy.[52] Seized by Soviet troops in Yugoslavia during World War II, he served twelve years in Soviet prison camps. Subsequently amnestied, toward the end of his life he argued that the Bolsheviks, *volens nolens*, had become Russian patriots.

Reflecting on these chaotic events, contemporary Ukrainian historian Kost Bondarenko says that the Galician politicians of that era were Austrians first, Galicians second, and Ukrainians last. It could also be said that the politicians in Kiev at the time were socialists first, Maloross second, and Ukrainians last. He tells a story of how Simon Petlyura once met Polish leader Jozef Pilsudski after the war, and chastised him for abandoning socialism. Pilsudski replied that, unlike Petlyura, when the train bound for socialism arrived at the Poland station, he realized that it was time to get off.[53]

In the end, this gave Ukrainians in Galicia exactly what they had been fighting *against* – Polish rule. Meanwhile, the Ukrainians who had aspired for independence in what was now the USSR saw their dreams crushed, but those who aspired to autonomy saw theirs partially fulfilled during the period of *korenizatsiya*. It is therefore not surprising that the lessons drawn by Galicia and Malor-

---

51 Andrei Sidorchik, "Posle nezalezhnosti," [After Independence] October 15, 2019, https://aif.ru/society/history/posle_nezalezhnosti_chem_zakonchili_ukrainskie_vozhdi_nachala_xx_-veka.

52 See his 1925 book *Tri stolitsy* [Three Capitals], reprinted in Moscow by Sovremennik publishing house in 1991.

53 Nikolai Podkopayev, "Konstantin Bondarenko: Obedinenie ZUNR i UNR uchit, chto ukraintsam nuzhno spokoino vosprinimat otlichiya drug druga," [Konstantin Bondarenko: The Union of the ZUNR and the UNR Teaches that Ukrainians Need to Calmly Accept Each Other's Differences] *Ukraina.ru*, January 22, 2018, https://ukraina.ru/exclusive/20180122/1019804567.html.

ossiya from this first failure to achieve statehood were very different, and would fuel future recrimination.

For Maloross socialists, it was the Galician nationalist's lack of proper (socialist) perspective that had doomed both Ukrainian and Russian democracy. Some later joined the *Smena vekh* movement, and embraced the Eurasianist view that the USSR, as unpalatable as its political regime may be, deserved to be supported because it was now the *de facto* Russian Empire. Those like philosophers Pyotr Savitsky and Nikolai Berdyaev, who were of Ukrainian origin, would later support the USSR in its fight against Nazi Germany.[54]

For Galician Ukrainians, by contrast, the central lesson was that there were too many foreign elements within Ukraine undermining its unity of purpose. In 1926 Dmytro Dontsov wrote his most influential work, *Nationalism*, specifically to identify Russians, Jews, Poles as foreign elements, and to demolish the notion that Ukraine should be tolerant of diversity. Such an assessment led to an understandable interest in fascism, which many Europeans at the time regarded as a very promising vehicle for promoting national unity. Soon this gave rise to sabotage and terrorism, which in western Ukraine was directed at the region's most accessible target – the Polish authorities.

2.5.1 Galician Unrest under Polish Rule

The Ukrainians were the only major European nationality left out of the Versailles Treaty. When the League of Nations, in deference to Poland, denied ZUNR's request for protectorate status, nearly seven million Ukrainians found themselves within the borders of a newly formed state, that was, at the time, preoccupied with reasserting its own national identity, often specifically against theirs. To secure these new territories for themselves, the Poles prohibited the use of Ukrainian in local government, shut down Ukrainian language schools, and resettled former soldiers and their families throughout the region.[55]

---

54 I.N. Sizemskaya, "Istoki evraziistva," [The Origins of Eurasianism] *Filosofskie nauki*, no. 3 (2013): 49 – 52; "Georges Florovsky," *Wikipedia*, October 10, 2021, https://en.wikipedia.org/w/index.php?title=Georges_Florovsky&oldid=1049143081; Andrey V. Ivanov et al., "The Ethno-Cultural Concept of Classical Eurasianism," *International Journal of Environmental and Science Education* 11, no. 12 (2016): 5155 – 5163. Notable Ukrainian Eurasianists included Prince Dimitry Petrovich Svyatopolk-Mirsky from Kharkov, and Russian religious philosopher Georges Florovsky, from Odessa.
55 Oleg Khavich, "Nakanune rezni," [On the Eve of the Massacre] *Ukraina.ru*, February 19, 2020, https://ukraina.ru/history/20200219/1026743222.html; Gordon M. Hahn, "Report: Maidan Uk-

The "Volyn Program," as this project was known, aimed at transforming Ukrainians into loyal Poles by separating them from the deleterious cultural and political influence of Lviv. As the region's military governor, Henryk Józewski, put it, "I rejected the idea of Lviv as the capital of Volyn. In this situation Lviv had nothing to say to Volyn, and the Polish and Ukrainian mentalities of Galicia could only poison life in Volyn."[56]

To build local support, Józewski labeled this assimilation policy "Ukrainianization." It included the imposition of the Ukrainian language in Orthodox churches, the impounding of books and periodicals published in Lviv, and the suppression in Volyn of any organizations headquartered in Lviv. Despite these efforts, the number of Orthodox communicants in Volyn continued to outnumber Catholics by four to one, so in 1937 the government began to assist the transfer of communities with more than 10,000 residents from the Orthodox faith into Catholicism.[57]

By the end of 1938 "Ukrainianization" was declared a failure and Józewski was transferred. It was replaced by a similarly Orwellian policy of "co-existence," whose objective was the "governmental and national assimilation of the non-Polish population."[58] Ukrainians were now prohibited from calling themselves Ukrainians. Blanket cultural restrictions were accompanied by pacification campaigns, during which hundreds of politically suspect Ukrainians and "Cossacks" were arrested.[59] These efforts, along with similar campaigns in Lviv and Lutsk, swelled the ranks of both Ukrainian nationalists and pro-Soviet sympathizers.

This brief overview helps us to better understand the rapid rise and militarization of the Organization of Ukrainian Nationalists (OUN). It also provides a bit of background to one of the most infamous mass killings of World War II: the Volyn Massacres of June–August 1943, in which the military arm of the OUN, the Ukrainian Insurgent Army, took the lives of an estimated 70,000–100,000 Poles, in their own effort to eradicate Polish influence in the region

---

raine, the Ultra-Nationalist Tradition, and Anti-Semitism," *Russian & Eurasian Politics*, January 17, 2016, https://gordonhahn.com/2016/01/17/report-maidan-ukraine-the-ultra-nationalist-tradition-and-anti-semitism-full-version-parts-1–3/.

56 Oleg Khavich, "Nakanune rezni."
57 Oleg Khavich, "Nakanune rezni."
58 "Bohdan Gud: Volin pered Volinnyu," [Bohdan Gud: Volyn before Volyn] *Istorichna pravda*, July 27, 2020, https://www.istpravda.com.ua/articles/2020/07/27/157862/.
59 Oleg Khavich, "Nakanune rezni"; Svyatoslav Lipovetsky, "Tri goda polskoi okkupatsii," [Three Years of Polish Occupation] *Zerkalo nedeli*, March 15, 2018, https://zn.ua/HISTORY/tri-goda-polskoy-okkupacii-278056_.html.

and re-assert "historical justice."[60] Ironically, the prior deportation by Soviet authorities of several thousand politically suspect Poles and Jews, who had been brought to the region as part of the Volyn Program, may have actually wound up saving their lives.[61]

2.5.2 The Rise of the Organization of Ukrainian Nationalists (OUN), 1923–1939

After World War I, tens of thousands of Ukrainian émigrés wound up in Czechoslovakia, Poland, and Germany. The more radically inclined among them joined the Ukrainian Military Organization (UVO), headed by Evhen Konovalets. Konovalets, located in Germany, coordinated his activities with German military intelligence, while coordination in Poland was left to Andriy Melnyk.[62] In the early 1920s, the UVO conducted numerous acts of railroad sabotage, targeted assassinations and arson against Polish businesses. Polish security forces responded by arresting more than 20,000 people.[63]

If the objective was to convince the Entente powers to grant Galicia independence from Poland, the UVO's actions had precisely the opposite effect. When diplomatic efforts to obtain recognition for Galicia in the League of Nations failed, many looked to the USSR for support. Those who did not, set up the OUN in 1929. With the death of its founder, Konovalets, the OUN split into

---

60 "Verkhovnaiya Rada osudila reshenie polskogo seima o 'genotside na Volyni,'" [The Verkhovnaia Rada Condemned the Decision of the Polish Seimas on the Genocide in Volyn] *Fokus*, September 8, 2016, https://focus.ua/politics/356747; Myroslav Shkandrij, *Ukrainian Nationalism: Politics, Ideology, and Literature, 1929–1956* (New Haven, CT and London: Yale University Press, 2015); Ivan Katchanovski, "The Organization of Ukrainian Nationalists, the Ukrainian Insurgent Army, and the Nazi Genocide in Ukraine," *Social Science Research Network*, July 15, 2019, https://papers.ssrn.com/abstract=3429340. The Ukrainian Rada rejected these conclusions because: (1) Poles also killed Ukrainians; (2) the number could not have exceeded 30,000 since there were not even that many people in Volyn at that time; (3) it is "well established" that the perpetrators were Soviet secret police agents (the NKVD) dressed as OUN-UPA fighters; and (4) raising this issue only serves Russian interests.
61 Aleksei Statsenko, "Getto: kak natsisty unichtozhali evreev Lvova," [Ghetto: How the Nazis Destroyed the Jews of Lviv] *Ukraina.ru*, November 8, 2020, https://ukraina.ru/history/20201108/1029539982.html.
62 Oleg Khavich, "Den v istorii. 11 iyulya: ukrainskie natsionalisty provozglasili sebya 'demokratami.'"
63 Oleg Khavich, "Den v istorii. 11 iyulya: ukrainskie natsionalisty provozglasili sebya 'demokratami.'"

the Melnyk's "Old Guard," still located mostly in Germany, and a group led by a young activist in Poland, Stepan Bandera.

The ideology of the OUN was an eclectic mix of authoritarian ideas popular in Europe at the time. A leading figure was Mykola Stsiborskyi, who argued for a Ukrainian form of corporativism that borrowed heavily from fascist Italy. The priority for Ukraine, he said, was to create a highly disciplined revolutionary organization capable of establishing a national dictatorship. He imagined that some day such a dictatorship might be replaced by the direct expression of the people's will, creating what he called a "Ukrainian spiritual totalitarianism."[64]

Another leading ideologist was Dmytro Dontsov, who argued that, in order to survive, Ukrainians needed to develop an indomitable will for life and political power, manifested in "active nationalism."[65] "Nature," Dontsov wrote, "does not know humanism and justice ... what we call endurance ... is simply the extermination of the weak."[66] The right of a nation to exist, he concludes, must therefore be "above the life of any given individual, above the blood and deaths of thousands, above the wellbeing of a given generation, above abstract mental calculations, above universal human ethics, above any imaginary concept of good and evil."[67]

According to Dontsov, the highest form of nationhood is the conqueror nation – a nation that is willing to transform the world in its own image, regardless of the cost. Ukraine must either become a conqueror nation, or suffer extinction. Its unifying national ideal must therefore be to destroy Russia, for only with Russia dismembered and its territories absorbed into Ukraine, can Ukraine achieve true security and greatness.

Dontsov quickly became one of the OUN's most popular and influential authors, but he never became its official ideologist, because he disagreed with the organization's pre-1939 focus on Poland, rather than Soviet Russia, as the most serious obstacle to Ukrainian statehood. His writings continue to serve as an inspiration and model for many contemporary Ukrainian nationalists.[68]

---

64 Mykola Stsiborskyi, "Natsiokratiya," [Natiocracy] *Ukrainske zhyttya v Sevastopoli*, accessed December 27, 2021, http://ukrlife.org/main/evshan/natiocracy.htm.
65 Georgiy Kasyanov, "Do pytannya pro ideolohiyu OUN," [On the Question of the Ideology of the OUN] *Litopys*, 2003, http://litopys.org.ua/kasian/kas201.htm#par3.
66 Konstantin Kevorkyan, "Oruell zhiv!," [Orwell Is Alive!] *Ukraina.ru*, December 27, 2017, https://ukraina.ru/opinion/20171227/1019719194.html.
67 Viktor Polishchuk, "Ponyatie integralnogo ukrainskogo natsionalizma," [The Concept of Integral Ukrainian Nationalism] *Maloros.ru*, September 1997, https://malorus.ru/ukrstor/piun.html.
68 "Mer Dnepra," [Mayor of the Dnieper] *IA Regnum*, September 8, 2018, https://regnum.ru/news/society/2478026.html; Konstantin Kevorkyan, "Ukraina kak anti-Rossiya," [Ukraine as

Although the OUN had no strong anti-Russian policy before 1939, this changed after the Molotov-Ribbentrop Pact, when the Soviets became Galicia's *de facto* overlords switched from the Poles to the Soviets. Although bitterness against the Poles lingered, there was simply no more need to fight against Poland and Polonization. The new targets were now Soviet Russia and Russification.

At its last pre-war gathering in August 1939, the OUN declared that the Ukrainian state would be constructed on the principle of national power. According to this "Stsiborskyi Constitution," Ukraine aspired to be a "sovereign, authoritarian, totalitarian, professional-class state." Full authority belonged to the Ukrainian Nation, but was realized by the Leader of the Nation. The sole ideology permitted was Ukrainian Nationalism, and the sole political organization permitted was the Organization of Ukrainian Nationalists. Ukrainian was to be the sole state language. Only two churches – the Ukrainian Autocephalous Orthodox Church and the Ukrainian Greek-Catholic Church – would be allowed, and their top hierarchs confirmed by the Leader of the Nation.[69]

Thus, on the eve of World War II, the OUN adopted a form of integral nationalism that was fairly commonplace in Eastern Europe at the time.[70] John Armstrong, an early student of Ukrainian nationalism, notes five key similarities of such movements: (1) a belief in the nation as an absolute value; (2) a belief in the mystical unity of the people who comprise the nation; (3) the subordination of analytical reasoning to intuition and correct emotions; (4) a reliance on a charismatic leader who incarnates the will of the nation; and (5) a cult of action, war, and violence that express the spiritual vitality of the nation.[71]

Anti-Russia] *Ukraina.ru,* August 4, 2021, https://ukraina.ru/history/20210804/1031989027.html. Serhiy Kvit, Ukraine's Minister of Education from 2014 to 2016, wrote the introduction for Dontsov's book *Nationalism.*

69 Mykola Stsiborskyi, "Natsiokratiya"; S.V. Kulchytskyi and O.M. Veselova, eds., *OUN v 1941 Rotsi: Dokumenty* [OUN in 1941: Documents] (Kiev: Instytut istorii Ukrainy NAN Ukrainy, 2006), 201; Evhen I. Hishchynskyi, ed., *Za volyu Ukrainy: antolohiya pisen nacionalno-vyzvolnych zmahan* [For the Freedom of Ukraine: An Anthology of Songs of National Liberation Competitions], 2nd ed. (Lutsk: Vydavnyctvo Volynska Knyha, 2007).

70 Orest Subtelny, *Ukraine: A History,* 442–444. Similar movements included the Croatian *Ustashi,* the Romanian Iron Guard, the Slovakian *Hlinkova garda,* the Polish ONR (Obz Narodowo-Radykalny), and the Hungarian Arrow Cross Party (*Nyilaskeresztes Párt*). According to Subtelny, Ukrainian integral nationalism "clearly contained elements of fascism and totalitarianism" and proposed "the creation of a new breed of 'super' Ukrainians."

71 John A. Armstrong, *Ukrainian Nationalism,* 3rd ed. (Englewood, CO: Ukrainian Academic Press, 1990), 13.

Its ideological orientation made the OUN a natural ally of the Axis powers, and leading OUN members were quite candid about their sympathies for both German Nazism and Italian fascism.[72] Despite these sympathies, however, Evhen Onatsky, the OUN representative in Rome, and a regular contributor to Sziborsky's journal *Postroenie Natsii* (The Construction of the Nation), argued that one important distinction should always be kept in mind: "Fascism" he wrote, "is the nationalism of a nation-state hostile to any irredentists, ready to sacrifice everyone and everything to the cult of its already created state. Ukrainian nationalism is, by contrast, the nationalism of a non-state nation, which only lives by irredentism and is ready to sacrifice everyone and everything in order to destroy the cult of those states that prevent it from living."[73]

One cannot therefore simply label the OUN a copy of Italian fascism or German Nazism. Rather, it was part of a like-minded group of political association which existed in many countries, each with its own specific national priorities. For the major Axis powers, like Germany and Italy, the priority was to gain territory and influence by exploiting the weaknesses of their foes (and allies). For lesser powers, like Hungary and Romania, the goal might be the same, but the opportunities to do so much more limited. At the bottom of the heap were allies like Ukraine and Croatia, which had no state of their own. Their first priority was simply to create a state.

In the case of the Croatian *Ustashi*, they succeeded. The Germans supported Croatia's declaration of independence, and supported their efforts to institute a full-fledged fascist regime allied with Nazi Germany. In Ukraine, however, the Nazi leadership sought colonization, not alliance. They therefore arrested the

---

72 "Ideologiya organizatsii ukrainskikh natsionalistov," [The Ideology of the Organization of Ukrainian Nationalists] *Wikipedia*, accessed June 21, 2021, https://ru.wikipedia.org/w/index.php?title=Ideologiya_Organizatsii_ukrainskikh_natsionalistov; Per A. Rudling, "Historical Representation of the Wartime Accounts of the Activities of the OUN-UPA," *East European Jewish Affairs* 36, no. 2 (2006): 163–189, https://doi.org/10.1080/13501670600983008; Georgiy Kasyanov, "Do pitannya pro ideolohiyu OUN." Dontsov, in an article "Are We Fascists?," written after Hitler's seizure of power in Germany, wrote: "The political and psycho-moral spirit that inspires Ukrainian nationalists is, undeniably, fascism." Bandera would write in 1940 that "These new nationalistic movements have different names in different countries: in Italy – fascism, in Germany – Hitlerism, and for us – Ukrainian nationalism."

73 Aleksandr Zaitsev, "Ukrainskyi integralnyi natsionalizm v poiskakh 'osobogo puti,'" [Ukrainian Integral Nationalism in Search of a Special Path] *Novoye Literaturnoye Obozreniye (NLO)*, no. 2 (2011), https://magazines.gorky.media/nlo/2011/2/ukrainskij-integralnyj-naczionalizm-v-poiskah-osobogo-puti-1920–8212–1930-e-gody.html; Evgenii Antonyuk, "Den v istorii. 27 oktyabrya: v Argentine umer nastoyashchiy ukrainskiy fashist," [A Day in History. October 27: A True Ukrainian Fascist Dies in Argentina] *Ukraina.ru*, October 27, 2020, https://ukraina.ru/history/20201027/1029395160.html.

OUN leadership when it declared an independent Ukraine state in Lviv on June 30, 1941, even though it too declared itself an ally of Nazi Germany.

Was the OUN fighting primarily for the freedom of Ukraine in World War II or as an ally of the Third Reich? This question has vexed several generations of Ukrainians, and become a litmus test of political loyalty since 2014. In truth, the OUN was fighting for Ukraine's freedom to be a part of the Third Reich.[74] As they saw it, this was the best civilizational choice available for Ukraine at the time. Subsequently, as the Third Reich began to collapse, they altered this civilizational choice to that of becoming part of the anticommunist West. This tactical shift, however, merely highlights the consistency of OUN's overarching ideological message – that Ukraine can ally with anyone, except Russia.

This second failure to achieve Ukrainian independence, just three decades after the first, added new fuel to the conflict between the Galician and Maloross visions of Ukraine. In the Galician interpretation, the OUN-UPA (Organization of Ukrainian Nationalists-Ukrainian Insurgent Army) were heroes who fought for Ukrainian freedom. Necessity forced them to establish a temporary alliance with the Nazis, but toward the end of the war, when they fully understood the true nature of the Nazi regime, they embraced Western ideals. Since then they have fought alongside the West against the common Soviet/Russian menace.[75]

In the Maloross interpretation, the OUN-UPA were traitors and war criminals. They point out that three million Ukrainians fought in the Red Army, compared to perhaps 80,000 in the Ukrainian Insurgent Army.[76] They dismiss the ideolog-

---

74 Georgiy Kasyanov, "Do pitannya pro ideolohiyu OUN"; Per A. Rudling, "The OUN, the UPA and the Holocaust: A Study in the Manufacturing of Historical Myths," *The Carl Beck Papers in Russian and East European Studies*, no. 2107 (December 21, 2011), 3, https://doi.org/10.5195/cbp.2011.164; Ivan Katchanovski, "The Organization of Ukrainian Nationalists, the Ukrainian Insurgent Army, and the Nazi Genocide in Ukraine." Katchanovski estimates that 63 percent of top UPA and OUN-B leaders, and at least 74 percent of top UPA commanders, collaborated with Nazi Germany. The close collaboration between the military wing of the OUN and Nazi authorities should be no surprise, given their ideological affinity, and the collaboration between Ukrainian exiles and German intelligence established during the early 1920s. Intelligence reports suggest that Konovalets met with Hitler twice in the early 1930s, among other things to discuss the training of Ukrainians at a Nazi Party School in Leipzig.
75 Grzegorz Motyka, *Ukraińska Partyzantka 1942–1960: Działalność Organizacji Ukraińskich Nacjonalistów i Ukraińskiej Powstańczej Armii* [Ukrainian Partisans 1942–1960: Activities of the Organization of Ukrainian Nationalists and the Ukrainian Insurgent Army], Wyd. 1, Seria Wschodnia (Warszawa: Instytut Studiów Politycznych PAN : RYTM, 2006).
76 Gordon M. Hahn, *Ukraine over the Edge: Russia, the West and the "New Cold War"* (Jefferson, NC: McFarland, 2018), 41. According to Hahn, in 1944–1945 pitched battles took place between 30–40,000 OUN-UPA partisans and Soviet forces. In order to deprive them of their support base, the Soviet NKVD blockaded and depopulated large swaths of Galicia, Volhynia, and the Trans-

ical transformation of the OUN at the end of the war as nothing more than an attempt to find new sponsors in the West, and save their own skins.

What stands out most in both narratives is their remarkable consistency. For Galician Ukrainians, despite the shift in rhetoric from integral nationalism to pro-Western nationalism, the basic elements of hostility toward Russia and Russian expansionism hardly changed since the time of the Austro-Hungarian Empire. For Maloross Ukrainians, despite Soviet Communism, the Holodomor, and collectivization, Russia and Ukraine are still seen as sharing a common destiny, even during the most difficult trials.

More than three-quarters of a century have passed since the end of World War II, yet the memory of these events continues to poison political emotions in Ukraine to an extent rarely seen elsewhere. Efforts in 2005 by the Institute of History of the Ukrainian Academy of Sciences in Kiev to bring some closure to this division were dismissed in Galicia as an effort to discredit the struggle for Ukrainian independence; while efforts by the Ukrainian Institute of National Memory after 2014 to re-define World War II as a liberation struggle are typically seen in Malorossiya as an attempt to glorify Nazi collaborators.[77]

One reason for this, of course, is that how one interprets the past has implications for the type of Ukraine that is being built today. For example, Yana Primachenko, a researcher at the Ukrainian Academy of Sciences, argues that the OUN and UPA cannot be considered racist, chauvinist, or fascist because "however radical they may have been, without the institutional resources of the state it was impossible to realize that potential."[78] This is the very same argument that Onatsky made in the 1930s, and conveniently sidesteps the question of what type of society the OUN wanted to establish after it had achieved power.

It is precisely this issue, however, that became a concern for Maloross Ukrainians after independence, when prominent Ukrainian politicians routinely began referring to OUN-UPA leaders as national heroes and role models.[79]

---

carpathian foothills, deporting families and even entire villages. It is estimated that as many as 500,000 persons may have been deported to Siberia from these regions between 1946 and 1949.
77 "Stanislav Kulchytskyi: 'Bilykh plyam' shchodo diyalnosti UPA vzhe ne isnue," [Stanislav Kulchytskyi: "White Spots" on the Activities of the UPA no Longer Exist] *Ukraina moloda*, no. 3, January 10, 2007, https://www.umoloda.kiev.ua/number/833/169/30322/; Aleksej V. Pogorelov, *Izgibaniya poverkhnostei i ustoichivost obolochek*, [Bending of Surfaces and Stability of Shells] 2nd ed. (Kiev: Naukova Dumka, 1998).
78 Yana Primachenko, "Istoricheskaya spravka ob izmeneniyakh v ideologii OUN," [Historical Background on Changes in the Ideology of the OUN] *Likbez*, [no date] https://likbez.org.ua/historical-information-about-the-changes-in-the-ideology-of-the-oun.html.
79 Krzysztof Janiga, "Minister zdrowia Ukrainy: w pracy zastanawiamy się, co by na naszym miejscu zrobił Bandera," [Minister of Health of Ukraine: At Work We Ask What Bandera Would Do in Our

2.5.3 The Ukrainian SSR: Soviet-Style Ukrainianization or Ukrainian-Style Sovietization?

While many Galician intellectuals in Poland and Germany embraced radical nationalism as a means to obtain nationhood after World War I, their counterparts in Soviet Ukraine, by and large, did not. This is often attributed to the suppression of Ukrainian national identity and culture in the USSR, but it would be more accurate to say that Soviet nationality policy in Ukraine swung between two extremes: violent suppression of local national identity and violent imposition of it.

At first, the Bolsheviks sought to undermine "Great Russian chauvinism," which they viewed as a pillar of the former tsarist regime. To this end, in April 1923, the *12th Congress* of the Russian Communist *Party* (Bolsheviks) adopted "indigenization" (*korenizatsiya*) as its official stance toward non-Russian nationalities. The same policy was adopted by the Ukrainian Communist Party later that month under the name "Ukrainianization."[80] Ukraine's People's Commissar for Enlightenment, Aleksandr Shumsky, appointed writer Nikolai Khvylevoi to be the main ideologist of Ukrainianization. A century later Khvylevoi's phrase "Away from Moscow!" (*Het vid Moskvy*) was adopted by Ukrainian President Petro Poroshenko.[81]

Khvylevoi, Shumsky, and his successor Nikolai Skrypnik, initiated a three-year plan for "total Ukrainianization," which included shutting down all Russian-language schools, theaters, and media outlets, as well as requiring the use of Ukrainian by all party members in all state organizations. Anyone unable to pass a Ukrainian language exam had to attend classes to learn it. Refusal to do so could result in being fired and denied employment benefits. It could also result in being labeled politically unreliable.[82]

———
Place] *Kresy* (blog), August 7, 2017, https://kresy.pl/wydarzenia/spoleczenstwo/minister-zdrowia-ukrainy-pracy-zastanawiamy-sie-by-naszym-miejscu-zrobil-bandera/; Mat Babiak, "Poroshenko: 'UPA Are Heroes,'" *Euromaidan Press*, September 26, 2014, https://euromaidanpress.com/2014/09/26/poroshenko-to-consider-giving-upa-veterans-legal-status/; "Nalyvaichenko: SBU budem reformirovat po obrazu OUN-UPA," [Nalyvaichenko: We Will Reform the SBU Along the Lines of the OUN-UPA] *Ukraina.ru*, April 1, 2015, https://ukraina.ru/news/20150401/1012608625.html; "Poroshenko obyavil UPA 'drugim frontom' borby s fashizmom," [Poroshenko Declared the UPA "Another Front" in the Fight against Fascism] *Ukraina.ru*, May 9, 2015, https://ukraina.ru/news/20150509/1013015597.html.
80 V.I. Lenin, "K voprosu o natsionalnostiyakh ili ob avtonomizatsii," [On the Question of Nationalities or Autonomization] *Library.maoism.ru*, December 30, 1922, http://library.maoism.ru/Lenin/Lenin-autonomisation.htm.
81 "Poroshenko: 'Het vid Moskvy, dayesh Yevropu,'" [Poroshenko: "Away from Moscow, Give Us Europe"] *BBC News Ukraina*, May 14, 2017, https://www.bbc.com/ukrainian/news-39914781.
82 V. Chernyshov, "Ukrainizatsiya kak ona byla," [Ukrainianization As It Was] *Maloros.ru*, https://malorus.ru/ukrstor/czernyszew-ukrainisazija.html.

The official goal of Ukrainianization, according to Skrypnik, was to "make the Ukrainian peasantry equal to the city proletariat," but it was widely viewed as an assault on the language and culture of the cities, which were then primarily Russian-speaking.[83] When Soviet policy shifted from pacification of the cities to pacification of the countryside, the pace of Ukrainianization slowed, but the policy was never formally abandoned.[84] Russian language instruction in school was permitted again only in 1938, the same year that the very first Ukrainian-wide newspaper in the Russian language, *Ukrainska pravda*, was established.

A second wave of Ukrainianization began in the 1950s. Its unlikely hero, according to historian Serhyi Hrabovskyi, was Stalin's notorious head of state security, Lavrenty Beria. As Hrabovsky tells it, shortly after Stalin's death, Beria prepared a report for the Politburo on "gross perversions by the party and Soviet leadership" in Lithuania and western Ukraine. Beria condemned the small number of Ukrainians among professors and school directors, and the fact that the vast majority of instruction was still done in Russian. Beria argued that this encouraged the "bourgeois-nationalist underground," and could potentially undermine Soviet rule there. In response, the Politburo passed a secret resolution to restore *korenizatsiya* in western Ukraine, but rescinded it a month later, when Beria himself fell from grace.[85]

Another Ukrainian historian, Petro Kralyuk, however, argues that parts of Beria's plan were later implemented by Nikita Khrushchev. He cites as evidence the appointment of Petro Shelest to head the Ukrainian Communist Party in June 1963.[86] Shelest encouraged the elaborate commemoration of Ukrainian literary figures like Taras Shevchenko, Ivan Kotlyarevski, and Lesi Ukrainka, and established

---

83 "Nikolai Skripnik i ukranizatsiya 'Odesskikh izvestii,'" [Nikolai Skrypnik and the Ukrainianization of "Odesskiye Izvestia"] *Ukraina.ru*, April, 25, 2020, https://ukraina.ru/history/20200425/ 1027520304. A resolution passed by the III Plenum of the Central Trade Union Bureau in March 1930 noted that "Ukrainization is facing fierce resistance from the great-power Russian elements," especially students and university professors.

84 Vasilii Azarevich, "Galitskoe ukrainstvo." For example, the Ukrainian cultural organization "Prosvita" (Enlightenment) was set up in Austro-Hungary in 1868 for the express purpose of encouraging Ukrainians to "feel their civic and national dignity and to realize the necessity of the existence of the nation as a separated national individualism," and remained active in the USSR through 1939.

85 "I vsyozh: okupatsiya chy kolonizatsiya?," [So Which Is It: Occupation or Colonization?] *Den*, accessed November 8, 2021, https://day.kyiv.ua/uk/article/istoriya-i-ya/i-vse-zh-okupaciya-chy-kolonizaciya.

86 Petro Kralyuk, "Ukrainizatsiiya vid Petra Shelesta," [Pyotr Shelest's Ukrainianization] *Radio Svoboda*, June 9, 2020, https://www.radiosvoboda.org/a/30656654.html.

national museums for Ukrainian folklore and architecture.[87] Most remarkable of all, he distributed dissident Ivan Dzyuba's book *Internationalism or Russification* (1965) to all regional party heads in Ukraine, along with his own critique of it. In 1970 he published *Our Soviet Ukraine,* which was later criticized by communist officials for trying "to revise the past, praise antiquity and the authority of the hetmans, and adapt all this to serve the interests of nationalism. There were obvious attempts to rehabilitate Mazepa, and to present Bohdan Khmelnitsky as a traitor, to re-evaluate the role of Petlyura, and the Central Rada."[88] Kralyuk calls this book Shelest's "personal credo." If so, it was also, effectively, the credo of Soviet-era Malorossiya.

Efforts to restore elements of the past did not end with Shelest's removal in 1972. His successor, Vladimir Shcherbitsky, introduced even stricter language quotas in mass media and shifted almost all local television to the Ukrainian language, all the while claiming that he himself took "the same position as Bohdan Khmelnitsky."[89]

Grabovsky and Kralyuk both agree that Ukrainian nationalism could not have survived the Soviet period without tacit support within the senior leadership of the Ukrainian Communist Party. Shcherbitsky himself wound up holding Soviet Ukraine's top political office longer than anyone, nearly to Ukraine's withdrawal from the USSR. Under his rule, one generation passed the baton to the next, until the generation that came of age in the late 1980s set up the pro-independence Ukrainian Rukh Movement.

Given the tremendous suffering caused by the communist regime in Ukraine (collectivization, the Holodomor famine, mass deportations), this persistent closeness to Russia seems puzzling, but many Maloross Ukrainians point out that it had its benefits for Ukrainians. One was the periodic resurgence of Ukrainianization, which gave "socialism" a much more local flavor. Historian Oleg Nyomensky argues that within the upper echelons of the Ukrainian Communist

---

87 Serhii Hrabovskyi, "Ukrainska mova v chasy SRSR," [The Ukrainian Language in Soviet Times] *Radio Svoboda,* July 6, 2020, https://www.radiosvoboda.org/a/30709133.html.
88 Oleg Izmailov, "Kogda konchilos lekarstvo ot natsionalizma," [When the Medicine for Nationalism Came to an End] *Ukraina.ru,* September 28, 2019, https://ukraina.ru/history/20190928/1025147739.html.
89 Dmitry Gubin, "Rokovaya oshibka tovarishcha Shcherbitskogo," [Comrade Shcherbitsky's Fatal Mistake] *Ukraina.ru,* February 18, 2020, https://ukraina.ru/history/20200218/1026726106.html; Oleg Izmailov, "Kogda konchilos lekarstvo ot natsionalizma."

Party, "Ukrainianism became the foundational consciousness of the Ukrainian SSR bureaucracy, its corporate ideology."[90]

A second benefit of Soviet rule for Ukraine was the dramatic expansion of its physical territory after 1939. With the annexation of parts of Poland, Hungary, and Rumania. Ukraine added 15 percent to its territory, and another 5 percent in 1954 when Khrushchev transferred Crimea from Russia to Ukraine.[91] It was not until Ukraine was under Soviet rule, some Maloross Ukrainians point out, that the nationalist dream of having both Galicia and Greater Ukraine together in a single territory was fulfilled.

Third, Ukrainians benefited from Soviet industrialization. During Shcherbitsky's seventeen-year reign, Ukraine's industrial production increased fivefold, its agricultural production doubled, and its population increased from 43.1 million in 1961 to its all-time high – 52 million.[92]

In the local media these Soviet achievements were portrayed as Ukrainian achievements. As Galician journalist Oleh Khavich notes, "many people from Ukraine were at the head of the Soviet state and the Soviet party – Brezhnev, Podgorny, Khrushchev. Chernenko was considered Brezhnev's man, working together in Dnepropetrovsk. ... [F]rom 1953 to 1985, the country was ruled by Ukrainian clans in the Central Committee and the Politburo of the CPSU [Communist Party of the Soviet Union]."[93] According to his speechwriter, Fyodor Burlatsky, Khrushchev was a great admirer of the former head of Central Rada, Vinnichenko, and said that it was one of Vinnichenko's stories that had inspired him to make his famous 1956 speech denouncing the cult of Stalin.[94]

Finally, the view that Russians and Ukrainians shared a common history and culture was reinforced by the Soviet narrative that Stepan Bandera had been a Nazi collaborator, supported by only a very small group of western Ukrainians, now mostly émigrés. This view persists among many older Ukrainians.[95]

---

90 "Chtoby byt Rusi bez Rusi," [Let Rus Be without Rus] accessed November 8, 2021, http://www.perspektivy.info/book/chtoby_byt_rusi_bez_rusi_ukrainstvo_kak_nacionalnyj_projekt_2012-05-22.htm.
91 Orest Subtelny, *Ukraine*, 482.
92 Oleg Izmailov, "Kogda konchilos lekarstvo ot natsionalizma."
93 Oleg Izmailov, "Kogda konchilos lekarstvo ot natsionalizma."
94 Evgenii Antonyuk, "Den v istorii. 6 marta: umer ukrainsky natsional-kommunist, kotorogo obozhal Khrushchev," [A Day in History. March 6: The Ukrainian National Communist Adored by Khrushchev Dies] *Ukraina.ru*, March 6, 2020, https://ukraina.ru/history/20200306/1026941421.html.
95 "V Ukraine zarabotal ekspertnyi sovet," [An Expert Council Is Launched in Ukraine] *Vesti*, September 22, 2017, https://vesti.ua/strana/257555-knihi-zapreshchajut-iz-za-knjazej-i-stalina.

All these factors combine to form an enduring "Soviet Ukrainian consensus" that widely shared outside of historical Galicia, as is evident in the starkly divided voting patterns in Left-Bank and Right-Bank Ukraine after independence.[96]

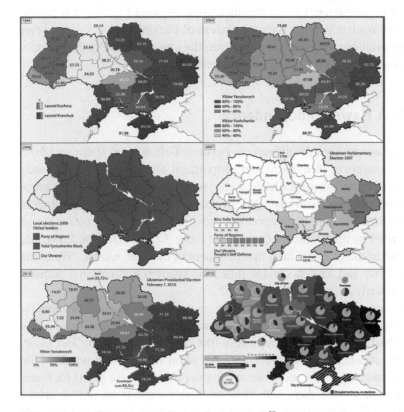

Map 2.1: Electoral Divisions in Ukraine (1994–2019).[97]

96 Lech Haydukiewicz, "Historical and Geographic Regionalization versus Electoral Geography," *Procedia: Social and Behavioral Sciences* 19 (2011) 98111, http://t.ly/bVbQ; "The Geographical (and Historical?) Divisions Underlying Ukraine's Political Strife," *Observationalism*, January 27, 2014, https://observationalism.com/2014/01/27/the-geographical-and-historical-divisions-underlying-ukraines-political-strife; Daniel J. Mitchell, "Ukraine, Ethnic Division, Decentralization, and Secession," *Forbes*, March 3, 2014, https://www.forbes.com/sites/danielmitchell/2014/03/03/ukraine-ethnic-division-decentralization-and-secession/?sh=4e2798a04035.
97 *Sources:* 2019: Author: No-itsme, https://commons.wikimedia.org/wiki/File:Ukraine_presi dential_elections_1994,_second_round.png. 2004: Author: Illuvatar~commonswiki, https:// commons.wikimedia.org/wiki/File:Ukraine_ElectionsMap_Nov2004.png. 2006: Author: Data-stat, https://commons.wikimedia.org/wiki/File:Ukr_local_elections_2006.PNG. 2007: Author:

In independent Ukraine, the co-existence of these two distinct narratives about Ukraine within a single state, the one focusing on total separation from Russia, the other on expanding mutually beneficial ties with it, has dramatically heightened the political stakes whenever issues of national identity, language, culture, and religion are discussed. I stress this dichotomy because I believe it is important to remind readers that the Galician version of Ukrainian identity was never the only one available. Indeed, it was not even the one espoused by the majority of Ukrainians on the eve of Ukrainian independence.

2.6 1991: A Flawed Independence

The Cold War accentuated the differences between Galician and Maloross Ukrainians, adding layers of ideological and geopolitical antagonism to the already existing cultural and religious divisions. So, when independence finally came in 1991, it did not deal honestly with the complexities of Ukrainian identity and regional diversity due, in no small measure, to the fact that it was initiated and shepherded by the Ukrainian Communist Party (UCP). As Leonid Kravchuk, then the head of the UCP, and later first president of Ukraine, recalls: "We in the Communist Party had already divided into conservatives and national-patriots, or more accurately national communists."[98]

In 1990 these national communists were trying to negotiate a better deal for themselves within the renewed Union of Sovereign States being proposed at the time by Mikhail Gorbachev. The party elite (the *nomenklatura*) and "Red Directors" – heads of major factories that comprised many of the crown jewels of Soviet industry and ship-building – were seeking to privatize these assets for themselves, rather than share them with Moscow. Kiev's rhetoric on independence was, however, still quite tentative. The "Act of Sovereignty" proclaimed on July 16, 1990 fell well short of declaring independence, focusing instead on claiming

---

DemocracyATwork, https://commons.wikimedia.org/wiki/File:Ukrainian_parliamentary_elec tion_2007_%28HighestVote%29.PNG. 2010: Author: Ivangricenko, https://commons.wikimedia. org/wiki/File:Ukraine_ElectionsMap_2010-2_Yanukovich.svg. 2019: Author: 沁水湾, https:// commons.wikimedia.org/wiki/File:2019_Ukrainian_presidential_election,_round_2.svg.
98 Viktoriya Venk, "Uvazhenie k yazykam i nikakogo NATO," [Respect for Languages and no NATO] *Strana.ua*, July 16, 2020, https://strana.one/news/279033-deklaratsija-o-suverenitete-uk rainy-chto-nam-obeshchali-30-let-nazad.html.

Ukraine's share of the Soviet Union's economic wealth, while simultaneously dis-associating it from obligations to any other Soviet republic.[99]

As the various national factions of the Soviet nomenklatura bickered over how to divide up the spoils of the Soviet economy, Mikhail Gorbachev tried to bolster the Union by holding a nation-wide referendum in March 1991. It posed the following question: "Do you consider it necessary to preserve the USSR as a renewed federation of equal sovereign republics, in which human rights and the freedoms of all nationalities will be fully guaranteed?" In Ukraine, 71.5 percent answered affirmatively.[100]

To offset this expected defeat, Kravchuk cunningly added an additional question: "Do you agree that Ukraine should be part of a Union of Soviet Sover-eign States on the basis of the Declaration of State Sovereignty of Ukraine?" This was approved by 80.2 percent of Ukrainian voters. He then allowed for a ques-tion on outright independence for Ukraine to be put on the ballot, but only in the three regions of historical Galicia, where it predictably received 88.4 percent approval. The purpose of this maneuver was to send a signal to Moscow that it had better make a deal with loyal Ukrainian communists, like Kravchuk himself, before Ukrainian nationalists gained the upper hand.

All of this changed after the August 1991 coup attempt in Moscow. In re-sponse, the Ukrainian Supreme Soviet convened an emergency session on Au-gust 24 and declared Ukraine to be independent. This served as insurance, both against revenge from the Communist Party of the Soviet Union (CPSU), should it gain the upper hand and try to re-establish the USSR, as well as against any efforts to remove the communist Old Guard in Kiev, should Boris Yeltsin emerge victorious.

Independence provided Communist Party elites, Red Directors, and ardent nationalists in Ukraine with a compromise they could all live with: it saved the Communist Party elites from political retribution; it set the stage for the pri-vatization of industrial assets; and it jumpstarted the process of Ukrainian na-tion-building. To offset complaints about its suddenness, a referendum was to be held later that year, organized to coincide with the country's first presidential elections.

---

99 "Deklaratsiya pro derzhavnyi suverenitet Ukrainy," [Declaration of State Sovereignty of Uk-raine] *Ofitsiinyi vebportal parlamentu Ukrainy*, https://zakon.rada.gov.ua/go/55‒12; Viktoriya Venk, "Uvazhenie k yazykam i nikakogo NATO."
100 "1991 Soviet Union Referendum," *Wikipedia*, September 25, 2021, https://en.wikipedia.org/w/index.php?title=1991_Soviet_Union_referendum&oldid=1046305576.

This second referendum of the year showed overwhelming support for independence from the USSR, although its results hinted at the geopolitical fault lines that still divided the country.[101]

Table 2.1: Percentage of the Electorate Approving the 1991 "Act of Independence."

Historical Galicia	
Ternopil	95.81%
Ivano-Frankivsk	94.22%
Lviv	92.82%
All Ukraine	**76.03%**
Historical Donbass	
Lugansk	67.63%
Donetsk	64.38%
Crimea	**36.58%**
Sevastopol	36.38%

Source: "1991 Ukrainian Independence Referendum," in *Wikipedia* (English) https://perma.cc/ J6N5-SK92; and *Wikipedia* (Russian) https://perma.cc/7XQF-7D35, accessed August 31, 2022.

Noted Ukrainian journalist and publisher Igor Guzhva has argued that the vote for independence reflected a compromise among regional Ukrainian elites to prevent further chaos in the face of an already collapsing USSR.[102] But while each constituent could agree to independence as a starting point, once past the starting gate they quickly began to pursue their own agendas.

By far the most influential political actor was the former nomenklatura, which, despite splitting into Communist and Socialist parties, continued to dominate political life. Under the first two presidents of Ukraine, Kravchuk and Kuchma, these two parties routinely received between 15 and 20 percent of the seats in parliament, and were indispensable to the formation of any government coalition. The Communist Party of Ukraine received the most seats in both 1994 and

101 "Vseukrainsky referendum (1991)," [The All-Ukrainian Referendum (1991)] *Wikipedia*, May 18, 2021, https://ru.wikipedia.org/w/index.php?title=Vseukrainsky_referendum_(1991).

102 Igor Guzhva, "Ot kompromissa k voine," [From Compromise to War] *Strana.ua*, November 19, 2017, https://strana.today/articles/istorii/105724-istorija-ukrainy-ot-1991-do-2017-hoda.html.

1998, and was the only party represented in all sessions of parliament, until it was banned in 2015.[103]

Another prominent group, the Red Directors, quickly established fiefdoms in the industrial regions of eastern Ukraine. Relying on their old ties to Soviet industry, they forged new transnational industrial conglomerates that benefited both the southeastern regions of Ukraine and themselves personally. In 1997 they established the Party of Regions to lobby for their political interests in Kiev, which included stronger commercial ties with Russia. But while striving for closer economic ties with Russia, they also insisted on Ukrainian political independence, since it prevented hostile takeovers by wealthier Russian competitors. Their patriotism was based not on religion or language, but on profit, says pro-Maidan journalist Vitaly Portnikov, ensuring that they would always be more pro-Donbass, than pro-Russian.[104]

The final component of this post-independence constituency, the Ukrainian nationalists, would seem to be the odd man out. According to Guzhva, however, in exchange for accommodating the business interests of eastern Ukraine, they were given free rein to pursue Ukrainianization in education, arts, culture, humanities, and religion, with the full support of the state.[105]

This division of responsibilities allowed each constituency to expand its influence in the areas of greatest interest to it, and to establish *de facto* control over key geographical regions. The goal was to share dominion over Ukraine in a way that would prevent its different constituencies from stepping on each other's toes. By its very design, however, it also prevented the creation of a common cultural and civil framework capable of unifying the country.

---

103 "Kommunisticheskaya partiya Ukrainy," [Communist Party of Ukraine] *Wikipedia*, October 23, 2021, https://ru.wikipedia.org/w/index.php?title=Kommunisticheskaya_partiya_Ukrainy; Volodymyr Ishchenko and Loren Balhorn, "An Election for the Oligarchs," *Rosa Luxemburg Stiftung*, April 3, 2019, https://www.rosalux.de/en/publication/id/40116/an-election-for-the-oligarchs-1/?fbclid=IwAR2ooCpoYyWbnjuxFvqPs0St-iQ1K1BwfafQhx6qqRHj_xiydG_6yZnmBxw; "Hlava derzhavy pidpysav zakony pro dekomunizatsiyu," [The Head of State Signed the Decommunization Laws] *Ofitsiine predstavnytstvo Prezydenta Ukrainy*, https://www.president.gov.ua/news/32869.html.
104 "Ukraina dlya lyudei," [A Ukraine for People] August 15, 2008, *Vitaly Portnikov's Journal*, https://vokintrop.livejournal.com/660016.html.
105 Igor Guzhva, "Ot kompromissa k voine."

2.6.1 The Backlash of the East: the Party of Regions

The Party of Regions, which dominated Ukrainian politics from 2006 to 2014, arose from the merger of several left-of-center and agrarian parties. It initially contained diverse ideological outlooks (suffice it to say that Petro Poroshenko was among its founders), but as it grew, it explicitly adopted the political and cultural agenda of Maloross Ukraine, which included increased social spending, a neutral foreign policy, and, most importantly, the reining in of forced Ukrainianization.

It did not achieve much electoral success until after the presidency of Viktor Yushchenko, who sharply accelerated the pace of Ukrainianization. The party now had a clear cause around which to rally its electorate – giving regions the local right to use Russian. By embracing this message, it quickly recovered from its electoral defeat in 2004, and from then on was the most popular party in every region of the country, outside of historical Galicia and Volyn.[106]

At first glance, language usage seems like an unlikely topic to stir political passions, since widespread usage of Ukrainian is largely limited to historical Galicia and Volyn. Russian is much more common in cities, while a mélange of the two known as *surzhyk* is common in the countryside.[107] Since these communities rarely overlap, in principle, they should have little reason to enter into conflict.

What makes the language issue such a hot-button political issue, however, is the national debate over whether Ukraine's *de facto* bilingualism came about "naturally," as a consequence of its close cultural affinity to Russia, or as the result of "colonialism." Those who take the former view, resent the implication that they must now give up their "colonial culture." For them this issue is one of freedom of choice.

On the other side, advocates of the colonial view see themselves as righting a historical injustice and ensuring the country's cultural, political, economic, and religious independence. For them, this issue is a civilizational imperative, and individuals must submit to this imperative for the benefit of the entire nation.

---

106 "Party of Regions," *Wikipedia*, July 20, 2021, https://en.wikipedia.org/w/index.php?title=-Party_of_Regions&oldid=1034622068; "Rezultaty Mstsevykh Vyboriv," [Results of the Local Elections] *Ukrainska pravda*, November 8, 2010, http://www.pravda.com.ua/articles/2010/11/8/5552584/.
107 Nicolai N. Petro, "Ukraine's Ongoing Struggle with Its Russian Identity," *World Politics Review*, May 6, 2014, https://www.worldpoliticsreview.com/articles/13758/ukraine-s-ongoing-struggle-with-its-russian-identity. Of Ukraine's eleven largest cities, all but the seventh largest, Lviv, is predominantly Russian speaking.

One's choice of language thus often serves as a *de facto* litmus test of having the "proper" Ukrainian identity.

The strongest advocates of total Ukrainianization tend to be located in the historical regions of Galicia. Here, the perception of Ukraine's history as "colonized" has been woven into the political culture since the late nineteenth century, and often carries with it the ideological imperative to reverse its unjust suppression. By contrast, the most ardent advocates of the view that the use of Russian and Ukrainian should be a personal choice and carries no ideological implications tend to be located in Maloross Ukraine.

Table 2.2: How Important for Ukraine Is the Problem of Developing the Ukrainian Language? (September 2020)

	West	South	East
Of primary importance	42.1%	5.8%	4.3%
Of secondary importance	9.4%	46.3%	55.2%

Source: Hanna Chabarii, "Po rusyfikovanykh mistakh. Shcho ukraintsi dumayut pro movnyi zakon ta 'utysky rosiiskomovnykh,'" *Tyzhden.ua*, September 15, 2020, https://m.tyzhden.ua/publication/247731.

Recognizing the potential of fragmenting the country along this cultural divide, the 1990 Act of Ukrainian Sovereignty proposed mutual respect for local language usage. While providing for the "national cultural renaissance of the Ukrainian people, its historical consciousness and traditions, national-ethnographic peculiarities, [and the] functioning of the Ukrainian language in all spheres of public life," it also guaranteed to all nationalities living within Ukraine the right to their own national-cultural development.[108] This principle was later restated in the 1996 Ukrainian Constitution, with Article 10 specifically guaranteeing "the free development, use and protection of Russian."[109]

Given the widespread use of Russian, and the mutually exclusive views on whether or not this is compatible with Ukrainian identity, it is not surprising that the issue of how to implement this "guarantee" has come up in every election. During their electoral campaigns, every candidate for president, including Yushchenko, Poroshenko, and Zelensky, has pledged to promote the free and

---

108 "Deklaratsiya pro derzhavnyi suverenitet Ukrainy."
109 "Konstytutsiya Ukrainy," [Constitution of Ukraine] *Ofitsiinyi vebportal parlamentu Ukrainy*, https://zakon.rada.gov.ua/go/254k/96-vr.

equal ability to use Russian.[110] The most famous of these pledges was Leonid Kravchuk's "Appeal to Russian Co-citizens," which was distributed on the eve of the referendum on Ukrainian independence. In it he described the 12 million Russians living in Ukraine as "full-fledged owners" of the country and vowed that "under no circumstances will the violent Ukrainization of Russians be tolerated. Any attempts to discriminate on ethnic grounds, he said, would be resolutely suppressed."[111]

When the Ukrainian Constitutional Court, in 1999, interpreted Article 10 in the narrowest possible way, it handed the Party of Regions a rallying cry that has served it, and its successor parties, ever since.[112] In 2012 a parliament dominated by the Party of Regions passed the Kivalov-Kolesnichenko Law, permitting the use of languages other than Ukrainian in local matters, if their regional parliaments allowed it. Half of Ukraine's regions immediately voted to do so. The passage of this law, however, similarly galvanized Ukrainian nationalists, whose very first act, in the rump Rada that removed Yanukovych from power in February 2014, was to rescind the Kivalov-Kolesnichenko Law.

These interminable language debates effectively strangled the development of healthy regionalism in Ukraine. Since 2014 the language issue has become, if anything, more toxic, with several leading political and cultural figures openly declaring that for a Ukrainian to use Russian is tantamount to treason.[113] The result has been the exact opposite of the tolerance for cultural diversity advocated in the 1990 Act of Sovereignty – and a persistent reminder of how the attempt to resolve one injustice through another injustice perpetuates the tragic cycle.

---

110 Viktoriya Venk, "Ostanovit zakrytie russkikh shkol," [Stop the Closure of Russian Schools] *Strana.ua*, July 18, 2020, https://strana.one/news/279217-kak-poroshenko-russkij-jazyk-zashchishchal.html; Bohdan Nahaylo, "Toward the Rule of Law – Ukraine," *RFE/RL Research Report* 1, no. 27, 3 (July 1992): 50 – 56. Curiously, Ukraine has also signed and ratified a number of international obligations guaranteeing the use of minority languages, including Russian. In 1991 it even passed a Declaration of the Rights of Nationalities of Ukraine that pledged to grant official status to the mother tongue of any ethnic group living compactly in any of Ukraine's regions.

111 "Obrashchenie L.M. Kravchuka 'K Russkim sootechestvennikam,'" [L.M. Kravchuk, "An Appeal to Russian Compatriots"] [1991] or [no date] https://perma.cc/CG8D-SBZ3.

112 In his dissent, judge Oleksandr Mironenko prophetically predicted that this ruling would eliminate the private sphere entirely and restore totalitarianism, masquerading as patriotism. As president, Yushchenko would later use this 1999 ruling to impose language restrictions that went well beyond previous practices.

113 Oleksandr Aleksandrovich, "Movne pytannya," [The Language Question] *Censor.net*, August 19, 2020, https://censor.net/ru/resonance/3214449/pro_movne_pitannya_v_ukran.

2.6.2 Rukh: The Moderate Galician Alternative

It did not have to be this way. As mentioned previously, a division of spheres of influence among regions served as the basis for social compromise for the better part of two decades, even as it avoided dealing with the issue of just what sort of identity Ukraine was building for itself. If, on the one hand, Maloross Ukrainians seemed quite comfortable with a Ukraine that, in many respects, did not differ dramatically from Soviet Ukraine, for many Galicians such an outcome was totally unacceptable. After independence, tensions increased not only between Galician and Maloross Ukraine, but also within the nationalist movement itself over how to achieve a Ukraine that was truly Ukrainian.

The unexpected death in 1999 of the leader of the People's Movement of Ukraine (Rukh) Viacheslav Chornovil (Chernovol in Russian) proved to be a decisive turning point in the evolution of Ukrainian nationalism. Despite being a noted Soviet-era dissident, Chornovil did not want to sever all ties with Russia. As one of the founders of Rukh (the Movement), he saw federalism as the best way to guarantee the individual and cultural rights enshrined in the Ukrainian Constitution.

Rukh emerged from the "Popular Movement in Support of Perestroika" set up by Gorbachev to overcome opposition within the CPSU to perestroika. From the outset, however, it was riven by disputes between those who saw it as a platform for Ukrainian nationalism, and those who saw it as a vehicle for the renewal of socialism. Like all official political movements at that time, it had to be sponsored by the Ukrainian Communist Party. At its first conference in September 1989, it dutifully supported the new Union Treaty proposed by Gorbachev, as well as the restoration of religious rights, and the "democratization" of economic and political life.[114] But, as Yeltsin's radical notion of declaring Russian independence from the USSR began to gain traction among Russian communists, so too did the idea of Ukrainian independence within Rukh.[115]

Chornovil himself wanted to see Ukraine become a federation of regions, the model for which he had created in the Galician Assembly, a gathering of the three regional Soviets in western Ukraine – Lviv, Ivano-Frankivsk, and Ternopil. Although it met only twice, and was primarily engaged with coordinating relief efforts to prevent food shortages in Galicia, Kievan authorities immediately at-

---

114 Aleksandr Chalenko, "Zapadnaya Ukraina nakanune GKChP," [Western Ukraine on the Eve of the State Committee on the State of Emergency] *Ukraina.ru*, August 22, 2016, https://ukraina.ru/exclusive/20160822/1017307218.html.

115 Vasilii Stoyakin, "Yubilei Rukha," [The Anniversary of Rukh] *Ukraina.ru*, September 8, 2019, https://ukraina.ru/history/20190908/1024904935.html.

tacked it as a separatist forum.[116] The obvious parallels with ZUNR did not help, nor did the occasional references in the Assembly to the Baltic Assembly of the Popular Fronts of Estonia, Latvia, and Lithuania. What Chornovil actually wanted for Ukraine, however, was a "unity of historical regions along the lines of the federation of lands of the FRG [Federal Republic of Germany]."[117]

"I imagine," Chornovil wrote, "the future Ukraine as a federated state, a Union of Lands, which have developed historically and that contain the natural-climatic, cultural-ethnographic, cultural-dialectical, trade and economic, and other differences that create the uniquely differentiated face of a Unified People." He envisioned Donbass as part of that Ukraine, but saw Crimea as "an independent neighbor, or an autonomous republic in alliance with Ukraine."[118]

At this point Rukh was still tolerant of religious, linguistic, and ethnic diversity. And even though, in 1992, Chornovil staged an elaborate "new Pereyaslavl Rada," where he demonstratively tore up the agreement Khmelnitsky had signed in 1654, he saw the solution to the security dilemma posed by the country's biculturalism in the creation of a second, upper chamber of the Rada that would give a permanent voice to each region (since its independence Ukraine has had a unicameral legislature).[119]

Rukh reached the height of its political popularity in 1998, when it won the second largest number of seats in the Rada, after the Communist Party of Ukraine. Its popularity, however, relied heavily on the charisma of Chornovil, and after he died in a car accident in March 1999, the moderate wing of Rukh collapsed. His death thus marks the end of the era when the former Communist

---

116 Ihor Solyar, *Ukraina: Kulturna spadshchina, natsionalna svidomist, derzhavnist* [Ukraine: Cultural Heritage, National Consciousness, Statehood] (Lviv: Natsionalna Akademiya Nauk Ukrainy, Institut Ukrainoznavstva, 2019), http://www.inst-ukr.lviv.ua/download.php?portfolioitemid=145; "Halytska Asambleya 1991," [The Galician Assembly 1991] *Wikipedia*, https://uk.wikipedia.org/w/index.php?title= Halyts′ka_Asambleya_1991.

117 "Zhurnalist napomnil, chto raspad Ukrainy mog sostoyatsya 20 let nazad," [A Journalist Recalls that the Dissolution of Ukraine Could Have Taken Place 20 Years Ago] *Rossiiskaya gazeta*, accessed November 9, 2021, https://rg.ru/2015/01/14/ruina1.html.

118 Igor Guzhva, Olesya Medvedeva, and Maksim Minin, "Vtoroi srok Kuchmy, gibel Chernovola, krakh Lazarenko, novaya strategiya Zapada," [The Second Term of Kuchma, the Death of Chernovol, the Collapse of Lazarenko, the New Strategy of the West] *Strana.ua*, August 3, 2021, https://strana.one/news/345889 – 1999-hod-v-istorii-ukrainy-vtoroj-srok-kuchmy-lazarenko-v-tjurme.html.

119 Vitaly Zakharchenko, "Federalizatsiya Ukrainy vmesto kolonizatsii Zapadom," [Federalization of Ukraine Instead of Colonization by the West] *Ukraina.ru*, April 6, 2015, https://ukraina.ru/analytics/20150406/1012650922.html.

Party elite of Malorossiya, now turned businessmen and factory managers, supported independence in exchange for personal control over Ukraine's portion of the Soviet patrimony.

Many in Ukraine's intellectual and cultural elite made common cause with them because they envisioned independence as an opportunity to build a more prosperous form of socialism in one country. Kravchuk relied on the support of both groups to argue against any devolution of authority from Kiev to the regions. The wing of Rukh represented by Chornovil, however, feared that the void left by the departure of Muscovite centralism would now be filled by Kievan centralism.[120]

National unity was preserved, but the threat of regional separatism remained because the very real cultural differences between Galician and Maloross Ukraine were never incorporated into the new political system, as Chornovil hoped they would be. Chornovil's death thus marks the end of the consensus on building a modern form of socialism in one country. The era of Socialist Nationalism was about to be replaced by the era of Nationalist Socialism.

2.6.3 Why the 2004 Maidan Failed

The Orange Revolution of 2004 is the story of how a popular government with enthusiastic Western government support became the most unpopular government in Ukrainian history. The short answer is that, in an effort to unite all Ukrainians, it promoted Galician identity as the only legitimate identity for all Ukrainians, and wound up uniting the rest of Ukraine against it. It is an instructive story, because it reflects one of the most persistent tragic patterns in Ukrainian history.

The 2004 presidential campaign was the first one in which the two top electoral candidates sought to portray each other as irredeemable enemies of Ukraine, rather than as merely political opponents. Western Ukrainians were all portrayed as neo-Nazis, while eastern Ukrainians were all criminals and communists. In their respective media outlets, each side appealed to its own regional constituency not to allow the other side to destroy Ukraine. After such demonization, conceding the election to the other side would be tantamount to permitting Evil to triumph over Good. Therefore, in a pattern that we will see repeated in 2014, local councils in the western regions and Kiev refused to accept any elec-

---

120 "Chornovil Vyacheslav Maksymovych," *Wikipedia*, October 4, 2021, https://uk.wikipedia.org/w/index.php?title=Chornovil_V'yacheslav_Maksymovych.

tion result that gave the victory to Yanukovych, while his supporters in Maloross Ukraine threatened to secede, if their candidate was not installed.[121]

Acting as the European Union's intermediary, Polish president, Alexander Kwasniewski, arranged a face-saving compromise: new elections in exchange for a weaker presidency. Since two-thirds of Rada deputies were now dollar millionaires, a weaker presidency that allowed them to secure their winnings suited most of them just fine. Swedish economist Anders Aslund aptly summed up the deal as a "revolt of the millionaires against the billionaires."[122]

It was also the first time that Western governments took an active and open interest in changing the course of Ukrainian politics. The groundwork for this had been laid back in 2003, when U.S. Secretary of State Condoleezza Rice, dissatisfied with the timid proposals of her Policy Planning staff, brought in Stephen Krasner, a Stanford scholar who argued that the sovereignty of weak states should be limited because of the threat they pose to the international order.[123] Together with Carlos Pascual, a former director in the National Security Council responsible for Russia, Ukraine, and Eurasia as well as US ambassador to Kiev (2000–2003), they devised a strategy of anticipatory US intervention in the domestic affairs of such weak states.[124]

A list of countries liable to collapse due to internal conflict was drawn up, and "reconstruction blueprints" prepared for them. Any state willing to "share sovereignty" with "an external actor such as another [obviously, Western] state or a regional or international organization" could expect to receive Western financial, political, and military assistance.[125] Pascual later explained that this assistance could be provided quickly by rapid-response teams composed of private companies, NGOs, and think tanks, shaving three to six months off the typical

---

121 Igor Guzhva, "Ot kompromissa k voine."
122 Sławomir Matuszak, "The Oligarchic Democracy: The Influence of Business Groups on Ukrainian Politics." *OSW Studies*, September 2012, http://aei.pitt.edu/58394/1/prace_42_en_0.pdf.
123 Stephen D. Krasner "Sharing Sovereignty: New Institutions for Collapsed and Failing States," *International Security* 29, no. 2 (2004): 85–120, https://doi.org/10.1162/0162288042879940; Peer Schouten, "Theory Talk #21: Stephen Krasner," October 2008, http://www.theory-talks.org/2008/10/theory-talk-21.html; Stephen D. Krasner "The Case for Shared Sovereignty," *Journal of Democracy* 16, no. 1 (2005): 69–83. https://doi.org/10.1353/jod.2005.0013.
124 Stephen D. Krasner and Carlos Pascual, "Addressing State Failure," *Foreign Affairs* (2005): 156–157; "Carlos Pascual, "Next US Ambassador, an Expert on 'Failed States,'" *La Jornada*, March 27, 2009, http://www.walterlippmann.com/docs2357.html.
125 Stephen D. Krasner, "Building Democracy after Conflict: The Case for Shared Sovereignty," *Journal of Democracy* 16, no. 1 (2005): 70, https://doi.org/10.1353/jod.2005.0013.

government response time. The goal of such intervention would be to "change the very social fabric of a nation."[126]

Ukraine was an obvious candidate for "shared sovereignty" from the start. USAID-funded groups, like Development Associates, Inc., later claimed to have "played a decidedly important role in facilitating Ukraine's turn to democracy in 2004."[127] Working alongside NDI, IRI, Freedom House, InterNews, and ABA/CEELI, the Strengthening Electoral Administration in Ukraine Project (SEAUP) "directly trained 7,405 individuals at the territorial election commission level … over 95,000 polling station commissioners [and] 1,350 election judges," as well as three justices of the Ukrainian Supreme Court. Given the Court's role in interpreting the Constitution to allow for a third round of elections, the claim that this "facet of the training component … proved to be extremely fortuitous" seems almost too modest.[128]

Technocratic reconstruction and shared sovereignty were expected to lead to rapid economic growth, and take Ukraine out of Russia's orbit permanently. Unfortunately, Yushchenko himself undermined these plans almost immediately, by appointing his business and political rival Yulia Timoshenko prime minister. Timoshenko undermined Yushchenko at every turn. He later repaid her by testifying against her for exceeding her powers in signing a ten-year gas agreement with Russia. Relations became so tense between them that Yushchenko was eventually forced to appoint his archrival Viktor Yanukovych, whose Party of Regions had just won the March 2006 parliamentary elections, prime minister. These two unlikely bedfellows signed a "Universal of National Unity" which, among other things, stipulated that Ukraine would refrain from seeking NATO membership.

What Yanukovych was not told, however, was that an agreement had already been reached to submit Ukraine for a NATO Action Plan at the next NATO summit in Bucharest in 2008. Thus, at the same time that Yanukovych, as prime minister,

---

126 Naomi Klein, "The Rise of Disaster Capitalism," accessed November 9, 2021, https://naomi-klein.org/rise-disaster-capitalism/.

127 Bohdan Nahaylo, *The Ukrainian Resurgence* (London: C. Hurst & Co. Publishers, 1999), 502; Camille Gangloff, *L'import-export de la democratie: Serbie, Georgie, Ukraine* [The Import-Export of Democracy: Serbia, Georgia, Ukraine] (Paris: Editions L'Harmattan, 2008), 47, http://www.vle-books.com/vleweb/product/openreader?id=none&isbn=9782296192577; "Berezovsky 'Funded Revolution,'" *The Independent*, November 12, 2005, https://www.independent.co.uk/news/world/europe/berezovsky-funded-revolution-514948.html. Berezovsky claims that he personally provided $21 million to the opposition in Ukraine during these contested elections.

128 Jeffrey Clark, *Elections, Revolution and Democracy in Ukraine: Reflections on a Country's Turn to Democracy, Free Elections and the Modern World* (Washington, DC: Development Associates, 2005), 11, 17.

was trying to promote better relations with Russia, Yushchenko, as president, was undermining them by challenging the Black Sea Fleet Agreement, and blocking agreement with Russia on supply transfers to Transnistria. The country was now being pulled in opposite directions not only culturally and linguistically, but also economically and geopolitically.[129]

At this point, rather than honoring the terms of the "Universal of National Unity," Yushchenko made his second major political mistake – he adopted Galicia's regional identity as the national model for all Ukrainians. With the collapse of Rukh, Ukrainian nationalists saw an opportunity to promote a much more ambitious political agenda, one that would end the country's cultural, linguistic, and religious divisions once and for all. Implementing this agenda, however, required the support of an establishment political figure with nation-wide legitimacy and Western support.

President Yushchenko served this purpose admirably. He provided Galician nationalism with its first nation-wide platform, and aggressively promoted three of its core themes: "Army, Language, Faith." He declared OUN-UPA leaders to be national heroes, reversed more than a decade of tolerance in linguistic policy ("only occupants, slaves and fools do not speak the national language"), and actively supported the offshoot Kievan Patriarchate in its efforts to become the sole Orthodox Church of Ukraine.[130] While avoiding any personal association with the Far Right, by his actions he brought Far Right views into the political mainstream.

To establish the Galician interpretation of Ukrainian history as the new national standard, Yushchenko created two new state agencies dedicated to promoting the view that the collaboration of the OUN-UPA with Nazi Germany during World War II was a struggle for Ukrainian independence: the Institute of National Memory (INP) and the OUN-affiliated Center for the Study of the Liberation Movement. The INP's first director, academician Ihor Yukhnovskyi, publicly supported the neo-Nazi, Social Nationalist Party of Ukraine, and argued that all government policies should be "based on the Ukrainian idea."[131] The Institute

---

129 "2007: God semnadtsatyi. Rospusk parlamenta, novyi krizis i novyi kompromiss," [2007: Year Seventeen. Dissolution of Parliament, New Crisis and New Compromise] *Ot kaidaniv do Maidaniv* (blog), accessed December 27, 2021, https://oko.cn.ua/blackzone/polit-linki/ot-kajda-niv-do-majdaniv/.

130 Tadeusz A. Olszański, "The Language Issue in Ukraine: An Attempt at a New Perspective," *OSW Study*, no. 40/2012 (May 2012), http://www.osw.waw.pl/en/publikacje/osw-studies/2012–05–16/language-issue-ukraine-attempt-a-new-perspective.

131 Aleksandr Burakovskiy, "Holocaust Remembrance in Ukraine: Memorialization of the Jewish Tragedy at Babi Yar," *Nationalities Papers* 39, no. 3 (May 2011): 382, https://doi.org/10.1080/

went so far as to depict the OUN-UPA as organizations that welcomed Jews and fought against Hitler. It even financed the erection of monuments to OUN-UPA fighters at Jewish memorial sites.[132]

Yushchenko also arranged for the State Archives of the Security Services of Ukraine (SBU) and the Center for the Study of the Liberation Movement to be headed by the young, revisionist historian Volodymyr Vyatrovych. His task, according to SBU director Valentyn Nalyvaichenko, was to "liberate Ukrainian history from lies and falsifications and to work with truthful documents only."[133]

After his humiliating defeat in the first round of the 2010 presidential election, where he received less than 6 percent of the vote, in his final act as president, Yushchenko rehabilitated OUN leader Stepan Bandera and declared him to be a national hero. Although a Ukrainian court later reversed this decision, it was widely interpreted as a gesture of contempt for the war time sacrifices of Ukrainians who had served in the Red Army, and contributed to a lasting enmity toward the 2004 Orange Revolution among Maloross Ukrainians, which carried over to the 2014 Maidan.

2.6.4 Yanukovych and the 2014 Maidan

A 2007 USAID report triumphantly declared: "the Orange Revolution is considered irreversible. Wherever we went and no matter whom we talked with, everyone agreed that the Orange Revolution had changed the political landscape permanently."[134] Three years later president Yushchenko got just 5.5 percent of the popular vote, and the percentage of Ukrainians who trusted the courts and the parliament was even lower.[135]

Not only had Yushchenko's propaganda of Galician narratives failed to transform Ukraine, it had spawned a counterreaction. A 2012 Kiev International Insti-

---

00905992.2011.565316; Per A. Rudling, "The OUN, the UPA and the Holocaust: A Study in the Manufacturing of Historical Myths."

132 Per A. Rudling, "The OUN, the UPA and the Holocaust: A Study in the Manufacturing of Historical Myths," 26–38.

133 Gordon M. Hahn, *Ukraine over the Edge*, 143.

134 "Ukraine Local Government Assessment," produced for USAID by Democracy International, Inc. under Task Order #DFD-I-07–04–00229–00, February 19, 2007, https://democracyinternational.com/media/Ukraine%20Local%20Government%20Assessment.pdf, 5.

135 Serhiy Kudelia, "Politics and Democracy in Ukraine," in Taras Kuzio and Daniel Hamilton, eds., *Open Ukraine: Changing Course towards a European Future* (Washington, DC: Paul H. Nitze School of Advanced International Studies, Johns Hopkins University, 2011), http://www.taraskuzio.com/books4_files/Open_Ukraine.pdf, 2.

tute of Sociology (KIIS) survey found that, when asked whom they would have supported in World War II, 75 percent said the Soviet Army, and only 8 percent said the Ukrainian Insurgent Army (UPA).[136]

Every post-Soviet election has demonstrated this traditional Galician-Maloross divide, but the 2010 presidential and 2012 parliamentary elections revealed that the split was now wider than ever.[137] While Yanukovych's victory in 2010 was seen as a return to normalcy in Maloross Ukraine, for Galician Ukraine it was seen as a betrayal that proved that elections alone could no longer be relied upon to guarantee Ukrainian independence. As a result, many Ukrainian nationalists began to seek alternative forms of political action, to ensure the type of change that they knew the country needed.

After his election, Yanukovych did indeed begin to reverse some of Yushchenko's pro-Galician policies. He dismissed Vyatrovych and Yukhnovskiy, the chief ideologists of Galician Ukrainian history, and restored the traditional policy of not enforcing a unitary version of Ukrainian identity. On the other hand, just like his predecessors, Yanukovych failed to keep his campaign promise to designate Russian a second official language.

In July 2012, however, the issue was taken out of his hands by his own party. The Party of Regions pushed through the Rada a law that allowed any region with an ethnic minority constituting more than 10 percent of the local population, to allow its language to be used for official purposes within that region. Within weeks (and in the city of Odessa, the very next day), thirteen of Ukraine's twenty-seven regions designated Russian as a second official language.[138]

For its proponents, the Kivalov-Kolesnichenko Law, as it was known, merely restored the Grand Compromise among regions. For Ukrainian nationalists, however, it was an assault on the Ukrainian language, Ukrainian identity, and Ukrainian sovereignty. Having tasted the fruits of political power under Yushchenko, they were no longer satisfied with playing second fiddle to former Communist Party bosses and Red Directors (now called oligarchs). They were now far better

---

136 Ivan Katchanovski, "The Politics of World War II in Contemporary Ukraine," *The Journal of Slavic Military Studies* 27, no. 2 (April 3, 2014): 210–233, 225, https://doi.org/10.1080/13518046.2013.844493. Curiously, half of Svoboda's supporters said they would have supported the Red Army over the OUN.
137 I.E. Bekeshkin, "Parlamentskie vybory v Ukraine," [Parliamentary Elections in Ukraine] in *Yezhegodnaya nauchno-prakticheskaya sotsiologicheskaya konferentsiya "Prodolzhaya Grushina"* (Moscow: VTsIOM, 2012), 413–415, accessed 28 November 2015, http://wciom.ru/fileadmin/file/nauka/grusha_2013/7.pdf.
138 Richard Sakwa, *Frontline Ukraine: Crisis in the Borderlands* (London and New York: I.B. Tauris, 2015), 59.

politically organized, dominated several regional parliaments in western Ukraine, and had even captured 10 percent of the seats in the Rada.[139] With each
electorate now solidly entrenched in its respective region, Ukraine's body politic
was increasingly being whipsawed, back and forth, over issues of language, religion, and political orientation.

The critical event turned out to be, quite unexpectedly, Ukraine's negotiations over association with the European Union. I say unexpectedly because,
as many of his critics now acknowledge, Yanukovych seemed to be handling
these difficult negotiations quite skillfully. It is worth recalling that it was Yanukovych who, in 2010, had signed the law making EU membership a fundamental
aspiration for Ukraine, and who, at the EU summit on February 25, 2013, had reiterated Ukraine's determination to sign an Association Agreement.[140] At home,
however, he was hearing more and more complaints from industrialists and oligarchs about the EU's insistence that the Association Agreement also meant that
Ukraine had to withdraw from the Customs Union, a trade agreement among CIS
(Commonwealth of Independent States) states. Without some form of compensation, two-thirds of the country's exports would lose their current trade preferences with Russia – a devastating blow for Ukrainian industry.[141]

Yanukovych's strategy was to play Russia and the EU against each other. He
delayed signing the EU Association Agreement at the Vilnius summit in November, and asked for a loan of 27 billion dollars. When the EU offered him the paltry
sum of 833 million dollars, Yanukovych turned to Russia to try to obtain a deal
that would put more pressure on the EU negotiators.[142] A month later, Ukraine
received a 15 billion dollar multiyear loan from Moscow, and the EU then countered with a comparable offer.[143] Yanukovych had actually achieved what many
other Ukrainian politicians had only dreamed of: getting Russia and the West to
compete with each other for Ukraine's favor.

But for this negotiating strategy to bear fruit, it needed domestic political
support, which Yanukovych's opponents were determined not to give him. In a
telling sign of how frayed social discourse had become, Yanukovych's refusal

139 David Stern, "Svoboda: The Rise of Ukraine's Ultra-Nationalists," *BBC*, December 26, 2012, https://www.bbc.com/news/magazine-20824693.
140 Gordon M. Hahn, *Ukraine over the Edge*, 169.
141 Gordon Hahn, "Russia – Ukraine – EU," *Russia: Other Points of View*, November 4, 2013, https://perma.cc/WQC6-VVA2?type=image.
142 "Ukraine 'Still Wants to Sign EU Deal,'" *Al Jazeera*, November 29, 2013, https://www.alja-zeera.com/news/2013/11/29/ukraine-still-wants-to-sign-eu-deal.
143 Luke Baker, "EU Offers Ukraine $15 Billion, but Help Hinges on IMF Deal," *Reuters*, March 5, 2014, https://perma.cc/47R5-MCQG.

to sign with the EU and get an even more advantageous deal with Moscow was interpreted as a betrayal of Ukraine's only proper "civilizational choice."[144]

It was to affirm this choice, in favor of Europe and against Russia, that the first protesters gathered on Kiev's Independence Square (*Maidan nezalezhnosti*) at the end of November 2013. This first phase of the Maidan, popularly known as the Euromaidan, was an expression of popular discontent with Yanukovych's refusal to ratify the EU Association Agreement. According to the official narrative, when police intervened to disperse the protesters, the Ukrainian people rose to defend them, and after bloody street battles in January and February 2014, forced the flight of Yanukovych and his henchmen.

This reflects a strictly Galician view of events. As several researchers pointed out at the time, the participants in the 2014 Maidan were not only overwhelmingly from western Ukraine, but saw their participation in it as an integral part of Galicia's long historical struggle to overcome Russian colonialism, which Yanukovych was trying to reimpose.[145]

Less than two weeks into the movement, on December 1, 2013, armed radicals from a little known group calling itself the Right Sector tried unsuccessfully to storm the presidential administration building. Although they denied it at the time, this attack was coordinated with the leaders of the political opposition.[146] On January 19, 2014 they attacked the police and internal militia on Hrushevsky street. Over the next few days, nearly a hundred people were killed by snipers some of whom, the Ukrainian State Prosecutor's Office would later determine, were located in buildings controlled by the Maidan protesters.[147]

---

144 Tatyana Izhvenko, "Yevrointegratsiyu v Kieve travili gazom," [European Integration Was Gassed in Kiev] *Nezavisimaya gazeta*, November 26, 2013, http://www.ng.ru/cis/2013–11–26/ 1_ukraina.html; Gordon M. Hahn, "Violence, Coercion and Escalation in the Ukraine Crisis, Parts 1–5: November 2013 January 2014," *Russian & Eurasian Poltics*, April 8, 2015, https://perma.cc/8UPL-NY33.

145 Oleksander Andreyev, "Power and Money in Ukraine," *OpenDemocracy*, February 12, 2014, https://www.opendemocracy.net/en/odr/power-and-money-in-ukraine/; Mark R. Beissinger, "Why We Should Be Sober about the Long-Term Prospects of Stable Democracy in Ukraine," *The Washington Post*, March 11, 2014, https://www.washingtonpost.com/news/monkey-cage/ wp/2014/03/11/why-we-should-be-sober-about-the-long-term-prospects-of-stable-democracy-in-ukraine/; "Ukraine's Maidan Curse," *Russia Insider*, March 16, 2015, https://russia-insider.com/ en/node/4516. Some research has suggested that actual residents of Kiev made up only 12 percent of protestors; 55 per cent came from western, predominantly rural regions, 24 percent from the center, and another 12 percent from southern and eastern Ukraine.

146 Igor Guzhva, "Ot kompromissa k voine."

147 Ivan Katchanovski, "The 'Snipers' Massacre'" accessed November 10, 2021, https://www. academia. edu/8776021/The_Snipers_Massacre_on_the_Maidan_in_Ukraine; Gordon M. Hahn, "Report: The Real Ukrainian 'Snipers' Massacre', 20 February 2014," *Russian & Eurasian Politics*,

The very next day, in what the Commandant of the Maidan, Andriy Parubiy, later described as a coordinated effort to throw the regime into turmoil, regional administrations in several western regions of the country were seized by right-wing groups loyal to the Maidan.[148] The arsenals of several police stations were looted, and their contents distributed to the protesters on the Maidan. As Yanukovych dithered, discontent rose in the east and south of Ukraine, with regional assemblies demanding an end to the violence and, if necessary, martial law.[149]

Despite the bloodshed, many Western observers, including this author who was in Kiev at the time, still clung to the belief that the country's regional elites would somehow once again manage to step back from the brink of civil war. Compromise seemed to be the most likely outcome because, while oligarchs and radicals were temporarily united in wanting Yanukovych removed, the oligarchs wanted nothing more than a return to business-as-usual. In retrospect, we grossly underestimated the influence of the Far Right, which was not just seeking to sweep away the current political establishment, but the entire political system.

On February 20, 2014, the foreign ministers of Germany, France, and Poland (later joined by a former Russian ambassador) flew to Kiev to broker a peace

March 9, 2016, https://gordonhahn.com/2016/03/09/the-real-snipers-massacre-ukraine-february-2014-updatedrevised-working-paper/.

148 "Ostanavlival russkuyu vesnu v Odesse," [I Stopped the Russian Spring in Odessa] *Timer-Odessa*, September 23, 2019, https://perma.cc/GPJ6–3LYA; "Parubiy govorit, chto na Maidane byl zapasnoi 'lvovskiy plan,'" [Parubiy Says There Was a Back-Up "Lviv Plan" for the Maidan] *Ukrainskaya pravda*, October 2, 2018, http://www.pravda.com.ua/rus/news/2018/10/2/7193828/; "Sozdanie vooruzhennykh gruppirovok," [Creation of Armed Groups] *Strana.ua*, September 23, 2019, https://strana.one/news/223761-parubij-odessa-2-maja-v-chem-obvinjaet-hbr-byvsheho-spi-kera-rady.html.

149 Uwe Klussmann and Matthias Schepp, "How Moscow Is Moving to Destabilize Eastern Ukraine," *Der Spiegel*, March 18, 2014, https://www.spiegel.de/international/europe/how-moscow-is-moving-to-destablize-eastern-ukraine-a-959224.html; Valeriy Kalnysh, "V Kharkove reshili otdat vlast mestnym sovetam," [Kharkiv Decided to Give Power to Local Councils] *Kommersant*, February 22, 2014, https://www.kommersant.ru/doc/2414773; Konstantin Kevorkyan, "Pervaya stolitsa protiv vtoroi," [The First Capital against the Second] *Ukraina.ru*, March 30, 2019, https://ukraina.ru/opinion/20190330/1023139281.html; "Dobkin i Shishatsky na syezde yugo-vostochnykh regionov uveryayut, chto oni – za tselostnost Ukrainy," [Dobkin and Shishatsky at the Congress of the Southeastern Regions Assure that They Are for the Integrity of Ukraine] *Ukrainskaya pravda*, February 22, 2014, http://www.pravda.com.ua/rus/news/2014/02/22/7015689/; "'Samooborona' Maidana uderzhivaet 12 adminzdanii," ["Self-Defense" of the Maidan Holds 12 Administrative Buildings] *Ukrainskaya pravda*, July 15, 2014, http://www.pravda.com.ua/rus/news/2014/07/15/7031971/.

deal. By that time, however, nearly a hundred people had been killed in another round of sniper fire coming, again, it now seems, from the area controlled by the Maidan forces.[150] Two days later, a demoralized Yanukovych relinquished his presidential powers and agreed to early presidential elections. In the interim, the acting head of the opposition party Fatherland, Arseniy Yatseniuk, agreed to serve as prime minister.

This agreement, however, was immediately rejected by the Maidan radicals. They stormed the Rada and, without a quorum, and in violation of the impeachment procedures stipulated in the Ukrainian Constitution, they voted to remove Yanukovych from office and replace him immediately with their own candidate, Oleksandr Turchynov.

As Guzhva puts it, for the first time in modern Ukrainian history, a change of regime had taken place through the assault of one part of the country on the rights of another part, rather than through a compromise of regional elites.[151] It is therefore no surprise that the influence of the Galician nationalist agenda soon reached unprecedented levels.

Overnight, the Party of Regions and all left-of-center parties were declared illegal, disenfranchising half the country's electorate. The new ad hoc government was pointedly staffed by western Ukrainians who rejected the idea of a "government of national unity."[152] The 2014 Maidan became a watershed moment for Ukrainian politics, the moment when national politics shifted from the pursuit of consensus, to the pursuit of explicit Galician political and cultural dominance. This explains why so many Maloross Ukrainians at the time regarded it as a coup.[153]

---

150 Ivan Katchanovski, "The Maidan Massacre in Ukraine: Revelations from Trials and Investigations," NYU Jordan Center for the Advanced Study of Russia, December 8, 2021, https://jordanrussiacenter.org/news/the-maidan-massacre-in-ukraine-revelations-from-trials-and-investigation/#.Ywkuyd8pDb0. Over time, several people have come forth to claim responsibility for these shootings, which directly contradicts the official narrative that "The Heavenly Hundred" were victims of the Yanukovych regime. The investigation is formally still ongoing, but now largely defunct because, as the former Prosecutor General of Ukraine Iryna Venediktova put it, society may not be ready to hear the truth. "Genprokuror predlozhila ukraintsam opredelitsy s delami Maidana," [The Prosecutor General Tells Ukrainians To Make Up Their Minds On the Maidan Cases} *Korrespondent.net*, May 30, 2020, https://korrespondent.net/ukraine/4235072-henprokuror-predlozhyla-ukrayntsam-opredelytsia-s-delamy-maidana.
151 Igor Guzhva, "Ot kompromissa k voine."
152 Richard Sakwa, *Frontline Ukraine: Crisis in the Borderlands*, 97–98.
153 "Zhiteli yuga Ukrainy shchitayut Evromaidan perevorotom," [Residents of Southern Ukraine Believe the Euromaidan Is a Coup] *Timer-Odessa*, February 14, 2017, https://perma.cc/N85C-DWYC; Alexei Zhmerinsky, "Vosem voprosov liberalam i dirizhistam," [Eight Questions for Liberals and Managers] *Ukrainska pravda*, February 26, 2016, https://businessforecast.by/

Ukrainians would soon witness many acts of violence by armed nationalist militias, in open defiance of the judiciary, law enforcement, the president, and the parliament.[154] The precedent for such impunity was set by the blanket amnesty that the rump parliament passed for all acts of violence committed on behalf of the Maidan, including looting, rape, and even murder.[155]

Such an all-out assault on state and legal institutions would be a challenge for any new government. To shore up its uncertain authority, the post-Maidan government in Kiev had to rely on the radical nationalist elements that had brought it to power, and would be beholden to them, whether it wanted to be or not.

partners/publication/vosem-voprosov-liberalam-i-dirizhist/; "Otnoshenie zhitelei Ukrainy i Rossii k sobytiam v Ukraine," [The Attitude of the Citizens of Ukraine and Russia to Events in Ukraine] *Levada.ru*, March 3, 2014, https://www.levada.ru/2014/03/03/otnoshenie-zhitelej-ukrainy-i-rossii-k-sobytiyam-v-ukraine/.

154 Gordon M. Hahn, "Violence, Coercion, and Escalation in Ukraine's Maidan Revolution" Russian & Eurasian Politics, May 8, 2015, https://gordonhahn.com/2015/05/08/violence-coercion-and-escalation-in-ukraines-maidan-revolution-escalation-point-6-the-snipers-of-february/; Volodymyr Ishchenko, "Denial of the Obvious," *Vox Ukraine*, April 16, 2018, https://voxukraine.org/en/denial-of-the-obvious-far-right-in-maidan-protests-and-their-danger-today; Jonathan Marshall, "Nazi Roots of Ukraine's Conflict," *Consortium News*, January 28, 2016, https://consortiumnews.com/2016/01/28/nazi-roots-of-ukraines-conflict/.

155 Elena Lukash, "Maidanu – amnistiyu, Donbassu – zakon?" [Amnesty for the Maidan, Legal Consequences for Donbass?] *Ukraina.ru*, April 3, 2017, https://ukraina.ru/news/20170403/1018485691.html.

Chapter Three
The Fatal Attraction of the Far Right

The spectrum of Ukrainian politics is fifty shades of brown.
Nikolai Azarov, Prime Minster of Ukraine (2010 – 2014)[1]

We have no information about any kind of radical far-right parties, organizations or groups … There are probably unofficial groups that share such views, but then we are dealing with individual cases. Ultra-radical groups and organizations are neither registered, nor identified [in Ukraine].
Vasily Vovk, head of the Central Investigation Department of the Security Service of Ukraine (2014–)[2]

The problem lies with us. The problem lies in the strange and incomprehensible transformation – which demands further study – that occurred with people here in Ukraine, who were recently still Ukrainians, and became Galicians.
Vasily Volga, Rada MP (2006 – 2007)[3]

President Petro Poroshenko's stunning transformation as president of Ukraine, from an opponent of Ukrainian nationalism into one of its prime sponsors, highlights the extent to which the Far Right has set the tone for national politics since 2014. It is why his Minister of Transportation, Volodymyr Omelyan, confidently predicted that by the end of his presidency, Volodymyr Zelensky would be similarly transformed:

Each new president of Ukraine begins his cadence with the conviction that he is the one who can conduct a constructive dialogue with Moscow, and that he has been given the role of peacemaker, who will do business and develop good relations … And every president of Ukraine has ended up becoming a de facto follower of Bandera and fighting the Russian Federation.[4]

---

1 Zakhar Vinogradov and Iskander Khisamov, "Nikolai Azarov: Ukraina segodnya," [Nikolai Azarov: Ukraine Today] *Ukraina.ru*, December 12, 2016, https://ukraina.ru/exclusive/20161212/1017986126.html.
2 "Kiev Says 'No Extreme Right Organizations in Ukraine,'" *RT.com*, April 21, 2015, http://rt.com/news/251545-ukraine-ultra-right-extremism/.
3 "Problema kroetsya v nas," [The Problem Lies with Us] *TV Zvezda.ru*, May 20, 2020, https://tvzvezda.ru/news/vstrane_i_mire/content/20205291330-fEvFS.html.
4 "Ukrainskiy ministr predskazyvaet banderovskiy put prezidentu Zelenskomu," [Ukrainian Minister Predicts Bandera's Path for President Zelensky] *Novorosinform.org*, June 10, 2019, https://novorosinform.org/ukrainskij-ministr-predskazyvaet-banderovskij-put-prezidentu-zelenskomu-38947.html.

https://doi.org/10.1515/9783110743371-007

Figuring out why Ukrainian politics is so enthralled to a Far Right nationalist agenda that is, at least according to the ballot box, very much in the minority nationwide, is of central importance to understanding the persistence of the tragedy of Ukraine.

3.1 The Parliamentary Far Right: Svoboda (Freedom Party)

With financial assistance from the Ukrainian émigré community in the West, many Far Right nationalist organizations re-emerged in western Ukraine on the eve of its independence. Their legacy of underground struggle against Soviet authorities well after the end of World War II encouraged the view that achieving true independence for Ukraine now might also require military activities against the remnants of Soviet rule. The creation of new political organizations therefore often went hand-in-hand with the creation of parallel paramilitary structures.

Typical in this regard is the UPA-UNSO, which claimed a direct linkage to the Nazi-era OUN-UPA through its leader Yuri Shukhevich, the son of UPA leader Roman Shukhevich. Members of its military wing, the Ukrainian National Self-defense (UNSO), participated in military conflicts in Transdnistria, Abkhazia, and Chechnya, and helped to organize the infamous "friendship trains" sent to intimidate the population of Crimea in 1992.[5] Rukh also had a military wing, known as *Varta* (the Watch). It formally separated from its parent organization in 1993, though some analysts see this as an effort to provide plausible deniability against the potential charge of military activity against the state.[6]

Among the scores of such groups, perhaps the most visible was the Social-National Party of Ukraine (SNPU), established on October 13, 1991 in Lviv. As its inverted name suggests, it promoted a Ukrainian form of national-socialism based on the "Ten Commandments of the Ukrainian nationalist" composed in 1929 by OUN ideologist Stepan Lenkavsky.[7] It adopted the Teutonic Wolfsangel

---

5 LN – Pozitivnaya, "1 marta 1992 g. 'Poezd druzhby' UNSO v Sevastopole," [March 1, 1992. The UNSO "Friendship Train" in Sevastopol] *Liveinternet.ru*, September 18, 2017, https://perma.cc/DG7Z-C5ET.

6 Vladislav Maltsev, "'Pravyi Sektor' i ego metastazy," ["The Right Sector" and Its Metastases] *Ukraina.ru*, accessed November 10, 2021, https://ukraina.ru/exclusive/20200119/1026369954.html.

7 Evgenii Antonyuk, "Bolshim potom i bolshoi krovyu," [Through Much Sweat and Much Blood] *Ukraina.ru*, September 29, 2020, https://ukraina.ru/history/20200929/1029064245.html; "Organizatsiya ukrainskikh natsionalistov," [Organization of Ukrainian Nationalists] *Wikipedia*, January 7, 2022, https://ru.wikipedia.org/w/index.php?title=Organizatsiia_ukrainskikh_natsionalistov.

as its party symbol, and had its own military wing, the National Self-defense battalions, which were modeled after the guard of the German Nazi Party. Its most famous alumnus, Andriy Parubiy, became Commandant of the Maidan in 2014, and later, the Speaker of the Ukrainian Parliament.

In 2004, however, Parubiy lost the leadership struggle within the party to Oleh Tyahnybok, who renamed the unpalatable sounding SNPU the Freedom Party (*Svoboda*). Parubiy meanwhile left to join Yushchenko's newly created "Our Ukraine" party (*Nasha Ukraina*), all the while publicly underscoring his faithfulness to his earlier political beliefs.[8] With Yushchenko's victory in the presidential election of 2004, therefore, the Far Right had at least some persons in high office who could be relied on to be sympathetic to their cause. This encouraged more to try to enter the political mainstream.

The first party from Galicia to make a bid for national political legitimacy was Svoboda, whose name also had a coded meaning for nationalists: "We live in our own God-given country" ("My zhyvemo v SVOii BOhom DAniy kraini").[9] Svoboda's leader, Oleh Tyahnibok, had served in the Lviv Regional Council, and was then elected to the Rada in 1998, as a member of the SNPU. He was re-elected in 2002, this time as a member of Viktor Yushchenko's *Nasha Ukraina*, but was expelled from the latter in July 2004, after saying that a "Moscow-Jewish mafia" was running Ukraine.[10]

Tyahnibok became well known during the 2014 Revolution of Dignity. As one of the three public faces of the Maidan opposition, along with Vitaly Klichko and Arseny Yatsenyuk, he met frequently with top Western politicians.[11] The US Embassy in Kiev at the time was telling reporters that Svoboda's ideology had

---

8 "Spiker Rady schitaet zhitelei Donbassa okkupantami," [The Speaker of the Rada Considers the Residents of Donbass Occupiers] *Ukraina.ru*, June 2, 2016, https://ukraina.ru/news/20160602/1016520748.html; Vladislav Maltsev, "'Pravyi Sektor' i ego metastazy."

9 Aleksandr Sabov, "Zhurnalist napomnil, chto raspad Ukrainy mog sostoyatsya 20 let nazad," [A Journalist Reminds Us that the Split of Ukraine Could have Taken Place 20 Years Ago] *Rossiiskaya gazeta*, January 14, 2015, https://rg.ru/2015/01/14/ruina1.html.

10 Peter Lee, "The Scary Side of the Ukraine Troika," *CounterPunch.org*, March 13, 2014, https://www.counterpunch.org/2014/03/13/the-scary-side-of-the-ukraine-troika/; Conn Hallinan, "The Dark Side of the Ukraine Revolt," *The Nation*, March 6, 2014, https://www.thenation.com/article/archive/dark-side-ukraine-revolt/.

11 Sabina Zawadzki, Mark Hosenball, and Stephen Grey, "In Ukraine, Nationalists Gain Influence – and Scrutiny," *Reuters*, March 18, 2014, https://www.reuters.com/article/ukraine-crisis-far-right-idINDEEA2H07 J20140318.

changed. Tyahnybok himself, however, insisted that his views had not changed, and that he would repeat his words today.[12]

Svoboda's political program was, in fact, an updated version of Sziborsky's 1935 book *Natiocracy*, which called for "Ukrainian spiritual totalitarianism."[13] For Svoboda, the first task of the new Ukrainian nation must be "a radical cleansing" that ensures its spiritual-blood unity.

According to Svoboda, there is to be a minimum quota of ethnic Ukrainians in every sphere of society, even business ownership. The percentage of Ukrainian in the media must correspond to the percentage of Ukrainians among the population, and "anti-Ukrainian activities" must be subjected to legal penalties, including the loss of voting rights.[14] All political parties, associations, and divergent ideological groups are to be banned, and full political power vested in "the Ukrainian nation." The executive, legislative and judicial branches are to be combined in one individual – the Head of State – who will be personally responsible for the nation's "blood and property."[15]

In foreign policy, Svoboda calls for restoring Ukraine's nuclear arsenal, and aligning Ukraine's foreign policy with a "Balto-Black Sea Axis." The party opposes cosmopolitanism and multiculturalism, and advocates a policy of "European Ukrainocentrism" aimed at creating a "living space for the Ukrainian nation."[16]

Svoboda rejected the Minks Accords, and insisted on a complete blockade of the rebel regions and Crimea. It also demanded that after liberation, the residents of Donbass and Crimea undergo a loyalty exam before regaining Ukrainian

---

12 Peter Lee, "The Scary Side of the Ukraine Troika"; Natasha Shevchenko, "'Pravyi Sektor' prizval vladeltsev ognestrelnogo oruzhiya vyiti na Maidan," ["The Right Sector" Called on the Owners of Firearms to Go to the Maidan] *Zerkalo nedeli*, February 18, 2014, https://zn.ua/UKRAINE/pravyy-sektor-prizval-vladelcev-ognestrelnogo-oruzhiya-na-maydan-138997_.html.
13 Mykola Stsiborskyi, "Natsiokratiya," [Natiocracy] *Ukrainske zhyttya v Sevastopoli*, accessed December 27, 2021, http://ukrlife.org/main/evshan/natiocracy.htm.
14 Alexey Tokarev, "The Electoral History of the Post-Soviet Crimea," *Cyberleninka.ru*, 2015, https://cyberleninka.ru/article/n/elektoralnaya-istoriya-postsovetskogo-kryma-ot-ussr-do-rossii.
15 Gordon M. Hahn, *Ukraine Over the Edge: Russia, the West and the "New Cold War"* (Jefferson, NC: McFarland, 2018), 150.
16 Emmanuel Dreyfus, "Ukraine beyond Politics," *Le Monde diplomatique*, March 1, 2014, https://mondediplo.com/2014/03/02ukraine; "Intervyu Sobchak s Tyagnibokom," [Sobchak Interviews Tyahnybok] *Telegraf*, February 12, 2014, https://telegraf.com.ua/ukraina/politika/1109726-intervyu-sobchak-s-tyagnibokom-video.html. According to Tyahnybok, "the liberals' biggest problem is that they focus on the rights of individuals. For us the rights of the nation, of society, take precedence over individual rights" (at 44:00), that is why "liberals are our ideological opponents" (at 46:20).

citizenship. Only after these regions are thoroughly cleansed of Russian influence, should local elections there be considered.[17]

3.2 The Extra-Parliamentary Far Right: The Right Sector

If Svoboda represents the branch of Far Right Ukrainian nationalism that, as US officials put it in 2014, was trying to "become a modern, European mainstream political party," then the Right Sector represents its extra-parliamentary constituency.[18] There is a great deal of confusion about the relationship between Svoboda and the Right Sector, since their ideologies are virtually indistinguishable.[19] Some of this confusion derives from the idea that there were two distinct Maidans in 2014, one liberal and one nationalist. According to this narrative, Svoboda was assigned the role of the moderate Far Right that wanted to remain politically relevant, while the Right Sector was given the role of the "lunatic fringe," which was doomed to political irrelevance.[20]

A leading scholar of radical movements in Ukraine, Volodymyr Ishchenko, challenges this view. His analysis of over 3,000 Maidan protests nationwide, shows that both Svoboda and the Right Sector, far from being marginal to the success of the Maidan, were its primary actors, albeit at different times.[21]From

---

17 "Vernut siloi, pasporta – zabrat," [Return by Force, Take away Passports] *RIA Novosti Ukraina*, September 17, 2017, https://rian.com.ua/analytics/20170917/1027756703.html.

18 Sabina Zawadzki, Mark Hosenball, and Stephen Grey, "In Ukraine, Nationalists Gain Influence – and Scrutiny."

19 Petro Ivanishin, "Ukrainian National Revolution," *Ukrainian Crusade*, January 28, 2017, https://ukrainiancrusade.blogspot.com/2017/01/ukrainian-national-revolution-some.html; Dmitro Yarosh, "Ukrainska revolyutsiya XXI stolittya," [Ukrainian Revolution of the XXI Century] *Banderivets.org.ua*, https://perma.cc/LEF6-W6RR. According to Yarosh, "Taras Shevchenko, Mykola Mikhnovskyy, Dmytro Dontsov, Evhen Konovalets, Mykola Stsiborsky, Andriy Melnyk, Stepan Bandera, Oleh Olzhych, Jaroslav Stetsko, Lev Rebet, Stephan Lenkavsky, Vasyl Ivanyshyn – these above-mentioned persons are the heart of nationalism, the basic ideological postulates of which cannot be depreciated under any circumstances."

20 "Ukraine's Right Sector Radical Group, Eyes Power after Ukraine Protest," *The Epoch Times*, August 9, 2014, https://perma.cc/9WT3-WLKH?type=image.

21 Volodymyr Ishchenko, "Denial of the Obvious," *Vox Ukraine*, April 16, 2018, https://voxukraine.org/en/denial-of-the-obvious-far-right-in-maidan-protests-and-their-danger-today; Volodymyr Ishchenko, "Far Right Participation in the Ukrainian Maidan Protests: An Attempt of Systematic Estimation," *European Politics and Society* 17, no. 4 (October 1, 2016): 457–458, https://doi.org/10.1080/23745118.2016.1154646. Of the more than 3,000 "protest events" that took place between October 2009 and December 2016, Ishchenko found that two-thirds occurred in the west and center, with the preponderance of violent encounters occurring in the west.

November 2013 to January 2014, before the onset of large-scale violence, Svoboda was the most frequently mentioned social agent in the Ukrainian media. It played an indispensable role in mobilizing the Euromaidan, and defining what it stood for. After the bloody events of January 19, 2014, however, it was the Right Sector that dominated all other groups and parties in Ukrainian media accounts.[22]

Ishchenko also challenges the view that Svoboda's lack of electoral success is proof of its irrelevance. As a party with an ideology that was deeply offensive to most Maloross Ukrainians, Svoboda was never really competing for national leadership, he says. Instead, it sought to establish its own unassailable base of support in the core regions of historical Galicia – Lviv, Ternopil, and Ivano-Frankivsk. As part of the western Ukrainian political establishment, it would then automatically became part of the national political dialogue as well.[23]

Finally, says Ishchenko, relying on the national electoral performance metric alone overlooks the unprecedented influence that the Far Right, through both its parliamentary and extra-parliamentary wings, has been able to exert in shaping the country's media, cultural, and religious discourse. Working in tandem, they have also been able to place their own candidates in key law enforcement and security positions.[24] Indeed, Ishchenko suggests, their coordination can be traced back several years.

For example, as early as 2009, in his book *Ukrainian Revolution: XXI Century*, the leader of the Right Sector, Dmitry Yarosh outlined the steps needed to hasten the national revolution. These included: (1) the development of a National Order of dedicated revolutionaries, (2) the creation of a unified nationalist movement, (3) increased awareness of the timing of the national revolution, and (4) the con-

22 Volodymyr Ishchenko, "Denial of the Obvious"; Volodymyr Ishchenko, "The Limits of Change and Wishful Thinking: Lessons from Ukraine's Euromaidan Uprising," *European Politics and Society* 17, no. 4 (2016): 453–472, https://doi.org/10.1080/23745118.2016.1154646. Ishchenko believes that the Western perception of the prominence of liberals in the Maidan movement is due to the way that it was covered by the Kievan-based Western press. The crucial role of the protests in western Ukraine was typically overlooked, even though those protests were no less massive and no less radical than the protests in the capital. As Ishchenko points out, it was in western Ukraine, not in Kiev, that Yanukovych first lost power.
23 Oleg Tkachuk, "Kak vystupili na vyborakh natsionalisty," [How the Nationalists Fared in the Elections] *Vesti*, November 12, 2020, https://vesti.ua/strana/na-pravom-flange-pochemu-natsionalisty-imeyut-shansy-v-ukrainskoj-politike.
24 Volodymyr Ishchenko, "Nationalist Radicalization Trends in Post-Euromaidan Ukraine," *PONARS Eurasia*, no. 529 (May 2018), https://www.academia.edu/36666257/Nationalist_Radicalization_Trends_in_Post_Euromaidan_Ukraine.

solidation, expansion, and development of a truly independent Ukraine.[25] He also described how the upcoming 2012 parliamentary election cycle fit into this strategy. Having set up national-revolutionary indoctrination centers throughout Ukraine, the parties of the Right would then consolidate during the pre-election phase and, after the election, initiate the revolutionary phase by galvanizing "demonstrations of citizens in the capital and in regional centers."[26]

Although this stage was delayed, the political and media influence that Svoboda gained from its spectacular electoral success in 2012, when it gained 10 percent of seats in the Rada, opened up political opportunities further to the right, that were later filled by the Right Sector. The Right Sector began to appeal to young people as the new, more radical version of Svoboda. It now seems that these differences were largely staged, and that the escalation of violence at the Maidan was coordinated by Svoboda and the Right Sector, acting together "as a united front."[27]

This would explains why, despite a European Parliament resolution of December 13, 2012 condemning it for espousing "racist, anti-Semitic and xenophobic views," Svoboda was heavily courted as a coalition partner in the Rada.[28] The promotion of Svoboda, and of Tyahnybok personally, by more moderate opposition parties, like *Batkivshchyna* and *Udar*, was part of their strategy for toppling the Yanukovych regime. On the one hand, it gave moderate parties a degree of credibility with the more radical electorate; on the other hand, it strengthened their negotiating position vis-à-vis Yanukovych by intimating that they could either restrain violence, if the regime were willing to cede power, or unleash it, if it did not.

To cement this relationship, liberals and nationalists jointly supported the nationwide protest action "Rise up, Ukraine!" in early 2013.[29] Defending this alliance against critics, liberal journalist Yegor Sobolev (later turned politician) ar-

---

25 Petro Ivanishin, "Ukrainian National Revolution."

26 Petro Ivanishin, "Ukrainian National Revolution."

27 Stephen D. Shenfield, "Ukraine: Popular Uprising or Fascist Coup?," *Johnson's Russia List*, April 6, 2014, https://russialist.org/stephen-d-shenfield-ukraine-popular-uprising-or-fascist-coup/.

28 "European Parliament Resolution of 13 December 2012 on the Situation in Ukraine," accessed November 10, 2021, https://www.europarl.europa.eu/doceo/document/TA-7–2012–0507_EN.html; David Stern, "Svoboda: The Rise of Ukraine's Ultra-Nationalists," *BBC*, December 26, 2012, https://www.bbc.com/news/magazine-20824693. Batkivschyna leader, and later Prime Minister, Arseniy Yatsenyuk is said to be close to Tyahnybok, even appearing at the Svoboda Congress, to congratulate the party on its parliamentary success.

29 "Svoboda (partiya, Ukraina)," *Wikipedia*, October 30, 2021, https://ru.wikipedia.org/w/index.php?title=Svoboda_(partiya,_Ukraina).

gued that Svoboda, unlike other parliamentary parties, understood that "one cannot act in a civilized way with this government ... one needs to act as with a robber who has broken into your home." If it cannot be stopped by legal means, Sobolev wrote, then "people should follow the example of the Afghans, and take parliament by storm."[30]

The distinctions that were drawn in the Ukrainian media between Svoboda and other Far Right groups during the 2014 Maidan were thus largely tactical. They aimed at: (1) accomplishing specific military objectives, such as defending the supply lines for the Maidan in Kiev, and preparing a fall back position in Galicia should it fail; and (2) offering the West a narrative that would allow it to support "moderate" political parties, instead of militarized "radicals."[31]

This tactic of creating multiple versions of the same organization, that could then act simultaneously and in a coordinated fashion in the political, economic, and military arenas, is well established among Ukrainian nationalists. The OUN, for example, was established as the legal political wing of the Ukrainian Military Organization (UVO) in 1929. After independence, the UPA set up a militant wing, Ukrainian National Self-defense (UNSO), so that its Rada deputies could continue their activities, even after criminal proceedings were initiated against the UNSO.

In the 1990s, the "Patriots of Ukraine" split off from its parent, the SNPU, in order to become the military wing of Svoboda, and then later, the Azov battalion. After 2015, Azov itself spawned multiple new social organizations, including the National Corp, National Detachments (*druzhiny*), Youth Corps, Sports Corps, Veterans Brotherhood, and the publishing house "Orientir." Nevertheless, as its leader Andriy Biletsky put it in late 2014, "Everything that Azov represents spiritually, proceeds from the legacy of 'Patriots of Ukraine.'"[32]

Svoboda and Right Sector thus form flip sides of the same nationalist coin, minted in Galicia. As a mainstream political party, Svoboda was welcomed into the liberal Euromaidan coalition, while staying true to its ideology and to the

---

30 Liza Monina, "Fashistskiy spetsnaz v tylu oppozitsii," [Fascist Special Forces behind Opposition Lines] *From-UA*, January 9, 2013, https://from-ua.com/articles/256768-fashistskii-specnaz-v-tilu-oppozicii.html.
31 "Parubiy govorit, chto na Maidane byl zapasnoi 'lvovskiy' plan," [Parubiy Says that There Was a Backup "Lviv" Plan on the Maidan,] *Ukrainskaya pravda*, October 2, 2018, http://www.pravda.com.ua/rus/news/2018/10/2/7193828/; Andreas Umland, "Is Tiahnybok a Patriot?," *Geopolitika*, Vilnius Centre for Geopolitical Studies, January 6, 2014, https://www.academia.edu/5693544/Is_Tiahnybok_a_Patriot_How_the_Spread_of_Banderite_Slogans_and_Symbols_Undermines_Ukrainian_Nation_Building.
32 Vladislav Maltsev, "Povsyudu 'Azov'" ["Azov" Is Everywhere] *Ukraina.ru*, June 16, 2021, https://ukraina.ru/exclusive/20210616/1031638423.html.

agenda of national revolution, which was coordinated with the more violent Right Sector. This symbiotic relationship continued in the post-Maidan transition government, where Svoboda was given several senior security positions as part of its government quota. The heads of these agencies then looked the other way as the Right Sector organized its own regional militia units.[33]

The Role of the Right Sector During and After the 2014 Maidan

After mid-January 2014, according to Russian pro-Maidan journalist Evgenii Kiselyov, the Right Sector *was* the face of the Maidan; if not in the Western media, then certainly in Ukraine.[34] Its stated objective was the removal of Yanukovych's government, which would set the stage for the national revolution they had been preparing for years.[35] Had Yanukovych remained in power, Far Right leaders were prepared to conduct a "prolonged guerrilla warfare" from western Ukraine, where several regional administrations were already on record as supporting armed insurrection and, if necessary, secession.[36]

33 Ekaterina Stulen, "'Pravyi sektor' ukhodit s oruzhiem v regiony," [The "Right Sector" Heads for the Regions with Weapons] *Vesti*, April 4, 2014, https://vesti.ua/strana/45844-pravyj-sektor-uhodit-s-oruzhiem-v-regiony.
34 Vera Kopti, "Evgenii Kiselev: ispokhablennoe kremlevskoi propagandoi ponyatie 'russkii mir' vse-taki sushchestvuet," [Evgenii Kiselev: The Notion of "Russian World" Corrupted by Kremlin Propaganda Still Exists] *Postimees*, April 25, 2015, https://perma.cc/R7AZ-HY8T.
35 Max Blumenthal, "Is the U.S. Backing Neo-Nazis in Ukraine?," *Voice of Detroit*, February 24, 2014, https://voiceofdetroit.net/2014/03/02/is-the-u-s-backing-neo-nazis-in-ukraine/; Stephen Shenfield, "Ukraine: Popular Uprising or Fascist Coup?" During the 1990s various right-wing groups had trained anywhere from several hundred to up to 5,000 fighters, and were therefore well prepared for a violent confrontation with Yanukovych, if necessary. Five days after the first demonstration on Maidan, four nationalist organizations (UNA-UNSO, Stepan Bandera's Trident, White Hammer, and the Social National Assembly) joined forces to form the Right Sector. In January they numbered only 300–350 people, but by early February, one local observer estimated that 30 percent of the demonstrators in Kiev were marching under Right Sector banners.
36 Alexey Tokarev, "Institutsionalizatsiya Ukrainskogo Natsionalizma," [The Institutionalization of Ukrainian Nationalism] 2014, https://yaznanie.ru/a/hIbs29 ha; Robert Parry, "NYT Discovers Ukraine's Neo-Nazis at War," *Consortium News*, August 10, 2014, https://consortium-news.com/2014/08/10/nyt-discovers-ukraines-neo-nazis-at-war/; "U SBU zayavyly pro kradizhku trokh kulemetiv, 268-my pistoletiv i 15-ty tysyach patroniv," [In SBU Announces the Theft of Three Machine Guns, 268 Pistols and 15 Thousand Cartridges] *TSN.ua*, February 19, 2014, https://tsn.ua/politika/u-sbu-zayavili-pro-kradizhku-troh-kulemetiv-268-mi-pistoletiv-i-15-ti-tisyach-patroniv-335355.html; "U Rivnomu shturmuyut bazu 'Berkutu,'" ["Berkut's" Base Is Stormed in Rivne] *Ukrainska pravda*, February 18, 2014, http://www.pravda.com.ua/news/2014/02/18/7014576/; "Ofitsiino: Z militsii Lvova vyneseno maizhe 1200 odynyts vohnepalnoi

The intensity of the Right Sector's determination to remove the Party of Regions from power may be gauged by its willingness to stage false flag operations to arouse outrage that would bolster public support for revolution.[37] The most iconic of these, the killing of "The Heavenly Hundred" in February 2014, was widely attributed to Yanukovych, even though from the outset there were suspicions that it had been staged by the Far Right.[38] In the intervening years, eight

―――――
zbroi," [Official: Nearly 1200 Firearms Have Been Taken from the Lvov Militia] *Zikua.tv*, February 14, 2019, http://zikua.tv/news/2014/02/19/ofitsiyno_z_militsii_lvova_vyneseno_mayzhe_1200_o-dynyts_vognepalnoi_zbroi_462336; "Frankivtsi kydayut kokteili Molotova v prymishchennya oblasnoho SBU," [Ivano-Frankivsk Residents Throw Molotov Cocktails onto the Premises of the Regional SBU] *Halytskyi Korespondent*, February 18, 2014, https://gk-press.if.ua/x11229/; Shaun Walker, "Ukrainian Far-Right Group Claims to Be Co-Ordinating Violence in Kiev," *The Guardian*, January 23, 2014, https://www.theguardian.com/world/2014/jan/23/ukrainian-far-right-groups-violence-kiev-pravy-sektor; Pavel Sheremet, "Dmitry Yarosh: Ya na voine komfortno sebya chuvstvuyu," [Dmitry Yarosh: I Feel Comfortable at War] *Ukrainskaya pravda*, accessed January 12, 2022, http://www.pravda.com.ua/rus/articles/2015/09/22/7082096/; Tereza Abis, "Pravyi sektor: My ishly ne za yevrointehratsiyu, a za te, shchob zvershyty natsionalnu revolyutsiyu," [The Right Sector: We Went Not for European Integration, but to Complete the National Revolution] *Newsland*, January 19, 2014, https://perma.cc/FV7U-DTUY; Roman Kabachiy, "Ukrainian Nationalism," *Open Democracy*, January 18, 2011, https://www.opendemocracy.net/en/odr/ukrainian-nationalism-are-russian-strategies-at-work/. Many, like the head of the Lviv Regional Council, Vasil Pavlyuk, were already on record as vowing "to defend all that is Ukrainian, meaning, if necessary, by armed insurrection."

37 "Bulatova nikto ne pokhishchal," [Nobody Abducted Bulatov] *Korrespondent.net*, November 20, 2014, https://korrespondent.net/ukraine/politics/3446285-bulatova-nykto-ne-pokhyschal-lyder-avtomaidana; L. Melnikova, *Facebook*, November 18, 2015, https://www.facebook.com/mlnkv/posts/1002533856477859?fref=nf. A famous example is the kidnapping and torture in January 2014 of the leader of AutoMaidan, Dmitriy Bulatov. His deputy, Sergei Poryakov, later admitted that the entire incident had been staged, which did not prevent Bulatov from being named Ukraine's Minister of Sport and Youth. Around that same time, a Kiev journalist reported that one of the leaders of White Hammer had told her that the first two Maidan protesters were killed in January 2014 by their own side, and that such false flag murders were one of the reasons that White Hammer eventually left the Right Sector.

38 Michael Bergman, *Breaking: Estonian Foreign Minister Urmas Paet and Catherine Ashton Discuss Ukraine over the Phone*, 2014, https://www.youtube.com/watch?v=ZEgJ0oo3OA8; Gabriel Gatehouse, "The Untold Story of the Maidan Massacre," *Information Clearing House*, February 13, 2015, https://perma.cc/5CAU-VXEY; Moritz Gathmann and Matthias Schepp, "Maidan-Jahrestag in Kiew: Das unaufgeklärte Massaker," [Maidan Anniversary in Kiev: The Unsolved Massacre] *Der Spiegel*, February 18, 2015, https://www.spiegel.de/politik/ausland/maidan-jahrestag-in-kiew-das-unaufgeklaerte-massaker-a-1019044.html; Stephen Stuchlik, Olga Sviridenko, and Philipp Jahn, "The Shootings in Kiev Were Responsible for the Bloodbath on the Maidan?," *Wikispooks*, April 10, 2014, https://wikispooks.com/w/images/5/52/Maidan_snipers.pdf; Steve Stecklow and Oleksandr Akymenko, "Reuters Special Report: Flaws Found in Ukraine's Probe of Maidan Massacre," *New Cold War*, October 12, 2014, https://newcoldwar.org/reuters-special-

different Ukrainian state prosecutors have investigated this incident, but no official report has ever been released. Three years after the incident, Deputy Speaker of Rada, Oksana Syroyid, intimated that the reason was because current government officials would be implicated in the massacre.[39]

Some analysts, nevertheless, continue to minimize the role of the Right Sector during the Maidan, pointing to its small numbers. Ishchenko concedes that "numerically the far right had a minor presence, but they were dominant on the political and ideological level."[40] This dominance rested on three factors.

The first was the Far Right's regional power base in Galicia, established after Svoboda's victories in the 2009 regional elections. This provided a territory from which to promote their agenda throughout all of Ukraine and, if necessary, from which they could threaten central authorities with separatism. Second, the Far Right used social media far more effectively than its opponents. Right Sector and Svoboda relied on popular Russian social networking sites like *Vkontakte* (ironically, now banned in Ukraine) to condemn pacificism, and urge the seizure of government buildings.[41] Finally, unlike their more moderate political allies,

report-flaws-found-in-ukraines-probe-of-maidan-massacre/; Katya Gorchinskaya, "He Killed for the Maidan," *Foreign Policy,* February 26, 2016, https://foreignpolicy.com/2016/02/26/he-killed-for-the-maidan/; Gordon M. Hahn, "Violence, Coercion, and Escalation in Ukraine's Maidan Revolution," *Russian & Eurasian Politics,* May 8, 2015, https://gordonhahn.com/2015/05/08/violence-coercion-and-escalation-in-ukraines-maidan-revolution-escalation-point-6-the-snipers-of-february/; Ivan Katchanovski, "The 'Snipers' Massacre' on the Maidan in Ukraine," SSRN Scholarly Paper (Rochester, NY: Social Science Research Network, September 5, 2015), 63, https://papers.ssrn.com/abstract=2658245; Gian Micalessin, "La versione dei cecchini sulla strage di Kiev," [The Snipers' Version of the Kiev Massacre] *ilGiornale.it,* November 15, 2017, https://www.ilgiornale.it/news/politica/versione-dei-cecchini-sulla-strage-kiev-ordini-1463409.html; Gordon M. Hahn, "Escalation Points 1–5 in the Ukrainian Revolutionary Crisis, November 2013–January 2014," *Russian & Eurasian Politics,* February 26, 2016, https://gordonhahn.com/2016/02/26/working-paper-revisedupdated-edition-escalation-points-1–5-in-the-ukrainian-revolutionary-crisis-november-2013-january-2014/. In a leaked call with the EU Foreign Affairs chief Catherine Ashton, Estonian foreign minister Urmas Paet shared his suspicions that members of the Maidan opposition may have been behind the shootings. Similar suspicions have been voiced by the German media corporation ARD, American documentary maker John-Beck Hoffman, Reuters news agency, and *Foreign Policy* magazine.
39 "Syroid dopuskaet prichastnost predstavitelei segodnyashnei vlasti k sobytiyam, proiskhodivshim na Evromaidane," [Syroid Admits the Involvement of Representatives of the Current Government in the Events that Took Place on the Euromaidan] *112ua.tv,* February 18, 2017, https://112ua.tv/video/syroid-dopuskaet-prichastnost-predstaviteley-segodnyashney-vlasti-k-sobytiyam-proishodivshim-na-evromaydane-227708.html.
40 Volodymyr Ishchenko, "Ukraine's Fractures," *New Left Review,* no. 87 (June 1, 2014): 15.
41 Gordon M. Hahn, "Escalation Points 1–5 in the Ukrainian Revolutionary Crisis, November 2013 – January 2014."

the Far Right offered a clear political vision for the future – a Ukraine for Ukrainians – and a strategy for achieving it – the seizure of power.

According to Far Right leaders, Ukrainian independence was incomplete because there had never been a true nationalist revolution. Accomplishing this revolution was the historical mission of Galician Ukraine. Guided by a sense of historical destiny, the Far Right tipped the dynamic of the Maidan away from peaceful protest in January 2014, seizing regional and city administration buildings throughout western and central Ukraine. These seizures were typically accompanied by declarations that, if Yanukovych refused to relinquish power immediately, these regions would secede.[42]

Not everyone in the pro-Maidan coalition applauded the rising influence of the Far Right and its violent tactics. The current mayor of Kiev, Vitaly Klichko, at the time a prime candidate to lead the new government, said on February 1, 2014 that "after our victory and the change of regime we shall form new law enforcement bodies, which will deal firmly with radical groups. All members of the militarized bandit formations that are now fighting in the center of Kiev will be held criminally liable."[43] What in fact happened, however, is indicative of who now

---

42 Alisa Revnova, "Protestnaya Ukraina," [Protest Ukraine] January 24, 2014, https://www.segodnya.ua/spectopics/maidan2013/protestnaya-ukraina-regiony-strany-ohvatili-masshtabnye-putchi-491015.html; "Militsiya zaderzhala 58 chelovek posle zakhvata Cherkasskoi oblastnoi administratsii," [Police Detained 58 People after the Seizure of the Cherkasy Regional Administration] *TVRain.ru*, January 24, 2014, https://tvrain.ru/teleshow/novosti_sajta/militsija_zaderzhala_58_chelovek_posle_zahvata_cherkasskoj_oblastnoj_administratsii-361247/; Fosgen Zarinyan, "Vinnitsa. Zakhvat oblastnoi gosudarstvennoi administratsii," [Vinnitsa. Seizure of the Regional State Administration] *YouTube*, January 26, 2014, https://www.youtube.com/watch?v=-qoRDfyZNCg; "V semi oblastyakh Ukrainy razgoraetsya narodnoe vosstanie," [Popular Uprisings Flare Up in Seven Regions of Ukraine] *Censor.Net*, January 24, 2014, https://censor.net/ru/video_news/267817/v_semi_oblastyah_ukrainy_razgoraetsya_narodnoe_vosstanie_aktivisty_shturmuyut_oga_i_vozvodyat_barrikady; "Vo Lvove zakhvatili OGA, SBU, prokuraturu, militsiyu, i nalogovuyu," [In Lvov, the Regional State Administration, the SBU, the Prosecutor's Office, the Police, and the Tax Administration Have Been Seized] January 19, 2014, *Ukraine News*, https://ukrainenews.fakty.ua/177020-vo-lvove-zahvatili-oga-sbu-prokuraturu-miliciyu-i-nalogovuyu-foto; Gianluca Mezzofiore, "Ukraine Facing Civil War," *International Business Times*, 19 February 2014, http://www.ibtimes.co.uk/ukraine-facing-civil-war-lviv-declares-independence-yanukovich-rule-1437092.
43 "Klichko poobeshchal privlech k otvetstvennosti aktivistov 'Pravogo Sektora,'" [Klitschko Vows to Bring the Right Sector Activists to Justice] *From-UA*, January 2, 2014, https://from-ua.com/news/298178-klichko-poobeschal-privlech-k-otvetstvennosti-aktivistov-pravogo-sektora.html.

set the agenda. Instead of pursuing criminal prosecutions, the Rada amnestied all violent crimes committed "in the name of the Revolution of Dignity."[44]

Once the transfer of power to a new nationalist elite was accomplished, according to Right Sector doctrine, the next task would be to extend the scope of the revolution and safeguard it against internal revanchism.[45] This task, however, was soon overtaken by the need to defend the territorial integrity of Ukraine, and here, again, the Right Sector played a decisive role.

During the 2014 Maidan, the Right Sector amassed a large arsenal of weapons and perhaps as many as 10,000 fighters.[46] The creation of what subsequently became known as volunteer battalions was, therefore, not just a response to Russian invasion, but also reflected the *a priori* view that force might be needed to consolidate and defend the revolution.[47] As the Right Sector's press spokesman pointed out even before Yanukovych's removal from office, "our group is fully capable of fighting a civil war."[48]

These armed units served three distinct purposes. First, to defend Ukrainian territory, a task they performed after the Ukrainian armed forces initially refused to fight the local populations in Crimea and Donbass. Yarosh claims to have per-

44 Dmitry Kovalevich and Zakhar Vinogradov, "Tri nerazgadannye tainy Evromaidana," [Three Unsolved Secrets of the Euromaidan] *Ukraina.ru*, January 4, 2021, https://ukraina.ru/exclusive/20210104/1030170033.html; Andrey Portnov and Elena Lukash, "Massovye falsifikatsii v spiske Nebesnoi Sotni," [Mass Falsifications in the List of the Heavenly Hundred] *Strana.ua*, February 17, 2020, https://strana.news/articles/analysis/250173-massovye-falsifikatsii-v-spiske-nebesnoj-sotni-rassledovanie-eleny-lukash-i-andreja-portnova.html; Andrei Portnov, "V programme "Prestuplenie i Nakazanie" [In "Crime and Punishment"], *YouTube*, 2019, https://www.youtube.com/watch?v=SECAs53Oov8; "Zakon pro amnistiyu," [Amnesty Law] *News24.ua*, April 25, 2018, https://news24ua.com/zakon-pro-amnistiyu-napravlen-na-nerassledovanie-vseh-prestupleniy-na-maydane-advokat-nebesnoy-sotni; "Turchinov podpisal 'amnistiyu' aktivistam Maidana," [Turchynov Signs an "Amnesty" for Maidan Activists] *Glavred.info*, February 26, 2014, https://glavred.info/politics/272287-turchinov-podpisal-amnistiyu-aktivistam-maydana.html.
45 Nadezhda Mainaya, "Lider 'Pravoho sektoru' Dmytro Yarosh," [Dmytro Yarosh, Leader of the Right Sector] *Glavred.info*, February 10, 2014, https://glavred.info/politics/270621-lider-pravogo-sektoru-dmitro-yarosh-mi-prosto-prirecheni-peremogti.html.
46 Simon Shuster, "Leader of Far-Right Ukrainian Militant Group Talks Revolution with TIME," *Time*, accessed November 11, 2021, https://time.com/4493/ukraine-dmitri-yarosh-kiev/; Vladislav Maltsev, "'Pravyi Sektor' i Ego Metastazy."
47 Gordon M. Hahn, "Coopting Neo-Fascism: Yarosh, Poroshenko, and the State's Monopoly on the Organs of Coercion," *Russian & Eurasian Politics*, March 29, 2015, https://gordonhahn.com/2015/03/29/901/. In addition to having its own Ukrainian Volunteer Corps (DUK) Right Sector members also entered other right-wing-dominated volunteer battalions such as Dnepr 1, Azov and Aidar, as well as the National Guard and the Armed Forces of Ukraine.
48 Doug Saunders, "Have Ukraine's Protests Been Taken Over by This Ultra-Right-Wing Group?," *The Globe & Mail* (Canada), February 7, 2014, https://perma.cc/EP4R-7CYY.

sonally led the first Ukrainian assault against the rebels in the Donbass on April 20, 2014. Although it was beaten back, he considers it a success because it torpedoed the Geneva peace process.[49]

Second, to pacify the local population in those areas of Donbass recaptured by Ukraine. This led to so many allegations of human rights abuses that the Ukrainian Military Prosecutors office was forced to disband the "Tornado" battalion.[50] Still, Yarosh believes that their experience will prove useful after the reintegration of Crimea and Donbass, where active resistance to Ukrainian rule, in his view, is likely to continue long after reintegration.[51]

The final purpose is ideological oversight of the Ukrainian government, which might also be labeled political intimidation. "If it's a question of bringing several thousand people to the Verkhovna Rada, and blocking its activity in case an important strategic bill is rejected, this will be perfectly realistic," says Yarosh, adding "the Right Sector has extensive experience in organizing such events."[52] In fact, before Yarosh became a senior advisor to the Minister of De-

---

49 Nikolai Podgorniy, "Vizitka po-kievski," [A Kiev-Style Business Card] *Lenta.ru*, April 28, 2016, https://lenta.ru/articles/2016/04/28/vizitka/; "Vizitka Yarosha," [Yarosh's Business Card] *Timer-Odessa*, April 22, 2016, https://perma.cc/7C58–8EA5; Yuri Butusov, "Dmytro Yarosh: 'Pershyi nastupalnyi bii viiny vidbuvsya 20 Kvitnya 2014-ho,'" [Dmytro Yarosh: "The First Offensive of the War Took Place on April 20, 2014"] *Censor.net*, April 22, 2016, https://censor.net/ru/resonance/385673/dmitro_yarosh_pershiyi_nastupalniyi_byi_vyini_vdbuvsya_20_kvtnya_2014go_-dobrovolts_atakuvali_blokpost.
50 "Matios: Dobrovoltsy na Ukraine nakhodyatsya vne zakona," [Matios: Volunteers in Ukraine Are Illegal] *Ukraina.ru*, October 30, 2017, https://ukraina.ru/news/20171030/1019448563.html; "Matios v pryamom efire rasskazal uzhasy o zverstvakh batalona 'Tornado,'" [Matios Told about the Horrors of the Atrocities of the "Tornado" Battalion] *Vesti*, June 19, 2015, https://vesti.ua/donbass/104244-matios-v-prjamom-jefire-rasskazal-uzhasy-o-zverstvah-batalona-tornado; "Voennye prestupleniya karatelei v Donbasse," [War Crimes of the Punishers in Donbas] *Ritm Evrazii*, March 17, 2020, https://www.ritmeurasia.org/news–2020–03–17–voennye-prestuplenija-karatelej-v-donbasse-skolko-verevochke-ni-vitsja-47996; "Yarosh prigrozil 'otrubit' golovy separatistam Nikolayevskoi oblasti," [Yarosh Threatened to "Chop off" the Heads of Separatists of the Nikolayev Region] *Vesti*, March 9, 2017, https://perma.cc/G2VB-U4BL.
51 Liliya Ragutskaya, "Yarosh: plokho, kogda stayu lvov vozglavlyayut barany," [Yarosh: It's Bad When a Flock of Lions Is Led by Sheep] *Obozrevatel*, March 26, 2015, https://perma.cc/K5Y9-NK2B; "Ukraina pokazhet, gde ukrainskaya zemlya," [Ukraine Will Determine Where Ukrainian Land Is] *Republic.com.ua*, March 11, 2018, https://republic.com.ua/article/ukraina-pokazhet-gde-ukrainskaya-zemlya-yarosh-rasskazal-chto-budet-posle-osvobozhdeniya-donbassa-i-kryima.html.
52 "Yarosh: I Can Send Several Battalions to Kiev and Resolve the Government Issue," *Euromaidan News*, October 18, 2014, http://euromaidanpress.com/2014/10/18/yarosh-i-can-send-several-battalions-to-kyiv-and-resolve-the-government-issue/.

fense in 2016, he routinely threatened to march his troops against Kiev.[53] They also routinely intimidated local officials, judges, religious leaders, journalists, teachers, entertainers, and sports figures they suspected of being disloyal to the new order.[54]

In sum, the Far Right, at first through the Right Sector, and then through the myriad civic organizations created out of their volunteer battalions, have become the day-to-day enforcers of loyalty to the Revolution of Dignity. Through vigilante action they foster just enough insecurity in the Ukrainian political, cultural, and religious establishment to keep alive what they call "the eternal spirit of elemental anarchy" (*dukh izvechnoi stikhii*), which must "be ever ready to mobilize the nation to new tasks, in the name of God's established truth and national justice."[55]

53 "Ukraine's Neo-Nazi Leader Becomes Top Military Adviser," *RT International*, April 6, 2015, https://www.rt.com/news/247001-ukraine-army-adviser-yarosh/; Valentina Ustyakhina, "'Pravyi sektor' grozit vooruzhennym pokhodom na Kiev," [The Right Sector Threatens an Armed Campaign against Kiev] *19Rus*, August 17, 2014, https://19rus.info/index.php/mir-v-pautine/item/16279-pravyj-sektor-grozit-vooruzhennym-pokhodom-na-kiev-trebuet-prekratit-ugolovnye-dela; "'Pravyi Sektor' Zakarpatya," [The "Right Sector" of Transcarpathia] *Zerkalo nedeli*, August 15, 2014, https://zn.ua/internal/pravyy-sektor-zakarpatya-razdvoenie-lichnosti-yavlyaetsya-li-zaschita-suvereniteta-rodiny-opravdaniem-dlya-ugolovnyh-prestupleniy-_.html; Gordon M. Hahn, "Coopting Neo-Fascism: Yarosh, Poroshenko, and the State's Monopoly on the Organs of Coercion."

54 "'Pravyi Sektor' otpustil mera Kurakhovo," ["The Right Sector" Released the Mayor of Kurakhovo] *Vesti*, July 10, 2014, https://vesti.ua/donbass/60410-pravyj-sektor-otpustil-mjera-kurahovo; "Ukraine Nationalists Attempt Storm on Kiev Supreme Court," *RT International*, April 7, 2014, https://www.rt.com/news/right-sector-supreme-court-825/; "Radikaly vorvalis v Kievskii gorsovet," [Radicals Broke into the Kiev City Council] *Ukraina.ru*, June 1, 2017, https://ukraina.ru/news/20170601/1018736694.html; "'Pravyi sektor' vorvalsya v gorsovet Nikopolya," ["The Right Sector" Broke into the Nikopol City Council] *Ukraina.ru*, May 4, 2018, https://ukraina.ru/news/20180504/1020299642.html; "Prepodavatelya zashchishchayut ot 'Pravogo Sektora,'" [Teachers are Being Protected from the "Right Sector"] *Odessa1*, July 7, 2016, https://odessa1.com/news/onu-protiv-pravogo-sektora.html; "V Odesse 'Pravyi sektor' sorval pokaz filma posvyashchennogo tragedii 2 maya," [In Odessa, the "Right Sector" Disrupted the Screening of a Film Dedicated to the Tragedy of May 2] *Strana*, October 23, 2016, https://strana.today/news/37296-v-odesse-pravye-radikaly-sorvali-pokaz-filma-posveshennogo-separatistam.html; Pavel Volkov, "Glavnoe iz doklada OON o narusheniyakh prav cheloveka na Ukraine v 2014–2020 godakh," [The Main Points of the UN Report on Human Rights Violations in Ukraine, 2014–2020] *Ukraina.ru*, December 2, 2020, https://ukraina.ru/exclusive/20201202/1029818181.html.

55 Igor Ivanchenko, "Natsionalnaya revolyutsiya trebuet revolyutsiya terminov," [National Revolution Requires a Revolution of Terms] *Banderivets*, January 16, 2014, https://perma.cc/C6HR-K38D; Vladislav Maltsev, "Povsyudu 'Azov.'"

The Right Sector, and the Far Right in general, should thus be viewed as a supra-institutional, rather than an institutional aspect of Ukrainian political life. Its objective is not to compete for voters' sympathies, and hash out a political compromise with other parties, but rather to establish the divinely pre-ordained Ukrainian national order. As Yarosh puts it, "For us, Ukrainian nationalists, the Laws of God, and the interests of our own nation, are far more important than any judicial norms." These must be vigilantly monitored by "modern Cossacks" who are willing to bring down the government at a moment's notice, should it swerve from the proper nationalist path.[56]

Skeptics will say that, while this may be the Far Right's intention, it is far too weak to actually accomplish it. Under normal circumstances, this might be true, but the circumstances in Ukraine since 2014 have been anything but normal, and it is in the interests of the Far Right to keep them that way. This has been accomplished by undermining any social, political or legal institution that might seek to curtail or dilute their efforts to establish a distinctively Ukrainian way of life in Ukraine.

To ensure that it has the ability to defend the national interest against these domestic traitors, the Far Right has insisted on maintaining its functional autonomy from the state, while at the same time infiltrating the state's law enforcement structures. In the first year after the Maidan, according to Yarosh, 90 percent of Right Sector's activities were coordinated with Ministry of Internal Affairs (MVD) and the Security Service of Ukraine, whose head, Valentyn Nalyvaichenko, wrote the foreword to Yarosh's book *Nation and Revolution*.[57]

With political power after 2014 now firmly in the hands of those sympathetic to the Far Right, the Right Sector was no longer needed in a specifically military capacity. New civic and social organizations were created on the basis of its volunteer battalions, in order to retain the same recognizable brand name. As civic organizations, they could conduct civilian oversight of state agencies, and re-

---

56 "Z Khrystom u sertsi," [With Christ in Our Hearts] *Banderivets*, [no date] https://perma.cc/ X79F-KR78; Petro Ivanishin, "Natsionalizm i prava politychna syla," [Nationalism and Rights Political Power] *Naukovo-ideolohichnyi tsentr imeni Dmytra Dontsova*, [no date] http://dontsov-nic.-org.ua/?m=content; "Yarosh: I Can Send Several Battalions to Kiev and Resolve the Government Issue"; Liliya Ragutskaya, "Yarosh: plokho, kogda stayu lvov vozglavlyayut barany"; Ivan Bukhtiyarov, "Ne tak strashen Pravyi sektor," [The Right Sector Is Not So Scary] *From-UA*, March 18, 2014, https://from-ua.com/articles/303602-ne-tak-strashen-pravii-sektor-ili-tak.html.
57 Pavel Sheremet, "Dmitry Yarosh: Ya na voine komfortno sebya chuvstvuyu"; Valentyn Nalyvaichenko, "Rozdil 'peredmova,'" [Preface] to *Natsiya i Revolyutsiya* (Lviv: LA Piramida, 2013).

ceive government funding to conduct military-patriotic training of young people and the armed forces.[58]

The Far Right has thus remained true to its core identity as a socio-religious National Order, for which armed insurrection, civic engagement, and political activism are all interchangeable aspects of the same struggle. As the new Right Sector leader, Andriy Denisenko, put it, "becoming a political party is an instrument for us, just as in self-defense a Kalashnikov rifle is an instrument for us."[59]

With the victory of the 2014 Maidan, the military part of the struggle to impose Galician nationalism on the rest of Ukraine was concluded. The political, legal, and socio-cultural part, however, was just beginning.

3.3 The Maidan in Power: Mainstreaming the Far Right

The Western negotiators who helped arrange Yanukovych's resignation in February 2014 feared that a defenseless Maidan would soon be overwhelmed by government forces, and therefore urged the opposition to make a deal as quickly as possible.[60] They were completely unaware of the degree to which the Far Right's organizational and military preparedness had leveled the playing field. The Far Right, meanwhile, was already looking toward the future. It understood perfectly well that, with the parliament, law enforcement, courts, and executive in complete disarray, any post-Maidan regime in Kiev would need their support to survive.

The most obvious beneficiary of this chaos was the Svoboda Party. Despite holding just a fraction of the seats in parliament, it was given senior positions on the parliamentary committees for national security and defense, and law enforcement, five regional governorships, and five government ministries in national and internal security.[61] As the conflict with Russia deepened, several local se-

58 Igor Serdyukov, "S14 i NABU: Natsistskii kontrol nad Ukrainoi," [C14 and NABU: Nazi Control over Ukraine] *Ukraina.ru*, May 31, 2018, https://ukraina.ru/exclusive/20180531/1020423731.html; Gabriel Gavin, "Ultranationalist Organizations Are Radicalizing Ukraine's Young People," *RT International*, December 2, 2020, https://www.rt.com/russia/508427-ultranationalist-organisations-kiev-government/.
59 "'Pravyi sektor' stal politicheskoi partiei," ["The Right Sector" Has Become a Political Party] *Vesti*, March 22, 2014, https://vesti.ua/strana/43784-pravyj-sektor-stal-politicheskoj-partiej.
60 "You'll All Be Dead," *On Demand News*, 2014, https://www.youtube.com/watch?v=PoKy-qoiq5b4.
61 "Ofitsiinyi portal Verkhovnoi Rady Ukrainy," [Official Portal of the Verkhovna Rada of Ukraine] *Rada.gov.ua*, http://w1.c1.rada.gov.ua/pls/site2/p_komity?pidid=2633; "Deputaty peretrusyly komitety pid Lyashka," [Deputies Restructured Committees to Suit Lyashko] *Ukrainska prav-*

curity positions were also filled by members of the Far Right. Vadim Troyan, a former member of "Patriots of Ukraine" and deputy commander of the Azov battalion, was first named head of police for the Kiev region, then promoted to deputy head of the national police, a position from which he supervised appointments throughout Ukraine.[62]

The Far Right also helped to promote an important ideological innovation in government – the nationalist narrative of perpetual war with Russia. According to this narrative, while the military conflict with Russia technically began with the seizure of the Supreme Soviet in Crimea, it was actually part of a long-established Russian plan to destabilize and absorb all of Ukraine.[63] It follows from this that the secessions of Crimea and Donbass, albeit externally instigated, are also aspects of "the Russian world" that, according to Ukrainian nationalists, still infects the souls of Russophile Ukrainians. These twin dangers – external aggression and internal sedition – require eternal vigilance, which makes the Far Right indispensable for Ukraine's survival. Thus, what began as a series of interim repressive measures vital for national security, has gradually become the regime's new ideological banner.

Laying the blame for Russian aggression squarely on the Maloross Ukrainian population became a prominent theme of Petro Poroshenko's presidency. After

da, December 11, 2014, http://www.pravda.com.ua/news/2014/12/11/7051672/; Richard Sakwa, *Frontline Ukraine: Crisis in the Borderlands* (London and New York: I.B. Tauris, 2015), 91, 95, 223–224; Anton Shekhovtsov, "Security Threats and the Ukrainian Far Right," *Open Democracy*, July 24, 2012, https://www.opendemocracy.net/ern/opensecurity/security-threats-and-ukrainian-far-right/; "Eks-glava SBU rasskazal, kto vinovat v potere Kryma Ukrainoi," [The Former Head of the SBU Said Who Is to Blame for Ukraine's Loss of Crimea] *RIA Novosti Krym*, March 30, 2019, https://crimea.ria.ru/20190330/1116330506.html; Inna Zolotukhina, "General Zamana: 'Nakanune godovshchiny anneksii Kryma vlastyam nuzhna novaya zhertva,'" [General Zamana: "On the Eve of the Anniversary of the Annexation of Crimea the Authorities Need a New Victim"] *Strana.ua*, February 25, 2019, https://perma.cc/QE5H-KU9Q.

62 "Troyan pohodyvsya staty pershym zastupnykom Dekanoidze," [Troyan Agrees to Become Dekanoidze's First Deputy] *Ukrainska pravda*, March 2, 2016, http://www.pravda.com.ua/news/2016/03/2/7100934/.

63 Lucy Fisher and Deborah Haynes, "Leaked Emails Expose Russian Dirty Tricks," *The Times*, April 2, 2018, https://www.thetimes.co.uk/article/leaked-emails-expose-russian-dirty-tricks-cmfkskj82; "Kravchuk rasskazal, pochemu Ukraina byla obrechena poteryat Krym," [Kravchuk Explains Why Ukraine Was Doomed to Lose Crimea] *RIA Novosti*, March 1, 2017, https://ria.ru/20170301/1489023466.html; "GPU rasskazala, kak 'Kreml gotovil perevorot v Odesskoi oblasti,'" [The GPU Reveals How "the Kremlin Was Preparing a Coup in the Odessa Region"] *Timer-Odessa*, August 23, 2016, https://perma.cc/YQU3-LK3 L; Stanislav Prokopchuk, "Kreml proty Ukrainskoi derzhavy," [The Kremlin against the Ukrainian State] *Uryadovyi Kuriyer*, December 22, 2020, https://ukurier.gov.ua/uk/articles/kreml-proti-ukrayinskoyi-derzhavi/.

running as a peace candidate who would end the rebellion in the East "in a matter of hours," he later blamed his failure to do so on the disloyalty of the local population. He contrasted their disloyalty with the loyalty of Galicians, whom he singled out as "the foundation of Ukrainian statehood."[64]

Poroshenko's persistent use of the term "Fifth Column" to describe Maloross Ukrainian political and religious leaders (see Table 3.1) encouraged other senior government officials to refer to Russophile Ukrainians, as "cancerous," backward-looking," *faux* Ukrainians, whose "genetics" were incompatible with the "national code" of the rest of Ukraine.[65]

Table 3.1: President Petro Poroshenko on the Ukrainian Fifth Column.

I don't know how to work with the parliament where the majority of people represent a "Fifth Column" which is controlled from abroad, whole factions. And this danger is only rising.[66]

64 Cicero, "Galitskaya istoriya Ukrainy" [Ukraine's Galician History] *Live Journal*, March 29, 2016, https://cycyron.livejournal.com/4278510.html.
65 Konstantin Kevorkyan, "Chrezmerno khitro sdelannye," [Overly Crafty] *Ukraina.ru*, February 10, 2021, https://ukraina.ru/opinion/20210210/1030508727.html; Konstantin Kevorkyan, "Smelost ostavatsya soboi," [The Courage to Be Yourself] *Ukraina.ru*, July 16, 2020, https://ukraina.ru/opinion/20200716/1028270703.html; Maxim Minin and Ekaterina Terekhova, "Donbass – rakovaya opukhol," [Donbass Is a Cancerous Tumor] *Strana.ua*, June 8, 2021, https://strana.one/news/337360-donbass-kak-rakovaja-opukhol-est-li-eto-v-dnevnikakh-olesja-honchara.html; Yuri Lutsenko, "Formula 'avtonomìya zamìst vtorgnennya' smertelno nebezpechna dlya Ukraini," [The Formula "Autonomy Instead of Invasion" Is Deadly for Ukraine] *Pravda Ukrainy*, December 10, 2021, https://blogs.pravda.com.ua/authors/lucenko/61b332fdabc75/; Georgi Luchnikov, "Gotovy k radikalnym deistviyam," [Ready for Radical Actions] September 17, 2019, *Ukraina.ru*, https://ukraina.ru/exclusive/20190917/1025010770.html; "Tuka: V Kieve 75 % lyudei s vatoi v golove," [Tuka: In Kiev, 75 % of People Have Cotton in Their Heads] November 7, 2015, *Ukraina.ru*, https://ukraina.ru/news/20151007/1014481939.html; "Zhebrivskiy naznachil mestnye vybory v chasti Donbassa na 29 noyabrya," [Zhebrivsky Appointed Local Elections in the Donbass on November 29] *Zerkalo nedeli*, August 19, 2015, https://zn.ua/POLITICS/zhebrivskiy-naznachil-mestnye-vybory-na-chasti-donbassa-na-29-noyabrya-186076_.html;_ "Yushchenko pro Krim i Donbas," [Yushchenko on Crimea and Donbass] *Pravda Ukrainy*, December 26, 2014, https://www.pravda.com.ua/news/2014/12/26/7053324/; "Ministr kultury Ukrainy oskorbil milliony sograzhdan," [The Minister of Culture of Ukraine Insulted Millions of Fellow Citizens] *1tv-ru*, November 23, 2016, https://archive.ph/jvQtR; Pavel Volkov, "Kod natsii protiv demokratii," [The Code of the Nation against Democracy] *Ukraina.ru*, January 2, 2022, https://ukraina.ru/exclusive/20220102/1032845562.html.
66 "Poroshenko Blasts MPs as Fifth Column after E. Ukraine 'Terrorist' Bill Fails," *RT.com*, August 2, 2014, https://www.rt.com/news/177560-ukraine-poroshenko-terrorist-east/.

It's no a secret that the Fifth Column consists of dozens of supposed people's deputies. Only they obviously do not represent the interests of the people who elected them. How can this be tolerated? How can a war be won this way?[67]

The Kremlin aims at internal political destabilization. The openly anti-Ukrainian Fifth Column has been subjected to, if not complete defeat, then significant losses. You are witnesses to this. In most regions, this pro-Russian Fifth Column has lost its social base and gone deep underground.[68]

I am convinced, we have enough sense of mind and strength to keep the political struggle inside the country within the framework of European standards of relations between government and opposition. This is necessary so that the enemy cannot undermine us from the inside; so that the Fifth Column does not raise the head.[69]

At the front it is very easy to recognize the enemy by his black and orange band or Russian tricolor flag. It is harder to determine here, inside Ukraine. The enemy is camouflaged, masked, acts in disguise, insidiously, through the Fifth Column … The words coming out of his mouth seem patriotic, and on his forehead it is not written that sometimes he is not shy about taking money, even from Moscow.[70]

We see how the Fifth Column is raising its head, trying to unite its various ranks, taking advantage of democracy, becoming active in the media arena.[71]

We have no right to repeat and permit the loss of unity; to allow Moscow's Fifth Column to separate us into different corners.[72]

---

67 "Poroshenko: v Rade zasedayut soobshchniki separatistov," [Poroshenko: Accomplices of Separatists Sit in the Rada] *Ukrainska pravda*, August 25, 2014, https://www.pravda.com.ua/rus/news/2014/08/25/7035758/.

68 Olga Novikova, "Poroshenko: My ne mozhem pozvolit sebe razdora," [Poroshenko: We Cannot Afford Discord] *Objective.tv*, December 14, 2015, http://archive.objectiv.tv/141215/122203.html.

69 Denys Rafalsky, "Razshifrovka rechi prezidenta na Den sobornosti," [Deciphering the Speech of the President on Unity Day] *Strana.ua*, January 23, 2018, https://strana.one/articles/analysis/119181-tsar-obedinitel-poroshenko-opredeljaetsja-s-messedzhami-dlja-budushchej-prezidentskoj-kampanii.html.

70 Vitaly Plakhotnyi, "Na lbu ne napisano," [Its Not Written on One's Forehead], *Fakty.com.ua*, March 26, 2018, https://fakty.ictv.ua/ru/ukraine/20180326-na-lobi-ne-napysano-poroshenko-zayavyv-pro-p-yatu-kolonu-v-ukrayini.

71 "Pyataya kolonna, armiya i tserkov," [The Fifth Column, Army and Church] *BBC.com*, September 20, 2018, https://www.bbc.com/ukrainian/features-russian-45587393.

72 "Poroshenko priravnyal poluchenie tomosa k pobede na fronte," [Poroshenko Equated Getting the Tomos with a Victory at the Front] *Ukrainska pravda*, January 15, 2019, https://www.pravda.com.ua/rus/news/2019/01/15/7203856/.

It is a matter of principle that there be no representative of the Kremlin Fifth Column seated in the presidium of the ninth session of the Verkhovna Rada.[73]

Today there are two threats. The first is the Fifth Column on which a lot of money is being spent for the purchase of media, the creation of portals, channels, social network groups, and the bribing of politicians. I am talking about generating chaos inside the country, to encourage the opinion that Russia is really not that terrible.[74]

The Fifth Column of the Kremlin has begun a large-scale special operation against Ukraine. By dragging us into the American electoral campaign, they are trying to undermine Ukraine's bipartisan support of Ukraine in the United States.[75]

Today, on behalf of our team, I am presenting several new initiatives aimed at counteracting Russian aggression, including tough measures against the "Fifth Column" of the Kremlin which operates in Ukraine.[76]

Since Poroshenko's new found nationalistic fervor came with a foreign and economic policy designed to tear Ukraine away from Russia's orbit, it was largely applauded by the West.

Its impact inside Ukraine, however, has been tragic.

One such consequence has been the loss of faith in nearly all political and social institutions, with the exception of the church, the military, and select NGOs.[77] Part of this is due to factors that are common to all regions of Ukraine,

---

73 "Poroshenko ne pustit nardepa OPZZh v prezidium, Rady," [Poroshenko Will Not Let the People's Deputy of the "Opposition Platform – for Life" into the Presidium of the Rada] *Korrespondent.net*, August 24, 2019, https://korrespondent.net/ukraine/4132727-poroshenko-ne-pustyt-nardepa-opzzh-v-prezydyum-rady.

74 "Poroshenko: prorossiiskaya pyataya kolonna vnutri gosudarstva i eroziya mirovoi solidarnosti," [Poroshenko: The Pro-Russian Fifth Column within the State and the Erosion of Global Solidarity] *Espreso.tv*, February 15, 2020, https://ru.espreso.tv/news/2020/02/15/poroshenko_-prorossyyskaya_pyataya_kolonna_vnutry_gosudarstva_y_erozyya_myrovoy_solydarnosty_eto_-glavnye_ugrozy_dlya_ukrayny.

75 Anna Pavlova, "Spetsaoperatsiya Kremlya," [The Kremlin's Special Operation] *Vesti.ua*, May 20, 2020, https://vesti.ua/strana/plenki-poroshenko-i-bajdena-eks-prezident-opravdalsya-za-skandal.

76 "Poroshenko prigrozil 'pyatoi kolonne Kremlya' novymi initsyativami," [Poroshenko Threatened the "Kremlin Fifth Column" with New Initiatives] *Ukraina.ru*, February 10, 2021, https://ukraina.ru/news/20210210/1030516060.html.

77 Andrei Yermolayev, "V Ukraine – totalnoe nedoverie ko vsem politicheskim lideram," [Ukraine Totally Distrusts All Political Leaders] *Spaces.ru*, October 24, 2020, https://spaces-blogs.com/diary/read/comm/souzmira/v_ukraine_totalnoe_nedoverie_ko_vsem_politicheskim_lideram-2063667915/.

such as poverty, corruption, and elected officials who fail to keep their promises. Still, the notably higher levels of distrust in Maloross Ukraine compared to western Ukraine may be attributed, in part, to the more prominent role of the Far Right in national politics and the military.[78]

At the beginning of the conflict in Donbass, the Ukrainian military refused to shoot at the local population. At this critical juncture, the Right Sector stepped in to ensure that the conflict would not end in a negotiated settlement that gave the region greater autonomy.[79] According to the chief military prosecutor of the Ukrainian military, Anatoly Matios, these volunteer battalions also routinely engaged in punitive expeditions against the local population.[80] Although some of these individuals were later prosecuted and their units disbanded, most were re-integrated into the regular military, the Ministry of Internal Affairs, or the police.

A second consequence is that it has now become perfectly acceptable to limit the rights of Ukrainian citizens based on their residency and suspected political sympathies. In the 2020 and 2021 municipal and regional elections, for example, Ukrainian citizens living in Donbass were denied the ability to vote for their own regional officials. The government argued that going to the polls was unsafe, even though Zelensky himself said at the time that the region had never been safer.[81] Such examples, along with statements by senior Ukrainian officials that the full reintegration of Donbass into Ukraine will require mass re-education, restrictions of political rights, the pre-emptive detention without trial of those who hold Russian passports (which is the majority of Donbass

78 Grigore Pop-Eleches and Graeme Robertson, "Ukraine Isn't Unified Yet," *Washington Post*, November 13, 2015, https://www.washingtonpost.com/news/monkey-cage/wp/2015/11/13/ukraine-isnt-unified-yet-these-4-charts-explain-how/; "Ukraini – 29. De my zaraz ta kudy priamuiemo?," [Ukraine – 29. Where Are We Now and Where Are We Going?] Fond "Demokratychni inisiatyvy" im. Ilka Kucheriva, August 21, 2020, https://dif.org.ua/article/ukraini-29-de-mi-zaraz-ta-kudi-pryamuemo; "Monitorynh hromadskoy dumky naselennia Ukrainy," [Public Opinion Monitoring of the Population of Ukraine] Tsentr "Sotsialnyi Monitorynh," March 4, 2021, https://smc.org.ua/monitoryng-gromadskoyi-dumky-naselennya-ukrayiny-lyutyj-2021-roku-2141/.
79 Nikolai Mikhailenko, "Yarosh bez vizitki" [Yarosh without a Business Card], *Filolingvia*, June 7, 2014, http://filolingvia.com/publ/jarosh_zhutko_sovetskij/441–1–0–6722.
80 Andrei Manchuk, "Deti dostoinstva," [Children of Dignity] *Ukraina.ru*, June 2, 2021, https://ukraina.ru/opinion/20210602/1031544519.html; Konstantin Kevorkyan, "Obydennost natsizma," [Everyday Nazism] *Ukraina.ru*, October 15, 2019, https://ukraina.ru/opinion/20191015/1025325571.html.
81 Igor Denisenko, "Demokraiya v typike," [Democracy Is at a Dead End] *Zerkalo nedeli*, February 8, 2022, https://zn.ua/internal/demokratija-v-tupike-zhizn-v-hromadakh-bez-vyborov.html; "Zelensky on Donbas Truce Achievements," *Unian*, June 12, 2020, https://www.unian.info/war/donbas-truce-zelensky-says-combat-losses-down-90-on-year-11245502.html.

and Crimean residents), and the deployment of Ukrainian troops there for at least twenty-five years, have been widely publicized in the rebel held territories.[82]

But blaming the rise of the Far Right exclusively on the disloyalty of Maloross Ukrainians is too simplistic, for it overlooks the attraction that nationalism now holds for many Ukrainians, whether liberal Europhiles, Galician nationalists, or even Maloross Ukrainians. To understand this fatal attraction, one must go back to the late 1980s, to the origins of Soviet Ukrainian civil society. At the time, one overarching goal united both liberal reformers and nationalists – Ukrainian independence. Rukh, led at the time by national communists, actively encouraged the blurring of ideological boundaries between them, hoping to thereby make demands for democracy and sovereignty mutually reinforcing.

Each side relied on this tactical dependence during times of extreme political crisis, such as the 2004 and 2014 Maidans. This allowed civil society to unite briefly, muster enough support to oppose existing oligarchical arrangements, and reshuffle the political deck. At the same time, however, their fundamental ideological incompatibility prevented the emergence of any long-term alternative to oligarchy, which therefore always regained power. This lack of clear political and ideological boundaries wound up benefiting the Far Right far more than it

---

82 Anatoly Sharii, "Reintegratsiya prodlitsya 25 let," [Reintegration Will Last 25 Years] *Sharij.net*, September 18, 2020, https://www.youtube.com/watch?v=5TjYhytrB44; Andrei Manchuk, "Rossiyu sozdali pod pulemetami" [Russia Was Created under Cannon Fire] *Ukraina.ru*, June 6, 2020, https://ukraina.ru/opinion/20200606/1027917013.html; "Zhebrivskiy prosit Poroshenko sozdat VGA vo vsekh raionakh donetskoi oblasti," [Zhebrivsky Asks Poroshenko to Create a CAA in All Districts of the Donetsk Region] *Ukrainskaya pravda*, August 13, 2015, http://www.pravda.com.ua/rus/news/2015/08/13/7077754/; "Zhebrivskiy priglasil 500 patriotov na rabotu v Donetskuyu OGA," [Zhebrivsky Invited 500 Patriots to Work in the Donetsk Regional State Administration] *Zerkalo nedeli*, July 7, 2015, https://zn.ua/UKRAINE/zhebrivskiy-priglasil-500-patriotov-na-rabotu-v-doneckuyu-oga-181720_.html; Oleg Shankovsky, "Zhebrivsky govorit, chto khochet bolshoi voiny s Rossiei za Donbass," [Zhebrivsky Says He Wants a Big War with Russia over Donbass] *Ukrainskaya pravda*, April 8, 2016, http://www.pravda.com.ua/rus/news/2016/04/8/7104896/; "Zolotarev rasskazal, chto na Ukraine na samom dele dumayut o zhitelyakh Kryma i Donbassa," [Zolotarev Said What Ukrainians Really Think of the Inhabitants of Crimea and Donbass] *Ukraina.ru*, December 9, 2020, https://ukraina.ru/news/20201209/1029890131.html; Anastasiya Tovt, "Nichego ne znayu pro genetiku," [I Don't Know Anything about Genetics] *Strana.ua*, November 23, 2016, https://strana.one/articles/special/41886–nichego-ne-znayu-pro-genetiku-ya-politeh-zakanchival.html. Governor Zhebrivsky called for martial law in Donbass, after coming to the conclusion that the number of civil servants loyal to the Ukrainian state in Donetsk had shrunk to "an insignificant number." After the liberation of Donbass Ukraine, he said, Ukraine will need to "impose … a normal democratic agenda on those people" by stationing a garrison of Ukrainian troops in each of the major cities there. Internment camps without trial are proposed to the Cabinet in Bill 4327, sponsored by Prime Minister Shmygal.

did the liberal wing of civil society, since it legitimized both their nationalistic agenda and their use of violence to achieve it. The reluctance of liberals to condemn violence, when it was aimed at their opponents, has severely eroded trust in public institutions and in the rule of law.[83]

Sociologist Volodymyr Ishchenko gives two examples of how the Far Right has benefited from this liberal codependency. The first is former Ukrainian prime minister Oleksiy Honcharuk's attendance at a neo-Nazi rock concert, shortly after his appointment. Ishchenko writes:

> nothing in Honcharuk's lived experience, would warn him against speaking and endorsing extreme nationalists. Because this is a norm in Ukrainian civil society and Honcharuk is a typical representative of this civil society ... what could he know about Ukrainian far right in these circles? That Ukrainian fascism is a Russian propaganda myth? That, perhaps, Ukrainian far right do exist but they are small, marginal, unpopular, insignificant and any other opinion is treacherous and helps Putin?[84]

His other example is the sympathetic coverage given to paramilitary groups such as C14 by Ukrainian-language media such as BBC-Ukraine, Radio Liberty, and Hromadske Radio. The name C14 refers to the Fourteen Words coined by American white supremacist David Lane – "We must secure the existence of our people and a future for White children."[85] In recent years, C14 members have received Ukrainian government grants to conduct "national patriotic education."[86] Since the start of Russia's February 2022 invasion of Ukraine, Western media have extended such sympathetic coverage to the Azov battalion, and other Far Right groups fighting against Russia.[87]

At the same time, many Ukrainian liberals contend that Far Right groups in Ukraine have modernized, and are therefore now less likely to succumb to fascism than during the interwar period. Let us examine this claim in depth.

---

83 Volodymyr Ishchenko, "Nationalist Radicalization Trends in Post-Euromaidan Ukraine."
84 "How to Mainstream Neo-Nazis," *MediaWell*, October 21, 2019, https://mediawell.ssrc.org/2019/10/21/bellingcat-how-to-mainstream-neo-nazis-a-lesson-from-ukraines-new-government-bellingcat/.
85 "Neo-Nazi Threat in New Ukraine," *BBC Newsnight*, February 28, 2014, https://perma.cc/8N4C-QXMX; "David Lane," *Southern Poverty Law Center*, accessed January 13, 2022, https://www.splcenter.org/fighting-hate/extremist-files/individual/david-lane.
86 Christopher Miller, "Ukrainian Militia behind Brutal Romany Attacks Getting State Funds," *Radio Free Europe/Radio Liberty*, June 14, 2018, https://perma.cc/9W63-3D8K.
87 Munsif Vengattil and Elizabeth Culliford, "Facebook Allows War Posts Urging Violence against Russian Invaders," *Reuters*, March 11, 2022, https://www.reuters.com/world/europe/exclusive-facebook-instagram-temporarily-allow-calls-violence-against-russians-2022-03-10/.

According to Vasyl Ivanishin, the founder of the Trident of Stepan Bandera, the forerunner of Right Sector, modern Ukrainian nationalism affirms "the Ukrainian path" – the centuries-long struggle to instill Ukrainianism in all spheres of life. At its heart is the Nation, which should not be confused with "cosmopolitan" concepts like "political nation," which is the mere mechanical unification of citizens. It should instead be thought of as "a conscious and active unity of people, united around the idea of freedom, based on ethnic-social and spiritual-cultural factors ... the defense, development, and reproduction of the Nation is based on the imperative of the nation, [it is] a categorical mandate."[88]

The Right Sector exists to infuse the various social institutions of the Nation with a single Ukrainian worldview. Its ultimate historical mission is "the completion of the national revolution and the construction of the Ukrainian Independent and Conciliar State (*Ukrainskoi Samostiynoi Sobornoi Derzhavy*)."[89] In this aspiration, the Far Right today, says Ivanishin, does not differ in the slightest from its predecessors.

The *sine qua non* of modern Ukrainian nationalism is the designation of Russia as the Eternal Enemy. The Ukrainian state will never be secure until the Russian state is destroyed. War with Russia, therefore, is to be welcomed because it will "arouse the militaristic spirit of the nation," a point also made by several Ukrainian government officials.[90] Given the large number of Ukrainians who view Russian cultural affinity as compatible with their own Ukrainian identity, this will require a great deal of public finesse, says Yarosh, but it is entirely in keeping with the approach taken by Stepan Bandera, who repeatedly admonish-

---

88 Petro Ivanishin, "Natsionalizm i Prava Politychna Syla."
89 Petro Ivanishin, "Natsionalizm i Prava Politychna Syla."
90 Tatyana Shpaikher, "Dmitry Yarosh: Ya veryu v parad pobedy Ukrainy v Moskve," [Dmitry Yarosh: I Believe in a Ukrainian Victory Parade in Moscow] *Apostrof*, September 30, 2016, https://apostrophe.ua/article/politics/2016 – 09 – 30/dmitriy-yarosh-ya-veryu-v-parad-pobedyi-ukrainyi-v-moskve/7539; Andrei Manchuk, "Rossiyu sozdali pod pulemetami"; "Dmitro Yarosh: 'Rano ili pozdno, no my obrecheny voevat s Moskovskoi Imperiei,'" [Dmitro Yarosh: "Sooner or Later, We Are Doomed to Fight with the Moscow Empire"] *Censor.net*, August 25, 2008, https://censor.net/ru/forum/2416274/dmitro_yarosh_rano_ili_pozdno_no_my_obrecheny_voevat_s_-moskovskoyi_imperieyi; Arsen Avakov, "V eti paru dnei mnogo govoril s nashimi v zone ATO," [In These Past Few Days I Spoke with a Lot of Our People in the ATO] *Facebook*, June 22, 2014, https://www.facebook.com/login/?next=https://www.facebook.com/arsen.avakov.1/posts/65728145102863; Alexei Arestovich, "Inaya Ukraina," [Another Ukraine] *Cowo.guru*, March 20, 2020, https://www.youtube.com/watch?v=6zySM-idKdQ (at 18:30). Arestovich, later president Zelensky's press spokesman, argues that, given its many enemies, Ukraine should be thinking of itself as a military fortress ("Israel squared"), rather than deceiving itself with hopes of peace with Russia.

ed Ukrainians to regard all Russians as invaders, and warned that "the sharpness of the Ukrainian anti-Russian front must not be blunted."[91]

Judging by such statements, the type of society that modern Ukrainian nationalists aspire to create does not seem to differ substantially from the fascist state that its founders sought, but were unable to realize because of their defeat in World War II. It is therefore not surprising that, as members of the Far Right have entered the state apparatus, violence has become an increasingly accepted means of dealing with one's opponents, be they members of the political opposition, the opposition media, or the opposition Ukrainian Orthodox Church (Moscow Patriarchate).[92]

Another aspect of political and ideological continuity with the past, which extends from the Galician Ukrainian elite more broadly, is the use of violent and dehumanizing rhetoric against all Maloross Ukrainians. The common use of the derogatory terms such as "not Ukrainian enough" (*nedoukraintsy*) and "cotton-heads" (*vatniki*) since 2014, has led to an overall rise social animosity.[93] So long as this animosity does not directly threaten the territorial integrity of the state, many leaders on the Far Right consider it a vital part of the purging that the Ukrainian nation must undergo to become worthy of its destiny.[94]

---

91 Nikolay Mikhailenko, "Yarosh bez vizitki."
92 "'Pravyi sektor' pregradil put krestnomu khodu," ["The Right Sector" Blocked the Religious Procession's Path] *Ukraina.ru*, July 18, 2016, https://ukraina.ru/news/20160718/1017015489.html; "'Pravyi sektor' ugrozhaet uchastnikam krestnogo khoda," ["The Right Sector" Threatens the Participants of the Procession] *Timer-Odessa*, July 19, 2016, https://perma.cc/B2G3 – 27SC; "Avakov o veruyushchikh s portretami tsarya," [Avakov about Believers with Portraits of the Tsar] *Korrespondent*, July 13, 2016, https://korrespondent.net/ukraine/3716553-avakov-o-veruui-schykh-s-portretamy-tsaria-ymeuit-pravo; "Avakov zhdet teraktov vo vremya krestnogo khoda v Kieve," [Avakov Expects Terrorist Attacks during the Religious Procession in Kiev] *Ukraina.ru*, July 13, 2016, https://ukraina.ru/news/20160713/1016973887.html; "Ukrainian Far-Right MP Declares 'Hunt' for Moscow-Loyal Priests after Split," *RT International*, December 17, 2018, https://www.rt.com/news/446630-ukraine-mp-hunt-priests/; "V SBU sovetuyut 'ukrainofobam' umenshit svoyu ritoriku 'do nulya,'" [SBU Advises "Ukrainophobes" to Reduce Their Rhetoric to Zero] *RT na russkom*, April 21, 2015, https://russian.rt.com/article/86874.
93 "Konstantin Kevorkyan," *Ukraina.ru*, https://ukraina.ru/authors/kevorkyan/; "Vasyl Rasevich," *Zaxid.net*, https://zaxid.net/blogger/vasil_rasevich_u5243/. Former Kharkov journalist Konstantin Kevorkyan, now in exile, has written poignantly about the current ideology, in his column for *Ukraina.ru*. On the other side, the pro-Maidan journalist Vasyl Rasevich has echoed some of these concerns in his regular column for the Lviv based *Zaxid.net*.
94 Pavel Sheremet, "Dmitry Yarosh: ya na voine komfortno sebya chuvstvuyu."

Table 3.2: Ukrainian Officials on the Treasonous Nature of Maloross Ukrainians.

My grandmother … told me about how millions of Ukrainians were killed in eastern Ukraine by these same Muscovite occupiers from the Kremlin. Millions of our grandfathers were killed on those territories, which were then settled by migrants from all corners of the other state. And today you appeal to the local population, to the opinion of the people who live there?
Andriy Parubiy, Speaker of the Ukrainian Rada (2016 – 2019).[95]

It would be politically useless to talk to these people who are, in fact, field commanders and not Ukrainians in the full sense of the word.
Vadim Prystaiko, Deputy Foreign Minister of Ukraine, later Foreign Minister (2019 – 2020).[96]

Speaking of pro-Russian attitudes, they are very high. In some settlements 95 %, in some 80 %, 30 % at the very least, and that is in the Ukrainianized part of the [Lugansk] region … Back in 2006, when I was head of the Lugansk administration, I told Yushchenko that this region was mentally distant from Ukraine. But it didn't register then, and it doesn't register now.
Gennady Moskal, Head of the Lugansk Military-Civilian Administration (2014 – 2015).[97]

It's not only the GRU [Russian military-intelligence – NP] there, you know. There are fully cognizant fellows who, from the age of twenty, hate Ukraine and want to live in the Soviet Union … A generation will have to change before you and I can say that the restoration of Ukrainian authority on those territories, has also overcome the discord in their heads.
Oleksiy Reznikov, at the time Deputy Prime Minister responsible for the Reintegration of Temporarily Occupied Territories, later Minister of Defense.[98]

The president believes that the cancerous tumor [of Donbass] must be subjected to blockade.
Yuri Lutsenko, at the time presidential representative to the Rada, later Prosecutor General of Ukraine.[99]

---

95 "Parubiy zayavil, chto mnenie zhitelei vostoka Ukrainy mozhno ignorirovat," [Parubiy Said that the Opinion of the Inhabitants of the East of Ukraine Can Be Ignored] *Vesti*, June 2, 2016, http://vesti-ukr.com/donbass/151294-parubij-zajavil-chto-mnenie-zhitelej-vostoka-ukrainy-mozhno-ignorirovat.
96 "RF Insists on Kiev's Dialogue with Donetsk," *TASS*, March 26, 2015.
97 "Gennady Moskal: Prorossiiskie nastroyeniya v Luganskoi oblasti 80 – 95 %," [Gennady Moskal: Pro-Russian Moods in the Luhansk Region are 80 – 95 %] *Ukrainska pravda*, October 30, 2014, https://www.pravda.com.ua/rus/articles/2014/10/30/7042701/.
98 Pavlo Vuets and Stanislav Gruzdev, "Oleksiy Reznikov: Bezpecha reintehratsiya Donbasu zaime minimum 25 rokiv," [Oleksiy Reznikov: A Safe Reintegration of Donbass Will Take at Least 25 Years] *Glavcom.ua*, July 11, 2020, https://glavcom.ua/interviews/oleksiy-reznikov-bez-pechna-reintegraciya-donbasu-zayme-minimum-25-rokiv-692369.html.
99 "Vsemu Donbassu gotovyat pravilo 'Moskalya,'" ["Moskal" Rule Is Being Prepared for the Whole Donbass] *Vesti.ua*, June 2, 2015, https://vesti.ua/donbass/101944-vsemu-donbassu-gotov-jat-pravilo-moskalja.

There is only one political problem in the country, and it would be resolved if war were declared. In wartime your faction [the Opposition Bloc – NP] would, of course, be shot, and the political problem thereby eliminated.
Nikita Poturayev, Rada MP (2019–present) and head of the Committee on Humanitarian and Information Policy.[100]

One cannot negotiate with the pro-Russian "Fifth Column," they understand only the language of force.
Arsen Avakov, Minister of Internal Affairs (2014 – 2021).[101]

These people, call them agents of influence if you want, call them spies, scouts, "the Fifth Column," whatever you like. These agents of the enemy state are present throughout our country. Their concentration in Donetsk or Luhansk is no less than in the Supreme Rada or in Transcarpathia.
Georgy Tuka, Head of the Lugansk Military-Civilian Administration (2015 – 2016).[102]

Those who were for Ukraine have all left. Those who remain have accepted occupation … [They are] traitors and separatists, even if they have a Ukrainian passport in their pocket. For me and for millions of those who opposed the traitors who invited the invaders into our country, they will be scum forever.
Andriy Reva, Minister of Social Policy (2016 – 2019).[103]

Leading the attack on the Ukrainian language is the Opposition Bloc. They are helped by individual "Servants of the People" and a high concentration of ideological cotton-heads. I am convinced that the people who are fighting our language are fighting Ukraine itself.
Petro Poroshenko, President of Ukraine (2014 – 2019)[104]

The fewer [Russian-speakers], the better, because experience shows that where the Russian language is, for some reason the "Russian world" also appears.
Maj. Gen. Viktor Yahun, Deputy Director of the Security Service of Ukraine (2014 – 2015).[105]

---

100 Konstantin Kevorkyan, "Patrioty po vyzovu," [Patriots on Demand] *Ukraina.ru*, May 7, 2021, https://ukraina.ru/opinion/20210507/1031320666.html.
101 Konstantin Kevorkyan, "Garant dostizhenii Maidana," [Guarantor of the Achievements of the Maidan] March 3, 2021, https://ukraina.ru/exclusive/20210303/1030730012.html.
102 "Tuka o vezdesushchikh agentakh Kremlya," [Tuka on the Ubiquitous Kremlin Agents] *RIA Novosti (Ukraina)*, November 28, 2017, https://rian.com.ua/video/20171128/1029844792/tuka-ob-agentakh-kremlia-v-ukraine.html.
103 "Ostanutsya mrazyami i podonkami," [They Will Always Be Scum and Bastards] *Dnr24.su*, October 22, 2019, https://perma.cc/PC4U-KGC5.
104 "Poroshenko v zashchitu yazykovogo zakona," [Poroshenko Defends the Language Law] *Obozrevatel.com*, July 7, 2020, https://perma.cc/9NC9-NCHX.
105 Konstantin Kevorkyan, "Spasti cherez pobedu," [Saved through Victory] *Ukraina.ru*, January 2, 2022, https://ukraina.ru/exclusive/20220102/1033014994.html.

[In these lands] there is almost nothing Ukrainian, there is practically none of our language, none of our memories; our church and our culture are not there … It is an alien territory, where much of what forms a whole and indivisible nation has been lost … This is my land, and I will do everything in my power to prevent any piece of this earth falling into anyone else's hands. At the same time, you feel there are people, very many people, who see it differently.
Viktor Yushchenko, President of Ukraine (2005–2010)[106]

After they [Donbass and Crimea] return to the bosom of Ukraine, they will have to undergo full de-separatization and re-passportization. Every person who wants to be in the Ukrainian state, and have the right to anything, will have to prove his loyalty to Ukraine … Only when it is really Ukraine, and not citizens who hate Ukraine, can you hold elections there … [Meanwhile] block the water, block electricity, no trade, don't supply them anything. Let them howl to their own government, that is destroying them. We should not feed them! Don't give them any pensions!
Oleh Tyahnybok, Rada MP (1998–2006 and 2012–2014).[107]

Until there is a garrison of Ukrainian troops in Donetsk, Snezhny and Torez … that will de facto impose … a normal, democratic agenda on those people, we will be pulling them out of their coma … for a very long time.
Pavel Zhebrivsky, Head of the Donetsk Military-Civilian Administration (2015–2018)[108]

The current nationalist policies of the Ukrainian government are therefore not simply a spontaneous reaction to Russian aggression in Crimea and Donbass. They are also part of the conflict between two Ukraines – Galician and Maloross – that have been fighting for generations over which one of them has the right to define what it means to be Ukrainian. Feelings on this issue run so high that, for many, compromise is simply out of the question. As Semyon Semenchenko, the former commander of the volunteer "Donbas" battalion put it, those who hoped, back in 2014, that the Revolution of Dignity would be enough to transform Ukraine, must come to terms with the fact that the "Maloross rot" within Ukrainian society is so deep, that only a "proper civil war" will fix it.[109]

Even before the 2022 Russian invasion, therefore, we could expect the Far Right to expand its influence in Ukrainian politics at the expense of its more liberal elements, since it had a number of advantages in this contest:

106 "Yushchenko pro Krym i Donbas," [Yushchenko on Crimea and Donbass], *Ukrainska pravda*, December 26, 2014, http://www.pravda.com.ua/news/2014/12/26/7053324/.
107 "Tyagnibok: lyudey na Donbasse nuzhno zastavit vyt," [Tyahnybok: People in Donbass Must Be Made to Howl] *Dnr24.su*, October 15, 2019, https://perma.cc/MGU2-LXFX.
108 Oleg Shankovsky, "Zhebrivsky govorit, chto khochet bolshoi voiny s Rossiei za Donbass."
109 "Ne grazhdane," [Not Citizens] *Antikor,* May 26, 2017, https://antikor.com.ua/articles/170745-ne_grazhdane_semenchenko_razgromil_hitelej_donbassa.

1) Nationalists build long-term ideological parties, whereas liberal activists tend to form temporary political alliances.

2) Liberal parties and NGOs are advocacy organizations, rather than community mobilizers. They rely heavily on government and Western funders for support, whereas nationalist organizations mobilize locally and thereby strengthen their local base of support.

3) After establishing a strong local base, nationalists integrate it into a nationwide network of ideologically committed activists. These activists can then be moved around the country, even into Maloross regions, giving the impression of greater numbers and influence.

4) Far Right nationalism consciously associates itself with an important segment of Ukrainian historical tradition, Cossack freedom, which glorifies the struggle for nationhood and confrontation with Russia. Liberalism, by contrast, has almost no historical tradition to rely on in Ukraine. Even worse, it stems from the liberal intellectual tradition of the Russian Empire.[110]

5) Finally, the Far Right does not see itself as in any way subordinate to the government, but rather, as a parallel instrument of popular control. So long as the government follows the path of Galician development, the Far Right will focus on civic activism and cultural education. But should the government swerve from this path, the Will of the Nation will be justification enough for the Far Right to remove it from power.

Since 2014, all Ukrainian governments have kowtowed to Far Right nationalism, believing that its implicit threat to public order will never be directed at them.[111] Indeed, many in the liberal wing of Ukrainian politics are convinced that they are using the Far Right to achieve liberal reform objectives, just as the Far

---

110 Volodymyr Ishchenko, "Nationalist Radicalization Trends in Post-Euromaidan Ukraine."
111 "Komandir DUK 'Pravyi Sektor' Stempitskii," [Commander of the DUK "Right Sector" Stempitsky] *Gordon.ua*, January 30, 2016, https://gordonua.com/news/society/komandir-duk-pravyy-sektor-stempickiy-v-svyazi-s-zaklyucheniem-horvata-io-zamkomandira-duk-ps-naznachen-mirnyy-117816.html. Two prominent political figures, Georgiy Tuka, former Deputy Minister for Occupied Territories and Displaced Persons and governor of the Luhansk Oblast, and Hennadiy Moskal, former governor of both the Transcarpathian and Luhansk oblasts, engaged in a telling debate over the morality of violence in Ukraine today. Tuka distanced himself equally from the violence perpetrated by the "Tornado" battalion and corrupt judges, but added that the fighters should be presumed innocent, while the judges should be presumed guilty. Moskal, speaking of attempts by right-wing activists to exonerate themselves for attacking the owners of a restaurant, suggested that their only mistake was that they got the wrong person, not that such an assault is in and of itself wrong.

Right is convinced that it is using the liberals to forge a more nationalistic Ukraine.

Meanwhile, the underlying clash of political visions remains intact and largely benefits the Far Right, whose core strengths – ideological purity, a monistic view of Ukrainian identity, and a strong regional base of support in Galicia – offer a simple solution to the disorder, chaos, and corruption that continue to plague the country. This solution is succinctly summarized in the popular nationalist slogan: "Bandera will come, and bring order!" (*Bandera priide – poryadok navede!*).

3.4 Searching for a Better Nationalism

Morgenthau, Arendt, and others have argued that the very same aspects of nationalism that can bolster national unity are also often used to suppress cultural, political, and religious pluralism, thus leading to a renewal of domestic conflict. This, in a nutshell, is what has been happening in Ukraine since 2014. According to Ukraine's first president, Leonid Kravchuk, a Galician version of Ukrainian identity has been promoted through the "very aggressive attacks of one region, which often believes that its ideology is the most correct, the most essential for the Ukrainian people; [it] encounters the opposition of all regions of Ukraine that have a different ideology, or maybe different views, to be more precise, on the situation in Ukraine."[112] His political opponent, former People's Deputy Evgenii Murayev, also sees this as an effort to transform all of Ukraine into a Greater Galicia with "no place for any sort of multiculturalism," and he worries that it will rekindle the cycle of resentment and violence.[113]

But couldn't a milder form of nationalism still be compatible with a liberal political order? *Washington Post* columnist Anne Applebaum has argued that, to achieve democracy, Ukraine actually needs more nationalism, not less. Nationalism today, she says, means no more than "patriotism, public spirit, national loyalty, national allegiance, whatever word you prefer: the sense that there

112 Anatoly Sharii, "Intervyu s Prezidentom," [Interview with the President] *YouTube Interview*, 2019, https://www.youtube.com/watch?v=uEFOHA2CLMI (at 13:40).
113 Evgenii Murayev, "Ediny ot yugo-vostoka dlya vsei Ukrainy," [United from the Southeast for All Ukraine] *Korrespondent*, May 18, 2018, https://blogs.korrespondent.net/blog/politics/3972140/.

was something special and unique about Ukraine." In the United States, she says, it goes by the name of American exceptionalism.[114]

Applebaum argues that democracy simply cannot work without a national identity to inspire public spiritedness. Donbass, she argues, is "what a land without nationalism actually looks like: corrupt, anarchic, full of rent-a-mobs and mercenaries." The crucial obstacle to democracy in Ukraine today is that, by the time Ukraine won its independence, most Ukrainians had already lost their true national identity. That is why "the tiny group of nationalists in Ukraine, whom perhaps we can now agree to call patriots, represent the country's only hope of escaping apathy, rapacious corruption, and, eventually, dismemberment."[115]

There are several problems with Applebaum's rosy view of nationalism, beginning with her assertion that nationalism is little more than a bout of patriotic fervor. In fact, what distinguishes nationalism from patriotism is that it exploits the deep-seated human instinct for hearth and home to exalt the Nation beyond any civil or legal constraints. That is why nationalism never embraces the full diversity of civil society, but only those who declare their unswervingly loyalty to the Nation.

A second problem is her attribution of modern democracy to nationalism. Building on the well established view that late nineteenth-century nationalist movements contributed to the emergence of the nation-state, Applebaum performs a sleight-of-hand by claiming the same for modern democracy. Most historians tend to take the opposite view.[116] True, at the very end of her article she mentions that nationalistic fervor should eventually be translated into "laws, institutions, a decent court system, and police training academies," but she seems blithely unconcerned about how this is supposed to happen in an environment that explicitly rejects "the kind of history, that was thought up by [Ukraine's] Russian-language citizens."

---

114 Anne Applebaum, "Nationalism Is Exactly What Ukraine Needs," *The New Republic*, May 13, 2014, https://newrepublic.com/article/117505/ukraines-only-hope-nationalism.

115 Anne Applebaum, "Nationalism Is Exactly What Ukraine Needs."

116 Maurizio Viroli, *For Love of Country: An Essay On Patriotism and Nationalism* (Oxford: Clarendon Press, 1995); John H. Schaar, *Legitimacy in the Modern State* (New Brunswick, NJ: Transaction Publishers, 1981); Margaret Canovan, *Nationhood and Political Theory* (Cheltenham, UK and Brookfield, VT: Edward Elgar, 1996); Anthony David Smith, *The Ethnic Origins of Nations* (Oxford and Malden, MA: Blackwell, 1986); Rogers M. Smith, *Stories of Peoplehood: The Politics and Morals of Political Membership, Contemporary Political Theory* (Cambridge and New York: Cambridge University Press, 2003); Bernard Yack, "Popular Sovereignty and Nationalism," *Political Theory* 29, no. 4 (2001): 517–536, https://doi.org/10.1177/0090591701029004003.

This highlights a third problem: her casual dismissal of the heritage of Maloross Ukraine which, she implies, is merely the result of cultural genocide against true Ukrainians. Her assumption that there is only one legitimate expression of Ukrainian culture leads her to ignore all the civic activism of eastern and southern Ukraine, both before and after 2014, most of which emerged as a direct result of efforts to impose a Galician face on Ukraine, rather than allow it to develop pluralistically. As one of the foremost historians of the region, Hiroake Kuromiya, notes, pluralism was always Donbass's distinctive contribution to the Ukrainian national movement. "The Donbass conception of Ukraine represented an alternative idea, a conception of Ukraine that differed from the idea of integral Ukrainian nationalism. Donbass meant 'Ukraine for all' as opposed to 'Ukraine only for Ukrainians.'"[117] By choosing to suppress this voice, he argues, Ukraine lost an important counterweight to authoritarian tendencies.

Looking back over Ukraine's fractious history, it is very tempting to concur with this bleak assessment offered by Albert Feldman, director of the Golda Meir Institute of Strategic Studies in Israel:

> The Ukrainian house is on fire, and one part, the one with the key to the front door, has locked itself in, does not acknowledge that it started the fire, and stubbornly refuses to give up the key. The other part understands that the fumes are spreading very quickly and everyone could burn up, but still hopes that the key holders will get wiser. Sometimes it seems to me that Ukraine has fallen into an eternal circle, doomed to repeat the same mistakes – two Maidans, war, elections and the re-elections have taught it nothing.[118]

The ancient Greeks, however, would have rejected such hopeless determinism, and would have used their knowledge of tragedy to explain why. One of the key lessons that tragedy seeks to impart is that it is never too late to restore social harmony, if one is willing to replace confrontation with dialogue. True dialogue assumes a willingness to recognize a part of one's self in the Other's narrative of you. This shared narrative framework is the "glue" that binds people and societ-

117 Denis Timoshenko, "Bez vtruchannya, bez viyny, bez anneksiy Krymu Rosieyu nichoho b ne bulo," [Without Intervention, without War, without Annexations of Crimea, Russia Would Be Nothing] *Radio Liberty (Crimean Realities)*, September 3, 2019, https://ua.krymr.com/a/khiroaki-kuromia-donbas-ukrainskyi-natsionalizm/30144401.html; Igor Piliayev, "The Nature of the Armed Conflict in Donbas: A Postnonclassical Viewpoint," *Ideology and Politics* 14, no. 3 (2019): 77–105, https://perma.cc/C644-LTVP?type=image. Mikhaylo Minakov, cited in Piliaiev, makes a similar point, saying that separatist movements in southeastern Ukraine are particularly "attentive to the peaceful coexistence of different ethnic and religious groups" (pp. 280–281) and that their political culture is based on a "non-ethnic statehood" (p. 280).
118 Albert Leizer Feldman, "Krizis ukrainskoi vlasti," [The Crisis of Ukrainian Governance] *Korrespondent*, September 20, 2017, http://blogs.korrespondent.net/blog/events/3888291.

ies together. It might be said that the ultimate purpose of dialogue is to encourage individuals to partake of that shared narrative and to expand it.[119]

In modern Ukraine *raison d'etat* has supplanted the commonweal. The state is seen as essential to the formation of the nation, rather than the other way around. State capture has become the ultimate objective of social and political groups in society and this inevitably leads to the temptation to view the enemies of the state as the enemies of the nation itself. This is a perennial problem of nationalistic ideologies, which, being a form of totalitarianism, strive to make the interests of state coextensive with the interests of society.

Nationalism is therefore never as beneficial in the long run as it appears to be in the short run, because it is fundamentally destructive of the dialogue needed for social harmony. It serves the purposes of revolution, but undermines the purposes of governance. To restore social harmony, nationalism must eventually be replaced with something that is more conducive to mutual understanding. That something could be civic patriotism.

---

119 David Bohm et al., "Difficult Dialogues," Clark University, https://www2.clarku.edu/difficultdialogues/learn/index.cfm.

Chapter Four
The Mental Habits of Nationalism

> Our state ideology now is Ukrainian integral nationalism ... Today it rules the roost, shaping decisions that contradict the interests of almost half the country's population.
> Mikhail Pogrebinsky, Ukrainian political analyst[1]

> I want Ukrainians to take a good look at the descendants of Yezhov, Beria, the bloody executioners of the Ukrainian people. These people [in the Rada] are the descendants of those who arranged the Great Famine, they killed millions of Ukrainians. Here they are! Here they are!
> Nikita Poturayev, Rada MP (2019–present), head of the Committee on Humanitarian and Information Policy[2]

> Why is the Institute of National Memory imposing the narrative of the regions of Lviv and Ivano-Frankivsk on the whole country? ... [I]f you try to build a nation on an Eastern European or Hungarian model, then sooner or later all territories will leave. They won't stay in a country where one narrative is imposed by two regions.
> Vadim Karasyov, Ukrainian political analyst[3]

Both patriotism and nationalism are powerful sentiments for political mobilization, but while nationalism mobilizes through an *exclusive* definition of "who belongs," patriotism mobilizes through an *inclusive* definition of "who belongs." Patriotism is inclusive because it is based on criteria that can be chosen. Nationalism is exclusive because it is based on criteria that are inherited. For the types of nationalism that are rooted in ethnicity or race, the principles of exclusion are obvious; it becomes somewhat murkier when cultural identity, language, or religion are used for exclusion. In such instances the individual's public choice of identity is often treated as a litmus test of belonging to the Nation.

Nationalism demands constant public demonstrations of identity allegiance because of its fear that cultural diversity will undermine national unity, leading eventually to disloyalty and treason. Patriotism, while it may not welcome cultur-

---

1 Anastasiya Kukova and Pyotr Slutsky, "Gradus nenavisti ko vsemu russkomy ne tot!" [The Degree of Hatred for Everything Russian Is Insufficient!] *360tv.ru*, February 28, 2019, https://360tv.ru/news/tekst/gradus-nenavisti-ko-vsemu/.

2 Konstantin Kevorkyan, "Spasite nashi ushi," [Save Our Ears] *Ukraina.ru*, November 14, 2019, https://ukraina.ru/opinion/20191114/1025669123.html.

3 Maksim Karpenko, "Karasyov potreboval obuzdat vezde suyushchikh svoi nos galichan," [Karasyov Demands That Galicians Stop Sticking Their Nose into Everything] *PolitNavigator.net*, April 18, 2020, https://m.politnavigator.net/karasev-potreboval-obuzdat-vezde-suyushhikh-svojj-nos-galichan.html/amp.

https://doi.org/10.1515/9783110743371-008

al diversity, is rarely frightened of it, since it views the loyalty of citizens as rooted in civic criteria, rather than culture, religion, or blood.

This distinction is relevant to Ukraine because, since 2014, the government has relied on nationalism, rather than patriotism, to unite society. Both can produce elements of social solidarity, but they affect the way that government policies are conceived and executed very differently. Whereas patriotism produces pluricultural and inclusive forms of social solidarity, nationalism produces ethnically and culturally exclusive forms of social solidarity. This difference lies at the heart of the tragedy of Ukraine.

If we look at the experience of other countries, we see that there are many ways to promote social harmony in divided societies. But whether we are talking about Canada, Belgium, South Africa, or Italy, what all these countries have in common is that their different ethnic constituencies have accepted their Other as a legitimate part of national society. This is the very first lesson of classical Greek tragedy: without compassion for the Other, true justice cannot be achieved, because some portion of society will continue to feel ostracized and resentful.

Fostering compassion is therefore essential to social healing. Each side must come to recognize the fears that drive its behavior – for Galician nationalists it is the fear of losing their identity within a Russophile Ukraine; for Maloross Ukrainians it is the fear of losing their identity within a Galician Ukraine. Both of these fears can be mitigated by shifting the country's political discourse away from one obsessed with establishing an exclusive Ukrainian nationalist identity, to one that focuses on creating an inclusive Ukrainian civic identity. But, as Ukrainian political scientist Andrei Yermolayev has aptly noted, this would require every part of Ukrainian society to undergo *catharsis*.[4]

Compassion and forgiveness, however, can only take former enemies so far. The crucial next step is restoring faith in social institutions. In *Eumenides*, Aeschylus suggests reconstituting political discourse so as to make reconciliation the foundational principle of the new social order. If we were to update his model, taking modern nationalism into account, it might look something like this:

---

4 "Esli Kiev ne proidet svoi katarsis," [If Kiev Does Not Go through Catharsis] *Ukraina.ru*, December 18, 2019, https://ukraina.ru/news/20191218/1026067559.html.

Table 4.1: The Cycle of Tragedy and Healing.

The Tragic Cycle	Results in …	Healing Therapies	Lead to …
Othering/dehumanizing	Social alienation	Compassion	Fora for reconciliation; the marginalization of hate speech
Refusal to engage in dialogue	Fear and aggression	Catharsis	Reunification on terms acceptable to all
Disdain for how one's own actions lead to catastrophe	Inability to communicate	Dialogue	Civic patriotism replacing nationalism

Nationalism tends to be especially damaging to social unity when it is applied to policy, because it privileges one group at the expense of all other groups. This invariably leads to resentment against the state, to which nationalist regimes typically respond by redoubling their ideological commitment. George Orwell refers to this insistence on ideological purity, even in the face of the visible harm it is doing to society, as part of "the mental habits" of nationalism.[5] It is also the quintessential definition of tragedy: the inability to recognize how one's own actions are leading to self-destruction.

Ideologically driven policy choices are certainly not unusual. Throughout history ideological failure has been masked by revolutionary fervor. The value of tragedy is that it rips away these masks and reveals the harm being done by ignoring reality. It does so, says Raymond Williams, by engaging the body politic "in such a way that the underlying disorder becomes apparent and terrible in overtly tragic ways. From the whole experience of this disorder, and through its specific actions, order is recreated."[6] This aptly summarizes what Ukraine has been going through since 2014: disorder is slowly giving rise to a new order, in which millions of Russophile Ukrainians no longer have a place.

The contours of this new order can be seen most clearly when one looks at how nationalism influences specific government policies. When the mechanisms of democratic government cannot check the nationalist imagination, economic policy is not about creating wealth, but about puffing up the national ego; cultural policy is not about balancing diversity with unity, but about eliminating competing views; and national security is not about promoting the national in-

---

5 O. Dag, "George Orwell: Notes on Nationalism," *Orwell.ru*, accessed November 27, 2021, https://orwell.ru/library/essays/nationalism/english/e_nat.
6 Raymond Williams, *Modern Tragedy* (Stanford, CA: Stanford University Press, 1966), 66.

terest in an interdependent world, but about portraying this interest as a struggle of Good against Evil. When overlaid onto a divided political and cultural matrix like that of Ukraine, nationalism thus promotes a vicious cycle that undermines national unity.

Yet there are still many in Ukraine today who insist on the primacy of nationalism. For example, Olga Mikhailova, a senior researcher at the Ukrainian Institute of National Memory, argues that the problems of Donbass and Crimea stem not from the nationalist policies of the government, but from the manipulation of concepts like "human rights" by those unwilling to join the new Ukraine. Such people, she explains, are irrational, and since rationality is more fundamental than human rights, building a liberal Ukraine does *not* mean that all people deserve equal rights. Individuals must first prove themselves worthy of civil rights, by demonstrating that they are rational in their choice of national identity.[7]

Proponents of a tragic view of politics warn that down this path lies endless heartbreak, because of the dangerous implications of linking nationalism to rationalism. As Reinhold Niebuhr explains, rationalism misses the ways in which inordinate self-love can distort reason itself, so that "the nation pretends to be God."[8] Morgenthau echoes this warning, describing modern nationalism as "essentially a political religion."[9]

Strengthening the bonds of loyalty within and to the state is no doubt vital to the success of any polity, the question really is, how can this be best accomplished, through nationalism or through patriotism? Nationalism is an ideology that serves the political purposes of the nation by strengthening national allegiance at the expense of all other allegiances.[10] The rise of the nation, and

---

7 Olga Mykhailova, "Liberalizm: utopiya, yaka zdiisnyuyetsya cherez nas," [Liberalism: A Utopia that Is Realized through Us] *Ukrainska pravda*, July 14, 2015, http://www.pravda.com.ua/columns/2015/07/14/7074453/; Taisiya Sleptsova, "Istorik Gritsak rasskazal, chto imenno mozhet obyedinit ukraintsev vostoka i zapada," [Historian Hrytsak Describes What Can Unite Ukrainians of the East and the West] *Natsionalnyi bank novostei*, February 6, 2020, https://nbnews.com.ua/obshchestvo/2020/02/06/istorik-gricak-rasskazal-chto-imenno-mojet-obedinit-ykraincev-vostoka-i-zapada/; Bohdan Ben, "Liberal Nationalism Is the Cure Ukraine Needs to Treat Its Post-Colonial Scars," *Euromaidan Press*, May 16, 2021, https://euromaidanpress.com/2021/05/16/liberal-nationalism-ukraine-riabchuk/. Historians Mykola Riabchuk and Yaroslav Hrytsak have offered more sophisticated versions of the same argument.
8 Daniel Lang, "Reinhold Niebuhr on Tragedy, Irony, and Politics," *SSRN Scholarly Paper* (Rochester, NY: Social Science Research Network, August 18, 2009), 18, https://papers.ssrn.com/abstract=1456940.
9 Hans Morgenthau, *The Tragedy of German-Jewish Liberalism* (New York: O Baeck Institute, 1961).
10 Tony Judt, "The New Old Nationalism," *The New York Review*, May 26, 1994, https://www.nybooks.com/articles/1994/05/26/the-new-old-nationalism/.

the concomitant expansion of the state, encouraged the rise of National Socialism and Fascism in the twentieth century. Prominent post-war refugees from
these regimes, like Arendt and Morgenthau, hoped that Europe's experience
would serve as a cautionary tale against the totalitarian potential of modern nationalism. But, as time has passed, and modern societies have drifted toward
anomie, nationalism's solution of conscripting vast armies of hopeless and isolated individuals into the service of the nation has once again begun to sound
appealing.[11]

Some common characteristics of state-sponsored nationalism are irredentism, the dismissal of individual and minority rights, and a dogged determination
to correct the wrongs of the past by re-writing culture and history. This need to
shape one's surroundings to make it conform to the proper ideological view of
reality invariably leads to violence against those who resist. It is precisely this
willingness to "repudiate civility," as Steven Grosby puts it, in order to achieve
national unity, that leads to violence.[12]

In the best of all possible worlds, the individual's subservience to the nation
would be voluntary, but if it is not, it is required nevertheless. As Elie Kedourie
puts it, "the members of a nation reach freedom and fulfillment by cultivating
the peculiar identity of their own nation and by sinking down their own persons
in the greater whole of the nation."[13] As the only goal worth pursuing, the Nation
demands unquestioned loyalty, and acknowledges no limits to that loyalty.

This view of nationalism dominated social science thinking through the latter half of the twentieth century. More recently, it has spawned two counter-argu-
ments. The first, cosmopolitanism, argues that there is a corruption inherent in
nationalism that makes it irredeemable. The emphasis placed on the sovereignty
of nation-states is immoral, and should be replaced by the view that humankind
is a single body.[14] The cure for nationalism is global citizenship, which should
become the new focus of civic education and replace national citizenship.[15]

11 Gregory Millard, "The Jealous God: A Problem in the Definition of Nationalism," *Ethnicities*
14, no. 1 (February 1, 2014): 3–24, https://doi.org/10.1177/1468796813484724; Josep Ramón Llo-
bera, "Recent Theories of Nationalism," in *Institut de Ciències Polítiques i Socials* (Barcelona,
1999).
12 Steven Grosby, *Nationalism: A Very Short Introduction* (Oxford and New York: Oxford University Press, 2005), 17.
13 Gregory Millard, "The Jealous God," 3–24.
14 Veit Bader, "For Love of Country," ed. Martha Nussbaum, Joshua Cohen, and Maurizio Viroli,
Political Theory 27, no. 3 (1999): 379–397, https://www.jstor.org/stable/192314; Marianna Papastephanou, "Cosmopolitanism Discarded: Martha Nussbaum's Patriotic Education and the Inward–Outward Distinction," *Ethics and Education* 8, no. 2 (July 1, 2013): 166–178, https://
doi.org/10.1080/17449642.2013.846057; Marianna Papastephanou, "Patriotism and Pride beyond

The other response has been to try to save nationalism from its own excesses by harnessing it to liberal institutions that will constrain it. Advocates of this view, like Yael Tamir, Michael Ignatieff, and Francis Fukuyama, argue that the United States, France, and Britain are all examples of this good kind of "civic nationalism," in which citizenship outweighs ethnic allegiance.[16]

Critics, however, argue that civic nationalism isn't really nationalism at all, because it privileges the interests of the individual over those of the community. Tamir and Ignatieff grudgingly concede this point, with the latter pessimistically concluding that: "it may be that liberal civilization runs deeply against the human grain and is only achieved and sustained by the most unremitting struggle against human nature."[17]

But such pessimism is based on a faulty premise – that nationalism and patriotism are essentially the same thing. This is an error common to both cosmopolitans, who argue that nationalism's destructive potential is often disguised as patriotism, and liberal nationalists, who describe a patriot's love of hearth and home as natural, and nationalism as the same thing on a larger scale.

The reason for this confusion is easy to understand – patriotism's distinctiveness from nationalism has been entirely swallowed up by the nation-state. This severely constrains the civic component of democracy, making it nothing more than an extension of the nation-state. Let us therefore take a moment to recall what made patriotism different from nationalism in the first place.

4.1 Patriotism versus Nationalism

Both patriotism and nationalism involve love of, identification with, and special concern for a specific entity. In the case of patriotism, that entity is one's *patria* or homeland; in the case of nationalism that entity is one's *natio* or birthplace,

---

Richard Rorty and Martha Nussbaum," *International Journal of Philosophical Studies* 25, no. 4 (August 8, 2017): 484–503, https://doi.org/10.1080/09672559.2017.1342684.

15 Martha Nussbaum, "Patriotism and Cosmopolitanism," *Boston Review*, October 1, 1994, https://bostonreview.net/articles/martha-nussbaum-patriotism-and-cosmopolitanism/.

16 John Agnew, "Nationalism," in *A Companion to Cultural Geography* (John Wiley & Sons, 2004), 221–237, https://doi.org/10.1002/9780470996515; Gregory Millard, "The Jealous God"; Francis Fukuyama, "A Country of Their Own: Liberalism Needs the Nation," *Foreign Affairs*, May/June 2022, https://www.foreignaffairs.com/articles/ukraine/2022–04–01/francis-fukuyama-liberalism-country.

17 Tony Judt, "The New Old Nationalism."

one's place of origin in the ethnic/cultural sense.[18] It may seem natural to think of the two as the same thing, but this is actually the result of the creative manipulation of history by nationalist elites. When a polity is not ethnically, culturally, or religiously homogeneous, patriotism and nationalism often part ways.

Classicist Mary Dietz, who has delved deeply into the origins of the term *patria*, traces it back to the city-states of ancient Greece. It was not a territorial concept (as Aristotle put it, "the identity of a polis is not constituted by its walls"), but rather, it meant that one participated actively in the life of the polis, which was the duty of every citizen. In the Roman Empire, she says, there were two *patriae* – the individual city (*patria sua*), and the city of Rome or common fatherland (*communis patria*).[19] Attachment to *patria* was thus from the outset "profoundly municipal, even domestic," says John Schaar.[20]

With the rise of Christianity, one's *patria* could be either political or spiritual, with the Pope connecting the two in his capacity as the Great Bridge Builder (*Pontifex Maximus*). Sometimes these two were deemed to be in harmony, as described by the Byzantine Emperor Justinian in his Sixth Novella; at other times they were seen as being in conflict, as described by St. Augustine, Bishop of Hippo, in his essay on *The City of God*.

The term *patria* was not widely used in English until the sixteenth century, when it became necessary to describe a particular political principle: the defense of the liberty and rights of Englishmen against tyranny. A patriot was someone who "took his stand with country (or, more exactly, with the constitution) and against absolutist kings."[21] By the eighteenth century, the term patriot was used to describe someone whose authority derived not from territory, but from a particular set of constitutional and political principles: a free republic, the love of liberty, the sanctity of property, and above all limited government. Well into the nineteenth century, Dietz says, patriotism in England therefore involved opposition to the centralized state and to the rising economic order of capitalism.

It is not until the latter half of the nineteenth century that patriotism became uncritical support for the nation-state. As the nation became the ultimate object of political loyalty, and the state the embodiment of the nation, patriotism was

18 Igor Primoratz, "Patriotism and Morality: Mapping the Terrain," *Journal of Moral Philosophy* 5, no. 2 (2008): 204–226, https://doi.org/10.1163/174552408X328984.
19 Mary G. Dietz, "Patriotism," in Terence Ball, James Farr, and Russell L. Hanson, eds., *Political Innovation and Conceptual Change* (Cambridge and New York: Cambridge University Press, 1989), 178.
20 John Schaar, "What Is Patriotism?," *The Nation*, July 15, 1991, https://www.thenation.com/article/archive/what-patriotism/.
21 Mary G. Dietz, "Patriotism," 183.

recast as duty and service to the state. This made the need for any direct civic engagement among citizens that sidestepped the state, superfluous. The inherent contradiction between the patriotic and nationalistic ways of thinking about politics was, nevertheless, still well understood. The *Oxford English Dictionary* traces the earliest known usage of the term "nationalism" back to 1844, when it was described as "another word for egotism."[22]

For many scholars today, the needs of modern society gave rise to the nation-state. This may be regrettable, they say, but it is nonetheless a fait accompli. Thus Ross Poole, who joins with Schaar and Dietz in criticizing nationalism, concludes that "the republican patriot will be a nationalist" because the battle to define a political role for *patria* apart from national boundaries has been lost.[23]

Maurizio Viroli is one of the few who disagrees. As the author of the only full-bodied study of the distinction between the republican tradition of patriotism and the statist tradition of nationalism, Viroli suggests that, even now, a rediscovery of patriotism could shift civic identity (citizenship) from the state back to local communities, and restore the traditional link between locality and politics that made it civic. Restoring the original meaning of patriotism, he argues, could thus be a powerful antidote to nationalism.

According to Viroli, patriotism demands a shift from a territorially based cultural identity, to an explicitly civic identity, which is why the creation of a republic was either repudiated, or regarded as an issue of secondary importance by early modern nationalists. While nationalism values above all else cultural, religious, and ethnic unity, patriotism values above all else the people's common liberty, which is enshrined in the republican ideal of equality before the law.[24]

The history of twentieth-century Europe illustrates the disastrous evolution that nationalism can take when it is mistaken for patriotism. Viroli's antidote against this is a patriotism divorced from nationalism; one in which political unity is based on the republican commitment to the ideal of the common good, rather than on cultural, religious, or ethnic homogeneity.[25]

---

22 Mary G. Dietz, "Patriotism," 189, fn. 18.

23 Ross Poole, "Patriotism and Nationalism," in Aleksandar Pavković and Igor Primoratz, eds., *Patriotism: Philosophical and Political Perspectives* (London: Routledge, 2016), chapter 8.

24 Michael Shalom Kochin, "The Constitution of Nations," *The Good Society* 14, no. 3 (2005): 68–76, https://doi.org/10.1353/gso.2006.0008.

25 Maurizio Viroli, *For Love of Country: An Essay on Patriotism and Nationalism* (Oxford: Clarendon Press, 1995), 183.

4.1.1 The Pros and Cons of Patriotism

For the Greeks, patriotism, or civic activism, went hand-in-hand with the cultivation of compassion. The main theme of *The Peloponnesian War*, according to Lebow, is understanding how the loss of compassion led to the loss of social harmony. The Greeks, yielding to their war frenzy, became inarticulate and unable to apply the language or thinking needed for communal deliberation. Upheaval (*kinesis*) undermined convention (*nomoi*) and encouraged savage deeds (*tolma*.) Thucydides wrote *The Peloponnesian War*, as "a grammar to aid in the reconstruction of the language of politics."[26] Could civic patriotism do the same today for our own frenzied societies?

As a path for restoring social harmony and civic discourse, reinvigorating the historical distinction between nationalism and patriotism has several advantages. The first is that instruction in civic patriotism would directly undermine the exclusivity of ethnic nationalism, by emphasizing that true citizenship means loyalty to pluralistic institutions and practices.[27]

Another advantage is that patriotism is deeply skeptical of the state. This stems from its premise that the values imposed by the state are only morally valid if they are universal.[28] For patriots, there is a crucial difference between values that derive from universal principles, and values that derive from a form of belonging, or a way of life.[29] While both nationalism and patriotism derive values from the same wellspring – "the people, places, and ways that nurture us" – for the patriot, devotion to these alone does not suffice to justify loyalty to the state. Such loyalty must rest on the limits, set forth in a covenant, or constitution, which gives primacy to shared interests over parochial identities.[30] "My country, right or wrong" is something that no patriot could ever say, states G.K. Chesterton. It would be like saying "My mother, drunk or sober."[31] For Szi-

---

26 Richard Ned Lebow, *The Tragic Vision of Politics* (Cambridge: Cambridge University Press, 2003), 299.
27 Szilárd Tóth, "Justifying Republican Patriotism," *Filozofija i Drustvo* 30, no. 2 (2019): 287–303, https://doi.org/10.2298/FID1902287T.
28 Igor Primoratz, "Introduction," *The Journal of Ethics* 13, no. 4 (2009): 293–299, https://doi.org/10.1007/s10892-009-9063-1.
29 Aleksandar Pavković and Igor Primoratz, *Patriotism*.
30 J. Toby Reiner, "Rediscovering Our Roots: John Schaar on Radical Politics Student Protest and the Amelioration of Alienation," accessed November 27, 2021, https://www.coursehero.com/file/51650625/Schaar-paper-draft-twodoc/; Steven Johnston, "This Patriotism Which Is Not One," *Polity* 34, no. 3 (2002): 285–312, https://www.jstor.org/stable/3235393.
31 Gene Veith, "Chesterton on the Virtue of Patriotism," *Cranach*, July 4, 2018, https://www.patheos.com/blogs/geneveith/2018/07/chesterton-on-the-virtue-of-patriotism/.

lárd Toth, the patriot's version of this would be: "my country for the values it realizes."[32]

A third advantage of patriotism is that it promotes one of the strongest and
most stable social bonds – civic solidarity. The argument for this view is as follows. If freedom is an inherent good, then upholding freedom in society is also a
collective enterprise that makes citizens dependent on each another. Turning this
abstract principle into everyday practice requires a personal commitment to civic
participation, which patriotism can produce, but nationalism cannot.[33]

A strong personal commitment to civic participation results from an education in civic values. Such an education will naturally lead to greater civic activism, while at the same time weaning citizens away from divisive nationalism.
For Juergen Habermas, this is a mutually reinforcing process, one that forms
the democratic will of the polity alongside the individual's recognition of his
or her role in it. An education in civic values thus makes citizens resistant to
the seduction of nationalistic ideologies, and is essential in any polity that
seeks a "constitutional patriotism" that embodies democratic principles.[34]

While Habermas emphasizes the rationality of fostering a common civic
identity, Simone Weil argues that it is no less important for civic patriots to foster
a compassionate view of their fellow citizens. Like other critics of modernity,
Weil saw the problem of alienation as the result of individuals being unable to
find meaningful "roots" in modern nations. Nations should therefore work to
re-establish their roots (*enracinement*), and expand them into an interconnecting
network of civic ties, within which individuals could feel a sense of belonging to
each other, and to their community as a whole.[35]

A final benefit that patriotism ostensibly has over nationalism is that it is inherently peaceful. Orwell insists that patriotism, unlike nationalism, "is of its nature defensive, both militarily and culturally."[36] Eighteenth-century English republican patriots were indeed generally hostile to colonialism, and supported

---

32 Szilárd Tóth, "Justifying Republican Patriotism."
33 Philip Pettit, *Republicanism: A Theory of Freedom and Government* (Oxford: Oxford University Press, 1999), https://doi.org/10.1093/0198296428.001.0001.
34 Aleksandar Pavković and Igor Primoratz, *Patriotism*.
35 Simone Weil, *The Need for Roots: Prelude to a Declaration of Duties towards Mankind*, Routledge Classics (London and New York: Routledge, 2002); Charles Taylor, "Why Democracy Needs
Patriotism," in Martha C. Nussbaum and Joshua Cohen, eds., *For Love of Country: Debating the
Limits of Patriotism*, ed. (Boston: Beacon Press, 1996), 120.
36 O. Dag, "George Orwell: Notes on Nationalism."

the American settlers claims against the Crown.[37] A century later, Little England-ers, like G.K. Chesterton, William Morris, Ernest Belfort Bax, C.F.G. Masterman, and J.A. Hobson, put anti-imperialism and opposition to the Boer War at the heart of their argument for patriotism. "What we really need for the frustration and overthrow of a deaf and raucous Jingoism is a renascence of the love of the native land," Chesterton wrote, specifically, he argued, a return to the city-patrio-tism of ancient Greece.[38]

At first glance, therefore, it might seem that a revival of patriotism, as an al-ternative to nationalism, is only to be welcomed, but skeptics have raised a num-ber of concerns. The first, and most common, is that there is no practical differ-ence between nationalism and patriotism today. "Most of what passes as patriotism in common parlance," says Michael Hechter, "are instances of state-building nationalism," hence the two are interchangeable.[39] Others are willing to concede that the difference may be real enough, but that they are used to promote simplistic arguments, such as cultural diversity is good, whereas cultural unity is bad.

A second objection is that while the objects of devotion for patriots, nation-alists, and cosmopolitans may not be the same, it is not clear why either of them should be inherently less violent. Patriotism is just as conflict-prone as nation-alism, says Ignatieff, because countries are contested places.[40] As patriotism forges bonds of solidarity, it also forges corresponding divisions among the friends and enemies of the republic. It is therefore just as likely as nationalism to bring about the ruin of said republic.[41]

---

37 Szilárd Tóth, "Justifying Republican Patriotism," 287–303; Joseph Priestley and Peter N. Mill-er, *Political Writings*, Cambridge Texts in the History of Political Thought (Cambridge and New York: Cambridge University Press, 1993), 140.
38 Anna Vaninskaya, "'My Mother, Drunk or Sober': G.K. Chesterton and Patriotic Anti-Imperi-alism," *History of European Ideas* 34, no. 4 (2008): 535–547, https://doi.org/10.1016/j.histeuroi-deas.2008.07.001. In *The Napoleon of Notting Hill*, Chesterton's hero wonders why his newly minted nation of Notting Hill should "condescend to be a mere Empire? Cannot you be content with that destiny which was enough for Athens, which was enough for Nazareth?"
39 Michael Hechter, *Containing Nationalism*, reprinted (Oxford: Oxford University Press, 2010), 17; Stephen Nathanson, "Nationalism and the Limits of Global Humanism," in Robert McKim and Jeff McMahan, eds., *The Morality of Nationalism* (New York: Oxford University Press, 1997), http://site.ebrary.com/id/10279248; Allan Craigie, "Unionism and Pan-Nationalism: Ex-ploring the Dialectical Relationship between Minority and Majority Sub-State Nationalism," in A. Lecours and L. Moreno, eds., *Nationalism and Democracy: Dichotomies, Complementarities, Oppositions* (London: Routledge), 231.
40 Mitja Sardoč, "The Anatomy of Patriotism," *Anthropological Notebooks* 23, no. 1 (March 30, 2017), http://notebooks.drustvo-antropologov.si/Notebooks/article/view/106.
41 Steven Johnston, "This Patriotism Which Is Not One," 285–312.

Patriotism's critics also point out that the nation is not merely an ideological construct. It is also drawn together by kinship and emotional attachments, especially to the territory considered home. Borders, says Veit Bader, are not derived from principles of liberty or democracy, but from primordial attachments. Ignoring these attachments results in a patriotism that is emotionally hollow and unconvincing.[42] The same problem arises when trying to translate one's emotional attachment for a particular culture, into an emotional attachment for humanity that is divorced from culture.

Viroli counters that, precisely because love of one's own liberty is so profound, it "easily extends beyond national boundaries and translates into solidarity."[43] But if the love of liberty can extend beyond national boundaries and present itself as an act of solidarity, then it can also become dangerously messianic, a criticism that is often leveled at American foreign policy. Schaar's confident assertion that patriotism is more peaceful than nationalism, because "patriots do not comfortably support wars of expansion or wars of 'principle,'" blithely ignores the reality that they routinely *do* support such wars.[44]

Finally, there is the argument that, even if a distinction between patriotism and nationalism were both valid and applicable, it is no longer practical.[45] What these critics object to most is the absence of concrete institutions for the formation of a patriotic, as distinct from nationalistic, polity. Proponents of patriotism, however, argue that education must precede institutions in establishing proper civic attitude. A proper patriotic education should promote compassion and social solidarity, which will then be transmuted into sentiments and actions that sustain liberty. Bader ridicules this as the social science equivalent of alchemy.[46]

Moreover, without an alternative in place, challenging national devotion risks undermining the role of the nation-state in global affairs. Habermas, Dietz, and Nussbaum have no problem with this, because they are convinced that the nation-stare has run its course as an instrument of human progress.[47]

---

42 Veit Bader, "For Love of Country: Review Essay," *Political Theory*, Vol. 27 No. 3, June 1999: 379–397, https://t.ly/696C; Steven Grosby, "Reviews the Book 'For Love of Country: An Essay on Patriotism and Nationalism,' by Maurizio Viroli," *Ethnic & Racial Studies* 20, no. 1 (January 1997).
43 Steven Johnston, "This Patriotism Which Is Not One," 306.
44 Steven Johnston, "This Patriotism Which Is Not One," 310.
45 Veit Bader, "For Love of Country: Review Essay."
46 Veit Bader, "For Love of Country: Review Essay," 388.
47 Aleksandar Pavković and Igor Primoratz, *Patriotism*. Similarly to Dietz and other cosmopolitans, Habermas is convinced that the main trends of the modern world are antithetical to the nation-state.

Others, however, see scant evidence of this, and worry about unleashing global chaos.

While critics of the revival of patriotism raise some valid concerns, they too tend to oversimplify their arguments. For example, the argument that there is no discernible distinction between patriotism and nationalism ignores the distinctive history of both terms. The argument that distinguishing between the two today is pointless because of the pre-eminence of the nation-state, dismisses the ability of education and information campaigns to alter public opinion. Finally, the argument that a renewal of patriotism without nationalism would have no practical benefit, if it is not accompanied by new institutions, puts the cart before the horse. Surely, societies must first recognize that they have lost social harmony and need to restore it, a process the Greeks referred to as *anagnorisis*, before thinking about the kinds of institutions that would uphold it. For patriots, this cannot take place without first shifting the locus of politics from the national to the local level.

Having examined the philosophical impact of Ukrainian nationalism (and alternatives to it), we can now trace its impact in areas such as foreign policy, cultural policy, economics, and even health policy. If the damage done by nationalism appears amorphous and abstract when discussing alternative historical narratives, it emerges much more concretely in the policy arena. It is here that nationalism tends to exacerbate already difficult reforms, and thereby further weakens Ukrainian sovereignty.

In the rest of this chapter we will look at how the mental habits of nationalism have manifested themselves in Ukrainian healthcare, economic, and foreign policy since 2014. Perhaps the most poignant example is Ukraine's tortuous efforts, in late 2020 and early 2021, to obtain a vaccine against Covid-19, from any country but Russia.

4.2 The Nationalist Struggle to Vaccinate Ukraine

The Ukrainian government's Covid vaccination effort encapsulates all the core ideological motifs of nationalism. First, the enemy Other – in this case Russia – is labeled as incompetent; its vaccine therefore destined to fail. Second, the enemy Other is labeled duplicitous, so that its apparent benevolence in offering the vaccine can be dismissed as a ruse. Third, any assertions to the contrary are defined as treasonous.

The tone was set by the American Embassy in Kiev, which on October 13, 2020 summoned Ukraine's Health Minister Maxim Stepanov to an urgent meeting, after he appeared to suggest that Ukraine would be willing to purchase any vaccine approved by the World Health Organization, even Russia's.[48] After this meeting the Embassy stated, on behalf of the minister, that "Ukraine will NOT be buying Russia's Covid vaccine, which has not passed clinical trials for safety!"[49] After that, both Minister Stepanov and the head of the Rada Committee for Health and Medicine, Mikhail Radutsky, then insisted discussions about purchasing the Russian vaccine were moot, since "the WHO would not purchase Sputnik V under any circumstances."[50]

In December 2020, opposition politician Viktor Medvedchuk, a friend of Russian President Vladimir Putin, reached a tentative agreement with the Russian government for the production of Sputnik V in Ukraine, which the government rejected.[51] As Ukraine's foreign minister Dmytro Kuleba put it, even if it were proven to be effective, Sputnik V would never be used in Ukraine because "Russia is not interested in the health of Ukrainians, but in imposing its propaganda and its ideology."[52]

By early January 2021, therefore, as most European countries were either producing their own vaccines, or arranging multiple suppliers, Ukraine had reached an agreement with just one supplier, the Chinese firm Sinovac Biotech, which said that it could provide doses of its own vaccine for only 2–5 million people. Ukrainian officials added that they also had pledges from the World Health Organization's COVAX consortium for several million more as yet unnamed vaccines to be delivered at a later date.[53]

---

48 "Minzdrav Ukrainy dopustil zakupku vaktsiny ot koronavirusa v Rossii," [The Ministry of Health of Ukraine Has Allowed the Purchase of a Vaccine against Coronavirus in Russia] *RIA Novosti*, October 13, 2020, https://ria.ru/20201013/koronavirus-1579661882.html.
49 U.S. Embassy Kyiv Ukraine, "CDA Kvien Hosted a Constructive and Collegial Dinner with Minister Stepanov," *Facebook*, October 16, 2020, https://www.facebook.com/usdos.ukraine/posts/10158431128031936.
50 L. Ksenz and E. Terekhova, "Nikto ne zhdet VOZ," [Nobody is Waiting for the World Health Organization] *Strana.ua*, December 15, 2020, https://perma.cc/TZ8P-NXZ5; "Ukraine Won't Buy Russian Coronavirus Vaccine," *UkrInform*, October 15, 2020, https://perma.cc/GSQ6-BGLL.
51 "RFPI gotov proizvodit vaktsinu 'Sputnik V' na Ukraine," [RDIF Is Ready to Produce the "Sputnik V" Vaccine in Ukraine] *Kommersant*, December 8, 2020, https://www.kommersant.ru/doc/4604712.
52 "Lish by pomogla," [If Only It Helps] *Timer-Odessa*, December 24, 2020, https://perma.cc/U87J-9WBL; "Ucrania pide ayuda a la UE para no tener que recurrir a la vacuna rusa," [Ukraine Asks the EU for Help so as Not to Have to Resort to the Russian Vaccine] *La Vanguardia*, January 13, 2021, https://www.lavanguardia.com/internacional/20210113/6181653/ucrania-pide-ayuda-ue-recurrir-vacuna-rusa.html.
53 Oleg Tkachuk, "Ukraina ne uspela zakazat vaktsiny ot koronavirusa," [Ukraine Failed to Order a Vaccine Against Coronavirus on Time] *Vesti*, January 4, 2021, https://vesti.ua/strana/za-kupki-vaktsiny-provaleny-kogda-mozhno-budet-privitsya-ot-koronavirusa; Aleksandra Ivankova,

A scandal erupted later that month, however, when the head of the National Medical Chamber of Ukraine, Sergei Kravchenko, who also directs the country's leading vaccine institute, declared that there were no actual contracts. As he explained it, the two competing Ukrainian purchasing agencies had agreed between themselves on what to purchase, but that Sinovac Biotech had not actually agreed to supply anything.[54]

When this became known, thanks to the investigative reporting of *112.ua*, one of several opposition networks subsequently taken off the air, the government decided to outsource its vaccine purchasing to the British firm Crown Agents. Thanks to the latter's efforts, 12 million doses of the CoviShield (AstraZeneca) and Novavax vaccines were purchased from the Serum Institute in India, with whom Crown Agents has a long standing relationship. This led to another scandal, however, when journalists noted that in 2008 the Serum Institute had produced an experimental vaccine against rubella and measles whose use in Ukraine had to be suspended after a child died.[55]

In an effort to find a way out of this debacle, on January 20, 2021 the Rada decreed that any vaccine approved for use in the USA, India, or any EU country would automatically be accepted in Ukraine.[56] This became problematic on the very next day, however, when Hungary approved the use of Russia's Sputnik V vaccine.[57] On February 8, therefore, the Cabinet of Ministers of Ukraine specifi-

"Ukraina zakupit kitaiskuyu vaktsinu ot koronavirusa," [Ukraine to Buy Chinese Coronavirus Vaccine] *Lenta.ru*, December 30, 2020, https://lenta.ru/news/2020/12/30/korona_ukraine/; L. Ksenz and M. Romanova, "Kitayskaya po tsene Amerikanskoy," [Chinese at the Price of an American] *Strana.ua*, December 30, 2020, https://strana.one/news/309533-ukraina-zakupit-kitajskuju-vaktsinu-coronavac-chto-o-nej-izvestno.html.

54 "Kitaitsy dazhe ne znayut o dogovore naschyot ikh vaktsiny ot koronavirusa dlya Ukrainy," [The Chinese Do Not Even Know about the Contract for Their Coronavirus Vaccine for Ukraine] *Khrabro.od.ua*, January 8, 2021, https://perma.cc/GH9G-MH3T.

55 Mariya Romanova, "Ne proshla ispytaniy," [It Didn't Pass the Test] *Strana.ua*, February 6, 2021, https://strana.one/news/316073-novavaks-podrobnoe-opisanie-vaktsiny-dlja-ukrainy.html. Unicef provided 9 million free vaccines to Ukraine, but Ukrainian doctors refused to certify it, saying it has not been tested. Ukraine's Chief Medical Officer, Nikolai Prodanchuk, however, allowed it to be administered anyway.

56 Evgeniya Kondakova, "Ukraina zaplatit zhiznyami lyudei za reshenie po vaktsine," [Ukraine to Pay with the Lives of People for its Decision on the Vaccine] *Ukraina.ru*, January 22, 2021, https://ukraina.ru/exclusive/20210122/1030322728.html.

57 Nick Thorpe, "Coronavirus: Hungary First in EU to Approve Russian Vaccine," *BBC News*, January 21, 2021, sec. Europe, https://www.bbc.com/news/world-europe-55747623; "Slovachchyna pidtverdyla kupivlyu 2 milioniv doz rosiiskoi Covid-vaktsyny," [Slovakia Has Confirmed the Purchase of 2 Million Doses of the Russian Covid Vaccine] *Euro Integration*, March 1, 2021, https://www.eurointegration.com.ua/news/2021/03/1/7120396/.

cally prohibited the registration in Ukraine of any Russian anti-Covid vaccine, or prophylactic measures, apparently unaware that 90 percent of Ukraine's PCR Covid test kits at the time came from Russia.[58]

In early February 2021, the British medical journal *The Lancet* published the positive results of the third round of clinical trials of Sputnik V. Publicly, however, Minister Stepanov continued to insist that "no one" believed in the vaccine's effectiveness, adding that "the Sputnik issue is a political one, any way you turn it."[59]

Then, unexpectedly, the National Anticorruption Bureau and the Specialized Anticorruption Prosecutor's office both opened criminal investigations into the Ministry of Health for ist purchase of the Chinese Sinovac vaccine.[60] Minister Stepanov immediately accused them of lacking patriotism, and of trying to force Ukraine to purchase Sputnik V. He warned ominously that this would lead to a sneak Russian attack on the Ukrainian military, weakened by its lack of vaccination.[61]

Having failed to obtain any vaccines by his own deadline of February 15, Stepanov flew to India himself to take personal possession of 500,000 doses of CoviShield that had been hastily purchased by the heretofore unknown intermediary firm "Grace of God" for 1.59 billion hryvnia (56.7 million USD).[62]

---

58 "Kabinet Ministriv Ukrainy – deyaki pytannya derzhavnoi reiestratsii vaktsyn abo inshykh medychnykh imunobiolohichnykh preparativ dlya spetsyfichnoi profilaktyky hostroi respiratornoi khvoroby COVID-19, sprychynenoi koronavirusom SARS-CoV-2, pid zobovyazannya dlya ekstrenoho medychnoho zastosuvannya," [Cabinet of Ministers of Ukraine – Some Issues of State Registration of Vaccines or Other Medical Immunobiological Drugs for the Specific Prevention of Acute Respiratory Disease Covid-19 Caused by Coronavirus Sars-Cov-2, under the Obligation for Emergency Medical Use] July 8, 2021, https://perma.cc/7PZ3-V9UH; Nikolai Storozhenko, "Ukraine prishlos prinyat srochnuyu pomoshch Rossii," [Ukraine Has Had to Accept Urgent Help from Russia] *Vzglyad*, February 16, 2021, https://vz-ru.turbopages.org/vz.ru/s/world/2021/2/16/1085348.html.

59 Yelena Poskannaya, "Stepanov: skolko lyudei privili v Rossii?" [Stepanov: How Many People Have Been Vaccinated in Russia?] *Gordon.ua*, February 9, 2021, https://gordonua.com/news/politics/stepanov-skolko-lyudey-privili-v-rossii-u-nih-samih-problemy-so-sputnikom-v-nikto-neverit-chto-eta-vakcina-effektivna-1539242.html.

60 Mariya Romanova, "Pervyi zhe kontrakt na grani sryva," [The First Contract Is on the Verge of Collapse] *Strana.ua*, February 16, 2021, https://perma.cc/A2DS-P5D5.

61 Dmitry Kovalevich, "Borba s rossiiskoi vaktsinoi," [The Struggle against the Russian Vaccine] *Ukraina.ru*, February 17, 2021, https://ukraina.ru/exclusive/20210217/1030578456.html.

62 "Minzdrav Ukrainy Zapretil Rasprostranyat Informatsiyu o Proizvoditelyakh i Postavshchikakh Vaktsin Ot COVID-19," [Ministry of Health of Ukraine Has Banned the Dissemination of Information about Manufacturers and Suppliers of Vaccines against COVID-19] *Gordon.ua*, March 3, 2021, https://gordonua.com/news/society/minzdrav-ukrainy-zapretil-rasprostranyat-informa-

A month later, however, India abruptly suspended all vaccine shipments to Ukraine. According to the head of the Rada Committee on Health and Medicine, Mikhail Radutsky, this was done, in part, because of "defamatory statements about India as a manufacturer of medicines" that had been made by Ukrainian politicians.[63] Meanwhile, the Sinovac vaccine that Ukraine had originally purchased from China in January began to arrive, but only one-tenth of the number ordered.[64] Health Minister Stepanov solved this problem by declaring that the time between the first and second shots of the vaccine would be extended from three weeks to twelve weeks in order, as he put it, to "increase its effectiveness."[65] This would not be possible for the Indian CoviShield vaccine, however, which expired in late June 2021.[66]

Given all these scandals, it is hardly surprising that the vaccine campaign itself met with widespread skepticism. The percentage of individuals vaccinated with even one dose was below 35 percent at the end of February 2022, compared with 73 percent in the European Union and over 50 percent in Russia.[67]

Because Ukraine's vaccine saga unfolded so quickly, it is easy to trace how the application of nationalism to policy led to Ukraine becoming the last country in Europe to begin mass vaccination. The arguments against the use of Russia's

---

ciyu-o-proizvoditelyah-i-postavshchikah-vakcin-ot-covid-19 – 1542329.html; "Pro dostup do publichnoi informatsii," [About Access to Public Information] *Ofitsiinyi vebportal parlamentu Ukrainy,* accessed November 30, 2021, https://zakon.rada.gov.ua/go/2939 – 17. Section II, Article 6, para 5: January 13, 2011, No. 2939–VI; Viktoriya Venk, "Nedoverie, util, prosrochka, novyi shtamm," [Distrust, Scrap, Delay, New Strain] *Strana.ua,* March 1, 2021, https://strana.one/news/320337-vaktsinatsija-v-ukraine-kak-ona-idet-na-1-marta-2021-koronavirus-novosti.html; "Minzdrav Ukrainy zapretil razglashat usloviya zakupki vaktsin," [The Ministry of Health of Ukraine Has Forbidden the Disclosure of the Conditions for the Purchase of Vaccines] *Ukraina.ru,* March 4, 2021, https://ukraina.ru/news/20210304/1030737437.html. It was never clarified whether this amount was paid only for the initial shipment or for all 12 million doses mentioned in the press, since on February 19 the Ministry of Health prohibited the release of all information regarding the producers, suppliers, or price of its vaccines.

63 "On odin raz skazal, a my raskhlebyvaem," [He Said It Just Once; Now We Have to Deal with It] *NV,* March 26, 2021, https://nv.ua/ukraine/politics/vakcina-covishield-maksim-stepanov-obvinil-petra-poroshenko-v-sryve-postavok-50150371.html.

64 Anna Kuznetsova, "Ocherednoi korruptsionnyi skandal," [Another Corruption Scandal] *NewsUa.RU,* March 26, 2021, https://is.gd/zLkPoi.

65 "V Kieve priznali, chto Ukraina ostalas bez indiiskoi vaktsiny ot COVID-19," [Kiev Acknowledges that Ukraine Has Been Left without an Indian Vaccine against COVID-19] *Novorosinform,* March 26, 2021, https://novorosinform-org.turbopages.org/novorosinform.org/s/852880.

66 Alla Kotlyar, "'Zolotaya Gora' ot Minzdrava," ["Golden Mountain" from the Ministry of Health] *Zerkalo nedeli,* March 1, 2021, https://zn.ua/Health/zolotaja-hora-ot-minzdrava-.html.

67 "Share of People Who Received at Least One Dose of COVID-19 Vaccine," *Our World in Data,* accessed May 10, 2022, https://ourworldindata.org/coronavirus-data-explorer.

Sputnik V vaccine, which by that time was already being administered in Hungary, Slovakia, and San Marino, shifted with such dizzying speed that their ideological nature became impossible to hide. When Vice-premier Oleksiy Reznikov referred to the Covid mortality rate in the rebel regions of Donbass as "medical genocide," then two weeks later said that administering the Sputnik V vaccine in the region to combat it was a "war crime," it fit the pattern perfectly.[68]

The government's ideological commitment to distancing itself from Russia at any cost, prevented it from realistically assessing Ukraine's chances of getting a vaccine quickly from any other source in such a cut-throat international environment. Disagreements within the Ukrainian medical community caused the government to issue mixed messages, further undermining public confidence. In May 2021, 70 percent of people surveyed said that the government's vaccination campaign had failed. Of these, 72 percent cited lack of professionalism in government, and political interests regarding vaccine selection, as the main reasons.[69]

Ukraine's vaccine debacle may be a particularly stark example of the ideological blinders that nationalism can impose on policy, but it is not atypical. The same pattern has unfolded in foreign policy, economic policy, and cultural policy. Despite its repeated failures, however, the government has continued to reaffirm its ideological commitments, rather than adjust its policies.

Social scientists who view policymaking as a rational decision-making process will find this disturbing. It calls into question their assumption that human beings act to maximize their own self-interest, which is driven largely, though not exclusively, by tangible benefits, rather than preconceived notions. But if one accepts that such notions are also a factor in policymaking, then a more hopeful prospect emerges. For example, if one set of cultural assumptions (e. g., nationalism) leads to policies that disrupt social harmony, then replacing it with an al-

68 "Reznikov o vaktsinatsii v Krymu i ORDLO," [Reznikov about Vaccination in Crimea and ORDLO] *RBC Ukraina*, February 25, 2021, https://news.rbc.ua/rus/politics/reznikov-vaktsinatsii-krymu-ordlo-eto-voennoe-1614265151.html; Anastasiya Tovt, "Indiiskaya vaktsina CoviShield kotoroi privivayut ukraintsev, byla zergistrirovana bez sertifikatsii," [The Indian CoviShield Vaccine That Ukrainians Are Being Vaccinated with, Was Registered without Certification] *Strana.ua*, February 26, 2021, https://strana.news/news/319955-vaktsina-covishield-zarehistrirovana-v-ukraine-bez-sertifikatsii.html. Reznikov initially described it as a war crime since it had not been certified for use in Ukraine, apparently unaware that the same was true for the Indian vaccine CoviShield, which was registered for use without the necessary certification of the State Medical Service.
69 "Dinamika sotsialno-politychnykh nastroiv ta otsinok naselennya Ukrainy," [Trends in the Socio-Political Sentiments and Assessments of the Ukrainian Population] *Center Social Monitoring*, May 2021, https://smc.org.ua/dynamika-sotsialno-politychnyh-nastroyiv-ta-otsinok-naselennya-ukrayiny-traven-2021-roku-2-2611.

ternative set of cultural assumptions (e.g., civic patriotism) should lead to policies that disrupt the tragic cycle, and promote social harmony. It is this proposition that we will now explore.

4.3 The Consequences of Economic Nationalism

I begin with the assumption that a modicum of economic growth is necessary for social stability. Even very modest, but predictable, growth allows citizens to look forward to a comfortable retirement, to a better future for their children, and thus creates a sense of confidence in the government and its institutions. Divided societies that experience steady economic growth have been able to translate this into social unity, since prosperity tends to shore up the support of the government in power, and put its critics on the defensive. Conversely, prolonged economic decline leads to questions about the government's competence and its choice of strategy.

One notable exception to this rule is if the government can blame the collapse of the economy on an external enemy. This can lead to a "rally round the flag" effect, as we have seen again since the Russian invasion of 2022. The problem with blaming an external enemy for hardships, however, is that it also implies that the causes of said hardships are artificial and temporary. If the hardships persist, and the government is still unable to deal with them, it calls into question not only the competence of the government, but also its claim that society's hardships are rooted in externalities.

In 1991, Ukraine was predicted to be one of the major beneficiaries of independence from the USSR. Some 40 percent of the Soviet military-industrial complex, and 60 percent of its heavy industry was located on Ukrainian territory.[70] Thanks to subsidies from central authorities, Ukraine's per capita level of consumer consumption was 12 percent higher than that of the Russian Soviet Federative Socialist Republic (RSFSR).[71] It also had a well developed agriculture, capable of ensuring enough food for itself as well as other nations.

---

70 Rostislav Ishchenko, "S treskom provalivsheesya gosudarstvo," [The Completely Failed State] *Odnako*, March 4, 2015, http://www.odnako.org/blogs/s-treskom-provalivsheesya-gosudarstvo/.

71 "Na moment obreteniya nezavisimosti dolya promyshlennosti v VVP Ukrainy byla 44%, segodnya – tolko 14%," [At the Time of Independence, the Share of Industry in Ukraine's GDP Was 44%, Today It Is Only 14%] *Finansovoe obozrenie*, October 12, 2016, https://finoboz.net/finances/na-moment-obreteniya-nezavisimosti-dolya-promyshlennosti-v-vvp-ukrainy-byla-44-segodnya-tolko-14/; Aleksandr Zapolskis, "Kto kogo kormil v SSSR," [Who Fed Whom in the USSR] *Kom-*

These were some of the arguments touted by supporters of Ukrainian independence. During the referendums of 1991, independence activists distributed leaflets comparing Ukraine's indigenous wealth to countries like Germany, Italy, and France, pointing out how, in many categories, Ukraine was better off than those countries. The difference they attributed to the transfer of Ukraine's wealth to Moscow.[72] Ukraine's first president, Leonid Kravchuk, predicted that it would take no more than ten years for Ukraine to become the wealthiest country in Europe, "a second France."[73]

It quickly became apparent, however, that Ukraine's economy was not developing as predicted. Five years into independence, the number of factories had shrunk by 80 percent.[74] Industrial production began a steady decline that resulted in Ukraine's GDP shrinking from $81.5bn in 1990 to just $31.6bn in 1999.[75] The population also fell precipitously, from a high of 52 million to just 43 million in 2021, although unofficially, observers consider 33–35 million a more realistic figure.[76] Starved of both financial resources and people, social services shrank as well: between 1991 and 2016, the number of hospitals declined by 56 percent, schools by 23 percent, and the number of books published by 71 percent.[77]

somolskaya pravda, August 21, 2017, https://www.kp.ru/daily/26571.7/3586720/; Andrei Polunin, "Den utrachennoi nezavisimosti," [Day of Lost Independence] Ukraina.ru, August 24, 2015, https://ukraina.ru/independence/20150824/1014059666.html.

72 Sergei Bondarenko, "Territorialnaya tselostnost i mezhdunarodnoe priznanie Ukrainy pod somneniem," [Territorial Integrity and International Recognition of Ukraine Is in Doubt] Odna Rodina, August 25, 2017, https://odnarodyna.org/content/territorialnaya-celostnost-i-mezhdunarodnoe-priznanie-ukrainy-pod-somneniem-i; Mikhaylo Krigel, "Mavra z hranatamy," [A Monkey with Grenades] Ukrainskaya pravda, December 3, 2020, https://www.pravda.com.ua/rus/articles/2020/12/3/7275645/. For the twentieth anniversary of Ukrainian independence in 2010, the Communist Party of Ukraine reprinted these leaflets.

73 "Ne slyshny v mozgu dazhe shorokhi," [Not Even a Rustle Is Heard in the Brain] Ukraina.ru, June 9, 2020, https://ukraina.ru/opinion/20200609/1027938143.html.

74 Aleksandr Dudchak, "Posol SShA prodolzhaet razdavat tituly Ukraine," [U.S. Ambassador Continues Handing out Titles to Ukraine] Ukraina.ru, March 10, 2016, https://ukraina.ru/analytics/20160310/1015841918.html.

75 Richard Sakwa, Frontline Ukraine: Crisis in the Borderlands (London and New York: I.B. Tauris, 2015), 51.

76 Sonya Koshkina and Diana Butsko, "Ruslan Stefanchuk: 'Use vyrishuie Zelenskyi,'" [Ruslan Stefanchuk: "Zelensky Decides Everything"] LB.ua, May 22, 2019, https://lb.ua/news/2019/05/22/427531_ruslan_stefanchuk_use_virishuie.html.

77 Svyatoslav Knyazev, "Ukraina protiv USSR," [Ukraine against the USSR] NK.org.ua, October 8, 2021, https://nk.org.ua/ekonomika/ukraina-protiv-ussr-shokiruyuschaya-statistika-pogroma-00279912.

The question is why? One group of analysts argues that it is because Ukraine failed to embrace truly radical economic and political reforms. This failure, which they often attribute to Russian influence, spawned corruption. Severing Ukraine's economy from Russia's would reduce this corruption, and promote much needed economic reforms. This view, strongly lobbied by Western governments, was supported by President Viktor Yushchenko, and later by Presidents Poroshenko and Zelensky.

But under these presidents the expected economic take-off never occurred because the pro-Western policies of Ukrainian governments never resulted in a corresponding level of Western investment. By contrast, pro-Russian policies generally did. This can be seen from the fact that real GDP in Ukraine grew under Kuchma, between 2000 and 2013, then shrunk under Yushchenko, then rose again, though not as dramatically, under Yanukovych.[78] The best years for economic growth in Ukraine were 2002 to 2004, when its economy grew by an astonishing 29.4 percent, on the basis of massive exports to Russia and the CIS.[79] The obvious implication, much to the chagrin of Ukrainian nationalists, is that Ukrainians benefit most from closer economic ties with Russia.

During the first twenty-five years of independence, for better or for worse, the Ukrainian economy was kept afloat largely thanks to its close integration with the Russian economy. Both countries suffered from the collapse of the Soviet Union and Western economic competition, but the preservation of Ukraine's Soviet-era industry and manufacturing gave it a competitive advantage in the markets of the former Soviet Union that it did not have elsewhere. Although preserving this infrastructure arguably delayed Ukraine's transition to a market economy, it also eased the social costs of that transition for the population.

---

78 German Bogapov, "V 2000–2004 VVP Ukrainy vozrastal v srednem na 8,4% v god, a v 2014–2017 padal na 4,8%," [From 2000–2004 Ukraine's GDP Increased by an Average of 8.4% per Year, and in 2014–2017 It Fell by 4.8%] *Zerkalo nedeli*, August 13, 2018, https://zn.ua/ECONOMICS/v-2000–2004-vvp-ukrainy-vozrastal-v-srednem-na-8–4-v-god-a-v-2014–2017-padal-na-4–8–291506_.html; "Investitsionnyi potentsial Ukrainy obnulilsya," [Ukraine's Investment Potential Has Been Reset to Zero] *Ukrainsky vybor*, August 31, 2018, http://is.gd/jXnfke; Fyodor Tikhii, "15 let s rynochnoi ekonomikoi," [15 Years with a Market Economy] *Ukraina.ru*, February 14, 2021, https://ukraina.ru/exclusive/20210214/1030533644.html; "Investory ne verya zayavleniyam Kieva o vosstanovlenii ekonomiki Ukrainy," [Investors Do Not Believe Kiev's Statements about the Restoration of the Ukrainian Economy] *Finanz.ru*, February 16, 2021, https://perma.cc/4G8F-GVUH.

79 Viktor Medvedchuk, "Ekonomika Ukrainy v srednesrochnoi perspektive ne sposobna vyiti na pokazateli dokrizisnogo 2013 goda," [In the Medium Term the Ukrainian Economy Will Not Be Able to Reach the Level of Pre-Crisis 2013] *Ukrainsky vybor*, July 7, 2017, http://is.gd/blJ1XO.

Russia was by far Ukraine's largest trading partner, accounting for more than 30 percent of its foreign trade in 2012, more than the entire EU combined.[80] Five million Ukrainians worked seasonally in Russia, sending back $7.5bn, which was 20 percent more than total foreign direct investment in 2012.[81] In addition, Ukraine earned a revenue of several billion dollars a year from the transit of Russian gas to Europe across its territory.

Russian Prime Minister Dmitry Medvedev puts the cumulative value of the tariff easements, trade preferences, and gas subsidies that Ukraine received from Russia between 1991 and 2014 at roughly $250bn.[82] Over this same period, Western financial institutions promised Ukraine $62bn in loans for implementing reforms, but actually disbursed less than half this amount. Such disbursements to Ukraine were routinely suspended due the country's failure to implement the reforms suggested by the West.[83]

4.3.1 Economic Relations with Russia and the DCFTA

On the eve of the 2014 Maidan, the main arguments in favor of signing the DCFTA (Deep and Comprehensive Free Trade Area), commonly known as the EU Association Agreement, were its presumed long-term benefits.[84] Pursuing business-

---

80 "Ukraina i Rossiya," [Ukraine and Russia] *TASS*, [no date] https://tass.ru/ukraina/predystoriya.

81 Richard Sakwa, *Frontline Ukraine*, 51.

82 "D. Medvedev podschital, skolko mlrd doll. SShA Rossiya podarila Ukraine," [D. Medvedev Has Calculated How Many Billions of US Dollars Russia Has Donated to Ukraine] *Neftegaz*, December 10, 2014, https://neftegaz.ru/news/politics/235589-d-medvedev-podschital-skolko-mlrd-doll-ssha-rossiya-podarila-ukraine/.

83 Halyna Kalachova and Samira Abbasova, "Komu i skilky vynna derzhava Ukraina," [To Whom and How Much Does the Ukrainian State Owe?] *Ukrainska pravda*, March 30, 2016, https://www.epravda.com.ua/cdn/cd1/2016/03/mvf/index.html.

84 Veronika Movchan and Ricardo Giucci, "Quantitative Assessment of Ukraine's Regional Integration Options: DCFTA with European Union vs. Customs Union with Russia, Belarus and Kazakhstan," *PP/05/2011*, German Advisory Group Institute for Economic Research and Policy Consulting, November 2011, 19, http://www.case-research.eu/sites/default/files/Movchan_0.pdf; Yuri Poluneev, "Ukraine: Ten Shocks," *Johns Hopkins Institute for Applied Economics, Global Health, and Study of Business Enterprise*, Studies in Applied Economics, 27 (March 2015): 10, https://sites.krieger.jhu.edu/iae/files/2017/04/Yuri_Poluneev_Ukraine_Ten_Shocks.pdf; E. Vinokurov et al., "Deadlock of Integrations Struggle in Europe *(Analytical Report)*," *Voprosy ekonomiki*, no. 8 (August 20, 2014): 4–25, https://doi.org/10.32609/0042–8736–2014–8–4–25; "Economic Impact of a Deep and Comprehensive FTA between the EU and the Ukraine," *Oxford Economics* (2012): 122–123, http://www.oxfordeconomics.com/my-oxford/projects/128886.

as-usual with Russia was portrayed as a pact with the devil, while the benefits of EU association were often wildly oversold to the Ukrainian public.[85]

Nearly all Western analyses favoring Ukraine's EU association assumed that Russia was bluffing when it said that it would re-impose tariffs on Ukrainian goods if it signed the exclusive trade agreement with the EU. The potential losses for the Ukrainian economy from the DCFTA were therefore often grossly underestimated. The Ukrainian government itself estimated that the country stood to lose $160bn if it left the free trade association with the Customs Union, as EU officials said it must, and signed the EU association agreement.[86] The EU, however, put Ukraine's estimated economic loses fifty times lower, and therefore offered a compensation package of just $3bn.[87]

What the EU sought in these negotiations was maximum political conditionality for Ukraine, with minimum economic responsibility for itself. While in theory both sides stood to benefit from the removal of tariffs and trade barriers, given their enormous economic disparity – 1.5 to 1 in trade, 11 to 1 in investment, and 40 to 1 in overall economic power – the requirement that Ukraine adopt EU institutional and regulatory standards meant that this disparity would initially increase.[88] Thus, in 2015, the one year that Ukraine benefited from a temporary suspension of export quotas, Ukrainian exports to the EU actually fell by 23 percent because of the inability of Ukrainian producers to meet EU certification requirements, and low demand for Ukrainian products.[89]

Yanukovych therefore went to the Vilnius summit in November 2013 in order to shame the EU into proposing a better deal. Not wanting to get caught up in a

---

85 Arkadiusz Sarna, "The Transformation of Agriculture in Ukraine: From Collective Farms to Agroholdings," *OSW Centre for Eastern Studies*, February 7, 2014, https://www.osw.waw.pl/en/publikacje/osw-commentary/2014 – 02 – 07/transformation-agriculture-ukraine-collective-farms-to. Note, for example, the contrast between Ukraine's Minister of Agriculture, Mykola Prysyazhnyuk's description of the DCFTA as providing an immediate increase in agricultural exports to EU markets, and the OSW's assessment that, "in reality, the agreement with the EU would not have created better export opportunities for Ukraine's agricultural products" in the short term.
86 Richard Sakwa, *Frontline Ukraine*, 87.
87 Robert Parry, "NYT Is Lost in Its Ukraine Propaganda," *Consortium News*, January 24, 2015, https://consortiumnews.com/2015/01/24/nyt-is-lost-in-its-ukraine-propaganda/; Mark Chapman, "Robert Kagan's 'The Jungle Grows Back,'" *The New Kremlin Stooge*, August 11, 2019, https://thenewkremlinstooge.wordpress.com/2019/08/11/book-review-robert-kagans-the-jungle-grows-back/.
88 Sean Guillory, "Ukraine's EU Association Is a Bad Deal," *SRB podcast*, December 3, 2013, https://srbpodcast.org/2013/12/03/ukraines-eu-association-bad-deal/.
89 Yuliana Romanishin, "Chto pomozhet bolshe prodavat v Evropu," [What Will Help to Sell More in Europe] *Ekonomicheskaya pravda*, March 11, 2016, https://www.epravda.com.ua/rus/publications/2016/03/11/584736/.

bidding war with Russia, EU delegates refused any further negotiations. At that point, according to Eduard Stavitsky, a member of the Ukrainian delegation, Ukraine proposed signing the political accord and leaving the details of the economic accord to be worked out later, in a trilateral format with Russia. Again, EU officials refused.[90]

The EU was trying to force Ukraine into a bleak choice: giving up its existing markets, in exchange for the nearly impossible challenge of breaking into new and protected markets. Moreover, it demanded that Ukraine cast its lot with the EU against Russia economically by insisting that it leave its current free trade association with the CIS, a position that was deeply divisive at home and fraught with economic uncertainty.[91] Supporters of the EU Association Agreement argued that these issues were all immaterial, compared to the symbolic value of making a civilizational choice in favor of Europe. This, of course, made the relationship between Ukraine and the EU one from which the EU could continue to extract one-sided benefits indefinitely.

Had Yanukovych's strategy of playing off the EU and Russia worked, it would have certainly been better for the Ukrainian economy in the short term, since it would have preserved the country's access to Russian markets, while also providing Ukraine with a stronger position in future negotiations with the EU.[92] Alas, Ukrainian society's wildly inflated popular expectations regarding the EU Association Agreement transformed the government's balanced strategy into a public relations nightmare.

To avoid the same fate, the new post-Maidan nationalist government decided to downgrade its economic ties with its main economic partner, Russia, despite not having secured any alternative sources of investment. Predictably, this led to economic collapse. Before 2014, more than 60 percent of Ukraine's exports went to the former countries of the Soviet Union. By 2017, despite a very slight rise in

---

90 Iskander Khisamov, "Eduard Stavitsky: tri stsenariya dlya Ukrainy," [Eduard Stavitsky: Three Scenarios for Ukraine] *Ukraina.ru*, October 21, 2016, https://ukraina.ru/exclusive/20161021/1017697180.html.

91 "Azarov zayavil ob obnishchanii ukraintsev," [Azarov Describes the Impoverishment of Ukrainians] *Ukraina.ru*, March 14, 2021, https://ukraina.ru/news/20210314/1030821985.html; "IMF Downgrades Ukraine Growth Outlook," *True Economics*, August 4, 2015, https://trueeconomics.-blogspot.com/2015/08/4815-imf-downgrades-ukraine-growth.html; Serhii Lyamets and Halyna Kalachova, "Uryad provalyv restrukturyzatsiyu zovnishnyoho borhu Ukrainy," [The Government Has Failed to Restructure Ukraine's Foreign Debt] *Ekonomichna pravda*, August 27, 2015, https://www.epravda.com.ua/publications/2015/08/27/557144/.

92 Christian Friis Bach, "Is Russia's Conflict with Ukraine Really about Trade? " *Reuters*, March 6, 2015, https://www.reuters.com/article/idIN353056739620150306.

exports to the EU, Ukrainian exports overall had fallen by 45.5 percent.[93] Opposition parliamentarian Vadim Novinsky estimates that, between 2014 and 2019, Ukraine lost $75 – 80 billion in trade with Russia, thanks to mutual tariffs and sanctions.[94]

With state revenues falling sharply, 10 percent of civil servants had to be laid off, pensions decreased, child support abolished, and the minimum wage frozen.[95] The percentage of the population living below poverty rose from 15 percent in 2014 to 25 percent in 2018.[96] Ukraine's GDP, already 30 percent below its pre-independence level in 2013, declined another 30 percent under President Poroshenko.[97] Now the poorest country in Europe, in 2020 the World Bank predicted that it would take Ukraine forty years of extraordinary growth to catch up to Russia's current level of GDP per capita; twice that to catch up to Germany's.[98]

Poroshenko cites the loss of Donbass and Crimea as the main reasons for this drop. It was, the head of the National Bank of Ukraine, Valeriya Gontareva, who first suggested that the loss of Donbass and Crimea had reduced Ukraine's

---

93 Viktor Medvedchuk, "ZST s ES: dva goda poter i provalov," [FTA and the EU: Two Years of Losses and Failures] *Ukrainsky vybor*, January 4, 2018, https://perma.cc/P7RK-ZZ5 V.

94 Olga Samofalova, "Ukraina smozhet vosstanovit svoyu ekonomiku tolko za schet Rossii," [Ukraine Will Be Able to Restore Its Economy Only Thanks to Russia] *Vzglyad*, May 19, 2019, https://vz.ru/economy/2019/5/19/978334.html.

95 "Minimum Wage: Ukraine," *Wage Indicator*, January–July 2016, https://wageindicator.org/salary/minimum-wage/ukraine. Minimum Wages in Ukraine with effect from 01–01–2016 to 30 – 07 – 2016.

96 "Bednykh v Ukraine seichas bolshe, chem pyat let nazad – Vsemirnyi Bank," [There Are More Poor People in Ukraine Now than Five Years Ago – World Bank] *Ukrinform*, July 17, 2018, https://www.ukrinform.ru/rubric-economy/2500637-bednyh-v-ukraine-sejcas-bolse-cem-pat-let-nazad-vsemirnyj-bank.html; Olga Samofalova, "Ukraina smozhet vosstanovit svoyu ekonomiku tolko za schet Rossii"; Fyodor Tikhii, "Pyat faktov, kotorye nuzhno znat ob Ukraine," [Five Facts You Need to Know about Ukraine] *Ukraina.ru*, March 20, 2021, https://ukraina.ru/exclusive/20210320/1030883980.html.

97 "25 shagov navstrechu samolikvidatsii," [25 Steps Toward Self-Destruction] *Flot XXI Vek*, April 3, 2016, http://blackseafleet-21.com/news/4 – 03 – 2016_25-shagov-navstrechu-samolikvidatsii; Fyodor Tikhy, "Pyatiletka Poroshenko," [Poroshenko's Five-Year Plan] *Zarya Novorossii*, March 31, 2019, http://novorossy.ru/articles/news_post/pyatiletka-poroshenko-itogi-pravleniya-v-tsifrakh-i-faktakh; Egor Leyev, "Tainstvennaya statistika," [Mysterious Statistics] *Ukraina.ru*, March 19, 2019, https://ukraina.ru/exclusive/20190319/1023014298.html. This picture becomes even more dire when one considers that Ukrainian FDI statistics typically include Russian investment in Crimea, since under Ukrainian law it is still part of Ukraine.

98 "Ekonomika Ukrainy nazdozhene Polshchu cherez 50 rokiv," [Ukraine's Economy Will Catch Up to Poland in 50 Years] *Volynski novyny*, February 17, 2019, https://www.volynnews.com/news/all/ekonomika-ukrayiny-nazdozhene-polshchu-cherez-50-rokiv-ministr-finansiv/.

GDP by 20 percent, a figure widely cited thereafter.[99] But even the loss of this territory cannot fully explain the depth or duration of Ukraine's overall economic collapse, particularly since the Ukrainian government was still receiving goods and tax revenues from these regions through the end of 2017. It was not until October 2017 that the Ukrainian government, under pressure from the Far Right, fully severed its economic ties with the rebel regions.[100]

Before that, there had been an attempt by the Far Right, on November 22, 2015, to end the supply of electricity from Ukraine to Crimea by blowing up the electricity pylons that served the region (as well as Kherson and Nikolayev). Although the blockade reduced trade between Crimea and the rest of Ukraine by half, and dramatically increased the cost of electricity throughout southern Ukraine, Poroshenko, who initially opposed it, later embraced it as his own idea.[101]

In the following months, the Right Sector seized control of the border crossings with Crimea, and cut off the water supply to both Crimea and Lugansk, relinquishing control of the border to Ukrainian authorities only after receiving assurances from the government that all trade between Ukraine and Crimea would end within a month.[102] When this did not occur, Ukrainian activists blocked all

99 "Gontareva nazvala ekonomicheskie poteri Ukrainy ot voiny na Donbasse," [Gontareva Cites Ukraine's Economic Losses from the War in Donbass] *Apostrof*, November 29, 2015, https://apostrophe.ua/news/economy/2015–11–29/gontareva-nazvala-ekonomicheskie-poteri-ukrainyi-ot-voynyi-na-donbasse/42889; "Poroshenko Nazval Ekonomicheskie Poteri Iz-Za Konflikta v Donbasse," [Poroshenko Cites Economic Losses Due to the Conflict in Donbass] *Ritm Eurasia*, March 23, 2018, https://www.ritmeurasia.org/news–2018–03–23–poroshenko-nazval-ekonomicheskie-poteri-iz-za-konflikta-v-donbasse-35569; Anton Pechenkin, "Maidan 2014," *Vesti*, February 18, 2020, https://vesti.ua/strana/vo-skolko-ukraine-oboshelsya-majdan. President Poroshenko gave a similar figure of 18.6 percent in 2018.
100 "Proekt zakonu pro stvorennyaneobkhidnykh umov dlya mirnogo vregulyuvannya situatsii v okremykh raionakh Donetskoi ta Luganskoi oblastei" [Draft Law on the Creation of the Conditions Necessary for the Peaceful Resolution of the Situation in Select Districts of the Donetsk and Lugansk Regions], *Verkhovna Rada Ukrainy*, October 6, 2017, http://w1.c1.rada.gov.ua/pls/zweb2/webproc4_1?pf3511=62641.
101 "Ukraina polnostyu prekrashchaet torgovye otnosheniya s Krymom," [Ukraine Completely Stops Trade Relations with Crimea] *Ukraina.ru*, December 6, 2015, https://ukraina.ru/news/20151206/1015013780.html; "Iz-za podryva LEP ostanovilis zavody Khersona i Nikolayeva," [Factories in Kherson and Nikolayev Have Stopped Due to Power Line Explosion] *Ukraina.ru*, December 5, 2015, https://ukraina.ru/news/20151205/1014992931.html; "Poroshenko initsiiruet ofitsialnuyu transportnuyu i torgovuyu blokadu Kryma," [Poroshenko Initiates Official Transport and Trade Blockade of Crimea] *Ukraina.ru*, November 23, 2015, https://ukraina.ru/news/20151123/1014900453.html.
102 "Ukraina otklyuchila LNR ot vodosnabzheniya," [Ukraine Has Disconnected the LPR from Its Water Supply] *Rambler*, January 4, 2016, https://news.rambler.ru/cis/32401666-ukraina-fakticheski-perekryla-podachu-vody-v-lnr/; "Uchastniki blokady Kryma snyali vse blokposty," [Partic-

rail and highway traffic to Donbass. Again, despite nearly unanimous condemnation by Ukrainian officials, the government was powerless to lift the blockade, and by the summer of 2017, simply adopted it as their own initiative.[103]

In response, the rebel authorities in Donbass seized the Ukrainian factories operating there. As a result, Ukraine lost an estimated $10bn- worth of economic assets, not to mention $2bn in tax revenues that these factories were still paying to Ukraine.[104] Since then, instead of buying Ukrainian coal from Donbass, Ukraine has been forced to purchase most of its coal supply from Russia, for an estimated additional $3bn a year.[105]

According to the Deputy Minister in charge of the Occupied Territories, Georgy Tuka, it was only after this exercise in economic nationalism that rebel-held Donbass decided to shift over entirely to the Russian ruble.[106] Pavel Zhebrivsky, the Kiev-appointed governor of the Donetsk region, noted angrily at the time that if local residents hadn't already enlisted with the rebels for political reasons, they would surely do so now for economic reasons.[107]

This policy of cutting off ties to the very regions that the government is ostensibly trying to woo, moreover in a manner that is dismissive of the costs to the

ipants in the Blockade of Crimea Have Removed All Checkpoints] *Korrespondent*, January 16, 2016, https://korrespondent.net/ukraine/3616084-uchastnyky-blokady-kryma-snialy-vse-blokposty; "Ukraine stellt Handel mit der Krim ein," [Ukraine Halts Trade with Crimea] *Zeit*, December 16, 2015, https://www.zeit.de/politik/ausland/2015–12/ukraine-russland-krim-tataren-handel.

103 "Ukraina polnostyu prekratila postavki elektrichestva v Donbass," [Ukraine Completely Cuts off Electricity Supplies to Donbass] *RIA Novosti*, 20170726T1346, https://ria.ru/20170726/1499191508.html; Galina Studennikova, "Igry Patriotov," [Patriot Games] *Strana.ua*, March 15, 2017, https://strana.one/articles/analysis/60635-igry-patriotov.html.

104 "Natsbank obrushil prognoz ekonomicheskogo rosta Ukrainy iz-za blokady Donbassa," [The National Bank Craters Ukraine's Economic Growth Forecast Due to the Blockade of Donbass] *Ukraina.ru*, March 21, 2017, https://ukraina.ru/news/20170321/1018437002.html.

105 Sergei Salivon, "Vtoroi god podryad Ukraina importiruet rekordnye obyemy uglya," [For the Second Year in a Row, Ukraine Imports Record Volumes of Coal] *Strana.ua*, January 20, 2020, https://strana.one/opinions/245415-vtoroj-hod-podrjad-ukraina-importiruet-rekordnye-obemy-uhlja.html; Brian Milakovsky, "Cut Off," *Wilson Center*, January 9, 2018, https://www.wilsoncenter.org/blog-post/cut-what-does-the-economic-blockade-the-separatist-territories-mean-for-ukraine; Nadezhda Rybalko, "My snimem blokadu Donbassa," [We Will Lift the Blockade of Donbass] *Tehnopolis*, August 16, 2018, https://tehnopolis.com.ua/index.php?option=com_content.

106 "V pravitelstve vystupili protiv ekonomicheskoi blokady Donbassa," [The Government Opposes the Economic Blockade of Donbass] *Vybor.ua*, September 30, 2016, https://perma.cc/PKE8-PSNE.

107 "Zhebrivsky: Na Donbasse – chetyre tysyachi voennykh RF," [Zhebrivsky: There Are 4,000 Russian Servicemen in Donbass] *Korrespondent*, May 5, 2017, https://korrespondent.net/ukraine/3847855-zhebryvskyi-na-donbasse-chetyre-tysiachy-voennykh-rf.

Ukrainian economy, forms part of a larger pattern of nationalist economic thinking that I call "suicide economics." Simply put, suicide economics refers to imposing an ideological imperative at the expense of economic rationality. It is not unique to Ukrainian nationalists. In her best-selling book, *The Shock Doctrine*, author Naomi Klein provides several examples of how capitalism, when pursued as an ideological imperative, can result in "disaster capitalism." At the other end of the political spectrum, British economist Peter Wiles has made a similar observation about the impact of communist ideology in the Soviet Union.[108]

There are, of course, many different ways to think of economic rationality.[109] Ukrainian nationalists might well argue that severing a dependent relationship with Russia, and replacing it with a dependent relationship with the EU, is an economically rational choice because it is generally more advantageous to gain access to a larger and wealthier market. They might also stress the non-tangible geopolitical benefits of EU alignment, presumably culminating in NATO membership. But societies as a whole tend to be more risk averse than individuals. Hence, a good criterion for gauging a policy's economic rationality is to consider to what degree its long-term objectives are put at risk by its short-term policies.

By way of illustration, let me use the example of a national health care policy. Its long-term objective would presumably be to improve the overall health of the nation. Among the mechanisms that might be used for this are – increasing access to health facilities, expanding health coverage, lowering healthcare costs. If the government were to choose to focus on the goal of increasing the number of persons covered, then a policy that results in fewer people being covered must

---

108 Naomi Klein, "The Rise of Disaster Capitalism," *Journalism*, April 15, 2005, https://naomi-klein.org/rise-disaster-capitalism/; Peter Wiles, *The Political Economy of Communism* (Cambridge, MA: Harvard University Press, 1964), 356. As Wiles put it, Soviet leaders regularly performed experiments upon the Soviet population, such as the collectivization of agriculture, that are difficult and disagreeable for both rulers and subjects. "No one is forced to perform them; no one in his right mind would want to perform them. Yet they have been achieved … The reason is of course that the Communist leaders are not in their right mind; they are in Marx's mind."

109 Shaun Hargreaves-Heap and Colin Clark, "Economic Man," in Steven Durlauf and Lawrence Blume, eds., *The New Palgrave Dictionary of Economics*, 2nd ed. (London: Palgrave Macmillan, 2008), 1–2. In neo-classical economic theory the "rational economic man … chooses the action that satisfies their preferences better (or at least no worse) than any other." The key assumption here is that reason will draw the individual to the selection of the most efficient means to a given end. If we assume that the *summum bonum* for the polity is preserving the country's independence, and if we further assume that this can be done only if the country is economically prosperous, then any policy that undermines that prosperity would seem to be irrational *prima facie*.

be considered a failure. Redefining the criteria for success *post facto*, or claiming that the policy was a success because it accomplished some other good, would clearly be an attempt to mislead the public and avoid accountability. It can, of course, still be claimed that while the current policy failed, other approaches are bound to be more successful, but unless the initial failure and the reasons for it are acknowledged, it will be difficult for society to have much confidence in the government's judgment.

The ability to acknowledge reality, and act in accordance with it, therefore goes to the very heart of faith in government, and its ability to recognize and adapt to circumstances that threaten social stability. That is why governments go to great lengths to avoid undermining their own credibility.

Countries that have a large reservoir of social capital to draw on tend to have an easier time getting their populations to wait patiently for the benefits of their policies to emerge. They have built this trust by fulfilling past promises. By contrast, in countries where trust is low, the government's claims of success in the face of daily adversity create a cognitive dissonance that often leads to conspiracy theories. These, in turn, result in distrust of social institutions, economic damage, and heightened social tensions. Over time, if these are not addressed, distrust can threaten the nation's survival.

The government's decision to sever all commercial ties with Ukraine's largest trading partner and investor, without giving any serious thought to what would replace these investments, is a textbook example of a policy pursued for short-term ideological advantage that puts at risk the long-term goal of a secure and prosperous Ukraine. Other examples of such government behavior, such as the country's foreign debt restructuring, the closing of Russian banks, unrestricted labor migration, de-industrialization, and self-destructive energy policies, are outlined in the sections below.

4.3.2 Debt Restructuring – the Tax on Growth

To avoid taking loans from Russia, the Ukrainian government had to negotiate a new debt agreement with private investors. The IMF made this a precondition for beginning negotiations for a new loan tranche. In 2015, Western corporate investors agreed to write off 20 percent of the debt, and renegotiate the repayment of the remainder.

The deal that was reached allowed Ukraine to forego debt repayments if its GDP falls below $125bn (as it last did in 2017). If its economy grows less than 3 percent year-on-year, then repayments will be capped at 1 percent of GDP between 2021 and 2025. After that, however, should Ukraine achieve an annual economic growth rate of 3 – 4 percent, foreign creditors will receive 15 percent of total GDP growth. Above 4 percent growth, creditors would receive a whopping 40 percent of each percent of national growth!

Economists Serhii Lyamets and Halyna Kalachova calculated the following comparative repayment rate for 2019, when Ukraine's GDP was S114.9bn:

Table 4.2: Ukraine's Projected Debt Repayment Schedule (2019).

Rate of Growth	Payment Amount	Growth Penalty
	(millions USD)	(% of growth paid to foreign investors)
3%	0	0%
4%	182.7	3.97%
5%	669.9	11.65%
6%	1,157	16.79%

According the Ukrainian Finance Ministry, the government's stated goal of increasing total GDP by 40 percent, between 2019 to 2024, would thus result in Ukraine paying twice as much as it owed before the restructuring – a long-term tax on growth that the country would continue to pay through 2041.[110]

A more immediate problem, however, is the very real possibility that, after a fall of 4.4 percent as occurred in 2020, the economy might rise sharply the next year (the Cabinet of Ministers predicted 4.6 percent for 2021). In this scenario, although the economy will have barely recovered the ground it lost, Ukraine's payments to its creditors would suddenly jump from $41 million to over $600 million.[111] It should also be noted that this arrangement with Western private investors, made in order to avoid borrowing from Russia, does not take into account the government debt that Ukraine has already accrued.[112]

---

110 Serhii Lyamets and Halyna Kalachova, "Uryad provalyv restrukturyzatsiyu zovnishnoho borhu Ukrainy"; Fyodor Tikhii, "Tainye operatsii i rost dolgov," [Secret Operations and Rising Debt] *Ukraina.ru*, March 24, 2021, https://ukraina.ru/exclusive/20210324/1030920138.html.
111 Fyodor Tikhii, "Tainye operatsii i rost dolgov."
112 Fyodor Tikhii, "Pyat faktov, kotorye nuzhno znat ob Ukraine." This does not include the repayment of $3bn that Ukraine received from Russia in 2013, which with interest now amounts to over $4.5bn. Ukraine has refused to acknowledge this debt, and the issue is now before a London arbitration court.

4.3.3 The Closing of Russian Banks in Ukraine

In 2017, at a time when half of all foreign direct investment (FDI) came into Ukraine through Ukrainian affiliates of Russian banks, the Ukrainian government decided it was time to impose sanctions on Russian banks and drive Russian capital out of Ukraine.[113] Both the head of the National Bank of Ukraine and Ukraine's Finance Minister objected to this, calling it a sign of "total anarchy," but their objections were overruled.[114] As a result, not only were Ukrainian companies starved of desperately needed capital, but it became more difficult for millions of Ukrainian migrant workers to transfer funds home from Russia, which was at the time Ukraine's largest source of foreign remittances, and foreign direct investment.[115]

4.3.4 Worker Exodus and Population Loss

At its peak in 1993, Ukraine's population was 52.2 million. In 2021 it was less than 44 million, even if one includes the occupied territories of Crimea and Donbass. Speculation that the actual number could be far less was fueled by Ruslan Stefanchuk, the Speaker of the Ukrainian parliament, who suggested back in 2019 that the real figure could be as low as 30 million.[116]

Again, this demographic crisis not unique to Ukraine. It has affected nearly all the former Soviet republics, with the Baltic states being among the hardest hit. In Ukraine, however, it is further exacerbated by the annual exodus of 7

113 "Natsbank Ukrainy pytaetsya dobratsya do rossiiskikh deneg," [The National Bank of Ukraine Is Trying to Get at Russia's Money] *Vesti*, March 15, 2017, https://www.vesti.ru/finance/article/1567996; "Ukraina poteryala bolee 25% otechestvennykh bankov," [Ukraine Lost More than 25% of Domestic Banks] *Novosti bankov Rossii*, September 26, 2015, https://piv-bank.ru/novosti-bankov/11033-ukraina-poteryala-bolee-25-otechestvennyh-bankov-novosti-bankov.html.

114 "Ukraina otkazalas vypolnyat trebovanie MVF," [Ukraine Has Refused to Comply with IMF Demands] *Ukraina.ru*, April 7, 2017, https://ukraina.ru/news/20170407/1018504689.html; "Natsbank Ukrainy prinyal storonu rossiiskikh bankov," [The National Bank of Ukraine Has Sided with Russian Banks] *Ukraina.ru*, March 20, 2016, https://ukraina.ru/news/20160320/1015931958.html.

115 "V Ukrainu bolshe vsego deneg pereveli iz Rossii v 2017," [2017 Saw the Most Money Transferred to Ukraine from Russia] *Capital.ua*, February 23, 2018, https://www.capital.ua/ru/news/108678-v-ukrainu-bolshe-vsego-deneg-pereveli-iz-rossii-v-2017; Yulia Samayeva, "V Rossii rabotaet 40% vsekh trudovykh migrantov iz Ukrainy," [40% of All Labor Migrants from Ukraine Work in Russia] *Ukrainskaya pravda*, October 9, 2016, http://www.pravda.com.ua/rus/news/2016/10/9/7123068/.

116 Sonya Koshkina and Diana Butsko, "Ruslan Stefanchuk: 'Use vyrishuie Zelenskyi.'"

to 9 million Ukrainians for seasonal labor. In 2019, every second Ukrainian spent at least some part of the year working abroad, and one in four sought permanent employment abroad.[117]

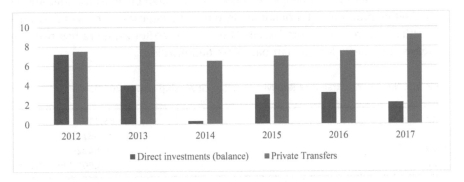

Figure 4.1: Private Transfers to Ukraine Compared to FDI in Billions of USD (2012 – 2017). *Source:* Based on data from: Aleksandr Moiseyenko, "Zarobitchane kak spasatelnyi krug," [Workers Abroad as a Lifeline] *Ekonomicheskaya pravda*, July 13, 2018, https://www.e-pravda.com.ua/rus/publications/2018/07/13/638675/.

This steadily rising exodus of workers, which gained speed dramatically after the EU lifted visa restrictions for Ukrainians in 2015, is a very troubling trend, according to labor expert Tatyana Pashkina, because Ukrainian migrant workers are increasingly establishing residency abroad and moving their entire families out of Ukraine. Between 2015 and 2019 Ukrainians were the largest recipients of long-term EU residency permits.[118] Whereas the number of births in Ukraine

---

117 "Minsotspolityky: ponad 3 mln ukraintsiv pratsiuye za kordonom na postiiniy osnovy," [Ministry of Social Policy: More than a Million Ukrainians Work Abroad on a Permanent Basis] *Radio Svoboda*, August 1, 2019, https://www.radiosvoboda.org/a/news-trudovi-mihran-ty-z-ukrainy/30087119.html; Alexander Sukov, "Nevidimye dengi," [Invisible Money] *MinProm*, September 27, 2019, https://minprom.ua/opinion/256237.html; Tatyana Bogdan, "Dolgovoe Is-toshchenie," [Debt Exhaustion] *Zerkalo nedeli*, November 15, 2019, https://zn.ua/finances/dolgo-voe-istoschenie-336243_.html; "Za god ukraintsev stalo menshe eshche na chetvert milliona che-lovek," [In One Year, There Were a Quarter of a Million Fewer Ukrainians] *Ukrainsky vybor*, February 18, 2020, https://perma.cc/YD9E-T9GC.
118 Anastasiya Pliyeva, "Kak naiti rabotu v 2021 godu," [How to Find Work in 2021] *Vesti*, January 11, 2021, https://vesti.ua/poleznoe/rabota/komu-povysyat-zarplaty-i-pochemu-zarobitchane-ne-vozv-rashhayutsya-prognoz; "Ukraintsy – na 3-mu mistsi za kilkistyu posvidok na prozhyvannya v ES," [Ukrainians are in 3rd Place for the Number of Residency Permits in the EU] *Eurointegration*, January 21, 2021, https://www.eurointegration.com.ua/news/2021/01/21/7118811/.

is falling, the number of births to Ukrainian residents in Poland increased by 60 percent in 2019.[119]

While western Ukrainians are increasingly fleeing westward, elsewhere in Ukraine large numbers of people are opting for Russian citizenship, after Russia simplified its procedures for obtaining it. While the largest numbers of new Russian citizens have come from Ukraine's occupied territories, there has been an increase in requests for Russian passports nationwide.[120]

Table 4.3: Number of Ukrainians Receiving Russian citizenship (2017–2020).

2017	85,119
2018	83,081
2019	299,422
2020	216,000 (first quarter)

But the most galling outcome of this policy of open migration, should it come to pass, is the prediction published in the British medical journal *Lancet* that, while both Ukraine and Russia will suffer significant demographic declines due to emigration, excess deaths, and low birth rates, by the end of the century the net result will be that the ratio of Russians to Ukrainians worldwide will double.[121]

---

119 Viktor Avdeyenko, "Mechty Shmygalya," [Shmygal's Dreams] *Apostrof*, February 4, 2021, https://apostrophe.ua/article/society/2021–02–04/mechtyi-shmyigalya-kogda-ukraina-dogonit-polshu-po-zarplatam/37629.

120 "V 2019 godu rossiysky pasport poluchili pochti 300 tysyach ukraintsev," [Nearly 300,000 Ukrainians Received Russian Citizenship Last Year] *Strana.ua*, January 24, 2020, https://strana.today/news/246167-v-2019-hodu-rossijskie-pasporta-poluchili-okolo-300-tys-ukraintsev-.html; Nikolai Storozhenko, "Rossiya zabiraet russkikh s Ukrainy," [Russia Gathers Russians from Ukraine] *Vzglyad*, January 21, 2020, https://vz.ru/world/2020/1/21/1019232.html; "Rossiya stala v 2,5 raza chashche predostavlyat grazhdanstvo," [Russia Is Now 2.5 Times More Likely to Grant Citizenship] *Kommersant*, May 19, 2020, https://www.kommersant.ru/doc/4348761; Violetta Chaikovskaya, "Ukraina rabotaet nad reformoi dvoinogo grazhdanstva," [Ukraine Is Working on Reforming Dual Citizenship] *Ukranews*, January 21, 2020, https://ukranews.com/news/678662-zelenskij-anonsiroval-vvedenie-dvojnogo-grazhdanstva-v-ukraine; Nataliya Magdyk, "Skolko rossiyan poluchili grazhdanstvo Ukrainy," [How Many Russians Received Ukrainian Citizenship] *Vesti*, March 25, 2021, https://vesti.ua/strana/stalo-izvestno-skolko-rossiyan-poluchili-grazhdanstvo-ukrainy. By comparison, just 181 Russians chose to become Ukrainian citizens in 2019, and fifty-six in 2020.

121 "K 2100 godu naselenie Ukrainy sokratitsya na 68% i sostavit 17 mln chelovek," [By 2100, the Population of Ukraine Will Decrease by 68% and Become 17 Million People] *Ukrainsky vybor*, July 16, 2020, http://vybor.ua/news/society/k_2100_godu_naselenie_ukrainy_sokratitsya_-na_68_i_sostavit_17_mln_chelovek.html.

4.3.5 Strategic De-industrialization

From 2005 to 2009, industrial production and agricultural production both accounted for roughly 13 percent of Ukraine's exports. Thereafter industrial production began a decline, which gained speed in 2016, after President Poroshenko revealed his plans to abandon some of Ukraine's largest export-oriented manufacturing industries, and shift government support to information technology and agriculture.[122] By 2020, agricultural products accounted for more than 50 percent of the country's exports, and industrial production for just 7 percent.[123]

What makes this choice perplexing from an economic standpoint is that the EU's tariff rate quotas (TRQs) are specifically designed to restrict the access of non-EU agricultural products to the European market. Signing such an agreement before preparing agricultural producers for the transition, therefore guaranteed that Ukrainian agricultural producers would fail to meet even these low quotas, which is precisely what happened. As President Poroshenko's former deputy chief of staff, Yuri Kosyuk, put it, "I believe Europe acted dishonestly with us ... there was never any opening of markets."[124]

More broadly, the problem with following the advice of former US ambassador Geoffrey Pyatt, that Ukraine should strive to become an "agricultural superpower," is that there is none.[125] As countries become wealthier, the weight of agricultural production in the economy tends to fall to about 1–3 percent.[126] By contrast, the weight of agriculture in the Ukrainian economy in 2020 was 16 percent and rising.[127]

---

122 "Za god kolichestvo storonnikov evrointegratsii sredi ukraintsev umenshilos," [In One Year, the Number of Supporters of European Integration among Ukrainians Has Decreased] *Unian*, March 11, 2016, https://www.unian.net/society/1287630-za-god-kolichestvo-storonnikov-evrointegratsii-sredi-ukraintsev-umenshilos-issledovanie.html.

123 Fyodor Tikhii, "MVF podschital," [The IMF Has Calculated] *Ukraina.ru*, October 22, 2020, https://ukraina.ru/exclusive/20201022/1029362166.html.

124 Viktor Medvedchuk, "ZST s ES: krakh nadezhd i prozrenie," [The FTA with the EU: The Collapse of Hopes and a Revelation] *Ukrainsky vybor*, April 12, 2016, http://vybor.ua/article/vneshnjaja_politika/zst-s-es-krah-nadejd-i-prozrenie.html.

125 "U.S. Envoy Urges Ukraine to Become Agricultural 'Superpower,'" *RFE/RL*, February 25, 2016, https://www.rferl.org/a/us-envoy-urges-ukraine-become-agricultural-superpower-cargill-/27572568.html.

126 "Value Added by Activity," OECD, accessed December 19, 2021, https://doi.org/10.1787/a8b2bd2b-en; "Countries by GDP Sector Composition 2017," *Statistics Times*, accessed December 19, 2021, https://statisticstimes.com/economy/countries-by-gdp-sector-composition.php.

127 Fyodor Tikhii, "MVF podschital."

Once again, the logic being applied here seems to be ideological, rather than economic. From the standpoint of Ukrainian nationalists, the attraction of defunding Ukrainian industry is that it significantly reduces Russian investment in Ukraine.[128] The government has therefore systematically dismantled Ukraine's industrial base, which is disproportionally concentrated in Maloross Ukraine, partly in order to prevent those regions from recovering the wealth and political influence they once had.

4.3.6 Suicide Economics and Energy Policy

Despite the government's best efforts to sever all ties between the Ukrainian and Russian economies, Russia remains among Ukraine's leading trading partners; whenever the government shuts down one area of profitable economic cooperation, another soon arises.

The energy sector is a good example of this. To fulfill the nationalist agenda of separating from Moscow, the government has imposed tariffs on a wide variety of energy imports from Russia. But while the government has touted these as examples of energy independence, in reality Ukraine remains as energy dependent on Russia as it ever was.

For example, after refusing to buy coal from Donbass, Ukraine has had to scramble to find other sources of coal to provide the country's need for heat and electricity. Ukraine tried to end its electricity purchases from Russia in November 2015, but had to renew them in again September 2019, when the national supply fell to a level not seen since 1972.[129] Since then, the Ukrainian parliament has routinely passed legislation to end all purchases from Russia, and then rou-

128 Yurasumy (Yuri Podolyaka), "Tse ostatochne proshchavai," [This Is the Final Farewell] *Livejournal*, March 12, 2019, https://yurasumy.livejournal.com/2344611.html; *Poroshenko – Ostatochne proshchavai feat. Twenty One Pilots* [Poroshenko – The Final Farewell Feat. Twenty One Pilots], 2017, https://www.youtube.com/watch?v=4zSRHp2gxXU. Popularized by Poroshenko as "the last good-bye to Russia."
129 Genby, "Ukraina dostigla urovnya proizvodstva elektroenergii 1972 goda," [Ukraine Has Reached the Level of Electricity Production of 1972] *Livejournal*, January 31, 2021, https://genby.-livejournal.com/898371.html; "ZE-ChERKNUTO," [Crossed Out] *AgitParokhod*, no. 28, 2019, https://www.youtube.com/watch?v=AlaL6kQbwMI (at 03:17). Valentin Zemlyanski says in 1990 Ukraine produced 296 billion KWh of electricity, and in 2018 only 159. Consumption meanwhile fell from 227 to 122.

tinely reversed itself. In 2020, Ukraine still received 62 percent of its coal producing electricity from Russia.[130]

Nuclear power, which provides roughly half of Ukraine's electricity supply, is likewise inextricably linked to Russia. Although the United States has been pushing Ukraine to sign a deal with Japanese-owned Westinghouse to provide alternative nuclear fuel, many scientists consider such a transition risky, pointing out that the reactors now using such a mixture of Russian and Western fuel have been shut down almost every month due to safety concerns.[131] In any case, the current government program to adapt nuclear plants to Westinghouse's standards will take at least a decade to realize, during which time Ukraine will have no alternative but to use Russian nuclear fuel.[132] Westinghouse's filing for bankruptcy protection in 2017 has raised additional questions about the long-term viability of its fuel supply.[133]

Likewise, in the area of natural gas, although President Poroshenko proudly declared Ukraine's total independence from Russian natural gas in 2016, the fact is that all the natural gas now being imported from Slovakia, Hungary, and Poland is actually natural gas from Russia. It is merely sent a few meters into these countries, then sent back into Ukraine.[134] For the privilege of misleading the public about its actual provenance, Ukraine pays a 30 percent premium over the regular price, which suits both these countries and Russia perfectly well.[135]

130 "Ukraine Cut Its Coal Import Bill Last Year by 40% Year-on-Year to $1.7 Billion," *UBN*, January 22, 2021, https://ubn.news/ukraine-cut-its-coal-import-bill-last-year-by-40-yoy-to-1 – 7-billion/; Fyodor Tikhii, "Kak Rossiya spasla Ukrainu ot kontsa sveta," [How Russia Saved Ukraine from the End of the World/the Light] *Ukraina.ru*, February 10, 2021, https://ukraina.ru/exclusive/20210210/1030508682.html. In Russian the word *svet* can mean either "the world" or "the light."
131 Fyodor Tikhii, "Kak Rossiya spasla Ukrainu ot kontsa sveta."
132 Natalia Michkovskaya, "Ukraina razorvala programmu ekonomicheskogo sotrudnichestva s RF," [Ukraine Has Torn Up its Program of Economic Cooperation with the Russian Federation] *KP in Ukraine*, March 21, 2018, https://kp.ua/economics/603920-ukrayna-razorvala-prohrammu-ekonomycheskoho-sotrudnychestva-s-rf-chto-dalshe.
133 L. Todd Wood, "Ukrainian Corruption Casts a Nuclear Pall over All of Europe," *The Washington Times*, March 30, 2017, https://www.washingtontimes.com/news/2017/mar/30/ukrainian-corruption-casts-nuclear-pall-over-all-e/.
134 Irina Koshanskaya, "My kogo khotim obmanut?," [Whom Are We Fooling?] *24 Kanal*, December 24, 2019, https://economy.24tv.ua/ru/my_kogo_hotim_obmanut_gerus_zajavil_chto_ukraina_pokupaet_rossijskij_gaz_n1253543.
135 "Poroshenko progovorilsya," [Poroshenko Let It Slip] *Ukraina.ru*, January 30, 2016, https://ukraina.ru/news/20160130/1015465217.html; O. Koshik, "Blef o nezavisimosti Ukrainy ot Rossiiskogo gaza," [Bluffing about Ukraine's Independence from Russian Gas] *Analitik*, May 23, 2016, http://www.analitik.org.ua/current-comment/economy/5739bd80913fd/.

Paradoxically, while Ukraine insists on being independent of Russian natural gas purchases, it insists on retaining Russian natural gas for transit, since Russian transit payments provide about 8 percent of Ukraine's annual fiscal revenue.[136] The West supports this because, while striving to make the EU and Ukraine less dependent on Russian gas, they want Russia to pay for the maintenance of the Ukrainian pipeline network. Before the Russian invasion of 2022, all sides but Russia were thus in the paradoxical position of supporting the continued use of a resource that they say they would rather be rid of.

Likewise, after a four-year hiatus, in 2020 Russia once again became Ukraine's largest supplier of oil, gasoline, and diesel fuel.[137] Even in the highly sensitive and symbolic area of military production, in 2020 Ukraine sold about 20 percent of its arms to Russia, more than any other country aside from China.[138]

Russia and Ukraine thus remain economically intertwined. The chief economist at VTB Capital estimated that, as late as 2020, modest economic shifts in Russia still accounted for up to 30 percent of the volatility in currency exchange rate, the rate of inflation, and interest rates in Ukraine.[139] The ideological imperative to separate from Russia persists, however, despite the fact that it typically results in direct harm to the Ukrainian economy. The blockade of Donbass imposed by Far Right activists went even further than that, and actually assisted the rebel economy.

Factories in Donbass that had previously paid taxes to Kiev now pay them to the rebel government instead. This influx of new cash expanded coal production, and resulted in the opening of eleven new veins in 2017. According to press reports, Donbass coal that had gone to Ukraine prior to the blockade, now goes

---

136 "Ukraine and Russia Signed 5 Year Long Package Deal on Gas Transit through Ukraine," *South Front*, December 31, 2019, https://t.ly/3VsH.

137 "Rossiiskaya 'Tatneft' vozobnovila postavki topliva ukrainskoi 'dochke' vpervye s 2014-go goda," [Russia's "Tatneft" Resumes Fuel Supplies to Its Ukrainian "Daughter" for the First Time Since 2014] *Ekonomicheskaya Pravda*, June 10, 2020, https://www.epravda.com.ua/rus/news/2020/06/10/661589/; Sergei Muslenko and Oleksandr Moiseyenko, "Kak rossiisky biznes 'vgryzalsya' v Ukrainu," [How Russian Business "Sunk Its Teeth" into Ukraine] *Ekonomicheskaya Pravda*, August 20, 2019, https://www.epravda.com.ua/rus/publications/2019/08/20/650787/.

138 Aleksei Kushch, "Torgovlya oruzhiem mezhdu Ukrainoi i Rossiyei ne prekrashchalas i v samye goryachie fazy voiny," [Arms Trade between Ukraine and Russia Never Stopped, Even During the Hottest Phases of the War] *Strana.ua*, April 13, 2021, https://strana.one/opinions/327881-torhovlja-oruzhiem-mezhdu-ukrainoj-i-rossiej-ne-prekrashchalas-i-v-samye-horjachie-fazy-vojny.html.

139 Ben Aris, "How Interconnected Are the Economies of Russia, Ukraine, Belarus and Kazakhstan?," *IntelliNews*, January 12, 2020, https://www.intellinews.com/how-interconnected-are-the-economies-of-russia-ukraine-belarus-and-kazakhstan-inflation-and-rates-outlook-for-2020 – 174374/.

to half a dozen other countries. The fact that high-grade coal exports from the nearby Russian port of Rostov rose by 50 percent after the blockade, while the Ukrainian ports of Mariupol and Berdyansk lost about a third of their coal cargo, appears to confirm this re-rerouting.[140] While coal mining in Ukraine continues to be heavily subsidized by the government, it actually became profitable again in Donbass, so that by the end of 2017 some coal mining factories began to repay the credit they had received from the rebel government – hardly the result the Ukrainian government was hoping for.[141]

According to Alexander Koltunovich, the former Chairman of the Subcommittee on the State Economic Policy of the Rada, each year Ukraine foregoes roughly half of its economic growth potential as a direct result of such nationalistic policies.[142] As enormous as this amount is, however, the cost to future generations could be even higher, since key global infrastructure projects have avoided Ukraine, because of the conflict there. For example, in 2016 it was decided that the EU's Via Carpathia transportation corridor would go around Ukraine rather than through it.[143]

In another blow to Ukraine's hopes of becoming an investment and transportation hub, in 2019 the international association of rail and freight transportation FERRMED agreed on the routes that would be developed for its Great Axis between China and the EU. Except for a spur to Kiev, it too avoids Ukraine entirely.[144] In the decade since the first container train traveled from China to Europe, the annual flow of commercial rail traffic through Russia has increased from seventeen trains to more than 10,000. By contrast, Ukraine began dedicated rail service between China and Ukraine only in 2021, to avoid having to pay for the use of the Russian railroads.

The policy of severing Ukraine from the Russian transportation system was the brainchild of Volodymyr Omelyan, one of the most Russophobic members of

140 Nadezhda Rybalko, "My snimem blokadu Donbassa"; Brian Milakovsky, "Cut Off."
141 Stanislav Medvedev, "Blokada Donbassa," [Blockade of Donbas] *Ritm Eurasia*, December 27, 2017, https://www.ritmeurasia.org/news–2017–12–27–blokada-donbassa-dlja-odnih-biznes-na-krovi-dlja-drugih-stimul-k-razvitiju-34258.
142 Olga Samofalova, "Ukraina smozhet vosstanovit svoyu ekonomiku tolko za schet Rossii."
143 Maksim Gardus, "Evropa stroit novuyu avtomagistral v obezd Ukrainy," [Europe Is Building a New Highway to Bypass Ukraine] *Apostrof*, March 10, 2016, https://apostrophe.ua/article/business/transport/2016–03–10/evropa-stroit-novuyu-avtomagistral-v-obyezd-ukrainyi-chem-eto-grozit-ekonomike/3662.
144 Aleksandr Kava, "Vdol granitsy Ukrainy," [Along the Border of Ukraine] *Strana.ua*, January 14, 2019, https://strana.one/opinions/181052-vdol-hranitsy-ukrainy-a-ne-cherez-ee-territoriju.html.

President Poroshenko's government.[145] As Minister of Infrastructure, he pledged to totally sever Ukraine from Russia's transportation network. In September 2015 he forbade all Russian carriers from flight, transit, and cargo shipments over Ukraine, and ended all Ukrainian air service to Russia.[146] This led to a 64 percent fall in passenger rail travel between Russia and Ukraine from 2014 to 2019.[147] The loss of these Russian routes has threatened the financial stability of Ukraine's national airline (MAU), since they were always the most profitable.[148] The economically self-destructive nature of these restrictions was well understood by presidential candidate Zelensky, who said "it is very strange that our trains go [to Russia] but our planes do not ... That, of course, is disadvantageous for us."[149] As president, however, he had done nothing to reverse this policy.

---

145 Ulyana Bezpalko, "Ukraina sovershila oshibku," [Ukraine Made a Mistake] *Obozrevatel*, August 8, 2017, https://news.obozrevatel.com/politics/omelyan-bolshoe-intervyu-2-chast.htm; "In the Decade since the First Container Train Traveled from China to Europe, the Annual Flow Has Increased from 17 Trains in 2011, to 10,000 Last Year," UBN, April 2, 2021, https://ubn.-news/in-the-decade-since-the-first-container-train-traveled-from-china-to-europe-the-annual-flow-has-increased-from-17-trains-in-2011-to-10000-last-year/; "Russian Trans-Continental Rail Freight Doubles in 2021," *Russia Briefing News*, March 30, 2021, https://www.russia-briefing.-com/news/russian-trans-continental-rail-freight-doubles-in-2021.html/. Omelyan ended all transportation ties with Crimea and occupied Donbass, saying "there is no justification for traveling to Russia. Except to visit family, if there is any there. If we are headed toward Europe, then we should go to Europe." By contrast, freight train shipments via Russia increased by 700 percent between 2016 and 2021, thanks to China's Belt and Road Initiative. Whereas ships take about 30–33 days to travel from East Asia to northern Europe, deliveries by rail take as little as nineteen days.
146 Georgii Luchnikov, "Plody propagandy," [Fruits of Propaganda] *Ukraina.ru*, October 25, 2019, https://ukraina.ru/exclusive/20191025/1025419477.html.
147 "Za 5 let chislo passazhirov na zheleznykh dorogakh mezhdu RF i Ukrainoi sokratilos pochti na 65%," [In 5 Years, the Number of Passengers on the Railways between Russia and Ukraine Has Decreased by Almost 65%] *Ritm Eurasia*, April 9, 2019, https://www.ritmeurasia.org/news–2019–04–09–za-5-let-chislo-passazhirov-na-zheleznyh-dorogah-mezhdu-rf-i-ukrainoj-sokrati-los-pochti-na-65–42078; "Tremya samymi pribylnymi poezdami 'Ukrzaliznytsi' okazalis napravleniya v Moskvu," [The Three Most Profitable Trains of "Ukrzaliznytsia" Turn Out to Be in the Direction of Moscow] *Strana.ua*, February 21, 2020, https://strana.one/news/251087-poezd-kiev-moskva-stal-samym-pribylnym-v-2019-hodu-ukrzaliznytsi.html; "Odessa – Moskva i Nikolayev – Moskva stali samymi napolnennymi poezdami v 2018 godu," [Odessa – Moscow and Nikolayev – Moscow Were the Most Popular Trains in 2018] *Timer-Odessa*, February 15, 2019, https://perma.cc/VSV8-WYYS.
148 Dmitry Ulyanitsky and Viktoriya Pokatis, "Novyi prezident MAU Evgenii Dykhne," [New UIA President Evgeniy Dykhne] *Delo.ua*, September 27, 2019, https://delo.ua/business/novyj-prezident-mau-evgenij-dyhne-aviabiznes-358520/.
149 Georgii Luchnikov, "Plody propagandy."

Nationalism aspires to a pristine separation among national economies, but nearly all large-scale international manufacturing today requires some form of transnational cooperation. Given the relative size of their markets, this will typically lead investors to favor Russia over Ukraine, although they would prefer to see them working together, and making products that can be used interchangeably in both Ukraine and Russia. A good example of this sort of synergy is Renault's Arkana car, which was to be assembled in Ukraine and then produced in Russia.[150]

In its effort to break the colonial ties with Russia that have ostensibly prevented Ukraine from prospering, the government has embraced nationalistic economic policies that have *de facto* reduced the standard of living, undermined confidence in the government, and fostered resentments among Maloross Ukrainians. We see the same patten at work in the government's cultural policy.

4.4 Jacob and Esau in Ukraine: Culture and Religion as Sources of Social Disunity

Cultural identity is rooted in such things as one's choice of language, religion, and historical perspective. While these become matters of choice later in a person's life, one is generally born into a particular cultural identity, which is typically adopted without question. When cultural identity overlaps with the territory of a sovereign nation, tensions over one's cultural identity tend to be minimal, since the perspectives of both the state and society on who is "native" and who is "foreign" will tend to coincide.

But this idyllic vision of the nation as a family writ large is largely a myth. In the nations that emerged from World War I, the cultural polity and the political polity were often significantly misaligned. The response of Ukrainian nationalists to this misalignment has been twofold. The first, was to establish a nation-state. This was finally achieved in 1991. The second, was to create a uniform culture within the borders of that nation-state. This task is as yet unfulfilled, and remains a top priority for Ukrainian nationalists.

For nationalists, the urgency of this task is dictated by the threat to national security ostensibly posed by the cultural identity Maloross Ukrainians. Since the Orange Revolution of 2004, the underlying assumption of the government's cul-

---

150 "Na Ukraine nachnut sobirat avtomobili iz rossiiskikh komplektuyushchikh," [Cars with Russian Parts Will Be Assembled in Ukraine] *Ukraina.ru*, September 17, 2020, https://ukraina.ru/news/20200917/1028936586.html.

tural policy has been that a multicultural Ukraine, by its very nature, undermines national unity and threatens national security. As former President Yushchenko put it, "there will never be peace unless we have harmony in memory, language, and culture."[151]

The Ukrainian government's cultural policy is premised on the assumption that cultural unity can be achieved only through the eradication of Russian culture, language, and identity within Ukraine.[152] This assumption lies at the heart of state policies in language, religion, and historical education, and it is a telling indication of their importance that the Svoboda Party was given these ministerial portfolios immediately after the 2014 Maidan.[153]

For Ukrainian nationalists, the Russian language and all its cultural by-products, no matter what era they come from, are part of an unhealthy colonial relationship. According to this narrative, Moscow usurped the name *Rus* and thereby stole Ukraine's birthright. The cradle of Slavdom ought to properly be called *Ukraina-Rus*, to distinguish it from modern Russia, which derives from the provincial outpost of Muscovy. It is therefore Muscovy, not Ukraine, that should be considered "at the border" (*u krainy*). This is, in essence, a Ukrainian retelling of the eternal brotherly conflict between Cain and Abel, between Jacob and Esau, between Romulus and Remus.[154] Only now it is between Kiev, "the mother of the cities of Rus," and the usurper Moscow.

As Ukraine struggles to re-acquire its own history, identity, religion, and language, just as in those ancient tales, it must do so at the expense of Russian history, identity, religion, and language. That is why Ukrainian nationalists are so insistent on re-branding everything that is Russian as Ukrainian – from borsch, to all desirable historical figures, both ancient and modern. This pattern of cul-

---

151 "Yushchenko: U nas neskolko yazykov i tserkvei – eto nenormalno," [Yushchenko: We Have Several Languages and Churches – That Is Not Normal] *NewsOne*, January 20, 2017, http://newsoneua.tv/news/politics/yushhenko-u-nas-neskolko-yazykov-i-cerkvej-eto-nenormalno.html.

152 Katerina Abrashina, "V Ukraine mnogo vnutrennikh vragov," [There Are Many Internal Enemies in Ukraine] *Vesti*, February 19, 2021, https://vesti.ua/politika/ya-nikogda-ne-dumal-chto-v-ukraine-tak-mnogo-vnutrennih-vragov-kravchuk; "Na Ukraine predlozhili gotovit molodyozh k 'voine s Rossiei,'" [In Ukraine, There Is a Proposal to Prepare Young People for "War with Russia"] *Regnum*, November 7, 2019, https://regnum.ru/news/2771018.html.

153 Volodymyr Ishchenko, "Ukraine and the Right a Year after Maiden [*sic*]," *The Real News Network*, November 26, 2014, http://therealnews.com/vishchenko1126ukraine.

154 *The Book of Genesis* 25:22–23, "And the children struggled together within her; and she said, If it be so, why am I thus? And she went to inquire of the LORD. And the LORD said unto her, Two nations are in thy womb, and two manner of people shall be separated from thy bowels; and the one people shall be stronger than the other people; and the elder shall serve the younger."

ture cleansing, which began in Galicia under the sponsorship of the Austro-Hungarian Empire as a means of curtailing Ruthenian pro-Russian sympathies, was later adopted wholesale by Ukrainian nationalists, who have extended it to the whole country.[155]

For Maloross Ukrainians, however, Russian culture is not a foreign imposition, but rather part of their historical identity. Their distinctive version of Ukrainian identity, which is neither wholly Great Russian, nor wholly Galician, existed within both the Russian Empire and in the Soviet Union. It is one of the many regional cultures that developed among the Eastern Slavs over the centuries. Perhaps its most notable cultural avatar is the nineteenth-century writer Nikolai Gogol, whose Russian national costume was, as Edyta Bojanowska puts it, "stitched from Ukrainian cloth."[156]

4.4.1 What Is Russian Culture for Ukraine?

By any conventional measure, Ukraine is a bilingual and bicultural country in which some Ukrainians identify themselves as Ukrainians, some as Russians, and some as both. Since independence, surveys have shown a steady decline in the number of Ukrainian citizens identifying themselves as Russian, from a high of 22.1 percent in 1989 to just 4.1 percent in 2020.[157] Other surveys, however, suggests that as many as 17 percent of Ukrainians may still identify themselves

---

155 "Lider Rusinov: Ukrainsky yazyk segodnya – krest inoyazychnykh," [Leader of the Rusyns: Ukrainian Language Today Is a Burden for Foreign Speakers] *Pravda*, July 23, 2019, https://www.pravda.ru/world/1422193-tjasko/; "Rusiny razocharovalis v Ukraine," [Ruthenians Disappointed in Ukraine] *Pravda*, June 19, 2019, https://www.pravda.ru/world/1421202-tjaskio/; Vasilii Azarevich, "Russkie bez Rossii," [Russians without Russia] *Ukraina.ru*, October 30, 2018, https://ukraina.ru/history/20181030/1021599648.html; Dmitry Teslenko, "Kak Avstriya iz rusinov Galitsii sozdala ukraintsev," [How Austria Created Ukrainians from Galician Ruthenians] *NK*, April 15, 2021, https://nk.org.ua/obshchestvo/kak-avstriya-iz-rusinov-galitsii-sozdala-ukraintsev-00302052. On the complicated relationship between Ruthenians and Ukraine.
156 "Taras Bulba," *InoSMI*, April 4, 2021, https://inosmi.ru/social/20210404/249477995.html.
157 Yulia Vityazeva, "Vina russkikh Ukrainy," [The Fault of Ukraine's Russians] *News Front*, September 27, 2017, https://news-front.info/2017/09/27/vina-russkih-ukrainy-yuliya-vityazeva/; Katerina Turenko, "Bolshinstvo ukraintsev ne vidyat izmenenii v svyazi s prinyatiem zakona o gosyazyke," [Most Ukrainians Do Not See Any Changes in Connection with the Adoption of the Law on State Language] *Vesti*, July 29, 2020, https://vesti.ua/strana/bez-izmenenij-ukraintsy-vynesli-verdikt-zakonu-o-gosyazyke.

ethnically as Russians.[158] Some of this discrepancy may be due to the inclusion or exclusion of pre-2014 statistics for Crimea and Eastern Donbass, but another wrinkle is added by the fact that, while 77 percent of ethnic Ukrainians describe themselves as belonging to only one nationality, only 39 percent of ethnic Russians in Ukraine feel that way; in other words, most of the latter see themselves as bicultural.[159]

The conventional measure of self-identification, language usage, is no more helpful in providing a clear sense of what distinguishes Russians from Ukrainians in Ukraine. Although an overwhelming majority indicate that Ukrainian is their native language (as many as 83 percent in 1996), only half say they use it on a regular basis, and then mostly in official settings, where they are required to do so by law.[160] Another problem is that the term "native language" is seen as ambiguous by those polled. A third of Ukrainians consider their best mastered language to be "native," another third consider it to be the language of their nation, while a quarter define as "native" the language spoken by their parents. Only 9 percent consider it to be the language they speak most often.[161]

But while surveys on language can yield widely divergent results, there are a few constants. When asked which language people felt most comfortable speaking, there has long been a 50/50 split, but when pollsters ask people to select a form to fill out in either Russian or Ukrainian, over 80 percent select Russian.[162] This corresponds to other surveys indicating that 22 percent of Ukrainian citizens describe their mastery of Ukrainian as "low."[163] Perhaps the most convincing

---

158 "Natsionalnyi sostav Ukrainy," [National Composition of Ukraine] *Racurs.UA*, July 28, 2020, https://racurs.ua/n141710-skolko-rossiyan-v-ukraine-nazvala-infografika-rady-o-nacionalnom-sostave-strany.html.

159 Olga Derkul, "Sotsiologiya podtverzhdaet etnotsid Russkikh na Ukraine," [Sociology Confirms the Ethnocide of Russians in Ukraine] *RitmEurasia*, April 23, 2017, http://www.ritmeurasia.org/news–2017–04–23–sociologija-podtverzhdaet-etnocid-russkih-na-ukraine-29764.

160 Taras Kuzio, *Ukraine: State and Nation Building* (London and New York: Routledge, 1998), 171; Hans van Zon, Andre Batako, and Anna Kreslavska, *Social and Economic Change in Eastern Ukraine: The Example of Zaporizhzhya* (Aldershot and Brookfield, VT: Ashgate, 1998), 54.

161 Tadeusz Andrzej Olszanski, *The Language Issue in Ukraine: An Attempt at a New Perspective*, ed. Wojciech Konończuk and Adam Eberhardt (Warsaw: Ośrodek Studiów Wschodnich im. Marka Karpia, 2012), 14–15, 19, 40.

162 Sergei Gradirovski and Neli Esipova, "Russian Language Enjoying a Boost in Post-Soviet States," *Gallup.com*, August 1, 2008, https://news.gallup.com/poll/109228/Russian-Language-Enjoying-Boost-PostSoviet-States.aspx.

163 Tadeusz Andrzej Olszanski, *The Language Issue in Ukraine*, 21–22.

measure of personal language preference in Ukraine today is personal internet usage, where 84 percent of text messaging is in Russian.[164]

Not surprisingly, Google and YouTube searches in Ukraine are also overwhelmingly in Russian, and for cultural content in Russian.[165] More worrying, from the Ukrainian government's perspective, is that, since blocking all major Russian televisions and social media sites in 2015, a third of Ukrainians have chosen to get their news through YouTube (obviously, prior to the global ban on Russian news sources it imposed after February 2022). Online, the popularity of Russian-language programming in Ukraine far exceeds that of Ukrainian in every news category (online news channels, social commentary, vlogs, journalists' blogs). To find a commercially viable audience online, marketing executive Mykola Rohinets admits, Ukrainian authors must produce their content in Russian.[166]

So, how widespread is the use of Russian in Ukraine? According to a 2017 Romir survey conducted by its Ukrainian partner KIIS, 95 percent of Ukrainians use Russian daily. Two-thirds speak it at home, 61 percent use it to communicate with friends and acquaintances, 39 percent watch Russian-language television and films, and 34 percent use it at work.[167]

While some Ukrainian officials optimistically predict that "in 10 – 15 years we will have a generation that know neither the Russian language nor the Russian Federation," the following chart suggests that Russian is not going anywhere soon.[168]

164 Maksim Mogilnitsky, "Kogda yazyk imeet znachenie," [When Language Matters] *Fokus*, January 16, 2021, https://focus.ua/opinions/471872-kogda-yazyk-imeet-znachenie-chego-hotya-ot-gosudarstva-te-ukraincy-kotorye-govoryat-po-russki.
165 Viktoriya Venk, "Zrada pod elochku," [Treason under the Christmas Tree] *Strana.ua*, January 2, 2021, https://strana.one/news/309931-chto-ukraintsy-iskali-v-google-i-smotreli-v-youtube-na-novyj-hod.html; Maksim Mogilnitsky, "Kogda yazyk imeet znachenie."
166 Yulia Moskalenko, "'Zerkalo Nedeli' voshlo v desyatku kachestvennykh Ukrainskikh media po versii IMI," ["Zerkalo Nedeli" is Among the Top Ten Quality Ukrainian Media According to IMI] *Zerkalo nedeli*, January 21, 2021, https://zn.ua/UKRAINE/zerkalo-nedeli-voshlo-v-spisok-media-s-kachestvennoj-informatsiej.html.
167 Mariya Nedyuk, "Lish 5% ukraintsev ne ispolzuyut russky yazyk," [Only 5% of Ukrainians Do Not Use the Russian Language] *Izvestiya*, February 27, 2017, https://iz.ru/news/666745.
168 "Na Ukraine predlozhili gotovit molodyozh k 'voine s Rossiei'"; Ekaterina Khroshchak, "Yazykovoi ombudsmen, Taras Kremen o pritesnenii russkogo yazyka na Ukraine," [Language Ombudsman, Taras Kremen on the Restriction of the Russian Language in Ukraine] *Ukrainska pravda*, July 8, 2020, https://life.pravda.com.ua/society/2020/07/16/241660/.

Table 4.4: What Language Do Ukrainians Ages 14–29 Speak at Home (2018)?

	Ukrainian	Russian	Both
West	93%	1%	3%
North	73%	5%	21%
Center	53%	19%	26%
Kiev	30%	50%	19%
South	6%	63%	30%
East	2%	84%	13%
Total for Ukraine *(without occupied territories)*			
	49%	33%	18%
Total for Ukraine *(with occupied territories)*			
	45%	37%	18%

Source: Radio Liberty Ukrainian language service (https://www.radiosvoboda.org/a/what-uk rainians-speak-at-home/28994291.html), January 29, 2018, omitting Crimea and areas of Donbass not under government control. My estimates for the population of Ukraine with these areas is taken from UkrStat (https://tinyurl.com/2bohk48a), November 1, 2015, and assumes equal age distribution across all regions, and that Crimean language preferences are the same as those of Eastern Ukraine.

Research done by the Ukrainian Academy of Sciences points to a similar conclusion. It notes that, although the number of wholly Ukrainian language schools in Ukraine has been over 90 percent for more than two decades, outside the classroom, children, teachers, and parents overwhelmingly speak Russian in all regions but historical Galicia.[169]

Although President Yushchenko took a number of new steps to discourage the use of Russian, including a 30 percent quota on foreign-language films and video cassette sales, and a decree in September 2009 that forbid school teachers to speak any language other than Ukrainian at work, the use of language quotas as an instrument of social policy truly took off after 2014.

A new language quota for radio broadcasters came into force on November 8, 2016. It imposed a three-year transition for broadcasting at least 75 percent

169 Egor Leyev, "Ukrainizatsiya na marshe."

songs in Ukrainian, as well as weekly television content in prime time. Quotas for regional channels were set at 50 percent, but must eventually move toward total Ukrainianization.[170]

Since 2021 the ability to use Russian language in public has been further curtailed by laws that prohibit initiating a conversation in a commercial or public setting in any language but Ukrainian (religious services being the only exception).[171] The parties may switch to another language afterward, if both sides consent. The implementation of this Orwellian provision is supervised by Ukraine's Language Ombudsmen, Taras Kremin, whose office can levy fines against repeat offenders. Kremin has said that his office regards any threat to the Ukrainian language as a threat to national security, and he has publicly urged those who disagree with this law to leave the country, since they pose a threat to the "code of the nation."[172]

Surveys taken before 2022, however, suggest that Ukrainians remain deeply divided about such restrictions. In the west, where Ukrainian dominates and thus no behavioral changes are demanded, they enjoy broad support. In Maloross Ukraine, however, they are widely viewed as a human rights violation, and been met with passive resistance.[173]

Why does the government insist on policies that are deeply unpopular in half the country? Although destructive of national unity, such policies become understandable in the context of nationalism. Nowhere is this more apparent than in the struggle over Ukraine's religious identity, which reached a new level of intensity in 2019, when Ukrainian President Petro Poroshenko decided to create a Ukrainian church loyal to the ideals of a nationalistic Ukrainian state.

---

170 Anastasiya Tovt, "Godovshchina kvot na radio," [One Year of Radio Quotas] *Strana.ua*, November 28, 2017, https://strana.one/articles/analysis/107008-sem-hlavnykh-posledstvij-kvot-na-radio-spustja-hod.html.

171 "Pro zabezpechennya funktsionuvannya ukrainskoy movy yak derzhavnoy stattya 30. Derzhavna mova u sferi obsluhovuvannya spozhyvachiv," [On Ensuring the Functioning of the Ukrainian Language as the State Language in Accordance with Article 30. The State Language in the Field of Customer Service] *Kodeksy*, Law No. 2704-VIII, April 25, 2019 (amended), https://kodeksy.com.ua/pro_zabezpechennya_funktsionuvannya_ukrayins_koyi_movi_yak_derzhavnoyi/30.htm.

172 Pavel Volkov, "Kod natsii protiv demokratii," [The Code of the Nation against Democracy] *Ukraina.ru*, January 2, 2022, https://ukraina.ru/exclusive/20220102/1032845562.html.

173 "Monitorynh hromadskoi dumky naselennya Ukrainy," *Social Monitoring Center.*

4.4.2 A State Church for the Ukrainian Nation

Throughout both the Imperial and Soviet eras, the Russian Orthodox Church was commonly regarded as the sole canonical Orthodox church in Ukraine. In October 1990, sensing the imminent collapse of the USSR, the Russian Orthodox Church granted its diocese in Ukraine "independence and autonomy in its administration."[174] This church, known informally as the Ukrainian Orthodox Church (Moscow Patriarchate), or UOC (MP), was recognized by all established autocephalous Orthodox churches as the sole canonical Orthodox church in Ukraine.

At the time, however, it was by no means clear that the dissolution of the USSR would result in the creation of an independent Ukraine, and many spiritual leaders hedged their bets. In 1992, the Metropolitan of Kiev, Filaret (Denisenko), having lost his bid to become Patriarch of Moscow, proclaimed himself Patriarch of Kiev, and set up his own Ukrainian Orthodox Church known as UOC (KP), or Kievan Patriarchate. Over the next quarter century the Kievan Patriarchate set up more than 4,000 parishes, many seized from the UOC (MP). Still, by the end of 2018, at least two-thirds of the 18,000 Orthodox Christian parishes in Ukraine swore allegiance to the UOC (MP).[175]

The fact that the majority of the country's faithful attended a church whose nominal head resides in Moscow has long troubled Ukrainian nationalists. On the wave of nationalism inspired by the 2014 Maidan Revolution, the National Institute for Strategic Research (NISS), a think tank closely affiliated with the presidential administration, elaborated a strategy for establishing a new Orthodox church in Ukraine that would be loyal to the post-Maidan regime.[176]

In 2015, Sergei Zdioruk and Vladimir Tokman, two senior analysts at the NISS, wrote a report about the threat that the UOC (MP) posed to Ukraine's statehood. They described it as a "channel for the clerical occupation of Ukraine," and suggested that it was assisting the rebels in eastern Ukraine and collaborating with the occupation in Crimea. These subversive activities, they argued, could be effectively countered by creating a new Ukrainian Orthodox church from the merger of the Kievan Patriarchate and the much smaller Ukrainian Autocephalous Orthodox Church, or UAOC. The authors predicted that the creation

---

174 Jesse Dominick, "What Rights Does the Ukrainian Orthodox Church Really Have?" *OrthoChristian.Com*, November 29, 2018, https://orthochristian.com/117556.html.
175 Vladislav Maltsev, "Mertvye dushi," [Dead Souls] *Ukraina.ru*, October 26, 2018, https://ukraina.ru/exclusive/20181026/1021565946.html.
176 "Natsionalnyi instytut stratehichnykh doslidzhen," *National Institute of Strategic Research*, http://www.niss.gov.ua/.

of such a new Orthodox church in Ukraine would lead to a "chain reaction" of demands for autocephaly from the Russian Orthodox Church throughout the former Soviet Union, which would make the new Ukrainian church the largest and most influential church in the Orthodox world, with all the corresponding political benefits.

To accomplish this, Zdioruk and Tokman proposed a nine-point government program, which included: rescinding the property rights of the UOC (MP) in key national shrines; preventing the participation of UOC (MP) hierarchs in all public celebrations; providing government support only to those Orthodox organizations that promote "the socio-patriotic education of their flock"; prohibiting visits to Ukraine by the "odious activists and functionaries of the Russian Orthodox Church"; and introducing a "system of concordats" that would oblige religious organizations to work "for the good of the entire Ukrainian people."[177]

When this plan was conceived, Ukrainian autocephaly seemed highly improbable. Not a single Orthodox hierarch, not even the Patriarch of Moscow's erstwhile rival, the Patriarch of Constantinople, recognized the legitimacy of either the Kievan Patriarchate or the UAOC. In early 2018, however, President Poroshenko's deputy chief of staff, Rostislav Pavlenko, reached a tentative agreement with the Patriarch of Constantinople, Bartholomew I. In exchange for Bartholomew's recognition of a new Orthodox Church of Ukraine, the latter would be placed under Constantinople's jurisdiction.

This was deemed a win-win scenario for all involved. The UOC (KP) would absorb the smaller UAOC and then be recognized, both politically and theologically, as the sole legitimate Orthodox Church of Ukraine. Constantinople, as a result, would gain effective control over a much larger flock, which included the wealthy expatriate communities in the United States and Canada. Finally, President Poroshenko could claim to have unified Ukrainian Orthodoxy, and expect a powerful boost entering the upcoming presidential elections.

Setting up the new church took about six months. On December 15, 2018, President Poroshenko took center stage at the Unifying Church Council, in the ancient cathedral of St. Sophia in Kiev, and proclaimed the final attainment of Ukrainian independence from Russia. "Not a single patriot," Poroshenko said, "can doubt the importance of an independent Ukrainian Orthodox Church for an independent Ukrainian state. Such a church is the spiritual guarantor of

---

177 Sergei Zdioruk and Vladimir Tokman, "Vydavlivaya Moskvu po kaple," [Squeezing Out Moscow, Drop by Drop] *Zerkalo nedeli*, October 23, 2015, https://zn.ua/internal/vydavlivaya-moskvu-po-kaple-_.html.

our sovereignty."[178] This nationally televised event served as a backdrop for the launch of the president's re-election campaign, which featured the slogan "Army, Language, Faith – the army defends our land. The language defends our heart. The church defends our soul."[179]

Overall, however, the creation of this new church, known as the Orthodox Church in Ukraine (OCU), has proved to be a serious disappointment for Ukrainian nationalists. It did not get Poroshenko re-elected. The prime instigator of its creation, Patriarch Filaret of Kiev, later withdrew his support and denounced the union. Finally, the prediction that the OCU would serve as a rallying point for all Orthodox Christians in Ukraine has not come to pass. In the first year just 3 percent of parishes switched over from the UOC (MP) to the new OCU.[180]

It is no secret that, in the eyes of the Ukrainian government, the cardinal political sin of the canonical Ukrainian Orthodox Church (Moscow Patriarchate) is its refusal to support the war in eastern Ukraine. Metropolitan Onufriy, the head of the UOC (MP), has routinely referred to the conflict in Donbass as "fratricidal" and a "civil war."[181] Under President Zelensky Ukrainian national security officials continue to label the UOC (MP) an enemy of the state, and urge the president to shut it down, as he has opposition parties and television channels.[182]

---

178 "Vystup prezydenta za rezultatamy Vseukrainskoho Pravoslavnoho Obiednavchoho Soboru," [Speech by the President Following the Results of the All-Ukrainian Orthodox Unification Council] *Ofitsiine internet-predstavnytstvo Prezydent Ukrainy*, December 15, 2018, https://www.president.gov.ua/news/vistup-prezidenta-za-rezultatami-vseukrayinskogo-pravoslavno-52050.

179 "Poroshenko ozvuchyv 'formulu suchasnoi ukrainskoy identychnosti,'" [Poroshenko Explains the "Formula of Modern Ukrainian Identity"] *Obozrevatel*, September 20, 2018, https://news.obozrevatel.com/ukr/politics/poroshenko-ozvuchiv-formulu-suchasnoi-ukrainskoi-identichnosti.htm.

180 Petro Poroshenko, "Pislya otrymannya Tomosu pro avtokefaliyu vzhe 320 parafii pryiednalysya do nashoi tserkvy," [After Receiving the Tomos on Autocephaly, 320 Parishes Have Already Joined Our Church] *Twitter*, February 18, 2019, https://twitter.com/poroshenko/status/1097477651244175362; "Episkop Baryshevsky Viktor rasskazal o realnoi statistike perekhodov obshchin iz Ukrainskoi Pravoslavnoi Tserkvi v PTsU," [Bishop Viktor Baryshevsky Spoke about the Real Statistics of the Transition of Communities from the Ukrainian Orthodox Church to the OCU] *Patriarchia.ru*, February 21, 2019, http://www.patriarchia.ru/db/print/5375891.html; Valeriya Malitska, "Skilky parafii UPTS (MP) pereishlo do PTSU," [How Many UOC (MP) Parishes Have Joined the OCU?] *Fakty ICTV*, January 6, 2020, https://fakty.com.ua/ua/ukraine/20200106-skilky-parafij-rpts-perejshlo-do-ptsu-karta/.

181 "Mitropolit Onufriy: Neobkhodimo prekratit voinu i perestat ubivat drug druga," [Metropolitan Onufriy: It Is Imperative to Stop the War and Stop Killing Each Other] *Ukraina.ru*, July 14, 2015, https://ukraina.ru/interview/20150714/1013658370.html.

182 "UPC (MP) perehovuvala rosiiskih diversantiv i vbivts–Parubiy," [The UOC (MP) Sheltered Russian Saboteurs and Assassins Says Paribiy] *RISU.ua*, October 7, 2018, https://risu.ua/upc-mp-

To sum up the impact of nationalism, if the tragedy of Ukraine's economic policy springs from its self-destructiveness, then the tragedy of Ukraine's cultural policy derives from lawlessness – the casual indifference to the right to use ones' native language, to freedom of expression, and to freedom of worship, all of which are explicitly guaranteed in the Ukrainian constitution. The government's subordination of the country's political and legal institutions to nationalistic objectives has effectively shattered trust in public institutions, not just in Maloross Ukraine, but nationwide.[183] With less public trust comes greater domestic instability, and increased dependence on foreign actors. It is this geopolitical aspect of Ukraine's tragedy, which has made the country a pawn in the larger conflict between Russia and the West, that we turn to next.

perehovuvala-rosiyskih-diversantiv-i-vbivc-parubiy_n93540; "Razvedka ubezhdena, chto RPTs na 99% kontroliruetsya spetssluzhbami RF," [Intelligence Is Convinced that the Russian Orthodox Church Is 99% Controlled by Special Services of the Russian Federation] *Ukrainskaya pravda*, January 24, 2019, http://www.pravda.com.ua/rus/news/2019/01/24/7204779/; Petro Poroshenko, "Derzhat shturval," [Stay the Course] *NV.ua*, January 1, 2019, https://nv.ua/opinion/derzhat-shturval-2515855.html.
183 Julie Ray and Neli Esipova, "Approval Ratings in Ukraine, Russia Highlight Differences," *Gallup.com*, July 31, 2009, https://news.gallup.com/poll/121976/Approval-Ratings-Ukraine-Russia-Highlight-Differences.aspx; Ben Aris, "Fear and Mistrust on the Ukrainian Campaign Trail," *IntelliNews*, March 25, 2019, https://www.intellinews.com/fear-and-mistrust-on-the-ukrainian-campaign-trail-158415/.

Chapter Five
The Tragedies of Crimea and Donbass

> Putin haunts eastern Donbass ... this territory is the weak link in our national unity. Because, when Putin wanders through Donbass, he hears the Russian language, he goes to Russian Church, he reads Russian newspapers, he goes to the Russian theater, he watches Russian television.
>
> Viktor Yushchenko, president of Ukraine (2005–2010)[1]

> Crimea was never on Ukraine's mental map ... it obviously didn't fit the concept of a mono-ethnic Ukrainian state ... [it] constantly forced us to feel the multiethnicity and multiculturalism of Ukraine, which led to cognitive dissonance in the minds of nationalists.
>
> Pavlo Zubyuk, Ukrainian journalist[2]

> Behind all of this lies the idea of turning Ukraine into Greater Galicia. That is where the danger lies. First, it is simply impossible to do. Second, such attempts will generate endless internal contradictions in the country ... It is impossible to clothe Donbass in Hutsul *hachy*, as trousers there are called.
>
> Pyotr Tolochko, Full Member, National Academy of Sciences of Ukraine[3]

Since its independence Ukraine has struggled to combine the economic advantages of economic integration with Russia and the CIS, with the security advantages of integration with the EU and NATO. To achieve this every Ukrainian president has tried to get the best deal that he could for his country by playing these suitors against each other. Meanwhile, the limits of integration, in either direction, were fixed in the Ukrainian Constitution, which prohibited the country from joining any military alliance, and committed it to neutrality. In practice, this meant "No" to membership in NATO and the Collective Security Treaty Organization (CSTO), but "Yes" to membership in the European Union and the Eurasian Customs Union.

The events of 2014 destroyed this two-pronged policy, splitting the country further along its historical and cultural fault lines. In the aftermath of what many Maloross Ukrainians deemed to be a nationalist coup inspired by the West, two of the most Russophile regions – Crimea and Eastern Donbass – sep-

---

1 "Yushchenko udivil zayavleniem o prisutstvii RF na Donbasse," [Yushchenko Surprised Everyone with His Statement about the Presence of the Russian Federation in Donbass] *Sud.ua*, September 3, 2018, https://sud.ua/ru/news/ukraine/124607-yuschenko-udivil-zayavleniem-o-prisutstvii-rf-v-donbasse.

2 Pavlo Zubyuk, "Nash nenash Krym," [Crimea – Ours and Not Ours] *Zaxid.net*, March 16, 2020, https://zaxid.net/nash_nenash_krim_n1499339.

3 Albina Petrova, "V strane tovarishcha mauzera," [In Comrade Mauser's Country] *Rossiiskaya gazeta*, March 14, 2014, https://rg.ru/2014/03/14/tolochko.html.

https://doi.org/10.1515/9783110743371-009

arated from Ukraine, raising fears that other parts of the country might soon join them. This fear, in turn, led to abandoning neutrality in favor of NATO membership, which is now mandated as a goal for all future Ukrainian governments, thanks to a constitutional amendment adopted in February 2019.

This ability to alter the Constitution on such a divisive issue without first putting the question to a popular vote underscores the new-found dominance of the Galician narrative in Ukrainian politics. In eastern and southern Ukraine 60 percent or more of the population traditionally supported closer ties with Russia, while in central and western Ukraine, 60 percent or more traditionally supported closer ties with NATO. Remarkably, as late as May 2022, the *Wall Street Journal* reported that only 59 percent of Ukrainians said they would vote in favor of joining NATO if a referendum were held today, a surprisingly low number, considering that the country was under assault by Russia and being armed by NATO.[4] Some of this hesitancy may be due to the fact that NATO membership for Ukraine would mean perpetual confrontation with Russia, which has long insisted that it sees Ukraine in NATO as an existential threat.[5]

The Ukrainian government's indifference to Russian security concerns is not accidental. It is inspired by Dmytro Dontsov's view that perpetual national mobilization for war with Russia would be an excellent way for Ukraine to develop the national will that it needs to survive in a hostile international environment.[6] In today's political parlance, it would (1) rally the country around a common enemy; (2) justify government censorship of foreign and opposition web sites; and (3) allow the suppression of the political and cultural rights of Maloross Ukrainians. As former Interior Minister Arsen Avakov wrote at the very outset of the conflict, back in June 2014, war with Russia should not be feared, because it

---

4 Daniel Twining, "What Ukrainians Think about the War with Russia," *Wall Street Journal*, May 6, 2022, https://www.wsj.com/articles/what-ukrainians-think-about-the-war-russia-putin-invasion-zelensky-victory-results-approval-rating-11651868038.
5 John J. Mearsheimer, "Why the Ukraine Crisis Is the West's Fault," *Foreign Affairs*, September/October 2014, www.foreignaffairs.com/articles/141769/john-j-mearsheimer/why-the-ukraine-crisis-is-the-wests-fault. Mearsheimer attributes Russia's decision to annex Crimea to its need to prevent the abrogation of the Black Sea Fleet Treaty which would have led to the expulsion of Russian naval forces from Sevastopol, and, more distantly, to it becoming a NATO base.
6 Wiktor Poliszczuk, *Gorkaya Pravda: Prestupnost OUN-UPA (ispoved Ukraintsa),* [The Bitter Truth: The Crimes of the OUN-UIA (a Ukrainian's Confession)] (Toronto, Warsaw, and Kiev, 1995), https://tinyurl.com/yykfr35n, 112–114.

would have a salutary and "cleansing" effect on the nation.[7] Many senior Ukrainian officials have voiced similar sentiments.[8]

But, unforeseen problems can arise when using conflict to inspire national unity. One is that, once animosity becomes institutionalized, it takes on a life of its own, leading to unintended escalations. In Ukraine this has happened at least twice in recent memory. First, during the Kerch Straits incident in August 2019, and again during the Wagner incident involving Belarus in August 2020. During the former, President Poroshenko started a maritime conflict with Russia in order to impose martial law on all of Maloross Ukraine. At the time many believed that he would use this as an excuse to suspend the 2019 presidential elections altogether, but was thwarted in his efforts by the concerted opposition of three former presidents of Ukraine.[9] In the latter incident, only the timely leak by a highly placed source within President Zelensky's administration (many suspect that it was his chief of staff, Andriy Yermak) prevented Ukrainian special forces from hijacking a Belarus plane with several dozen Russian mercenaries on board.[10]

---

7 Arsen Avakov, "V eti paru dnei mnogo govoril s nashimi v zone ATO," [In These Past Few Days I Spoke with a Lot of Our People in the ATO] *Facebook*, June 22, 2014, https://www.facebook.com/arsen.avakov.1/posts/657281451028631%20%5b25.

8 "Donbassu – konets, on razrushen," [Donbass Is Finished, It Is Destroyed] *Liga.net*, February 7, 2019, https://www.liga.net/politics/articles/donbassu—konets-on-razrushen-intervyu-s-gorbulinym-za-minutu; "Zhebrivsky govorit, chto khochet Bolshoi voiny s Rossiei za Donbass," [Zhebrivsky Says He Wants a Big War with Russia over Donbass] *Ukrainska pravda*, April 8, 2016, https://www.pravda.com.ua/rus/news/2016/04/8/7104896/; "Yushchenko naschital 24 voiny s Rossiei," [Yushchenko Counted 24 Wars with Russia] *Ukraina.ru*, April 5, 2017, https://ukraina.ru/news/20170405/1018493199.html; Georgy Luchnikov, "Logika parazita," [A Parasite's Logic] August 4, 2021, https://ukraina.ru/exclusive/20210804/1031994062.html.

9 Nicolai N. Petro, "Ukraine's Pinochet Scenario," *The Nation*, November 28, 2018, https://www.thenation.com/article/archive/ukraines-pinochet-scenario/.

10 "Na Ukraine raskryli detali 'Vagnergeita,'" [Details of "Wagnergate" Revealed in Ukraine] *Ukraina.ru*, December 23, 2021, https://ukraina.ru/news/20211223/1032953690.html; Marina Yakovenko and Oleg Tkachuk, "Operatsiya Vagner," [Operation Wagner] *Vesti*, November 17, 2021, https://vesti.ua/strana/ne-proshlo-i-goda-chto-rasskazali-bellingcat-v-nashumevshej-state-o-vagnere; Jonny Tickle, "33 Russian 'Mercenaries' Targeted by Ukrainian Sting Operation," *RT International*, November 18, 2021, https://www.rt.com/russia/540605-russians-detained-belarus-ukrainian-operation/; Matthew Chance and Zahra Ullah, "How Ukraine Planned to Lure Russian Mercenaries into a Trap," *CNN*, September 8, 2021, https://www.cnn.com/2021/09/07/europe/ukraine-belarus-russia-mercenaries-sting/index.html; Maksim Minin, "Opravdat Zelenskogo, Ermaka i TsRU," [Justifying Zelensky, Yermak and the CIA] *Strana.ua*, November 16, 2021, https://strana.news/news/362389-kto-provalil-operatsiju-po-vahnerovtsam-analiz-otcheta-tsk-bezuhloj.html; Maksim Minin, "Udar Burby," [Burba's Blow] *Strana.ua*, November 21,

A second problem is that while war unites some, it encourages the resistance of others. From the beginning of the 2014 Maidan, a large portion of the population in eastern and southern Ukraine blamed Ukrainian authorities for the conflict with Russia as much as they did Russian authorities.[11] According to some Western media reports, this conflict of loyalties persists even after Russia's military incursion of February 2022.[12]

A third problem is that it leads Ukrainian leaders to have unrealistic expectations of the West.[13] Despite being routinely disappointed, the current leadership clings to these unrealistic expectations because nationalism offers them no other alternative. Ukrainian foreign and defense policy is trapped by its own rhetoric, just as its economic policy is trapped into buying Russian gas at much higher prices across the border in Slovakia, to avoid calling it "Russian gas." Political figures from across the Ukrainian political spectrum, including some in the presidential administration, have lamented this loss of independence.[14]

2021, https://strana.one/news/363099-burba-na-shustere-obvinil-ofis-prezidenta-v-provale-operatsii-po-vahnerovtsam.html.

11 "Zhiteli yuga Ukrainy shchitayut Evromaidan perevorotom," [Residents of Southern Ukraine Consider the Euromaidan a Coup] *Timer-Odessa*, February 14, 2017, https://perma.cc/HMK3–2RPV; "Khto vynen u voiny," [Who Is to Blame for the War] *IMI.org*, January–March 2017, http://imi.org.ua/news/58070-kojen-pyatiy-meshkanets-pivdnya-ta-shodu-pidtrimue-avtonomiyu-okupovanogo-donbasu-opituvannya.html.

12 Erin Burnett, "'They've Found Traitors': Why Ukrainians Find It Hard to Hold Key Towns," *CNN*, May 12, 2022, https://us.cnn.com/videos/tv/2022/05/11/ukraine-pushback-on-russia-nick-paton-walsh-ebof.cnn/video/playlists/top-news-videos/; "As War Nears 6-Month Mark, Ukraine Struggles against New-Old Foes: Collaborators and Corruption," *Russia Matters*, July 22, 2022, https://www.russiamatters.org/blog/war-nears-6-month-mark-ukraine-struggles-against-new-old-foes-collaborators-and-corruption; Nabih Bulos, "In Eastern Ukraine, Some Stand against Their Defenders," *Los Angeles Times*, June 21, 2022, https://www.latimes.com/world-nation/story/2022–06–21/in-eastern-ukraine-some-back-the-russians.

13 Evgenii Vasilenko, "V MID ne ponimayut, pochemu Ukrainu ne priglasili na zakrytyi sammit NATO – Kuleba," [The Foreign Ministry Does Not Understand Why Ukraine Was Not Invited to Close NATO Summit – Kuleba] *NV.UA*, May 26, 2021, https://nv.ua/world/geopolitics/ukraina-v-nato-v-mid-vozmushcheny-chto-alyans-ne-priglasil-ukrainu-na-zakrytyy-sammit-50162253.html; Irina Sitnikova, "Ukraina ne mozhet vechno byt v zale ozhidaniya," [Ukraine Can't Stay in the Waiting Room Forever] *Hromadske.ua*, April 16, 2021, https://hromadske.ua/ru/posts/ukraina-ne-mozhet-vechno-byt-v-zale-ozhidaniya-zelenskij-prizval-prinyat-ukrainu-v-nato-i-es.

14 Pyotr Lavrenin, "Timoshenko rasskazala o bessmyslennom vneshnem yprvlenii Ukrainoi," [Tymoshenko Spoke about the Pointless External Administration of Ukraine] *Lenta.ru*, March 16, 2021, https://yandex.ru/turbo/lenta.ru/s/news/2021/03/16/vneshpol/; "Tatarov otreagiroval na aktsiyu pod OP i snova zayavil pro 'vneshnee upravlenie,'" [Tatarov Reacted to the Protest

The final problem with perpetual mobilization for perpetual war, is that it requires the current regime to hold onto power for a generation or more. Senior Ukrainian officials have said that it will take at least twenty-five years to transform Maloross Ukrainians into new, nationalistic Ukrainians.[15] Since truly democratic elections are likely to bring the opposition to power at some point, these officials candidly admit that the political rights of Maloross Ukrainians will have to be significantly curtailed during this time. In sum, the same divisive ideological imperative that characterizes economic, cultural, and religious policies is also at work in Ukraine's national security policy.

Russia's blatant intervention in 2014, and again in 2022, has given these nationalist arguments new legitimacy and urgency. Still, it is important to point out that they have existed for decades, and are therefore not the *result* of Russia's annexation of Crimea and intervention in Donbass. To paraphrase Voltaire, if Russian aggression had not existed, it would be necessary to invent it, because it allows all of Ukraine's problems to be explained as the product of Russian aggression.

None of this is meant to rationalize Russian military intervention in Ukraine since 2014, but only to point out that such intervention alone would not have been sufficient to sustain the rebellions in Crimea and Donbass, had there not already been very real differences with the rest of Ukraine, differences exacerbated by the nationalistic policies adopted after 2014. And since Russia and Ukraine share such a long and intertwined history, when internal differences become acute, it perforce leads to tensions between them.

5.1 Crimea's Quest for Autonomy

It is important to understand how the 2014 Maidan was perceived in Maloross Ukraine, because it explains why their rebellion against it met with so little local resistance. In the West, the separation of these regions from Ukraine is attributed exclusively to Russian intervention. But while it is certainly true that without Russian intervention they probably would not have succeeded, Russian intervention relied on considerable local support, and would have certainly

---

under the President's Office and Again Spoke of "External Administration"] *Ukrainska pravda*, December 5, 2020, https://perma.cc/ESR7-GYZJ.

15 Maria Yakovenko, "Tam zhivut prestupniki," [Criminals Live There] *Vesti.ua*, September 9, 2020, https://vesti.ua/politika/tam-zhivut-prestupniki-pochemu-vlasti-slivayut-vozvrashhenie-donbassa.

failed without it. This is true in both Crimea and Donbass, although the historical circumstances of each differed.

Crimea, also known as Tauridia, is among the oldest recorded settlements along the Black Sea coast. Archeological records reveal that there were Greek colonies there as far back as the ninth century BCE. During the Middle Ages it fell under the control of Genoese merchants, and then the Ottomans, until it was conquered by Russia in 1783. Crimea is the only region of Ukraine whose population identifies itself as primarily ethnically Russian. This, and the status of the indigenous Crimean Tatar population, were issues of contention throughout both the Soviet and post-Soviet eras.

Before 1945, Crimea was an autonomous republic within the RSFSR. In 1954, however, it was transferred from the Russian SFSR to the Ukrainian SSR as a "gift" to the Ukrainian people in honor of the three hundredth anniversary of the Pereyaslavl Rada that joined Ukraine to Russia. This decision to alter the internal borders was apparently a matter of some disagreement within the Soviet leadership, which may be why it was not submitted to a referendum, as required by the Constitution of the RSFSR.[16]

The question of holding a referendum to restore Crimean autonomy, however, never entirely went away and resurfaced at the end of the 1980s, thanks to three simultaneous events. First, Moscow unveiled plans to build a nuclear power plant in Crimea, and a local post-Chernobyl ecological movement mobilized to stop it. Second, in 1989 the USSR Supreme Soviet officially rehabilitated the Crimean Tatars, and simultaneously called for Crimean autonomy to be restored. Finally, in October 1989, the Supreme Soviet of the Ukrainian SSR passed a language law that made Ukrainian the sole official state language in Ukraine, at a time when Crimea was 97 percent Russian-speaking.[17]

In January 1991, as the USSR was visibly disintegrating, the Crimean regional government decided to hold its own referendum on restoring the autonomy of Crimea that had been abrogated in 1946. It sought to get Crimea recognized as an independent participant of the Union Treaty then being proposed by Mikhail

---

16 Grigory Tsykunov, "Historical and Legal Bases of Crimea's Inclusion in the Russian Federation," *Izvestiya Irkutskoi Gosudarstvennoi Ekonomicheskoi Akademii* 25, no. 3 (2015): 550–555, https://doi.org/10.17150/1993–3541.2015.25(3); Gwendolyn Sasse, *The Crimea Question: Identity, Transition, and Conflict*, Harvard Series in Ukrainian Studies (Cambridge, MA: Harvard University Press for the Harvard Ukrainian Research Institute, 2007).
17 Galiya Ibragimova, "Kiev otstupil," [Kiev Has Retreated] *Ria.ru*, January 20, 2021, https://ria-ru.turbopages.org/ria.ru/s/20210120/krym-1593733426.html; "Portret elektoratov Yushchenko i Yanukovycha," [Portrait of the Electorates of Yushchenko and Yanukovych] *Analitik*, January 18, 2005, https://perma.cc/JN5X-58CP?type=image.

Gorbachev. Nearly 84 percent of registered voters participated in this referendum, and 93 percent voted for Crimean autonomy from the Ukrainian SSR, opening the door to potentially separating Crimea from both the USSR and the Ukrainian SSR.[18]

On February 12, 1991, the Supreme Soviet of the Ukrainian SSR recognized these results, and in June it amended the Ukrainian Soviet Constitution accordingly. On September 4, 1991, the Supreme Soviet, of now the Autonomous Crimean Republic (ACR), proclaimed the region's sovereignty, but added that it intended to create a separate, democratic state *within* Ukraine. It is in this context that 54 percent of Crimeans voted in December 1991 in favor of Ukrainian independence, with a voter turnout of 65 percent, the lowest of any region in Ukraine.

In early 1992, however, buyers remorse began to set in. A quarter of a million residents, more than 10 percent of the population, signed a petition asking for a referendum on separation from Ukraine. By law, this was enough to mandate a referendum, but Ukraine's new president, Leonid Kravchuk, wary of the potential for bloodshed, refused to hold it.[19] Nevertheless, on May 5, 1992, the Supreme Soviet of the ACR adopted an "Act Proclaiming the State Sovereignty of the Crimean Republic," effectively declaring total independence from Ukraine, subject to approval by a referendum to be held in August 1992. The Ukrainian parliament responded by declaring Crimea's independence illegal, and authorizing President Kravchuk to use any means necessary to stop it. After two weeks of stalemate and threats, on May 20, 1992, the Crimean parliament rescinded its declaration of independence and suspended the independence referendum, in exchange for a negotiated devolution of power from Kiev to Simferopol, within the broad framework of the recently adopted Crimean Constitution.

This Constitution asserted extensive regional autonomy, including exclusive control of the land, resources, and "economic potential" of Crimea. Crimea was to have its own president and prime minister, as well as the authority to hold its own local referenda. The region's official language would be Russian, although Ukrainian and Tatar were also recognized as state languages. From the outset, however, both sides had diametrically opposed interpretations of what Crimean autonomy meant – Simferopol wanted maximum autonomy in local affairs,

---

18 "V Krymu nazvali pervyi shag na puti k vossoedineniyu s Rossiei," [Crimea Names the First Step Towards Reunification with Russia] *Ritm Eurasia*, January 19, 2021, https://www.ritmeurasia.org/news–2021–01–19–v-krymu-nazvali-pervyj-shag-na-puti-k-vossoedineniju-s-rossiej-52847.

19 Peter Hitchens, "Our Navy's Black Sea Antics Were Stupid," *Mail Online*, June 26, 2021, https://www.dailymail.co.uk/debate/article-9728423/PETER-HITCHENS-wont-popular-Navys-Black-Sea-antics-stupid.html.

while Kiev was aiming for a unitary state in which Ukrainian language and culture would be the norm.

When Kiev granted Crimea autonomy, contingent on its constitution eventually being brought into line with that of Ukraine, and a moratorium on referenda on secession, the crisis was averted, but only temporarily, since it did not deal with the core issue – the desire of a large portion of the Crimean population to be part of Russia rather than Ukraine. This desire, which was well known to British and American diplomats at the time, re-surfaced in 1994, when Yuri Meshkov won the presidency of Crimea on a platform of reuniting with Russia.[20]

After Meshkov's resounding victory (73 percent in the run-off), the Crimean parliament restored the 1992 constitution that had been revoked under pressure from Kiev, and decided to hold a non-binding referendum on the status of Crimea which, Meshkov later admitted, would have been the first step to joining Russia.[21] The results of the March 27, 1994 referendum, which Kiev declared illegal, were as follows: 82.2 percent supported dual citizenship with Russia; 78.4 percent supported increased autonomy for Crimea; and 77.9 percent favored giving Crimean presidential decrees the force of law.[22]

The new Crimean president and his majority party, "The Russia Bloc," were now headed for a direct confrontation with Kiev. On July 1, 1994, the Crimean parliament voted to assume full powers throughout Crimea, except for those that it voluntarily chose to delegate to Kiev, and on August 23, 1994, the Sevastopol City Council declared itself to be a Russian city, subject only to Russian law.

In the dead of night March 16 – 17, 1995, Ukrainian President Leonid Kuchma, after consulting with Boris Yeltsin and receiving his support, sent Ukrainian special forces to seize government buildings and arrest the Crimean government. Meshkov was immediately deported to Russia, and that same day the Rada abrogated the Crimean Constitution, and abolished the presidency, and term "Republic of Crimea."[23] Once again, a full-blown crisis had been averted.

---

20 Vladislav Maltsev, "Sovsem nevezhlivye 'chelovechki,'" [Very Impolite "Little Men"] *Ukraina.ru*, April 11, 2020, https://ukraina.ru/exclusive/20200411/1027359226.html; Nikolai Gorshkov, "UK and US Always Knew Crimea Wanted to Re-join Russia," *Sputnik News*, December 28, 2018, https://sputniknews.com/20181228/uk-us-crimea-russia-1071042343.html.
21 Vladislav Maltsev, "Sovsem nevezhlivye 'chelovechki.'"
22 Nikolai Malomuzh, "Razrushiteli mifov," [Myth Busters] *Apostrof*, December 12, 2019, https://apostrophe.ua/article/politics/2019 – 12 – 12/razrushiteli-mifov-kak-ukraine-pobedit-rossiyskuyu-propagandu/29790.
23 Sergei Mirkin, "Politicheskie 'svaty,'" [Political "Matchmakers"] *Ukraina.ru*, March 31, 2021, https://ukraina.ru/history/20210331/1031004260.html.

Despite having established control over the new Crimea parliament, however, it took three more years to pass a Crimean constitution that conformed to the Ukrainian Constitution. Again, the main sticking points were the status of the Russian language, and the issue of local referenda.[24] During these three tumultuous years, Crimean parliamentarians sought to push the envelope as far as they possibly could, bombarding Kievan authorities with requests for referenda on all sorts of matters, from such petty issues as having their own time zone (so that local time could be set to Moscow, rather than Kiev), to the perennial issue of granting the Russian language official status locally.

On February 4, 1998, the Crimean parliament once again voted to have a referendum on whether the region should return to Russian jurisdiction, to restore the 1992 Crimean Constitution, and adopt Russian as the region's official language.[25] Such exceptions, however, could not be tolerated in a unitary state seeking cultural homogeneity, and so, buckling to intense pressure from Kiev, on October 21, 1998, the Crimean parliament finally mustered enough votes to ratify a new constitution that declared Ukrainian the sole official language of Crimea, specified that Crimea was an inalienable part of Ukraine, and delimited its regional powers as deriving from the Ukrainian Constitution, Ukrainian laws, and the new Crimean Constitution.[26]

This did not, however, put an end to the region's discontent. Local deputies continued to push the two hot button issues of the 1992 Crimean Constitution and the Russian language, with the unstated goal of joining Russia. That, at least, is the view of the last Ukrainian appointed Prime Minister of Crimea, Anatoly Mogiloyv, who candidly calls Crimea "a Russian region."[27] Mogilyov says he warned publicly that, if Kiev refused to grant the region more autonomy, it would bolt to Russia, something that he believes the pro-Maidan leaders in 2014 secret-

---

24 Galiya Ibragimova, "Kiev otstupil." As Malgin recalls, Kravchuk initially opposed it because it would destabilize the USSR. He therefore amended the original question from "Are you in favor of recreating the Crimean ASSR?" to "… as a subject of the USSR and a party to the Union Treaty."

25 See entry for February 4, 1998 of the *Deutsche Presse-Agentur* in "Chronology for Crimean Russians in Ukraine," *Refworld*, accessed December 21, 2021, https://www.refworld.org/docid/469f38ec2.html.

26 *Refworld*, "Chronology for Crimean Russians in Ukraine."

27 Oksana Kovalenko, " Anatoly Mogilyov o potere Kryma," [Anatoly Mogilyov on the Loss of Crimea] *Ukrainskaya pravda*, February 27, 2018, http://www.pravda.com.ua/rus/articles/2018/02/27/7172941/.

ly welcomed, because they felt it would lessen Russian influence within Ukraine.[28]

Most surveys taken since 1991 highlight the salience of this issue for Crimeans. Anatoly Karlin has conveniently compiled a list of thirty surveys taken between 1994 and 2016. Twenty-five show Russophile sentiment at over 70 percent, and five at 25–55 percent.[29] Polls conducted by the United Nations Development Program (UNDP) in Crimea between 2009 and 2011 also show a majority of Crimeans favoring reunification with Russia.[30] One of Crimea's foremost sociologists, Natalia Kiselyova, says that the percentage of Crimeans who "yearned for Russia" between 1991 and 2014 was always greater than 50 percent, while the percentage that favored Crimean regionalism was never less than 55–60 percent.[31]

This highlights an important point when considering the events that lead up to its secession, namely the importance of Crimean regional identity, which often trumped the political differences between Russians, Ukrainians, and even Crimean Tatars.[32] Figure 5.1, from late 2013, reveals the striking extent to which Crimeans gave primacy to their own regional identity.

For the status quo to change from regional autonomy within Ukraine to separation from Ukraine, therefore, there had to be a significant increase in the perception of threat to that local identity. In early 2014, a number of factors coincid-

28 Sergei Malgavko, "Ukrainskogo generala vyzvali na dopros iz-za slov o Kryme," [Ukrainian General Summoned for Questioning Because of His Words about Crimea] *RIA Krym*, August 1, 2019, https://crimea.ria.ru/world/20190801/1117087776.html.
29 Anatoly Karlin, "Trump Is Factually Right on Crimea," *The Unz Review*, July 31, 2016, https://www.unz.com/akarlin/trump-right-on-crimea/. Karlin defines Russophile sentiment as "the single most 'Russophile' option in each case, with 'Don't Know' and N/A responses discounted. The 'Adjusted' version of the referendum results consider those who abstained from voting as having voted Against."
30 Hunter Cawood, "Five Reasons Why It's Time to Recognize Crimea," *Russian International Affairs Council*, March 11, 2020, https://russiancouncil.ru/en/analytics-and-comments/columns/political-life-of-usa/five-reasons-why-it-s-time-to-recognizesrimea/; "Kvartalnyi monitoringovyi otchet," [Quarterly Monitoring Report] *UNDP Crimea*, August 2009, https://web.archive.org/web/20140502000238/http://www.undp.crimea.ua/img/content/file/monitoring_ru_2009_10–12.pdf.
31 "Krymskyi sotsioloh u pryamomu efiri rozpovila ukraintsyam, chyi Krym," [Crimean Sociologist Tells Ukrainians on Live TV, Who Crimea Belongs To] *Golos Pravdy*, October 26, 2020, https://golospravdy.eu/krimskij-sociolog-u-pryamomu-efiri-rozpovila-ukraincyam-chij-krim/.
32 Pål Kolstø and Helge Blakkisrud, eds., *Russia before and after Crimea: Nationalism and Identity 2010–17* (Edinburgh: Edinburgh University Press, 2018), 287; Vladimir Kapitsyn, "'Mladorossiiskaya' identichnost," ["Young Russian" Identity] *Cyberleninka*, August 22, 2016, https://cyberleninka.ru/article/n/mladorossiyskaya-identichnost-krym-2014–2016-gody.

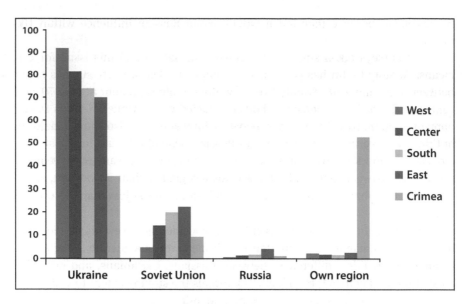

Figure 5.1: Regions Asked "What is Your Homeland?" (January 2013).
Source: Razumkov Center & Grigore Pop-Eleches and Graeme Robertson, "Do Crimeans Actually Want to Join Russia?," *The Washington Post*, March 6, 2014, https://perma.cc/Z59T-L7CD?view-mode=client-side&type=image.

ed to cause such a shift. First, the prominence of the Far Right during the Maidan. The inclusion of leading members of the Svoboda Party in the interim government afterwards only encouraged the melding of the images of the Maidan and the Far Right.[33]

---

33 "Vlasti Ukrainy priznali plan utopleniya Kryma v krovi," [Authorities in Ukraine Planned to Drown Crimea in Blood] *NK*, February 15, 2021, https://nk.org.ua/politika/vlasti-ukrainyi-priznali-plan-utopleniya-kryima-v-krovi-00294377; Aleksei Malgavko, "Eks-glava SBU rasskazal, kto vinovat v potere Kryma Ukrainoi," [The Former Head of the SBU Says Who Is to Blame for Ukraine's Loss of Crimea] *RIA Krym*, March 30, 2019, https://crimea.ria.ru/politics/20190330/1116330506.html; Inna Zolotukhina, "General Zamana: 'Nakanune godovshchiny anneksii Kryma vlastyam nuzhna novaya zhertva,'" [General Zamana: "On the Eve of the Anniversary of the Annexation of Crimea, the Authorities Need a New Victim"] *Strana.ua*, February 25, 2019, https://strana.one/articles/interview/188059-vladimir-zamana-intervju-s-opalnym-heneralom-kotoryj-ruhal-turchinova.html. In his deposition during Viktor Yanukovych's trial for treason, the former head of the general staff of the armed forces, general Yuri Ilyin, says that he appealed to the Maidan leaders for support, and was told that they intended to deal with Crimea in the harshest possible terms. According to Ilyin, Tyahnybok assured him that "They will be bathed in blood and all will understand. We will break them like a broom handle. On this issue we

Second, the violence of the Maidan itself, which evoked memories of the abusive "Friendship Trains" that Far Right activists had sent to Crimea in 1991. Expectations of similar violence in 2014 led to the organization of local self-defense forces, particularly after such prominent Far Right activists as Ihor Mosiychuk and Dmytro Korchinsky referred publicly to them.[34]

Finally, when authorities in Simferopol offered shelter in Crimea to the Ukrainian internal affairs troops and their families vilified during the Maidan, many took them up on this offer and shifted their loyalty accordingly.[35] The success of this strategy became apparent on February 27, 2014, when masked gunmen seized government buildings in Crimea. Widely reported at the time to be the work of Russian special forces, the former head of Ukrainian Security Services, Evgenii Marchuk, who had directed the take over of the Crimean parliament in 1995, insists that it was actually done by local Crimean forces.[36] The only correspondent who actually managed to get inside the building during the operation says that they identified themselves as "Self-defense of the Russian-speaking population of Crimea," a local veteran's group known to include ex-military, ex-security services, and ex-police.[37] Their actions were not so much an embrace

---

have solid support." At the time Tyahnybok's Svoboda Party was responsible for military appointments in the post-Maidan government.

34 Sergei Mirkin, "Politicheskie 'svaty'"; Vladislav Maltsev, "'Eks-pravosek' rasskazal, kak gotovil 'poezd druzhby' v Krym i Sevastopol v marte 2014-go," [Former Right Sector Activist Tells How He Was Preparing a "Friendship Train" to Crimea and Sevastopol in March 2014] *ForPost*, May 30, 2020, https://perma.cc/7NVT-42RM; *NK*, "Vlasti Ukrainy priznali plan utopleniya Kryma v krovi." Mosiichuk recalls that there was a firm intention to send volunteers to Crimea. Korchinsky, then head of the UNA-UNSO volunteer battalions, vowed that Crimea "would be either Ukrainian or depopulated."

35 "Parlament Kryma prizval yug i vostok Ukrainy vystupit edino protiv perevorota v strane," [The Parliament of Crimea Has Called on the South and East of Ukraine to Act in Unison Against the Coup in the Country] *NEWSru.com*, January 24, 2014, https://www.newsru.com/world/24jan2014/crimea.html.

36 "Krymsky parlament zakhvatil sevastopolsky spetsnaz," [The Crimean Parliament Captured By Sevastopol Special Forces] *NEWSru.com*, December 7, 2017, https://www.newsru.com/world/27feb2014/thecrimea.html; "Pryinyato postanovu 'pro utvorennya ta likvidatsiyu raioniv,'" [Resolution "On the Formation and Liquidation of Districts"] *Verkhovna Rada Ukrainy*, July 17, 2020, https://www.rada.gov.ua/news/Novyny/196122.html; "Chislennost i sostav naseleniya avtonomnoi Respubliki Krym po itogam vseukrainskoi perepisi naseleniya 2001 goda," [The Number and Composition of the Population of the Autonomous Republic of Crimea According to the Results of the All-Ukrainian Population Census of 2001] *Gosudarstvennyi komitet statistiki Ukrainy*, http://2001.ukrcensus.gov.ua/rus/results/general/nationality/crimea/.

37 "Zdaniya pravitelstva i parlamenta Kryma zakhvatili vooruzhennye lyudi v maskakh," [The Buildings of the Government and Parliament of Crimea Have Been Seized by Armed Men in Masks] *NEWSru.com*, December 7, 2017, https://www.newsru.com/world/27feb2014/crimea.html.

of Russia (although it may have been for some), and not so much a rejection of Ukraine (although it may have been a rejection of the Maidan for some), but first and foremost an affirmation of loyalty to Crimea, in light of events that made Kiev seem much more threatening.

5.1.1 Seven Days in February

According to the official Ukrainian version of events, Russian authorities had planned the annexation of Crimea for years. To this end, Russia planted moles throughout the Ukrainian military, security services, and government. The latter worked to systematically dismantle the Ukrainian military, and implemented the final stage of Russia's plan on February 20, 2014, the day before President Yanukovych agreed to relinquish power to the opposition. This day is now designated by Ukrainian law as the official beginning of the Russian military incursion.[38]

The official Crimean version of events, by contrast, stresses their initial loyalty to Ukraine, and puts the blame for their secession squarely on the unwillingness of other regions to restore law and order. They point to the Crimean parliament's appeals to Kiev throughout December and January to impose martial law in order to put an end to the seizure of government buildings by right-wing militias, the forced removal of governors, and the refusal to pay taxes to Kiev in western Ukraine.[39]

In a last ditch effort to preserve national unity, on February 12, the Crimean parliament invited the heads of all regional parliaments of Ukraine to meet in

---

38 "Pro vnesennya zmin do deyakykh zakoniv Ukrainy shchodo vyznachennya daty pochatku tymchasovoi okupatsii," [On Amending Certain Laws of Ukraine That Determine the Date of the Beginning of the Temporary Occupation] *Ofitsiinyi vebportal parlamentu Ukrainy,* September 15, 2015, https://zakon.rada.gov.ua/go/685–19; Artem Dekhtyarenko, "Viktor Yushchenko: u Zakharchenko net ni odnogo tanka," [Viktor Yushchenko: Zakharchenko Does Not Have a Single Tank] *Apostrof,* September 28, 2015, https://apostrophe.ua/article/politics/2015–09–28/viktor-yuschenko-u-zaharchenko-net-ni-odnogo-tanka-o-chem-myi-s-nim-dogovarivaemsya/2307. At the National Security and Defense Council meeting of February 28, 2014, Defense Minister Igor Tenyukh blamed former President Yushchenko for destroying the Ukrainian military. Yushchenko rejects this accusation, saying: "I think that Crimea was not taken by arms. At the time of the conflict, we had an army of 190 thousand people. It was one of the largest armies in Europe. And in terms of the number of tanks, armored personnel carriers, infantry fighting vehicles and other equipment, it had more than the armed forces of the leading Western countries. The issue was not the arsenal, obviously."

39 *NEWSru.com,* "Parlament Kryma prizval yug i vostok Ukrainy vystupit edino protiv perevorota v strane."

the Livadia Palace in Yalta, and try to find a common way forward. Konstantin Bakharev, a senior member of the Crimean parliament, notes that not a single parliament from western Ukraine responded to this invitation. After that, he says, "we understood that Crimea must take its own path."[40]

On February 20, the speaker and several members of the Crimean parliament visited government officials in Moscow. According to participant accounts, there was no mention of holding a referendum at that point, because President Yanukovych was expected at the Congress of Local Deputies from South-Eastern Ukraine in Kharkov two days later, and the Crimean delegates intended to support his efforts to form an interim government. On the day that Yanukovych left for Kharkov, however, a segment of the Maidan stormed the parliament and removed him from office. Yanukovych never actually made it to the Congress, which instead adopted a resolution encouraging local assemblies to assume full political authority until "constitutional order, and the law and rights of citizens" were restored in Kiev.[41]

February 23, however, saw a massive public protest in Sevastopol against the coup in Kiev. Its organizers demanded the right to elect their own mayor and city council, to have a local militia, and to withhold their taxes from Kiev.[42] That same day, Putin says, he and a group of four advisors began work on "returning Crimea to Russia."[43]

On February 25, several hundred protesters blocked the Crimean parliament and demanded a referendum on Crimea's independence. The next day, activists from the Crimean Tatar community also stormed the parliament. The Presidium

---

40 Yurii Snegirev, "My ne znaem, chto budet s Ukrainoi, no znaem, chto budet s Krymom," [We Do Not Know What Will Happen to Ukraine, but We Know What Will Happen to Crimea] *Rossiiskaya gazeta*, March 18, 2015, https://rg.ru/2014/03/18/baharev-site.html.

41 "Syezd deputatov v Kharkove," [Congress of Deputies in Kharkov] *NEWSru.com*, February 22, 2014, https://www.newsru.com/world/22feb2014/ukreast.html.

42 Lujack Skylark, "Russian Citizens Elect Sevastopol Pro-Russian Mayor amid Ukrainian Pro-EU Protestors," *The Moscow Times*, February 25, 2014, https://themoscowtimes.com/news/article/russian-citizen-elected-sevastopol-mayor-amid-pro-moscow-protests-in-crimea/495113.html; Taras Kuzio, ed., *Contemporary Ukraine: Dynamics of Post-Soviet Transformation* (Armonk, NY: M.E. Sharpe, 1998); Marina Perevozkina, "Aleksei Chalyi raskryl tainy prisoedineniya Kryma k Rossii," [Aleksei Chalyi Reveals the Secrets of the Annexation of Crimea by Russia] *ForPost*, March 16, 2019, https://sevastopol.su/news/aleksey-chalyy-raskryl-tayny-prisoedineniya-kryma-k-rossii. Sevastopol has no mayor. Instead, the Chairman of the Sevastopol City State Administration, who is appointed by the President of Ukraine, fulfills this role. The plan was to remove existing authorities in the city, then appeal for Russian support.

43 Aleksei Druzhinin, "Putin obyasnil, v svyazi s chem prinyal reshenie vozvratit Krym v sostav Rossii," [Putin Explains Why He Decided to Return Crimea to Russia] *TASS*, March 9, 2015, https://tass.ru/politika/1816491.

of the Crimean parliament issued a statement deploring these "incidents of pressure, intimidation and coercion," saying that they would only increase confrontation within society.[44]

On February 27, armed gunmen seized several government buildings in Crimea and raised the Russian flag. The Crimean parliament, meeting in emergency session, dismissed the Crimean government, and replaced its Kiev-appointed prime minister with Sergei Aksyonov, who backed Yanukovych as the legitimate president of Ukraine.[45] As one of its first acts, it set May 25 as the date of a referendum on restoring the 1992 Crimean Constitution, with Crimea as part of Ukraine.[46] According to Crimean parliamentary spokesman, Olga Sulnikova, the parliament had the concurrence of President Yanukovych for this referendum, and was therefore acting in accordance with Ukrainian law.[47]

5.1.2 The Interim Government Fails to Respond

On February 28, the National Security and Defense Council of Ukraine met in emergency session to decide what to do about Russia's military intervention, and possible annexation of Crimea. The transcript of this meeting was made public as part of Yanukovych's trial for treason.[48]

---

44 "Rossiiskie deputaty sobirayutsya zashchitit Krym ot 'politicheskogo Chernobylya,'" [Russian Deputies Are Preparing to Protect Crimea from a "Political Chernobyl"] *NEWSru.com*, February 25, 2014, https://www.newsru.com/world/25feb2014/crimea.html.

45 "Verkhovnyi sovet Kryma otpravil v otstavku pravitelstvo," [The Supreme Soviet of Crimea Dismisses the Government] *NEWSru.com*, February 27, 2014, https://www.newsru.com/world/27feb2014/krimsovmin.html.

46 "Krym poyasnil izmenenie voprosov referenduma 'zlymi slovami' Kieva," [Crimea Explains the Change in Referendum Questions as Due to Kiev's "Mean Words"] *NEWSru.com*, March 8, 2014, https://www.newsru.com/world/08mar2014/referendum.html.

47 "Novym premyerom Kryma izbran lider 'Russkogo Edinstva' Aksyonov," [The Leader of Russian Unity, Aksyonov, Is Elected the New Prime Minister of Crimea] *Business Information Network*, February 27, 2014, https://bin.ua/top/152391-novym-premerom-kryma-izbran-lider-russkogo.html; Aleksei Druzhinin, "Kandidatura Aksyonova na post glavy Kryma byla soglasovana s Yanukovichem v Fevrale 2014 Goda," [Aksyonov's Candidacy for the Post of Head of Crimea Was Agreed Upon with Yanukovych in February 2014] *TASS*, March 10, 2016, https://tass.ru/politika/2728698.

48 "Stenohrama zasidannya Rady natsionalnoi bezpeky i oborony pid holovuvannyam v.o. Prezydenta Ukrainy, Holovy Verkhovnoi Rady Ukrainy O.V. Turchynova," [Transcript of the Meeting of the National Security and Defense Council, Chaired by Acting President of Ukraine, Chairman of the Supreme Rada of Ukraine O.V. Turchynov] July 28, 2014, http://www.rnbo.gov.ua/files/2016/stenogr.pdf.

The head of the Ukrainian Security Service, Valentyn Nalyvaichenko, informed the participants that the Ukrainian armed forces in Crimea had rejected the authority of the Maidan and refused to execute its orders. Minister of the Interior Arsen Avakov stated that most Crimeans hold "a pro-Russian and anti-Ukrainian position."

This pessimistic assessment was confirmed when, on March 2, the head of the Ukrainian Navy, the Head of the Security Service of Crimea, the Head of Internal Affairs in the Crimea, and the Acting Chief of the Ukrainian Border Guard all switched their allegiance from Kiev to the Republic of Crimea and its people.[49] Over the next two weeks, 189 Ukrainian military units stationed in Crimea raised the Russian flag.[50] Igor Tenyukh, Ukraine's defense minister at the time, estimates that 80 percent of the Ukrainian army "immediately went over to the other side."[51] His successor, Viktor Muzhenko, later lowered this figure to 70 percent.[52]

Understanding that the military situation was hopeless, Acting Speaker and President Oleksandr Turchynov suggested an approach that has since become the official government position: "We need to dispel this myth that the Crimeans raised a rebellion against Ukraine. These are not Crimeans. It's solely a [Russian]

---

49 "Glava VMS Ukrainy kontr-admiral Berezovsky prines prisyagu na vernost narodu Kryma," [Rear Admiral Berezovsky, Head of the Ukrainian Navy, Swears Allegiance to the People of Crimea] *NEWSru.com*, March 2, 2014, https://www.newsru.com/world/02mar2014/vmc.html.

50 "Minoborony: flagi Rossii v Krymu podnyali 189 podrazdelenii vooruzhennykh sil Ukrainy," [Ministry of Defense: 189 Units of the Armed Forces of Ukraine Have Raised the Russian Flag in Crimea] *NEWSru.com*, March 23, 2014, https://txt.newsru.com/russia/23mar2014/flagi.html.

51 Olga Talova, "Viktor Tenyukh: 'Vmesto togo, chtoby strelyat po zakhvatchikam, 10 tysyach krymskikh voennykh srazu pereshli na storonu vrag,'" [Viktor Tenyukh: "Instead of Shooting at the Invaders, 10,000 Crimean Soldiers Immediately Went Over to the Enemy"] *Obozrenie Russky Dozor*, February 8, 2018, https://rusdozor.ru/2018/02/08/viktor-tenyux-vmesto-togo-chtoby-strelyat-po-zaxvatchikam-10-tysyach-krymskix-voennyx-srazu-pereshli-na-storonu-vraga_541984/; Ollie Richardson, "Former Ukrainian Defence Minister Igor Tenyukh: Ukrainian Troops Refused to Shoot Russians in Crimea in 2014," *Stalker Zone*, March 3, 2019, https://www.stalkerzone.org/former-ukrainian-defence-minister-igor-tenyukh-ukrainian-troops-refused-to-shoot-russians-in-crimea-in-2014/.

52 Alena Roshchenko, "Muzhenko: vo vremya zakhvata Kryma byl boi na materike," [Muzhenko: During the Capture of the Crimea There Was a Battle on the Mainland] *Ukrainskaya pravda*, March 10, 2017, http://www.pravda.com.ua/rus/news/2017/03/10/7137690/; "Turchinov zayavil, chto tolko 29,6% soldat i ofitserov VSU i 0,8% sotrudnikov MVD ne predali Ukrainu vo vremya okkupatsii Kryma," [Turchynov Says that Only 29.6% of the Soldiers and Officers of the Armed Forces of Ukraine and 0.8% of the Employees of the Ministry of Internal Affairs Did Not Betray Ukraine during the Occupation of Crimea] *Gordon.ua*, February 28, 2017, https://gordonua.com/news/crimea/turchinov-zayavil-chto-tolko-296-soldat-i-oficerov-vsu-i-08-sotrudnikov-mvd-ne-predali-ukrainu-vo-vremya-okkupacii-kryma-175897.html.

military operation against a sovereign country ... It is very important to recite and
to propagate this objective view of events to Ukraine and all the world."⁵³

5.1.3 The Tide Turns in Favor of Secession

On March 1, 2014, as the new Crimean Prime Minister, Aksyonov appeals to Russian President Vladimir Putin "to provide assistance in securing peace," and the
Russian upper house of the parliament quickly approved the use of Russian military forces in Ukraine.⁵⁴ Russia also submitted a letter by President Yanukovych,
dated March 1, to the UN Security Council, asking that Russian armed forces
enter his country to restore "law and order, and stability, and to protect the population of Ukraine."⁵⁵

Russia already had a significant military presence on the peninsula, although to this day Russian officials insist that they never exceeded the amount
permitted under the Black Sea Fleet Agreement with Ukraine, namely 25,000
troops.⁵⁶ Ukraine, however, puts the number of Russian troops in Crimea at

53 RNBO.gov.ua, "Stenohrama zasidannya Rady natsionalnoi bezpeky i oborony pid holovuvannyam v.o. Prezydenta Ukrainy, Holovy Verkhovnoi Rady Ukrainy O.V. Turchynova."
54 "Ukraine Crisis: Crimea Leader Appeals to Putin for Help," *BBC News*, March 1, 2014, http://
webcache.googleusercontent.com/search?q=cache:Yd4DHRHrossJ:https://www.bbc.com/news/
world-europe-26397323&hl=en&gl=ua&strip=1&vwsrc=0.
55 "Pismo postoyannogo predstavitelya Rossiiskoi Federatsii Organizatsii Obedinennykh Natsii
ot 3 Marta 2014 goda na imya generalnogo sekretarya," [Letter Dated March 3, 2014 from the Permanent Representative of the Russian Federation to the United Nations in the Name of the Secretary General] March 3, 2014; V. Yanukovich, "Prilozhenie k Pismu Postoyannogo Predstavitelya
Rossiiskoi Pri Organizatsii Obyedinennykh Natsii Ot 3 Marta Goda Na Imya Generalnogo Sekretarya," [Appendix to the Letter of March 3, Permanent Representative of the Russian Federation
to the United Nations, Addressed to the Secretary General], https://digitallibrary.un.org/record/
766526?ln=en.
56 "Spetspredstavitel prezidenta Rossii," [Special Representative of the President of Russia] *Uk-
raina.ru*, August 8, 2018, https://ukraina.ru/news/20180808/1020774436.html; "Russia's 25,000-
Troop Allowance & Other Facts You May Not Know about Crimea," *RT International*, March 4,
2014, https://www.rt.com/news/russian-troops-crimea-ukraine-816/; "V Krymu propadaet
svyaz, nebo zakryto dlya grazhdanskikh sudov, Moskvu obvinili v anneksii," [In Crimea, Communication Is Being Lost, the Sky Is Closed for Civilian Ships, Moscow is Accused of Annexa-
tion] *NEWSru.com*, February 28, 2014, https://www.newsru.com/world/28feb2014/telekom.html;
"Putin: nashi voennye 'vstali za spinoi' samooborony Kryma," [Putin: Our Military "Stood Behind" Self-Defense of Crimea] *BBC News Russkaya sluzhba*, April 17, 2014, https://
www.bbc.com/russian/russia/2014/04/140417_putin_phone_line; Robert Parry, "Crimeans Keep
Saying No to Ukraine," *Consortium News*, March 22, 2015, https://consortiumnews.com/2015/
03/22/crimeans-keep-saying-no-to-ukraine/.

the time at over 30,000.[57] Aksyonov, meanwhile, puts the number of Crimean self-defense forces loyal to the new government at roughly 11,000.[58]

Aksyonov then announces that the date of the referendum to restore the 1992 Crimean Constitution will be moved up, from May 25 to March 30. At that point, it still does not include an option to leave Ukraine.[59] Between March 1 and March 6, however, after it becomes clear that Ukrainian forces in Crimea are not going to fight, and are indeed switching sides, the popular mood in Crimea swings decisively in favor of secession.

On March 6, the Crimean parliament votes unanimously in favor of Crimea joining Russia, and to submit this decision to a referendum. The initial referendum is scratched, and a new referendum, this time on Crimea joining Russia, is now set for March 16, 2014. With a voter turnout of 83 percent, 97 percent vote to join Russia. While this referendum did not meet Western standards, there can be little doubt, Gwendolyn Sasse notes, that it reflected the will of the majority of the Crimean population at the time.[60]

When reflecting on why so many Crimeans chose to leave Ukraine in March 2014, analysts point to several factors. Some stress the role of the Russian military, while others point to Kiev's historical neglect of the region. Considering the long history of Crimean attempts to obtain greater autonomy from Kiev, I feel that Crimea left because a fractured Ukraine could no longer prevent it from leaving.[61]

By early March, Kiev's authority in Crimea had ceased to exist. The problem, as Sergei Pashinsky – at the time head of the Ukrainian presidential administration – points out, was that Ukrainian forces were mostly manned by locals. In

---

57 "Ukraine Says Russian Troops in Crimea Have Doubled to 30,000," *Independent*, March 7, 2014, https://www.independent.ie/world-news/ukraine-says-russian-troops-in-crimea-have-doubled-to-30000 – 30071613.html; "Moscow Asks for Restoration of Yanukovych-Signed Agreement as Kerry Heads for Kiev," *Fox News*, March 20, 2015, https://www.foxnews.com/world/moscow-asks-for-restoration-of-yanukovych-signed-agreement-as-kerry-heads-for-kiev.
58 "V protivostoyanii s Kievom Krym perekhodit ot samooborony k oborone," [In the Confrontation with Kiev, Crimea Is Moving from Self-Defense to Defense] *NEWSru.com*, March 4, 2014, https://www.newsru.com/world/04mar2014/crimea_ministery_defense.html.
59 "Referendum o statuse Kryma proydet 30 marta," [The Referendum on the Status of Crimea Will Be Held on March 30] *NEWSru.com*, March 1, 2014, https://txt.newsru.com/world/01mar2014/referendum.html.
60 Gwendolyn Sasse, "ZOiS Report – Terra Incognita – The Public Mood in Crimea," *Zois Berlin*, November 3, 2017, https://www.zois-berlin.de/fileadmin/media/Dateien/3-Publikationen/ZOiS_-Reports/2017/ZOiS_Report_3_2017.pdf.
61 Maksim Vruchnyi, "Politolog nazval glavnye prichiny poteri Ukrainoi Kryma," [Political Scientist Names the Main Reasons for Ukraine's Loss of Crimea] *Riafan*, October 2, 2020, https://riafan.ru/1317269-politolog-nazval-glavnye-prichiny-poteri-ukrainoi-kryma.

their mind, he says, they were righting a historical injustice by rejoining Russia.[62] The role of the Russian Black Sea Fleet was important, though not for the reasons usually attributed to it. It never actually had to enter into direct conflict with Ukrainian forces, but its mere presence reassured Crimeans that Russia would protect them, if necessary.[63]

Later, Putin would add an explicitly geopolitical motive for Russia's intervention:

> We were once promised ... that after the reunification of Germany NATO would not expand Eastward ... And then it began ... our decision on Crimea was partly related to this as well ... if we do nothing, then some day, guided by these exact same principles, Ukraine will be dragged into NATO, and then we'll be told: it is none of your business ... for us it has geopolitical significance – Russia will be practically pushed out of the Black Sea region.[64]

5.1.4 Assessing the Legitimacy of Annexation of Crimea

In the final analysis, one's assessment of the legitimacy of the annexation is rooted in one's assessment of who held legitimate authority in Crimea and in Kiev at the time. According to Kiev, the acting post-Maidan government that had ousted President Yanukovych was legitimate. Moreover, although the right to a referendum did exist under the Ukrainian Constitution, no legal mechanism for implementing this right had been developed. Such a referendum could, theoretically, be initiated by "a group of citizens," but not by a government body such as the Crimean parliament. Finally, the issue of secession could not be submitted to a popular vote.[65]

62 "Zamana: V 2016–2017 godakh v minoborony Ukrainy unichtozhili dokumenty, kotorye kasayutsya primeneniya Rossiiskoi armii v Krymu vo vremya anneksii," [Zamana: In 2016–2017, the Ministry of Defense of Ukraine Destroyed Documents Related to the Use of the Russian Army in Crimea during the Annexation] *Gordon.ua*, November 9, 2020, https://gordonua.com/news/politics/zamana-v-2016–2017-godah-v-minoborony-ukrainy-unichtozhili-dokumenty-kotorye-kasajutsja-primenenija-rossijskoj-armii-v-krymu-vo-vremja-anneksii-1526576.html.
63 "Premier Kryma priznal: vazhnye obekty okhranyayut rossiiskie voennye," [Prime Minister of Crimea Admits: Important Objects Are Being Guarded by the Russian Military] *NEWSru.com*, March 1, 2014, https://www.newsru.com/world/01mar2014/ruswarriors.html.
64 "Pryamaya liniya s Vladimirom Putinym," [Direct Line with Vladimir Putin], *Kremlin.ru*, April 17, 2014, http://kremlin.ru/events/president/news/20796.
65 "Zhiteli Kryma khotyat reshat sudbu poluostrova na referendume," [Residents of Crimea Want to Decide the Fate of the Peninsula in a Referendum] *NEWSru.com*, February 27, 2014, https://www.newsru.com/world/27feb2014/referendum.html.

The Crimean view, by contrast, is that the Crimean Constitution, approved by the Rada on October 21, 1998, gave Crimea the sovereign right to conduct local referenda.[66] In addition, the Crimean parliament viewed the new government in Kiev as illegitimate. It had therefore assumed plenipotentiary authority for the region, in accordance with the resolution of the Kharkov Congress of Local Deputies, "until constitutional order was restored in Kiev." When it became apparent that this was not going to happen, all that was left was to legalize Crimea's independence through the mechanism of a local referendum. According to Vladimir Konstantinov, the Head of the Crimean Parliament, that right existed in the 1998 Crimean Constitution, and could be invoked "if the Ukrainian State legally ceased to exist."[67]

At the same time, the government of Crimea also invoked the right to self-determination under Article 1 of the United Nations Charter. Although traditionally international law has given precedence to state sovereignty over those of separatist claimants, in its July 22, 2010 ruling on Kosovo, the International Court of Justice (ICJ) set a new standard, stating that international law contained no "prohibition on declarations of independence." Crimean separatists argued that, under this standard, they had the same right to declare their independence from Ukraine that the Kosovars did when they declared their independence from Serbia.[68]

---

66 "Konstitutsiya Avtonomnoi Respubliki Krym," [Constitution of the Autonomous Republic of Crimea] *Ofitsiinyi vebportal parlamentu Ukraini*, May 26, 2010, https://zakon.rada.gov.ua/go/rb239k002–98. The appointment and conduct of local referenda is the competence of the Crimean Autonomous Republic (CAR) [Sect. 2, chap. 5, art. 18, pt. 1, para. 7]. Local referenda supersede the authority of the Supreme Council of the CAR [Sect. 3, chap. 6, art. 26, pt. 1], and the decision to hold a republican referendum lies within the competence of the Supreme Council of the CAR [Sect. 3, chap. 6, art. 26, pt. 3, para. 3]. The conduct and authority of a local referendum could thus be interpreted as a sovereign right of the CAR. Finally, Sect. 5, art. 48, pt. 2, specifies that the Supreme Rada CAR may propose changes to the status and authority of the CAR on the basis of a "consultative republican (local) referendum." The word "consultative," presumably meaning in consultation with the Supreme Rada of Ukraine, appears only this once among seven other appearances of the word "referendum."

67 Vladimir Konstantinov, *To Go One's Own Way* (Simferopol: Salta, 2017), 36.

68 "Yury Fedotov: We Risk Danger by Granting Kosovo Independence," *The Independent*, December 19, 2007, https://www.independent.co.uk/voices/commentators/yury-fedotov-we-risk-danger-by-granting-kosovo-independence-765912.html. As Fedotov noted presciently in 2007, "Once the principle of self-determination has been established as being above the principle of territorial integrity, it will be hard to argue why any territory within any nation state should not be able to declare independence."

The legality of the annexation is of course only a small part of the argument over its legitimacy, which is dominated by great power rivalry. This is amply demonstrated by the ease with which the sides have flipped in their assessments of the new ICJ standard on self-declarations of independence when the object became Crimea instead of Kosovo. Russia flipped from opposition to support of the new standard, while many Western nations flipped from support to opposition. If more evidence were needed that nation-states take a purely utilitarian approach to international law, one need look no further that US Secretary of State Mike Pompeo's explanation of America's 2019 decision to recognize Israel's annexation of the Golan Heights. According to Pompeo, "We were simply recognizing that reality on the ground and the history that existed in that particular space" which, he then pointedly added, makes it completely different from Russia's annexation of Crimea.[69]

In a similar vein, while legal scholars have, by-and-large, argued that Crimea's declaration of independence from Ukraine was illegal, several senior statesmen have argued in favor of recognizing Russia's *de facto* jurisdiction over Crimea.[70] They typically base their arguments on Russia's historical ties

---

69 "Pompeo on Crimea and Golan Heights – Recognizing The Reality on the Ground and the History That Existed in That Particular Space," *U.S. Department of State*, November 16, 2019, https://www.state.gov/in-tribute-to-human-freedom/.

70 Legal scholars who have argued that the annexation could be considered legal, include: Luca J. Uberti, "Crimea and Kosovo – The Delusions of Western Military Interventionism," *Opendemocracy*, March, 24, 2014, https://www.opendemocracy.net/en/odr/crimea-and-kosovo-delusions-of-western-military-interventionism-nato-putin-annexation-legal/; Peter Hilpold, "Die Ukraine-Krise aus völkerrechtlicher Sicht," [The Ukraine Crisis from the Perspective of International Law] *Swiss Review of International and European Law* 25, no. 2 (2015): 171–181, http://www.szier.ch/index.php?id=99; Kirsten Engelstad, "Utsettes også vi for propaganda?," [Are We Being Exposed to Propaganda?] *Aftenposten*, November 17, 2017, https://www.aftenposten.no/meninger/debatt/i/79Wa8/krim-der-paastand-moeter-paastand-kirsten-engelstad; Vladimir T. Kabyshev and Tamara V. Zametina, "Prinyatie v Rossiiskuyu Federatsiyu Respubliki Krym i goroda Sevastopolya – vosstanovlenie istoricheskoi spravedlivosti: konstitutsionno-pravovoi analiz," [Admission to the Russian Federation of the Republic of Crimea and the City of Sevastopol – Restoration of Historical Justice: A Constitutional and Legal Analysis] *Vestnik SGYUA* 2, no. 97 (2014), https://cyberleninka.ru/article/n/prinyatie-v-rossiyskuyu-federatsiyu-respubliki-krym-i-goroda-sevastopolya-vosstanovlenie-istoricheskoy-spravedlivosti; Reinhard Merkel, "Die Krim und das Völkerrecht: Kühle Ironie der Geschichte," [Crimea and International Law: The Cool Irony of History] *Frankfurter Allgemeine*, April 8, 2014, https://www.faz.net/aktuell/feuilleton/debatten/die-krim-und-das-voelkerrecht-kuehle-ironie-der-geschichte-12884464.html; Paul Schreyer, "'Annexion der Krim': Prof. Merkel widerspricht Georg Restle," ["The Annexation of Crimea": Prof. Merkel Contradicts Georg Restle] *Paul Schreyer*, May 29, 2018, https://paulschreyer.wordpress.com/2018/05/29/annexion-der-krim-prof-merkel-widerspricht-georg-restle/; Reinhard Merkel and Jan Philipp Reemstma, "Von Nachbarn, Töchtern

to the peninsula, or the fact that the referendum, for all its flaws, clearly demonstrated the desire of the Crimean people. The list of political dignitaries who have said the same thing *after* leaving office is even more impressive, and includes two German chancellors, two presidents of France, two US presidents, the presidents of Czechia, Georgia, Kirgizia, Moldova, and Poland, as well the prime ministers of several NATO countries and Japan.[71]

Und Pistolen," [Of Neighbors, Daughters, and Pistols] *Eurozine*, September 3, 2014, https://www.eurozine.com/von-nachbarn-tochtern-und-pistolen/; "How the Badinter Commission on Yugoslavia Laid the Roots for Crimea's Secession from Ukraine," *EUROPP*, February 20, 2015, https://blogs.lse.ac.uk/europpblog/2015/02/20/how-the-badinter-commission-on-yugoslavia-laid-the-roots-for-crimeas-secession-from-ukraine/; Eric Posner, "What to Do about Crimea? Nothing," *Slate*, March 27, 2014, https://slate.com/news-and-politics/2014/03/sanctions-against-russia-why-everything-we-are-doing-about-crimea-is-completely-wrong.html; Georgii B. Romanovsky, "Itogi vossoedineniya Kryma s Rossiei: pravovye voprosy," [The Results of the Re-unification of Crimea with Russia: Legal Issues] *Nauka. Obschestvo. Gosudarstvo* 4, no. 3 (15) (2016): 8, https://cyberleninka.ru/article/n/itogi-vossoedineniya-kryma-s-rossiey-pravovye-vo-prosy; "Putin, Krim und Psychologie," [Putin, Crimea and Psychology] *Globus Deutschland*, March 13, 2019, https://www.globusdeutschland.de/2019/03/13/putin-krim-und-psychologie-funf-jahre-mit-russia/; Grigory Tsykunov, "Historical and Legal Bases of Crimea's Inclusion in the Russian Federation," 550–555; Bernd Murawski, "Die ungelöste Krim-Frage als Hemm-schuh," [The Unresolved Crimean Question as a Stumbling Block] *Heise online*, November 7, 2019, https://www.heise.de/tp/features/Die-ungeloeste-Krim-Frage-als-Hemmschuh-4578550.html; Norbert Rouland, "À qui la Crimée appartient-elle?," [Who Does Crimea Belong To?] *The Conversation*, July 23, 2020, http://theconversation.com/a-qui-la-crimee-appartient-elle-le-regard-dun-juriste-142927; Christian Marxsen, "Crimea's Declaration of Independence," *European Journal of International Law: Talk!*, March 18, 2014, https://www.ejiltalk.org/crimeas-declaration-of-independence/; Grigory Ivanov and Ivan Chikharev, "Diplomat s ruchkoi," [Diplomat with a Pen] *Ukraina.ru*, September 25, 2021, https://ukraina.ru/exclusive/20210925/1032316524.html; François Gruber Magitot, "The Crimean Referendum: A Democratic Secession or an Imperial Annexation?," 2017, https://www.academia.edu/35807218/The_Crimean_referen-dum_A_democratic_secession_or_an_imperial_annexation; Michael Geistlinger, "Der Beitritt der Republik Krim zur Russländischen Föderation aus der Warte des Selbstbestimmungsrechts der Völker," [The Republic of Crimea Joining the Russian Federation from the Point of View of the Right of Peoples to Self-Determination] *Archiv des Völkerrechts* 52, no. 2 (June 2014): 175–204; Peter Ørebech, "International Law and the Crimea," *Radikal Portal*, 8 June 2017.

71 "Rivoluzione di Maidan falsa e Crimea russa," [The Maidan Is a False Revolution and Crimea Is Russian] *Corriere della Sera*, July 22, 2018, https://www.corriere.it/politica/18_luglio_22/frasi-salvini-crimea-ucraina-convoca-ambasciatore-italiano-9222baf6–8dae-11e8–8382-fa27f64-b6a47.shtml; "Gerhard Schröder: Kein Russischer Präsident Wird Die Krim Wieder Aus Russland Ausgliedern," [Gerhard Schroeder: No Russian President Will Ever Let Crimea Leave Russia] *Os-texperte*, September 21, 2017, https://ostexperte.de/schroeder-bundeswehr-im-baltikum/; "Hel-mut Schmidt verteidigt in Krim-Krise Putins Ukraine-Kurs," [Helmut Schmidt Defends Putin's Ukraine Course in the Crimea Crisis] *Der Spiegel*, March 26, 2014, sec. Ausland, https://www.spiegel.de/politik/ausland/helmut-schmidt-verteidigt-in-krim-krise-putins-ukraine-kurs-a-

Given this vast gap between legal and political assessments, one might think that what the people in Crimea today think of their status would be of particular interest. Most Western politicians, however, have taken the position that Crimea's vote for Ukrainian independence in December 1991 trumps anything that has taken place in the region since then, and especially since 2014.[72] This is also the Ukrainian government's official position.[73]

960834.html; "Eks-premyer Yaponii – referendum v Krymu otrazil volyu naroda," [Ex-Prime Minister of Japan – the Referendum in the Crimea Reflected the Will of the People] *RT na russkom*, March 12, 2015, https://russian.rt.com/article/79030; "Lider prezydentskoi honki Moldovy zayaviv, schho Krym nalezhit Rosii," [The Leader of the Presidential Race in Moldova Says Crimea Belongs to Russia] *Evropeiskaya pravda*, October 25, 2016, https://www.eurointegration.com.ua/news/2016/10/25/7056403/; "Crimea Cannot Be Returned to Ukraine, Czech President Says," *Reuters*, September 9, 2016, https://www.reuters.com/article/us-ukraine-crisis-crimea-czech-idUSKCN11F184; Anna Sous, "Cherchil by skazal, chto Krym russki," [Churchill Would Say that Crimea Is Russian] *Radio Svoboda*, March 7, 2016, https://www.svoboda.org/a/27585655.html; Alberto Nardelli, "How Nicolas Sarkozy Went from Fierce Putin Critic to Ardent Admirer," *BuzzFeed*, November 19, 2016, https://www.buzzfeed.com/albertonardelli/tu-vuo-fa-l-americain; Isabelle Lasserre, "Beseda s Valeri Giscard D'Estaign," [Conversation with Valerie Giscard D'Estaign] *Inosmi.ru*, February 17, 2015, https://inosmi.ru/world/20150304/226636185.html; Alberto Nardelli and Julia Ioffe, "Trump Told G7 Leaders That Crimea Is Russian Because Everyone Speaks Russian in Crimea," *BuzzFeed News*, June 14, 2018, https://www.buzzfeednews.com/article/albertonardelli/trump-russia-crimea; "Jimmy Carter o vstreche s Vladimirom Putinym," [Jimmy Carter on His Meeting with Vladimir Putin] *E-News*, April 30, 2015, https://e-news.su/mnenie-i-analitika/56941-dzhimmi-karter-o-vstreche-s-vladimirom-putinym.html; John Helmer, "Radoslaw Sikorski Sees the Light in Eastern Ukraine," *Dances with Bears*, July 6, 2016, http://johnhelmer.net/radoslav-sikorski-sees-the-light-in-eastern-ukraine-why-he-dumped-kiev-for-washington/; "Sikorsky: vozvraschenie Donbassa i Kryma nevygodno Ukraine," [Sikorsky: The Return of Donbass and Crimea Is Disadvantageous for Ukraine] *Inosmi.ru*, May 20, 2016, https://inosmi.ru/politic/20160520/236607098.html; Aleksei Kovalsky, "Burdzhanadze: Krym – chast Rossii, u Ukrainy net shansov," [Burjanadze: Crimea Is Part of Russia, Ukraine Has No Chance] *24SMI*, July 10, 2015, https://24smi.org/news/27999-burdzhanadze-krym-chast-rossii-u-ukra-newsya-pol.html; Sergei Sidorenko, "Kvasnievsky: eta voina, esli sluchitsya, budet strashnoi, v tom chisle po kolichestvu zhertv," [Kwasniewski: This War, if It Happens, Will Be Terrible, Including in the Number of Victims] *NewsLand*, April 10, 2015, https://newsland.com/community/129/content/kvasnevskii-eta-voina-esli-sluchitsia-budet-strashnoi-v-tom-chisle-po-kolichestvu-zhertv/3404009.
72 "Rede von Bundeskanzlerin Merkel Beim 3. Deutsch-Ukrainischen Wirtschaftsforum am 29 November 2018 in Berlin," [Speech by Federal Chancellor Merkel at the 3rd German-Ukrainian Economic Forum on November 29, 2018 in Berlin] *Presse- und Informationsamt der Bundesregierung*, November 29, 2018, https://www.bundesregierung.de/breg-de/suche/rede-von-bundeskanzlerin-merkel-beim-3-deutsch-ukrainischen-wirtschaftsforum-am-29-november-2018-in-berlin-1555732. According to Merkel, "Ukraine decided by referendum after the collapse of the Soviet Union to become independent. Crimea participated in this referendum and Crimea also made the same choice, to belong to Ukraine." It would be more accurate to say that after Crimea

Despite this, recent polls, including those sponsored by Western organizations, consistently show a high level of support for reunification with Russia. Thus, a Pew poll from April 2014 showed that 91 percent of Crimean respondents believed the 2014 referendum was free and fair. While only 30 percent of Ukrainians overall felt that Kiev should accept the results of the Crimean referendum, 88 percent of Crimeans felt they should.[74] A June 2014 poll, this one from Gallup, found nearly 83 percent of the Crimean population (94 percent of ethnic Russians and 68 percent of ethnic Ukrainians) thought the 2014 referendum reflected

---

voted to separate from the USSR in its referendum in January 1991, it agreed to be part of Ukraine as an autonomous region with extensive local self-government. Its attempts to realize this autonomy, however, were repeatedly undermined by Kiev, and in 1995 undone by force. Since then, the region's elective representatives have been in more or less open confrontation with Kiev over issues of cultural identity that might have been resolved by restoring autonomy. When Kiev adopted an even more nationalistic stance in 2014, Crimea chose divorce.

73 "Pid chas psevdoreferendumu v Krymu naspravdi lyshe 15% hromadyan xotily pryyednannya do Rosiyi," [During the Pseudo-Referendum in Crimea, in Fact, Only 15% of Citizens Wanted to Join Russia] *TSN.ua*, May 5, 2014, https://tsn.ua/politika/pid-chas-psevdoreferendumu-v-krimu-naspravdi-lishe-15-gromadyan-hotili-priyednatisya-do-rosiyi-348108.html; Alexey Tokarev, "The Electoral History of the Post-Soviet Crimea: From USSR to Russia," *Cyberleninka.ru*, 2015, https://cyberleninka.ru/article/n/elektoralnaya-istoriya-postsovetskogo-kryma-ot-ussr-do-rossii; "Dynamyka otnosheniya naseleniya Ukrainy k Rossii i naseleniya Rossii k Ukraine," [Attitudinal Trends among the Population of Ukraine to Russia and the Population of Russia to Ukraine] *Kiev International Institute of Sociology*, June 27, 2013, http://www.kiis.com.ua/?lang=rus&cat=reports&id=177; Dmytro Kuleba, "The Peril of Polling in Crimea," *Foreign Affairs*, August 18, 2020, https://www.foreignaffairs.com/articles/ukraine/2020–04–21/peril-polling-crimea; John O'Loughlin, Gerard Toal, and Kristin M. Bakke, "To Russia with Love," *Foreign Affairs*, April 3, 2020, https://www.foreignaffairs.com/articles/ukraine/2020–04–03/russia-love. The Ukrainian press has also reported that a statement appeared briefly on the web site of the Russian Presidential Council for the Development of Civil Society and Human Rights, to the effect that only 30 percent of Crimeans participated in the referendum, and that only half of those voted for reunification. A telephone survey done two days before the referendum, by GFK Ukraine, however, reported that 70.6 percent intended to vote in favor of reunification, and only 10.8 percent against it.

74 "2015 Russia-Ukraine Conflict: Do People in Crimea Regret Their Decision to Be a Part of Russia?," *Quora*, accessed March 25, 2016, https://www.quora.com/2015-Russia-Ukraine-Conflict-Do-people-in-Crimea-regret-their-decision-to-be-a-part-of-Russia; James Bell, Katie Simmons, and Russ Oates, "Despite Concerns about Governance, Ukrainians Want to Remain One Country," *Pew Research Center's Global Attitudes Project*, May 8, 2014, https://www.pewresearch.org/global/2014/05/08/despite-concerns-about-governance-ukrainians-want-to-remain-one-country/.

the views of the people.[75] A spring 2017 survey conducted by the German-based Center for East European and International Studies (ZOiS), found that, if asked to vote again today, 79 percent would cast the same vote.[76]

Especially noteworthy are the surveys by Gerard Toal and John O'Loughlin (sometimes joined by Gwendolyn Sasse and Kristin Bakke) taken between late 2014 and 2019. They show that the decision to join Russia remains popular among all ethnic groups in Crimea.[77] Among the reasons they point to are that the majority of Crimeans do not experience Russian rule as oppressive, alien, or unwelcome, and that many Crimeans still hold a very negative opinion of the 2014 Maidan.[78] In addition, the Russian government's massive investment in Crimea's infrastructure has resulted in it becoming one of the fastest-growing regions of Russia, which has increased optimism among all ethnic groups.[79]

Most striking has been the turnaround in attitude of Crimean Tatars. Toal and his colleagues found that the proportion of Tatars who indicated that they thought being part of Russia would make them better off, rose from 50 percent in 2014 to 81 percent in 2019.[80] These figures are supported by a 2017 survey by Russia's Federal Agency for Ethnic Affairs, which showed that three-quarters of Crimean Tatars are pleased with their life since Crimea became a part of Russia.[81]

As with the general population, the reasons seem to stem from a mixture of pragmatism and new investments in areas of particular concern to them. *The Guardian* noted that "in the incomplete year of 2014, Russia spent as much as Ukraine did in the previous seven years on issues of housing and support for Cri-

---

75 Kenneth Rapoza, "One Year after Russia Annexed Crimea, Locals Prefer Moscow to Kiev," *Forbes*, March 20, 2015, https://www.forbes.com/sites/kenrapoza/2015/03/20/one-year-after-russia-annexed-crimea-locals-prefer-moscow-to-kiev/.
76 *Der Globus Deutschland*, "Putin, Krim und Psychologie."
77 Gerard Toal, John O'Loughlin, and Kristin M. Bakke, "Six Years and $20 Billion in Russian Investment Later, Crimeans Are Happy with Russian Annexation," *The Washington Post*, March 18, 2020, https://www.washingtonpost.com/politics/2020/03/18/six-years-20-billion-russian-investment-later-crimeans-are-happy-with-russian-annexation/; Gwendolyn Sasse, "ZOiS Report – Terra Incognita – The Public Mood in Crimea."
78 Gerard Toal and John O'Loughlin, "The Crimean Conundrum," *Open Democracy*, March 3, 2015, https://www.opendemocracy.net/en/odr/crimean-conundrum/.
79 John O'Loughlin, Gerard Toal, and Kristin M. Bakke, "To Russia with Love." In both 2014 and 2019, when asked if they trusted Putin, 85 percent of Crimeans said they did.
80 John O'Loughlin, Gerard Toal, and Kristin M. Bakke, "To Russia with Love."
81 "Survey Claims Most Crimean Tatars Satisfied with Living in Russia," *TASS*, February 28, 2017, https://tass.com/society/933346.

mean Tatars."[82] President Putin's decree of April 21, 2014 rehabilitated the deported peoples of Crimea, and provided additional federal funding for their national and cultural traditions. As a result, education in the Tatar language has expanded, and 150 new mosques have been built.[83] The Tatar language is now official in Crimea, alongside Russian and Ukrainian, which is something the Tatars never achieved under Ukrainian rule.[84]

Critics counter that Russia is only "trying to solve the Crimean Tatar question on paper."[85] In reality, they say, there has been a tenfold reduction in the number of Tatars in positions of authority in Crimea, because the Crimean Tatar *Mejlis* (Assembly) is now outlawed, and Tatars must run for office as members of different parties.[86] At the same time, it probably has not helped the overall popularity of the Mejlis in Crimea, that its exiled leaders in Ukraine have said that they do not recognize the rights of any other nationality in Crimea, and support their mass deportation, after Crimea is liberated from Russia.[87]

---

82 Shaun Walker, "Crimean Tatars Divided between Russian and Ukrainian Promises," *The Guardian*, March 17, 2015, https://www.theguardian.com/world/2015/mar/17/crimean-tatars-divided-between-russian-and-ukrainian-promises.

83 Kirill Yerchenko, "Krymsko-tatarskaya kultura v rossiiskom krymu," [Crimean Tatar Culture in the Russian Crimea] *Ritm Eurasia*, July 3, 2018, https://www.ritmeurasia.org/news–2018 – 07 – 03–krymsko-tatarskaja-kultura-v-rossijskom-krymu-o-chem-molchit-ukrainskij-agit-prop-37315.

84 Natylie Baldwin, "How Crimeans See Ukraine Crisis," *Consortium News*, February 11, 2016, https://consortiumnews.com/2016/02/11/how-crimeans-see-ukraine-crisis/; Shaun Walker, "Crimean Tatars Divided between Russian and Ukrainian Promises."

85 Natylie Baldwin, "How Crimeans See Ukraine Crisis."

86 Valentina Samar, "Ekzamen Na Krym Perenositsya," [The Exam on Crimea Is Postponed] *Zerkalo nedeli*, June 14, 2019, https://zn.ua/internal/ekzamen-na-krym-perenositsya-320868_.html; "Gafarov rasskazal, kak izmenilos otnoshenie krymskih tatar k sobytiyam 2014–go," [Gafarov Says How the Attitude of the Crimean Tatars to the Events of 2014 Has Changed] *RIA Krym*, February 28, 2019, https://crimea.ria.ru/vesna2019/20190228/1116156729.html; Arina Tsukanova, "Medzhlisovskaya krymsko-tatarskaya avtonomiya," [Mejlis Crimean Tatar Autonomy] *NK*, July 16, 2021, https://nk.org.ua/politika/medjlisovskaya-kryimsko-tatarskaya-avtonomiya-ugroza-i-kryimu-i-ukraine-i-evrope-00315417; "Chubarov Calls on Ukraine Authorities to Change Crimea's Status in Constitution," *Unian*, January 20, 2017, https://www.unian.info/politics/1734946-chubarov-calls-on-ukraine-authorities-to-change-crimeas-status-in-constitution.html; "Medzhlis vydvinul Poroshenko ultimatum po Krymu," [The Mejlis Gives Poroshenko an Ultimatum on Crimea] *RIA Novosti Ukraina*, March 16, 2018, https://rian.com.ua/politics/20180316/1033320047/medglis-vydvinul-Poroshenko-ultimatum.html.

87 Marina Shashkova, "Samuyu bolshuyu oshibku Ukraina sovershila za mnogo let do anneksii Kryma – Ilmi Umerov," [Ukraine Made Its Biggest Mistake Many Years Before the Annexation of Crimea – Ilmi Umerov] *Apostrof*, November 7, 2017, https://apostrophe.ua/article/politics/

The history of Crimea after 1991 offers yet another vivid illustration of how nationalism leads nations to self-delusion and tragedy. Knowing full well of the region's long-standing aspirations for autonomy, Kievan nationalist politicians tried to ignore or suppress them. This persistent clash of values and aspirations was vividly captured by Mustafa Nayem, who later became famous for sparking the 2013–2014 Maidan Revolution. After a visit to Sevastopol in 2009, he penned this remarkably candid assessment:

> This is a *Ukrainian* city in which Ukrainians are called occupiers. …
> This is a *Ukrainian* city in which the Ukrainian flag is called a "dirty cloth," and the Russian tricolor is hung proudly from windows.
> In this *Ukrainian* city it is almost impossible to encounter the Ukrainian state seal, even on the signs of many government agencies.
> In this *Ukrainian* city, sailors of the Ukrainian fleet cannot understand why they are paid 2–2.5 times less than their Russian counterparts.
> In this *Ukrainian* city people worship the Russian fleet because, if it leaves, twenty thousand people will be left without work.
> This is a *Ukrainian* city whose anthem glorifies the "pride of Russian sailors," and says not a word about Ukraine.
> In this *Ukrainian* city, representatives of official Kiev are referred to exclusively as "the worst nits." And I have a hard time believing that in this *Ukrainian* city one can find even a hundred people who, at the appearance of Russian tanks, would grab a rifle to proudly defend their right to be called Ukrainians … and if many [in Ukraine] will not vote because "they're all the same," in this *Ukrainian* city they will not vote because they do not understand why they should vote for the president of a foreign country.[88]

At the time Nayem proposed that, rather than trying to eradicate Russian identity, the government should encourage the locals to accept Ukrainian identity in exchange for a better standard of living. Unfortunately, his advice was ignored.

2017–11–07/samuyu-bolshuyu-oshibku-ukraina-sovershila-za-mnogo-let-do-anneksii-kryima—ilmi-umerov/15379; Yulia Bezpechnaya, "Ne lyublyu slovo 'deportatsiya,'" [I Don't Like the Word "Deportation"] *Segodnya.ua*, March 28, 2021, https://www.segodnya.ua/regions/krym/ne-lyublyu-slovo-deportaciya-reznikov-rasskazal-chto-budet-s-pereehavshimi-v-krym-rossiyanami-1515289.html. The deputy head of the Mejlis, Ilmi Umerov says "There is no Ukrainian population in Crimea. There are individual Ukrainians. But the 600 thousand Ukrainians who are statistically there do not exist. They are all Russians, or pro-Russians. In 1944, everyone was deported, and the current demographic situation in the Crimea was created artificially. If this can be changed, then it must be done. Right now Ukraine must fight not for population, but for territory. It must return its territory. For the majority that you are talking about, it really doesn't matter to them where they live." Ukraine's Vice-Premier Oleksiy Reznikov agrees that all who came to Crimea illegally will have to be deported after it is liberated.
88 Mustafa Nayyem, "Sevastopol – Ne Ukraina," [Sevastopol Is Not Ukraine] *Ukrainska pravda*, October 19, 2009, https://blogs.pravda.com.ua/authors/nayem/4adc22c19f1b6/.

Instead, many leading Ukrainian political and cultural figures, like writers Vasyl Shklyar, Yuri Andrukhovych, and former President Viktor Yushchenko, kept referring to Crimea (often, together with Donbass) as foreign to Ukraine, its multiculturalism a threat to the nationalist Ukraine they were trying to create.[89] After 2013, some continued to suggest letting these alien territories go their own way, but the danger of doing so now, according to President Poroshenko's permanent representative in Crimea, Boris Babin, is that "if we don't liberate Crimea and the East [militarily], then all of Ukraine will become the East and Crimea."[90]

To be clear, the crux of this aspect of Ukraine's tragedy is not that Ukraine insists on restoring its former territory, but that it has yet to acknowledge how much its own past policies contributed to the alienation of Crimea in the first place. Had Kiev accepted local patriotism, rather than sought to impose a form of Galician nationalism, many subsequent tragedies might have been avoided.

5.2 The Donbass Difference

While other regions of Ukraine were settled due to territorial disputes and conquests, the growth of Donbass is linked to the discovery in 1720 of Europe's largest coal basin and iron ore deposits that transformed it into the industrial heartland of the Russian Empire. With the help of British and French investors, Donbass was to become "a New America," to quote poet Alexander Blok, a region of industrial promise.[91] Its capital, Donetsk, was originally named Yuzovka

---

89 "Kievsky zhurnal zapretil intelligentsii Lvova obsuzhdat vozmozhnost otdelenita Kryma i Donbassa," [Kievan Magazine Forbids Discussion of the Possible Separation of Crimea and Donbass to Lviv intellectuals] *Novyi den*, February 9, 2013, https://newdaynews.ru/kiev/423752.html; "Vasyl Shklyar: Donbass ne vartiy zhyttiv naikrashchykh ukraintsiv," [Vasyl Shklyar: Donbass Is Not Worth the Life of the Best Ukrainians] *Volynski noviny*, May 29, 2017, https://www.volynnews.com/news/culture/vasyl-shkliar-donbas-ne-vartyy-zhyttiv-naykrashchykh-ukrayintsiv/; Mikhail Ryabov, "Ukrainsky pisatel predlagaet dat vozmozhnost otdelitsya Krymu in Donbassu," [Ukrainian Writer Proposes Giving Crimea and Donbass the Opportunity to Secede] *Novyi den*, July 22, 2010, https://newdaynews.ru/kiev/293271.html; "Vid referendum my nikudy ne denimosya," [We Can't Avoid a Referendum] *Radio Svoboda*, May 21, 2016, https://www.radiosvoboda.org/a/27689191.html; Pavlo Zubyuk, "Nash nenash Krym."

90 Olga Skorokhod, "Koly my zabiratimemo Krym, tam budut ruiny," [When We Take Back Crimea, There Will Be Ruins] *Censor.net*, June 30, 2019, https://censor.net/ru/resonance/3134577/koli_mi_zabiratimemo_krim_tam_budut_runi_rosyani_zaberut_use_ta_voni_navt_yayitsya_pokradut_u_kureyi. For Babin, "Crimea can be liberated only by military force."

91 Nikolai Protsenko, "Poslednyaya 'vnutrennyaya Amerika' Evropy," [Europe's Last "Inner America"] *Ukraina.ru*, May 29, 2020, https://ukraina.ru/history/20200529/1027833564.html.

(Hughes-ovka) in honor of its founder, Welsh industrialist John Hughes. Before 2014, the two regions of Donetsk and Lugansk that now comprise Donbass contributed nearly 16 percent of Ukraine's GDP, and as much as a quarter of its industrial output.[92]

Donbass resembled America in other ways as well. Thanks to the region's insatiable demand for new workers, it became a true cultural and ethnic melting pot. By some estimates, more than two million newcomers settled in the region after the opening of its first iron ore smelting plant in 1871.[93] Such a rapid influx of people facilitated the development of a cosmopolitan identity that fit well with the Soviet mentality that valued people for their abilities as laborers, rather than because of their place of origin, ethnicity, or language.[94] It is this local cosmopolitanism that Ukrainian nationalists point to dismissively when they say that Donbass is "not Ukrainian territory by content" and must be subjected to "positive, peaceful colonization."[95]

Another historical characteristic of this region is its rebelliousness, seen in periodic peasant uprisings that were fed, in part, by the half-a-million Old Believers that settled in this region during the latter half of the seventeenth century. During the Bolshevik Revolution, the descendants of these fiercely independent communities formed the back bone of anarchist Nestor Makhno's "Black Army"

---

92 Yuri Poluneyev, "Desyat shokiv Ukrainy," [Ten Ukrainian Shocks] *Ekonomichna pravda*, December 12, 2014, http://www.epravda.com.ua/publications/2014/12/12/512627/view_print/&us-g=ALkJrhizeiv1mTxjFgfZ3IW20aP_Wjjirw.

93 "Puti Gospodni," [The Ways of the Lord] *Ukraina.ru*, March 10, 2019, https://ukraina.ru/ex-clusive/20190310/1022920400.html.

94 Aleksei Makovtsev, "Donbass – predposylki i predystoriya narodnykh respublik," [Donbass – Background and Prehistory of the People's Republics] *Regnum*, March 22, 2017, https://regnum.-ru/news/2252676.html.

95 Boris Chervak, "Stanet li Donbas Ukrainskim?" [Will Donbas Become Ukrainian?] *Ukrainska pravda*, July 10, 2014, http://www.pravda.com.ua/rus/columns/2014/07/10/7031364/; "Professor DonNU Elena Styazhkina: 'Donbass ne vernetsya v Ukrainy potomu chto Donbass ne sushchest-vuyet,'" [Professor of Donetsk National University Elena Styazhkina: " Donbass Will Not Return to Ukraine Because Donbass Does Not Exist"] *Fakty.ua*, November 6, 2014, http://fakty.ua/190599-elena-styazhkina-Donbas-ne-vernetsya-v-ukrainu-potomu-chto-Donbasa-ne-sucshest-vuet; "Nikakogo Donbassa ne sushchestvuet," [There Is No Such Thing as Donbass] *Delo.ua*, March 24, 2021, https://delo.ua/econonomyandpoliticsinukraine/nikakogo-donbassa-ne-sus-chestvuet-danilov-prizv-379895/. Styazhkina's mantra that Donbass does not exist was later taken up by the head of Ukraine's National Security and Defense Council, Oleksiy Danilov.

which arose in defense of the brief-lived Donetsk-Krivoi Rog Soviet Republic, or DKR.[96]

The DKR represented a curious mix of industrialism and anarchism. The idea of regional autonomy for eastern Ukraine, along with parts of Rostov, Taganrog, and Novocherkassk regions, had long been a dream of the Council of Mining Industrialists of Southern Russia, which saw it as a way to rationalize the supply chain and increase profits.[97] Makhno's anarchists envisioned the region as a loose confederation of local communities, connected by economic interests, but completely independent in local matters such as religion, language, and cultural norms.[98]

In response to the creation of the Ukrainian People's Republic in Kiev, on February 12, 1918, the Congress of Regional Soviets in Kharkov established the DKR, and declared its intention to become an autonomous part of Soviet Russia. Its leaders condemned efforts by both Moscow and Kiev to increase their own authority at the expense of local autonomy, but eventually sided with Moscow for three reasons. First, because of the popularity of socialism. Second, because the Ukrainian nationalistic course chosen by Hetman Skoropadsky was inconsistent with the cosmopolitan identity of the region. Third, because the Red Army was the only force still fighting the Germans. On this last point, local historian Vladimir Kornilov sees a certain continuity between 1918 and 2014.[99]

Ultimately, the DKR was never offered autonomy, either in the USSR or the Ukrainian SSR, although the idea was apparently supported by one of the founding fathers of the Ukrainian SSR, Nikolai Skrypnik.[100] Instead, it was fully absorbed into the Ukrainian SSR in order to serve as a "proletarian counterbalance" to the more rural center and west. Forcing such a disparate region into the newly

---

96 "O teorii i istorii anarkhizma rasskazyvaet doctor nauk Aleksandr Shubin," [Dr. Alexander Shubin on the Theory and History of Anarchism] *Gazeta.ru*, June 9, 2014, http://www.gazeta.ru/science/2014/06/09_a_6064065.shtml.
97 Aleksandr Chalenko, "Kornilov izdal pervuyu istoriyu Donetsko-Krivorozhskoi Respubliki," [Kornilov Publishes the First History of the Donetsk-Krivoy Rog Republic] *Ukrainska pravda*, July 3, 2011, https://blogs.pravda.com.ua/authors/chalenko/4e89cc4aef953/.
98 Sergei Mirkin, "Pochemu Nestor Makhno ne mog byt soyuznikom ukrainskikh natsionalistov," [Why Nestor Makhno Could Never Be an Ally of Ukrainian Nationalists] *Ukraina.ru*, March 29, 2019, https://ukraina.ru/history/20190329/1023128197.html.
99 Sergei Mirkin, "Pochemu Nestor Makhno ne mog byt soyuznikom ukrainskikh natsionalistov"; Aleksandr Chalenko, "Kornilov izdal pervuyu istoriyu Donetsko-Krivorozhskoi Respubliki." On January 1, 1919, use of the Ukrainian language in the army, fleet, and all public institutions was made mandatory. In an echo of what was to come, the Rada also adopted a law "on the autocephaly of the Ukrainian church."
100 Aleksandr Chalenko, "Kornilov izdal pervuyu istoriyu Donetsko-Krivorozhskoi Respubliki."

established borders of Ukraine, however, placed a ticking time bomb within Ukraine, that would explode with renewed force after independence.

5.2.1 1991–2014: The Rise of Donbass Regionalism

Despite its generally loyal attitude toward the Soviet regime, on the eve of the collapse of the USSR, the Donbass region was engulfed by a wave of miners' strikes. Declining living standards, rather than ideological differences with the Soviet regime, led many to put their faith in assertions that Ukrainians would be much better off if they stopped sending their wealth to Moscow. Thus, even though the Ukrainian Communist Party, and it offshoot *Interdvizhenie*, opposed independence, 64 percent of the total electorate in Donetsk and 68 percent in Lugansk voted for it in December 1991.[101]

Disappointment, however, made itself know very soon afterwards. It is customary to think of Crimea as the first Maloross region to challenge the authority of Kiev, but Donbass was not far behind. Discontent with Kiev's decision to impose a unitary, rather than a federal state system, and to reject the Russian cultural heritage of Donbass, led to the creation of organizations calling for the reunification of Ukraine with Russia. These groups, organized around Cossack, Orthodox, and military-historical clubs, merged in April 1992 to form the Civic Congress of Ukraine. In September 1992, the Civic Congress joined with the Donetsk Strike Committee, which represented nearly all the coal miners in the region, to demand a federal state system for Ukraine.[102]

Knowing that they did not have the numbers to oppose the nationalist agenda nationwide, they concentrated instead on obtaining greater local autonomy for their region, unabashedly using its industrial importance to increase their leverage at the national level. The common notion that Donbass, unlike Galicia, lacked political activism, tends to ignore this history of grassroots organizations, because it aimed not at separating Ukraine from Russia, but rather at integrating the two countries, which contradicts Ukrainian nationalist mythology.

In September 1993, with the endorsement of the Donetsk Strike Committee, the Donetsk Regional Soviet decided to create a Regional Economic Self-government (REK) together with the regional soviets of Lugansk, Donetsk, and Zaporz-

---

101 "1991 Ukrainian Independence Referendum," *Wikipedia*, October 27, 2021, https://en.wikipedia.org/w/index.php?title=1991_Ukrainian_independence_referendum&oldid=1052206889.
102 Aleksei Makovtsev, "Donbass – predposylki i predystoriya narodnykh respublik."

hye. The formation of the Galician Assembly in western Ukraine two years earlier most likely served as a precedent, if not a direct inspiration.

In December 1993, the Donetsk Regional Soviet suspended payments to the central government in Kiev, until the latter agreed to pay its arrears to the region. Unable to reach a compromise on this issue, in March 1994 Donetsk began to form its own budget, independent of Kiev. That month both Donetsk and Lugansk decided to hold non-binding local referenda on federalism and the status of the Russian language. In Lugansk, 68 percent of registered voters participated, and in Donetsk 72 percent. The results are shown in Table 5.1.[103]

Table 5.1: Donetsk Referendum and Lugansk Opinion Poll of March 27, 1994.

	Donetsk oblast referendum (% in favor)	Lugansk oblast opinion poll (% in favor)
"Do you agree that the constitution of Ukraine should establish Ukraine's federal structure?"	79.6	not asked
"Do you agree that the constitution of Ukraine should establish Russian as another state language in Ukraine alongside the Ukrainian state language?"	87.2	90.4
"Do you agree that on the territory of the Donetsk/Lugansk oblast Russian should be a language of official correspondence and documentation, as well as education and science on equal footing with Ukranian?"	89.0	90.9
"Are you in favor of signing the CIS Charter and of Ukraine fully participating in the CIS economic union and interparliamentary assembly?"	88.7	90.7

Source: Poll and referendum results from *Luhanska Pravda*, April 2, 1994, 1; *Zhizn*, April 1, 1994, 1. Translation of questions adapted from "Constitution Watch," *East European Constitutional Review* 3(2):1.

President Kravchuk declared both referenda illegal, a decision that sparked the first mass rally in Donbass in support of Leonid Kuchma who, as a Rada deputy,

103 M.K. Flynn, "Political Mobilization in Eastern Ukraine: The Referendum of 1994 in the Donetsk Oblast," *The European Legacy* 1, no. 1 (March 1, 1996): 342–349, https://doi.org/10.1080/10848779608579417.

had abstained from voting for Ukrainian independence, and campaigned for maximum rapprochement with Russia.[104]

A month after he was elected president, however, Kuchma issued a decree making all heads of regional, city, and district administrations subject to his authority, thus putting Kiev on a collision course with local autonomy.[105] The subsequent political history of Donbass, like that of Crimea, is therefore, quintessentially, a struggle to assert regional political authority over central political authority, in order to safeguard the cultural and religious preferences of the local population, and the political and economic interests of local elites.

5.2.1.1 The Congress of Severodonetsk

The two most persistent demands of Donbass, as in Crimea, were: (1) official status for the Russian language; and (2) maximum regional autonomy. Always lurking in the background, however, was the implied threat that, if Kiev refused these demands, Donbass would seek reintegration with Russia. In fact, however, local elites had very little interest in joining Russia, where their influence would be diluted within a much larger political and economic arena. They insisted publicly on these two demands primarily to gain votes at election time.

This political dance lasted until the Orange Revolution of 2004, which many in Donbass interpreted as Viktor Yushchenko stealing the election from their candidate, Viktor Yanukovych. On November 26, 2004, the Lugansk Regional Council responded by calling for the creation of an "Autonomous Southeastern Ukrainian Republic," and summoned representatives from all Maloross regional councils to join it. Two days later nearly 4,000 local and regional officials from seventeen regions met in the town of Severodonetsk, and elected Evgenii Kushnaryov, the chairman of the Kharkov regional administration, as their leader.[106] Kushnaryov declared, "We want to live in a state where every individual is protected. His rights, his culture, his language, his history, his traditions and his customs should all be protected. We understand that the East is very different from Galicia. We do not intend to impose our way of life on Galicia, and we

---

104 Aleksei Makovtsev, "Donbass – predposylki i predystoriya narodnykh respublik."
105 M.K. Flynn, "Political Mobilization in Eastern Ukraine." Flynn points out that, earlier, both Kravchuk and Kuchma had supported a federal system with a bicameral legislature in which regional differences could be tempered by allowing for stable representation of regional interests in an upper house of parliament.
106 Aleksandr Nekrot, "Tsvetnye perevoroty na Ukraine," [Color Coups in Ukraine] *RitmEurasia*, November 22, 2019, https://www.ritmeurasia.org/news–2019–11–22–cvetnye-perevoroty-na-ukraine-kto-i-kak-obrek-stranu-na-rasterzanie-46107; Aleksei Makovtsev, "Donbass – predposylki i predystoriya narodnykh respublik."

will never allow Galicia to teach us how to live!"[107] After voting to make Kharkov the capitol of the new autonomous republic, the delegates appealed to Russian President Vladimir Putin for support.[108]

The regional councils of Donetsk, Lugansk, and Kharkov then voted to assume control of their local militias, and to stop all payments into the Ukrainian budget. Tent cities arose in Donetsk, Lugansk, and Mariupol, and opposition rallies were held daily. On December 5, 2004, the Congress declared that it would hold a referendum on the creation of a Southeastern Ukrainian Republic in one week, if Yanukovych was not sworn in as president. Yushchenko, in turn, promised to promote closer ties with Russia and allow the free use of the Russian language, but ultimately it was Yanukovych's personal appeal to the tent dwellers in Donetsk to stop before things went too far that defused the situation.[109]

Ukraine had never been closer to partition. According to the current head of the National Security and Defense Council of Ukraine, Oleksiy Danilov, the Congress in Severodonetsk, "was the precursor of all these separatist processes" with which Ukraine is now dealing.[110] As analyst Andrei Yermolaev sees it, "Severodonetsk gave birth to a new paradigmatic rivalry – cultural nationalism that veered into ethnic nationalism, versus a polycultural nation and patriotism."[111] When, as president, Yushchenko went back on his word, with tacit support of his prime minister, Viktor Yanukovych, political activists in Donbass began to adopt a much more radical stance, first in favor of independence, then in favor of reunification with Russia.

Many of the political leaders of the 2014 "Russian Spring," began their political careers at this time. A civic organization called "Donetsk Republic," whose black-blue-red tricolor flag is now the official flag of the Donetsk People's Republic (DPR), was registered at the end of 2005, and its first deputy head, Andrei Purgin, later became chairman of the People's Council of the DPR.[112] In Lugansk,

---

107 Aleksandr Nekrot, "Tsvetnye perevoroty na Ukraine."

108 "Kto i kogda vystupal s ideei federalizatsii," [Who Supported Federalism, and When] *Kommersant*, July 16, 2012, https://www.kommersant.ru/doc/1981569.

109 Aleksei Makovtsev, "Donbass – predposylki i predystoriya narodnykh respublik"; "Kuchma zaklykaie skhid Ukrainy ne rozvalyuvaty krainu," [Kuchma Urges Eastern Ukraine Not to Break Up the Country] *Korrespondent*, November 22, 2004, https://ua.korrespondent.net/amp/250755-kuchma-zaklikae-shid-ukrayini-ne-rozvalyuvati-krayinu.

110 Elena Galadzhii, "Chto novyi sekretar SNBO govoril o Donbasse, ES i Putine," [What the New Secretary of the National Security and Defense Council Said about Donbass, the EU and Putin] *KP in Ukraine*, accessed December 25, 2021, https://tinyurl.com/y3u2d284.

111 Yurii Tyurdo, "Ukraina Nesoborna," [Disunited Ukraine] *Zaxid.net*, March 14, 2008, https://zaxid.net/ukrayina_nesoborna_vikliki_syevyerodonetska_n1051027.

112 Aleksei Makovtsev, "Donbass – predposylki i predystoriya narodnykh respublik."

one of the members of the "Young Guard" youth group, Alexander Zakharchen-ko, would later become prime minister of the DPR. Dozens of like-minded civic organizations cultivated their own candidates within the establishment political structures of the Communist Party of Ukraine, the Progressive Socialist Party of Ukraine, and the Party of Regions. One of these was Pavel Gubarev, "People's Governor of Donetsk" in early 2014, who first entered politics as a deputy of the Kuibyshev local council in the Donetsk region.[113]

The existence of a ready-made ideology (Novorossiya as part of the "Russian World"), and of a romantic history linked to Nestor Makhno and the DKR, spawned a local identity and political culture that was distinct not only from the rest of Ukraine, but even, to a degree, from the rest of Malorossiya.[114] It manifested itself in elections and survey results that revealed a much more determined opposition to EU and NATO membership, and a more visceral rejection of Ukrainianization, and of Nazi collaborators being portrayed as Ukrainian heroes, than elsewhere in Ukraine.[115] All that was needed to re-ignite the flames of federalism was an opportune political crisis, which conveniently presented itself in the spring of 2014.

5.2.2 How the Donbass Rebellion Began

In light of this history, it is hardly surprising that the regional governments in Donbass strongly supported Yanukovych, that anti-Maidan meetings there gathered tens of thousands of supporters, and that the aforementioned civic groups

---

113 Nikita Sinitsin, "Kak nachalas voina na Donbasse," [How the War in Donbass Started] *Vesti*, March 14, 2021, https://vesti.ua/donbass/mart-kotoryj-nas-izmenil-7-let-nazad-donbass-prevrati-li-v-porohovuyu-bochku.
114 Elise Giuliano, "The Origins of Separatism: Popular Grievances in Donetsk and Lugansk," *Ponars Eurasia*, October 28, 2015, https://www.ponarseurasia.org/the-origins-of-separatism-popular-grievances-in-donetsk-and-luhansk/. The region of settlement along the Black Sea became known as Novorossiya, or "New Russia," in the early nineteenth century. It emerged as a political ideology in the early-1990s, as a fringe intellectual movement around Professor Alexei Surylov of Odessa National University, who argued for the establishment of Novorossiya as a separate state, based on the idea that the residents of southern Ukraine were a separate ethnos from Ukrainians.
115 Brian Milakovsky, "Understanding the 'Under Control' Donbas," *Kennan Cable*, no. 16 (April 2016), https://www.wilsoncenter.org/sites/default/files/media/documents/publication/kennan_-cable_no._16_understanding_the_under_control_donbas.pdf.

began to set up their own self-defense forces, in imitation of those set up at the Maidan in Kiev.[116]

On February 28, 2014 Gubarev, speaking to the Donetsk City Council, demanded that the new political authorities in Kiev be declared illegitimate.[117] The very next day he was acclaimed "People's Governor" of Donetsk at a public rally. At the same time, meetings in half a dozen other Donbass cities designated their own "People's Mayors," and organized local militia groups. These quickly reached an "understanding" with local Ukrainian security forces that the latter would not interfere.[118] In March 2014 alone, according to the head of the Ministry for Internal Affairs for the Donetsk region, there were 200 public gatherings, involving more than 130,000 participants.[119]

On March 2, Speaker and Acting President Turchynov tried to remove Donetsk governor Andrei Shishatsky. The next day the Donetsk Regional Administration not only voted to confirm Shishatsky as governor, but called for a local referendum on increasing local self-government and expanding "strategic partnership with the Russian Federation."[120] Later that week, Alexander Kharitonov

---

116 Andrei Liakhov, "Straight Talk about Russian Aggression in Ukraine," *Johnson's Russia List*, July 9, 2015, https://russialist.org/re-utexpertsdiscgrp-straight-talk-about-russian-aggression-in-ukraine/; "Donetsk patruliruyut otryady kazakov i veteranov-afgantsev," [Detachments of Cossacks and Afghan Veterans Patrol Donetsk] *Korrespondent*, January 26, 2014, https://korrespondent.net/ukraine/politics/3297360-donetsk-patrulyruuit-otriady-kazakov-y-veteranov-afhantsev; "Simonenko bolshe ne podderzhivaet Yanukovicha," [Symonenko No Longer Supports Yanukovych] *Delo.ua*, January 26, 2014, https://delo.ua/econonomyandpoliticsinukraine/simonenko-bolshe-ne-podderzhivaet-janukovicha-225502/.

117 Andrii Portnov, "How 'Eastern Ukraine' Was Lost," *Open Democracy*, January 14, 2016, https://www.opendemocracy.net/en/odr/how-eastern-ukraine-was-lost/. On the sabotage of the Maidan by local authorities in Donbass, see Portnov. Local oligarchs, he says, took a "neutral position," law enforcement and militia adopted an attitude of "passivity," while the vast majority of inhabitants chose to become "militantly self-absorbed" ("voinstvuyushchim obyvatel'stvom").

118 "Boi za Slavyansk," [Battle for Slavyansk] *Wikipedia*, December 18, 2021, https://ru.wikipedia.org/w/index.php?title=Boi_za_Slaviansk; Nikita Sinitsin, "Kak nachalas voina na Donbasse"; "Narodnyi mer Slavyanska," [People's Mayor of Sloviansk] *Regnum*, October 20, 2014, https://regnum.ru/news/1858546.html. The former people's mayor of Slavyansk Vyacheslav Ponomaryov says that a people's militia of 1,200 was organized in the city after Yanukovych's removal from office. "We did not want to live under the fascists and oligarchs, who, having usurped power, made important decisions for the state, not taking into account the interests of the people, violating all the norms of the Constitution and international law."

119 Nikita Sinitsin, "Kak nachalas voina na Donbasse."

120 "Ob obshchestvenno-politicheskoi situatsii v Donetskoi oblasti," [About the Socio-Political Situation in the Donetsk Region] *Donetsky oblastnoi sovet*, March 3, 2014, http://donbassrada.gov.ua/?lang=ru.

was acclaimed "People's Governor" of the neighboring Lugansk region, where his followers seized the regional administration building.[121]

When Gubarev was arrested on March 6, it appeared as if Kiev had gained the upper hand. In fact, however, the scenario increasingly began to resemble events in Crimea. Local government officials were turning against Kiev in increasing numbers, while the Ukrainian armed forces refused to engage the local population.[122] Inspired by what had happened in Crimea, many locals were confident that the same sort of peaceful separation from Ukraine would take place in Donbass.

5.2.2.1 The Anti-Terrorist Operation

On April 6–7, the rebels simultaneously seized government buildings in Donetsk, Lugansk, and Kharkov. Their intent, according to the People's Mayor of Slavyansk, was to demonstrate to the authorities in Kiev exactly how little support they had in the region and, as in Crimea, be forced to leave.[123] Instead, however, on April 14, Acting-President Turchynov announced the beginning of an Anti-Terrorist Operation (ATO). Turchynov explained that "blood has been spilled in war that the Russian Federation is conducting against Ukraine … This is not a war between Ukrainians. It is an artificial confrontation, with the goal of weakening and destroying Ukraine itself."[124]

The blood that Turchynov was referring to was actually spilled by the forces of the Right Sector in an operation conducted the previous day at Turchynov's behest.[125] Interviewed some years later, the Right Sector's Dmitry Yarosh recounts how he led the attack. Although he failed to capture his target, and lost several colleagues in the skirmish, he considers the mission a success because it was the first Ukrainian counterattack. Most importantly, he says, it tor-

121 Viktoriya Venk, "Konditsionera ne bylo," [There Was No Air Conditioning] *Strana.ua*, June 2, 2020, https://strana.one/news/270777-aviaudar-po-luhanskoj-oha-2-ijunja-2014-chto-my-znaem-o-trahedii-shest-let-spustja.html.
122 Nikita Sinitsin, "Kak nachalas voina na Donbasse."
123 *Regnum*, "Narodnyi mer Slavyanska."
124 Vasilii Stoyakin, "ATO: pyataya godovshchina," [ATO: The Fifth Anniversary] *Ukraina.ru*, April 13, 2019, https://ukraina.ru/exclusive/20190413/1023300658.html.
125 Vasilii Stoyakin, "ATO: pyataya godovshchina." Yarosh says he was given a direct order by Turchynov, and that he attacked with 150 Right Sector volunteers. This timing coincides with Avakov's April 13, 2014 post on Facebook.

pedoed the Geneva peace talks, and forced Ukraine to pursue the military liberation of Donbass, rather than a negotiated settlement with the rebels.[126]

For the rest of April, Ukrainian and rebel forces engaged in indecisive skirmishes. At this point, the Ukrainian forces consisted mostly of Far Right volunteers funded by oligarchs, since the acting Ukrainian government was still unsure of the reliability of the regular army.[127] By the end of April, most of the administrative centers in the Lugansk region had fallen to the rebels, and on April 27, the Lugansk People's Republic was declared.[128]

On May 7, however, Putin unexpectedly called on the rebels to delay their planned independence referenda, adding that he would recognize the results of Ukraine's presidential election later that month. Despite Putin's plea, the two rebel regions proceeded with their sovereignty referenda on May 11, which yielded the results shown in Table 5.2.

---

126 Anna Sokolova, "Lyubovnitsa arestovannogo Pashinskogo rasskazala, kto razvyazal voinu v Donbasse," [The Mistress of the Arrested Pashinsky Describes Who Unleashed the War in Donbass] *NewsUA.ru*, October 9, 2019, https://gorlovka.today/blogs/20078-lyubovnitsa-arestovanno go-pashinskogo-rasskazala-kto-razvyazal-vojnu-v-donbasse; "Nalyvaichenko priznalsya, chto eto on razvyazal voinu v Donbasse vopreki prikazu Turchinova," [Nalyvaichenko Admits that It Was He Who Unleashed the War in Donbass against Turchynov's Orders] *Ukraina.ru*, May 19, 2018, https://ukraina.ru/news/20180519/1020364371.html; Vasily Stoyakin, "ATO: pyataya godovshchina"; Yuri Butusov, "Dmytro Yarosh: 'Pershyi nastupalnyi bii viiny vidbuvsya 20 kvitnya 2014,'" [Dmytro Yarosh: "The First Offensive of the War was on April 20, 2014"] *Censor.net*, April 22, 2016, https://censor.net/ru/resonance/385673/dmitro_yarosh_pershiyi_nastupalniyi_-byi_vyini_vdbuvsya_20_kvtnya_2014go_dobrovolts_atakuvali_blokpost. "War with the Russian Federation was ongoing since February 2014," says Yarosh, "and in order to win it someone had to finally start shooting at the terrorists. You can't win a war by persuasion." It should be noted that Yarosh is not the only person trying to take credit for initiating hostilities in Donbass. There is also Sergei Pashinsky, then Turchynov's Chief of Staff who, according to the account of his confidante Tatyana Chernovol, gave the first military order to use force. Chornovol quotes Pashinsky as saying, "Not enough blood had been spilled during the Maidan to achieve a breakthrough in consciousness ... the only people ready to shoot were a handful of people from the Maidan, whose brothers had died, and that is precisely why the role of the volunteer battalions in the Ukrainian resistance of 2014 was decisive." Pashinsky called up the "Vega" special forces unit which was stationed in Ivano-Frankovsk and was therefore sufficiently radicalized by Ukrainian nationalism (dostatochno "obanderilis"). There is also Valentyn Nalyvaichenko, head of the Ukrainian Security Services (SBU) at the time. In a television interview five years later, he recalls how Turchynov ordered him to abandon the Lugansk headquarters of the SBU. He balked at this order, and instead sent his forces to attack Slavyansk. "I repeat: the order to retreat did not stop me," says Nalyvaychenko, "We attacked!"
127 "Kiev osoznal vliyanie 'Pravogo sektora' na politiku," [Kiev Is Now Realizing the Influence of the "Right Sector" on Politics] *DAN News*, February 2, 2016, https://perma.cc/7X8N-65N7.
128 Viktoriya Venk, "Konditsionera ne bylo."

Table 5.2: Donetsk and Lugansk Referenda of May 11, 2014.

Question posed in Donetsk oblast "Do you support the Act of State Self-rule of the Donetsk People's Republic?"	% in favor 89.7	% participation 74.87

Question posed in Lugansk oblast "Do you support the Declaration of State Independence of the Lugansk People's Republic?"	% in favor 96.2	% participation 81

Sources: Anna Revyakina, "Donbass v ocheredi za svobodoi. Kak èto bylo 11 i 12 maya 2014 goda," *Ukraina.ru*, May 11, 2021, https://ukraina.ru/exclusive/20210511/1031284571.html; "2014 Donbas Status Referendums," *Wikipedia*, November 12, 2021, https://en.wikipedia.org/w/index.php?title=2014_Donbas_status_referendums&oldid=1054909786.

These figures are disputed by the Ukrainian Ministry of Interior, which puts the participation rate at just 24 percent and 32 percent respectively.[129] Moscow, meanwhile, said that, while it respected the will of the people in these regions, it would not recognize these results.[130]

The election of Petro Poroshenko thus seemed to offer hope for a peaceful resolution to the conflict, and negotiations were launched, between Ukrainian negotiators Viktor Medvedchuk and Nestor Shufrich, and Donbass rebel leaders. As Shufrich recalls, the Donbass representatives voiced just three demands: to be able to use the Russian language in official documents, to be consulted on the appointment of the local state prosecutor, and to be consulted on the appointment of the regional governor.[131] By the latter half of June, Shufrich says, a for-

---

129 "Turchinov oproverg opisannye separatistami chudesa yavki na referendum," [Turchynov Contradicts the Miraculous Turnout for the Referendum Described by the Separatists] *Ukrainskya pravda*, May 12, 2014, http://www.pravda.com.ua/rus/news/2014/05/12/7025064/.
130 "Moscow Respects Will Expressed by Population of Donetsk and Lugansk Regions of Ukraine," *TASS*, May 12, 2014, https://tass.com/world/731214.
131 "Viktor Medvedchuk v programme 'Maga' na 112 Ukraina," [Viktor Medvedchuk in the "Maga" Program on 112 Ukraine], https://youtu.be/n__w6id84IE (at 01:27:20); "Nestor Shufrich o nachale konflikta na Donbasse," [Nestor Shufrich on the Beginning of the Conflict in Donbass] *NewsOne*, September 5, 2018, https://tinyurl.com/y2o25ltb. Medvedchuk also says that all the rebel leaders wanted was the same autonomy for Donbass that the Ukrainian Constitution provided for Crimea. Nestor Shufrich, speaking on the *NewsOne* television program "Ukrainsky Format," says that in negotiations on June 27, 2014, he, Kuchma, Zurabov, Tagliavini, and Medvedchuk undertook at Poroshenko's request, the Donbass representatives asked for just three things: (1) the right to use Russian in their official documents; (2) the right to consult with Kiev on the appointment of state prosecutor; and (3) the right to consult with Kiev on the appointment of their governor.

mula for ceasing hostilities and reintegrating into Ukraine had been found. The Russian parliament's decision on June 24 to rescind President Putin's authority to use Russian troops abroad added to the sense of optimism. The final details were to be worked out in Donetsk on July 1, but on June 30, President Poroshenko, apparently convinced by his Minister of Defense, Valery Heletey, that Putin's decisions had shifted the balance on the ground in Kiev's favor, launched a blitzkrieg to recapture all of Donbass.[132]

After initially gaining ground, the Ukrainian military offensive collapsed at the end of August when its forces were surrounded at Ilovaisk.[133] This debacle forced Poroshenko to sign the First Minsk cease fire agreement on September 5, 2014. A second defeat at Debaltsevo in January 2015 forced Poroshenko to agree to the Second Minsk Protocol on February 12. This set up the Minsk Process, in which France, Germany, and Russia tried to use their diplomatic leverage to force Kiev to accept local self-government and local language rights for Donbass, in exchange for restoring Ukrainian sovereignty over the region.

We will examine the reasons for the failure of the Minsk Process in the next chapter. First, however, let us review several competing explanations of why Donbass erupted in 2014, with an eye toward answering one of the key questions of this conflict: should it be viewed as an interstate or a civil conflict?

5.2.3 Why Did Donbass Revolt?

The dominant Western narrative aligns with the one proposed by Turchynov at the National Security and Defense Council meeting in Kiev on February 28, 2014, which he reiterated on April 14, 2014 when launching the ATO: there is no revolt, there is only Russian aggression. This view is echoed by Samantha Power, then US Permanent Representative to the United Nations, who said

---

132 "Shufrich: 'Donbass ne treboval nichego takogo, chego ne khotel by Lvov ili Ivano-Frankovsk,'" [Shufrich: "Donbass Did Not Demand Anything that Lvov or Ivano-Frankivsk Would Not Want"] *DNR24 Novosti*, January 8, 2018, https://perma.cc/Q8XX-US8D?view-mode=server-side&-type=image; "Shufrich o 'progibe' Poroshenko pered Heleteyem," [Shufrich on Poroshenko Kowtowing to Heletey] *Agenstvo Novostei Kharkova*, December 26, 2017, https://perma.cc/TLH9-VCL2.
133 Svyatoslav Knyazev, Irina Taran, and Elena Onishchuk, "Zhiteli yugo-vostoka poschitali lyudmi vtorogo sorta," [Residents of the Southeast Were Considered Second-Class People] *RT na russkom*, April 14, 2019, https://russian.rt.com/ussr/article/621255-ukraina-donbass-voina.

there is "nothing grassroots-seeming about it."[134] It follows from this that a single order from Russia's president would suffice to end the insurgency.

But, as we have seen, popular sentiment in Donbass has long identified with Russia, and rejected attempts by governments in Kiev to sever those ties, and to suppress their local identity and culture. Clearly, therefore, the roots of the present conflict go much deeper.[135] So, while it is not surprising that hostilities erupted there again in 2014, the question that still needs to be answered is why it went so much further *this* time.

Pro-Maidan historian Andrii Portnov suggests that the answer lies in the neutral stance taken by local financial and political elites; the passivity of local law enforcement; the loss of control over the border with Russia; and the indecisiveness of the new government in Kiev.[136] He agrees that the main actors in this drama were mostly locals, but I feel he underestimates the extent to which they became more disposed to fighting for independence from Kiev because of two additional factors: the violence displayed during the 2014 Maidan Revolution, and the bloodless separation of Crimea.

A survey of eight Russophone regions, conducted as the rebellion was still unfolding (April 8–16, 2014), found that:

- Two-thirds of Donbass residents saw the Right Sector as "a prominent military formation that is politically influential and poses a threat to the citizens and national unity";
- Of those polled in Donetsk and Lugansk, 60 percent and 52 percent, respectively, disagreed with the view that Russia is organizing the rebels and guiding their actions;
- While 70 percent did not support secession, only 25 percent wanted to join the EU, while 47 percent preferred the Russia-led Customs Union.[137]

---

134 Sergiy Kudelia, "New Policy Memo: Domestic Sources of the Donbas Insurgency," *Ponars Eurasia*, September 29, 2014, https://www.ponarseurasia.org/new-policy-memo-domestic-sources-of-the-donbas-insurgency/.

135 Aleksandr Nekrot, "Tsvetnye perevoroty na Ukraine." A second All-Ukrainian Congress of elected officials was held in Severodonetsk in 2008. It met to oppose NATO membership for Ukraine and the continued violation of the rights of Russian-speaking Ukrainians. Its impact, however, was much more muted than the first for three reasons. First, many of the key oligarchs were now in Kiev promoting their interests through the Party of Regions. Second, local groups were now following a grassroots agenda, and were dismissive of national politics. Third, Kuchma had already seized control of the Crimean government and curtailed its autonomy.

136 Andrii Portnov, "How 'Eastern Ukraine' Was Lost."

137 Yulia Mostovaya, Sergei Rakhmanin, and Inna Vedernikova, "Pesnya o Rodine," [Song about the Motherland] *Zerkalo nedeli*, December 26, 2014, https://zn.ua/internal/pesnya-o-rodine-slova-narodnye-_.html.

A follow up poll, conducted September 12–21, 2014, confirmed the vast gulf between popular attitudes in Donbass and western Ukraine. Thus, in answer to the question of whether Russia was responsible for the bloodshed and deaths of people in eastern Ukraine, only 19.1 percent of Donbass residents said "yes" (definitely or probably), while 62.8 percent said "no." In western Ukraine, by contrast, 81.6 percent said "yes," while only 15.8 percent said "no."[138]

Identical questions in both surveys, reveal that after six months of fighting even fewer people in Donbass believed that this was a war between Russia and Ukraine than at the outset of hostilities (19.4 percent compared to 28.2 percent); more felt that Russia was justified in defending the interests of Russophone citizens in eastern Ukraine (50.9 percent compared to 47 percent agreed; 8.1 percent compared to 33.4 percent disagreed). Meanwhile, the percentage favoring separation from Ukraine jumped dramatically, from 27.5 to 42.1 percent.[139]

It therefore seems more appropriate to describe local elites as hostile rather than "neutral" to what was happening in Kiev at the time. For regional law enforcement, this hostility manifested itself in deliberate acts of sabotage. Kiev's inability to get these forces to follow orders, forced it to rely on the militias of the Far Right.[140]

---

138 "Stavlennya naselennya do podii na Donbasi," [The Attitude of the Population to Events in Donbass] *Democratic Initiatives Fund*, October 7, 2014, https://dif.org.ua/article/stavlennya-naselennya-do-podiy-na-donbasi-tsina-miru-zagalnonatsionalne-opituvannya.

139 "Mneniya i vzglyady zhitelei yugo-vostoka Ukrainy," [Opinions and Views of Residents of Southeastern Ukraine] *Zerkalo nedeli*, April 19, 2014, http://zn.ua/article/print/UKRAINE/mneniya-i-vzglyady-zhiteley-yugo-vostoka-ukrainy-aprel-2014–143598_.html; *Democratic Initiatives Fund*, "Stavlennya naselennya do podii na Donbasi."

140 "Avakov: Kievskikh militsionerov mogli ubit boitsy UPA," [Avakov: Ukrainian Police Officers Might Have Been Killed by UPA Fighters] *Ukraina.ru*, May 4, 2015, https://ukraina.ru/news/20150504/1012959425.html; "Matios v pryamom efire rasskazal uzhasy o zverstvakh batalyona 'Tornado,'" [Matios Spoke on Live TV about the Horrors and Atrocities of the "Tornado" Battalion] *Vesti*, June 19, 2015, https://vesti.ua/donbass/104244-matios-v-prjamom-jefire-rasskazal-uzhasy-o-zverstvah-batalona-tornado; "Naiti 'rukopozhatnykh' liderov slozhno," [Finding "Respectable" Leaders Is Difficult] *Inosmi*, June 19, 2015, https://inosmi.ru/overview/20150619/228682333.html; Fyodor Koloskov, "Voennye prestupleniya karatelei v Donbasse," [War Crimes of Punishers in Donbass] *Ritm Eurasia*, March 17, 2020, https://perma.cc/BC89-QLM9; Iryna Shtohrin, "Khto natsyst?," [Who Is a Nazi?] *Radio Svoboda*, May 28, 2017, https://www.radiosvoboda.org/a/28512571.html; "Minoborony naznachilo rassledovanie v otnoshenii 'Aidara,'" [The Ministry of Defense Launches an Investigation into "Aidar"] *Vesti*, March 31, 2015, https://vesti.ua/donbass/94544-minoborony-naznachilo-rassledovanie-v-otnoshenii-ajdara; Aleksandr Chalenko, "Mikhail 'Berkut' Shatokhin," [Mikhail "Berkut" Shatokhin] *Ukraina.ru*, July 17, 2015, https://ukraina.ru/interview/20150717/1013685597.html; "Advokat Efremova Pokazal Video," [Yefremov's Lawyer Shows a Video] *Gordon.ua*, April 8, 2018, https://perma.cc/FRQ5-F5BU; Sergiy Kudelia, "Reply to Andreas Umland: The Donbas Insurgency Began at Home," *Po-*

Sergiy Kudelia, who has studied the Donbass uprising closely, also feels that the separatist movement emerged in response to the violent regime change in Kiev, and had the support of roughly a third of the population.[141] According to Kudelia, surveys in early April showed that the population of Donbass feared the spread of violence into their region, and viewed disarming the Far Right as essential for the restoration of law and order. When the government in Kiev failed to do so, and then actually mobilized these groups against Donbass, Kudelia says, it "hardened pre-existing local grievances, added to the sense of the illegitimacy of the Kiev government, and so strengthened the rebellion."[142]

Critics of this view, however, contend that it is the Russian government that is primarily responsible for driving a wedge between Donbass and the rest of Ukraine, by highlighting the dehumanizing rhetoric used by Ukrainian nationalists toward them.[143] While it is certainly true that Russian media amplified this rhetoric, there are far too many examples of it over the years to claim that it was invented by Russia in 2014. One example that stands out is President Poroshenko's promise, just six months after his election, that children in Donbass would cower in their cellars, while "our children will go to school, to kindergartens."[144] Many took note of the fact that the president no longer saw the children of Donbass as "our children."

Another critic, Andreas Umland, acknowledges that Donbass's grievances against Kiev run deep, but he points out that they had never before led to outright rebellion. The distinctive element contributing to this, he concludes, was Russian military intervention.[145] He also links the Donbass and Crimean upris-

nars Eurasia, October 8, 2014, https://www.ponarseurasia.org/reply-to-andreas-umland-the-donbas-insurgency-began-at-home/; Anna Sokolova, "Lyubovnitsa arestovannogo Pashinskogo rasskazala, kto razvyazal voinu v Donbasse." The Head of the Main Directorate of the Ministry of Internal Affairs (MVD) of Ukraine for the Lugansk region, Police Lieutenant General Volodymyr Guslavsky, apparently refused to act to prevent the seizure of the Lugansk Directorate of the Security Service of Ukraine (SBU) on April 6, 2014. After holding the building for six hours, they surrendered when it became clear that no support would be arriving.
141 Sergiy Kudelia, "New Policy Memo: Domestic Sources of the Donbas Insurgency."
142 Paul Robinson, "Origins of the War in Donbass," *Irrussianality*, September 14, 2016, https://irrussianality.wordpress.com/2016/09/14/origins-of-the-war-in-donbass/.
143 Sergiy Kudelia, "New Policy Memo: Domestic Sources of the Donbas Insurgency."
144 "Poroshenko: Donbas Children Will Sit in Cellars," *Sputnik International*, November 14, 2014, https://sputniknews.com/20141114/1014748940.html.
145 Sergiy Kudelia, "Reply to Andreas Umland: The Donbas Insurgency Began at Home"; Sergiy Kudelia, "New Policy Memo: Domestic Sources of the Donbas Insurgency." Umland sees the failure of the secessionist movement outside of Crimea and Donbass as evidence that Russian intervention was decisive. Kudelia, however, suggests that the secessionist movement failed to take root in towns where over 80 percent of the population were native Ukrainian speakers,

ings, saying that the latter was the first step in a sequence of events orchestrated by Moscow.[146]

Within Ukraine itself it has become impossible to discuss and contrast these distinct perspectives on the origins of this conflict. This further contributes to Ukraine's tragedy, since each view contains some essential truths, without which the conflict cannot be resolved. On the one hand, after the secession of Crimea, the new leadership in Kiev became even more fearful that Donbass's demand for greater autonomy would lead to the country's disintegration. On the other hand, Donbass leaders feared that a Kiev captured by Ukrainian nationalists would seek to destroy their distinctive culture and identity.[147]

Thus, two distinct responses to the Maidan revolt emerged in Malorossiya at the beginning of 2014. One, in those regions where opposition to the Maidan gathered steam, thanks to the support of local officials, security personnel, and oligarchs – Crimea, Donbass, and to a lesser extent Kharkov. The second, in those regions where opposition to the Maidan was resisted by local officials, security personnel, and oligarchs – Odessa, Dnipropetrovsk, and to a lesser extent Nikolayev, Kherson, and Zaporozhye. Although the anti-Maidan rebellion had the potential to succeed in any of these regions, it succeeded only in Crimea because it could rely on the Russian troops that were already stationed there. In the rest of Maloross Ukraine the rebellion failed.

In those regions where the rebellion failed, pro-Maidan forces relied heavily on the Far Right, who were able to intimidate local rebels long enough for the Ukrainian military and state institutions to rally. The Far Right was able to put some 1,500 well armed, combat personnel in the field at a time when the Ukrai-

---

but succeeded in Donbass towns where fewer than 20 percent were native Ukrainian speakers. He sees this as supporting the thesis that pre-existing beliefs and political orientations were crucial in determining whether or not locals took up arms. Such pre-existing beliefs, he notes, were particularly strong with respect to right-wing nationalist groups and parties.

146 Paul Robinson, "Origins of the War in Donbass." This assertion is based on Strelkov and Borodai's Russian citizenship, and on the revelations on the "Glazyev Tapes." Dual citizenship, however, is not that unusual in Ukraine. Many senior government officials retained Russian citizenship for years after the Maidan. Robinson contends that Strelkov was not an agent of the Russian state, but that he and other Russians who came to Ukraine acted on their own initiative. As for the Glazyev tapes, Kudelia points out that Glazyev is recorded speaking with activists in Odessa, Kharkov, and Zaporozhye, but not in Donbass. Furthermore, his conversations suggest that the activists were not in contact with any Russian representatives in Ukraine.

147 Sergiy Kudelia, "New Policy Memo: Domestic Sources of the Donbas Insurgency." An extraordinary 69.5 percent of Donetsk residents identified themselves primarily with their own region, rather than with Ukraine.

nian military was essentially paralyzed.[148] In Crimea and also partly in Donbass, by contrast, the Far Right was pre-empted by anti-Maidan groups, who were able to intimidate the pro-Maidan groups long enough for Russian forces to rally to their aid.

The precise number of Russian military personnel involved in the fighting in Donbass before 2022 is hotly contested. Russia still denies any official military involvement in the region, but does admit that Russians have gone to Donbass as private citizens to support the rebels.[149]

---

148 Vladislav Maltsev, "Mif i pravda o grazhdanskoi voine na Donbasse," [Myth and Truth about the Civil War in Donbass] *Ukraina.ru*, April 16, 2020, https://ukraina.ru/exclusive/20200416/1027404109.html; Aleksei Romanov, "Vspomnim, kak 5 let nazad razzhigali voinu na Donbasse," [Let's Remember How 5 Years Ago They Sparked a War in the Donbass] *Strana.ua*, October 18, 2019, https://strana.one/opinions/228427-vspomnim-kak-5-let-nazad-razzhihali-vojnu-na-donbasse.html; Heavenly Cat, "Fashisty rasstrelivayut mirnykh zhitelei," [The Fascists Are Shooting Peaceful Civilians] May 9, 2014, https://tinyurl.com/y47avf4n, alternatively https://perma.cc/WV2K-N2 A4.

149 Jonathan Ferguson and N.R. Jenzen-Jones, *Raising Red Flags: An Examination of Arms and Munitions in the Ongoing Conflict in Ukraine, 2014*, 2014, http://armamentresearch.com/Uploads/Research%20Report%20No.%203%20-%20Raising%20Red%20Flags.pdf; "How the Media Spins Story of Russian Soldiers in Ukraine," *Russia Insider*, May 15, 2015, https://russia-insider.com/en/node/6919; Lorenzo Cremonesi, "Ucraina, Tra i Russi al Fronte," [Ukraine, among the Russians at the Front] *Corriere della Sera*, February 18, 2015, https://perma.cc/AK4 V-7LZX?type=-image; Michael R. Gordon, "Armed with Google and YouTube," *The New York Times*, May 27, 2015, https://www.nytimes.com/2015/05/28/world/europe/videos-and-google-help-researchers-gauge-russias-presence-in-ukraine.html; "Forbes' 'Russian Casualties in Ukraine' Report That Set MSM on Fire Was a Fake," *Russia Insider*, August 31, 2015, https://russia-insider.com/en/node/9423; "1,500 Foreigners Making up 10 – 15 Percent of Forces Fighting for DPR," *Sputnik International*, September 10, 2014, https://sputniknews.com/20140910/1500-Foreigners-Making-Up-10 – 15-Percent-of-Forces-Fighting-for-DPR-192823434.html; "OSCE: No Russian Violations on Ukrainian Border," *RT International*, August 7, 2014, https://www.rt.com/news/178668-osce-russia-ukraine-border/; Alexander Reed Kelly, "Vladimir Putin Not Responsible for Ukrainian Civil War," *Truthdig*, March 21, 2015, https://www.truthdig.com/articles/vladimir-putin-not-responsible-for-ukrainian-civil-war-expert-says/; "Berlin Is Alarmed by Aggressive NATO Stance on Ukraine," *Russia Insider*, March 8, 2015, https://russia-insider.com/en/node/4203; Patricia Adam, "Hearing of General Christophe Gomart, Director of Military Intelligence, on the Draft Law on Intelligence" (2015), https://perma.cc/GY99-MMKE; Christian Weisflog, "OSCE Reports on Russian Soldiers," *Neue Zürcher Zeitung*, August 4, 2015, https://www.nzz.ch/international/osze-trifft-auf-russische-soldaten-1.18590107?reduced=true; Andrij V. Dobriansky, "Lackluster Journalism on Russo-Ukrainian War from PBS and Pulitzer Center," *Euromaidan Press*, July 10, 2016, https://euromaidanpress.com/2016/07/10/lackluster-journalism-on-russo-ukrainian-war-from-pbs-newshour-and-pulitzer-center/; "Around 90% of Donetsk Self-Defense Troops from Donbas," *Sputnik International*, June 4, 2014, https://sputniknews.com/20140604/Around-90-of-Donetsk-Self-Defense-Troops-From-Donbas—Commander-190338268.html; "OSCE Spokesman Says

Western government sources rarely provide specific numbers, but imply that Russian commanders are in charge of the rebel defense forces. Meanwhile, the OSCE observation teams inspecting the region have routinely reported finding no official Russian forces there. Official Ukrainian sources place the number of Russian forces in the region at 3,000 – 3,500, among a total rebel contingent of 30 – 35,000. This would suggest that troops from Russia constituted roughly 10 percent of the rebel forces, prior to 2022.[150]

The actual number of Russian troops, however, is far less important than the psychological perception of Russian support in explaining the different outcomes of the anti-Maidan rebellions of 2014. Just as the feeling of Russia's full psychological and logistical support was vital to the success of the rebellion in Crimea, Russia's half-hearted support for Donbass explains why it turned into a frozen conflict. The complexity of this crisis is thus best captured by the term "internationalized civil war."[151] While the Ukrainian government objects

Wrong to Call Ukraine's Independence Supporters 'Separatists,'" *Sputnik International*, August 6, 2014, https://sputniknews.com/20140806/OSCE-Spokesman-Says-Wrong-to-Call-Ukraines-Independence-191777262.html.

150 "Gensek OBSE: Nelzya tochno skazat, est li na Donbasse rossiiskie voennye," [OSCE General Secretary: It Is Impossible to Say for Sure Whether There Is Any Russian Military in Donbas] *Korrespondent*, February 12, 2015, https://korrespondent.net/ukraine/3478712-hensek-obse-nelzia-tochno-skazat-est-ly-na-donbasse-rossiyskye-voennye; "ARD: Rossiiskikh regulyarnykh voisk v Donbasse net," [ARD: There Are No Russian Regular Troops in Donbass] *Ukraina.ru*, February 10, 2015, https://ukraina.ru/news/20150210/1012062883.html; Patrick Jackson, "Ukraine War Pulls in Foreign Fighters," *BBC News*, August 31, 2014, https://www.bbc.com/news/world-europe-28951324; Nolan Peterson, "Foreign Fighters Vow to Support Ukraine against Russian Invasion," *Coffee or Die Magazine*, December 24, 2021, https://coffeeordie.com/foreign-fighters-ukraine-russian-invasion/; Gijs Weijenberg and Jeanine de Roy van Zuijdewijn, "The Forgotten Front," *International Center for Counter-Terrorism*, July 16, 2021, https://icct.nl/publication/the-forgotten-front-dutch-fighters-in-ukraine/; "Foreign Fighters in Ukraine," *Balkan Insight*, accessed January 15, 2022, https://balkaninsight.com/foreign-fighters-in-ukraine/; Amy Mackinnon, "Counting the Dead in Europe's Forgotten War," *Foreign Policy*, October 25, 2018, https://foreignpolicy.com/2018/10/25/counting-the-dead-in-europes-forgotten-war-ukraine-conflict-donbass-osce/. While Hug was deputy head of the OSCE's observer mission in Ukraine, a minor scandal arose because of his comment that "we did not see direct evidence (of Russia's involvement) ... We have seen convoys leaving and entering Ukraine on dirt roads in the middle of the night, in areas where there is no official crossing." The editors of *Foreign Policy* later removed this remark because, as they put it, "it did not convey his intended view" (clarification of October 25, 2018).

151 Paul Robinson, "Origins of the War in Donbass"; Robert H. Wade, "The Ukraine Crisis Is Not What It Seems," *Le Monde diplomatique*, March 31, 2015, https://mondediplo.com/outsidein/the-ukraine-crisis-is-not-what-it-seems.

to any use of the term "civil war," in this context it most accurately reflects the role that both internal and external actors have played in stoking this crisis.

5.3 Is There No Escape from Tragedy?

Both of these rebellions stem, in no small measure, from the Ukrainian government's persistent attempts after 2014 to narrow the definition of Ukrainian identity. This resulted in the marginalization of important constituencies within Ukraine, some of which then rebelled against the Ukrainian state. To regain their loyalty, Kiev will have to acknowledge the role that its own policies, most notably forcible Ukrainianization, have played in alienating this population.

What makes this a true tragedy, rather than merely a series of bad policy choices, is Kiev's insistence that there is no Maloross culture at all in Ukraine. This position is now codified in the 2021 law on the native peoples of Ukraine, which states that Russians are not indigenous to Ukraine, and therefore have no right to any state protection of their spiritual, religious, or cultural heritage.[152] This begs the question of whether Maloross Ukrainians should be considered "Russians" by virtue of their cultural identity, and therefore denied these rights, or "Ukrainians" by virtue of their citizenship and therefore afforded these rights. From a civic perspective, rights should presumably apply to all individuals, but Ukrainian courts have often ruled that primacy should be given not to individual rights, but to the promotion of Ukrainian nationhood.[153]

---

152 "Prezident podpisal zakon 'O korennykh narodakh Ukrainy,'" [The President Has Signed a Law "On the Indigenous Peoples of Ukraine"] *President.gov.ua*, July 21, 2021, https://www.president.gov.ua/ru/news/prezident-pidpisav-zakon-pro-korinni-narodi-ukrayini-69677.

153 Constitutional Court of Ukraine, Decision No. 10-rp/99 of December 14, 1999, "Po delu po konstitutsionnomu predstavleniyu 51 narodnogo deputata Ukrainy ob ofitsialnom tolkovanii polozhenii stati 10 Konstitutsii Ukrainy otnositelno primeneniya gosudarstvennogo yazyka organami gosudarstvennoi vlasti, organami mestnogo samoupravleniya i ispolzovaniya ego v uchebnom protsesse v uchebnykh zavedeniyakh Ukrainy (delo o primenenii ukrainskogo yazyka)," [In the case of the constitutional submission of 51 people's deputies of Ukraine on the official interpretation of the provision of Article 10 of the Constitution of Ukraine regarding the use of the state language by state authorities, local governments and its use in the educational process in educational institutions of Ukraine (case on the use of the Ukrainian language)] http://search.ligazakon.ua/l_doc2.nsf/link1/KS99010.html. The majority of the court interpreted the Article 10 guarantee of "the free development, use and protection of Russian" in the narrowest possible way. In his prescient dissent, judge A. Mironenko predicted that this would be used to eliminate its use in the private sphere entirely, and to restore totalitarianism, this time masquerading as patriotism.

Meanwhile, Kiev's visceral fear of separatism has led it to impose draconian sanctions on the very population it should be seeking to win over. The inherent contradiction between insisting that these territories are Ukrainian, while denouncing the people who live there as alien, has prevented the adoption of any coherent strategy that might actually appeal to people in Crimea and Donbass. As more than one former regional governor has pointed out, unless the country adopts a more inclusive approach, the liberation of these regions will simply result in a new cycle of violence there in the future.[154]

A shift from ethnic nationalism to civic patriotism would require escaping the cycle of mutual fear that drove the sides to separate in the first place: the fear that the violence of the Maidan evokes in Crimea and Donbass, as well as the fear that the separation of Donbass and Crimea evokes among Ukrainian na-

---

154 "Gennady Moskal, Prorossiiskie nastroeniya v Luganskoi oblasti 80 – 95%," [Gennady Moskal, Pro-Russian Attitudes in the Lugansk Region Are 80 – 95%] *Ukrainska pravda*, October 30, 2014, http://www.pravda.com.ua/rus/articles/2014/10/30/7042701/; Reinhard Veser, "Izvilistyi put kharkovskogo gradonachalnika Kernesa," [The Tortuous Path of Kharkov Mayor Kernes] *Inosmi*, April 17, 2019, https://inosmi.ru/politic/20190417/244953837.html; Tamila Varshalomidze, "Kharkiv's Pro-Russian Protesters Still Mistrustful of Kiev," *Aljazeera*, March 29, 2019, https://www.aljazeera.com/news/2019/3/29/kharkivs-pro-russian-protesters-still-mistrustful-of-kiev; Andrei Veselov, "Kolumbiiskie uroki dlya Ukrainy," [Colombia's Lessons for Ukraine] *RIA Novosti*, March 5, 2017, https://ria.ru/20170305/1489269030.html; "Navit Kherson bilsh proukrainsky," [Even Kherson Is More Pro-Ukrainian] *Inshe.tv*, February 22, 2017, https://inshe.tv/politics/2017-02-22/206294/; "Odessky gorsovet progolosoval protiv zakonoproektov Vyatrovicha," [Odessa's City Council Voted against Vyatrovich's Proposals] *Vesti*, March 24, 2017, https://vesti.ua/odessa/231237-odesskij-horsovet-proholosoval-protiv-zakonoproektov-vjatrovicha-; Mariya Razenkova, "Sotsiolog Golovakha," [The Sociologist Golovakha] *Vesti*, August 17, 2017, https://vesti.ua/strana/252417-sotsioloh-evhenij-holovakha; Vladislav Maltsev, "Eto ne pro nas," [This Is Not about Us] *Ukraina.ru*, November 16, 2017, https://ukraina.ru/exclusive/20171116/1019529997.html; Vladislav Maltsev, "Vtoroi Donbas," [A Second Donbas] *Ukraina.ru*, June 11, 2018, https://ukraina.ru/exclusive/20180611/1020471775.html; "Tuka: v Kieve 75% lyudei s vatoi v golove," [Tuka: 75% of People in Kiev Have Cotton in Their Heads] *Ukraina.ru*, October 7, 2015, https://ukraina.ru/news/20151007/1014481939.html; "Postpred Poroshenko: V Khersonskoi oblasti ischezayut priznaki ukrainskoi gosudarstvennosti," [Poroshenko's Permanent Representative: Evidence of Ukrainian Statehood Is Disappearing in the Kherson Region] *Ukraina.ru*, May 29, 2018, https://ukraina.ru/news/20180529/1020407567.html; Viktor Kuznetsov, "Chuzhaya rodina Poroshenko," [Poroshenko's Alien Homeland] *Ukraina.ru*, February 4, 2019, https://ukraina.ru/exclusive/20190204/1022556770.html; "Trukhanov prosit institut natspamyati razreshit vernut v Odessu prospekt Marshala Zhukova," [Trukhanov Asks the Institute of National Memory to Allow Marshal Zhukov Avenue to Be Restored to Odessa] *Timer-Odessa*, June 10, 2020, https://perma.cc/MB8W-YJ2B; "Mer Poltavy sdelal strannoe zayavlenie po ukrainskomu yazyku," [The Mayor of Poltava Made a Strange Statement about the Ukrainian Language] *Vesti*, April 28, 2016, https://vesti.ua/strana/146419-mjer-poltavy-sdelal-strannoe-zajavlenie-po-ukrainskomu-jazyku.

tionalists. So long as fear remains their predominant motivation, these two inter-pretations of Ukrainian national identity will always be mutually exclusive. Should one side ever succeed in imposing itself by force on the other, it will not mean the conflict is resolved. It will only mean that its re-emergence has been postponed for a later date.

There can be no solution to the tragedy of Ukraine without transforming both narratives: the Galician narrative in which Russia is the Eternal Enemy, and the Maloross narrative in which Russia is the Eternal Partner. If Ukrainians are to have any chance of establishing lasting social harmony, therefore, they must find a third narrative that can reconcile these two.

Chapter Six
A Flawed Peace

There is also an alternative view to what is happening – the view that this big war in Ukraine really hasn't changed … the framework of our customary habits and prejudices. From this perspective, February 24, 2022 looks not so much like a magical gateway into a new world, but more like a broken doorway, through which to drag all the baggage of the recent past: all the old fixations, insults, and recriminations that defined Ukraine's public agenda before … it took but a moment for the front lines to stabilize, for this traditional internal hate to re-emerge.
Mikhail Dubinyanski, Ukrainian historian and journalist[1]

There are quite a few who believe that peace will come when each soldier – from one side as well as the other – reaches across his pain and declares his willingness to extend his hand to his former enemy in the name of the future. When all sides start to think, not about vengeance, but about what unites them.
Vadim Novinsky, Rada MP (2013 – 2022)[2]

Amidst the wreckage of our culture, at the very bottom of hell, a single ray of sunlight, or even just a premonition of it, can illuminate the darkness, and tragedy will then cease to be hopeless.
Georgy P. Fedotov, Russian religious philosopher[3]

It is tempting to blame Ukraine's disastrous decline on eight years of war with Russia, but, as Zelensky advisor Mikhail Podolyak admitted not long ago, it is much more the consequence of "an immature state which for decades has failed the expectations of its citizens."[4] I would argue that part of this immaturity is reflected in recurring state policies that seek to ensure the victory of Galician Ukrainian identity over Maloross Ukrainian identity.

Since 2014 this has been a core consideration in national policymaking, not only in military and security matters, but also in cultural, educational, religious, linguistic, and economic policy. The alternative approach, of viewing cultural di-

---

1 Mikhail Dubinyanski, "Den, yakyi [ne] zminyv use," [The Day that Did [Not] Change Everything] *Ukrainska pravda*, March 24, 2022, https://www.pravda.com.ua/articles/2022/03/24/7334183/.
2 Nadiya Sukha, "Partiya yakoho myru?," [What Kind of Peace Party?] *Vybory*, November 9, 2018, https://vybory.pravda.com.ua/articles/2018/11/9/7149780/.
3 Georgy P. Fedotov, "Khristianskaya tragediya," [Christian Tragedy] *Novyĭ zhurnal* 23 (1950), https://azbyka.ru/otechnik/Georgij_Fedotov/hristianskaja-tragedija/.
4 "Ofis Zelenskogo Obyasnil, pochemu ukraintsy massovo uezzhayut," [Zelensky's Office Explains Why Ukrainians Are Leaving en Masse] *Smotrim*, December 30, 2021, https://smotrim.ru/article/2659043.

https://doi.org/10.1515/9783110743371-010

versity as a strength and using it to forge ties that could bind diverse populations to the Ukrainian state – an approach sometimes referred to as "liberal nationalism," but more accurately called "patriotism" – was briefly contemplated during the early 1990s, but has since fallen into disrepute due to Russia's military intervention, which Ukrainian nationalists have eagerly seized upon to promote their own agenda.

In this concluding chapter, I will examine what it will take to restore peace to Ukraine. In the past, such efforts have fallen into two broad categories: external efforts, such as the Minsk Accords; and internal efforts, such as the National Platform for Reconciliation and Unity. Both approaches failed because, they did not include any mechanisms for fostering social healing among Ukrainians themselves. That is why a greater awareness of classical Greek tragedy which saw social healing as one of it core therapeutic functions, can be so valuable for Ukraine. By ripping away all pretense, and exposing the devastating consequences of avoiding the issues at the heart of conflict, tragedy can help Ukrainian society move beyond self-consuming rage, and begin the long and arduous process of healing. It is a therapy that is still being actively used today, not on theater stages, but in the public works of Truth and Reconciliation Commissions.

I will conclude with an afterword about the Russian invasion of February 2022 and why, in my opinion, no matter how the invasion ends, it will not bring the country's tragic cycle to an end, unless Ukrainian elites also come to recognize how their own actions contributed to its perpetuation.

6.1 From Geneva to Minsk: Why Peace Failed

Attempts to negotiate a peaceful settlement between Kiev and Donbass began well before the latter's outright rebellion. On April 17, 2014, consultations between Ukraine, Russia, the United States, and the European Union led to the signing in Geneva of a "Declaration of Principles" for resolving the crisis there. It consisted of just three points:

1. All sides must refrain from any violence, intimidation or provocative actions. The participants strongly condemn and reject all expressions of extremism, racism and religious intolerance, including anti-semitism.
2. All illegal armed groups must be disarmed; all illegally seized buildings must be returned to their legitimate owners; all illegally occupied streets, squares and other public places in Ukrainian cities and towns must be vacated.

3. Amnesty will be granted to protestors and to those who have left buildings and other public places and surrendered weapons, with the exception of those found guilty of capital crimes.[5]

An OSCE Special Monitoring Mission was set up to supervise the implementation of de-escalation measures, and the Ukrainian government pledged to begin an "inclusive, transparent and accountable" process of constitutional review, that would include "the immediate establishment of a broad national dialogue, with outreach to all of Ukraine's regions and political constituencies."[6]

The Geneva Agreement had neither timetables nor mechanisms for its implementation. Its significance lay in setting down certain principles to be used in resolving the crisis. At this juncture, most international observers still viewed the conflict in Donbass as a civil conflict within Ukraine. The end of military hostilities was therefore to be followed by the negotiation of a new political framework that would grant more local autonomy to any region of Ukraine that wanted it. Russia's Foreign Minister Sergei Lavrov summed up the view of many that it was up to Kiev to "show the initiative, extend a friendly hand to the regions, listen to their concerns, and sit down with them at the negotiation table. Only then will Ukraine be a strong state, a proverbial bridge between the East and the West."[7]

Many hoped that the election in May 2014 of a new president, Petro Poroshenko, would bring about a speedy peace, since he had served under both presidents Yushchenko and Yanukovych, and had extensive business ties with Russia. But after just a month in office, Poroshenko abandoned the Geneva Agreement, and stepped up the Anti-Terrorist Operation (ATO) against Donbass, promising victory within hours.[8]

The Ukrainian army did, in fact, re-take a significant amount of rebel territory, but then it got bogged down. When it attempted to push forward again, it

---

5 "Full Text of Geneva Agreement on Ukraine," *Interfax-Ukraine*, April 18, 2014, https://en.interfax.com.ua/news/general/201277.html; Viktoriya Venk, "'Shkurnyaki' Poroshenko i familii strelkov Maĭdana," [Poroshenko's "Skeletons" and the Names of the Maidan Shooters] *Strana.ua*, December 18, 2019, https://strana.today/news/240033-elena-lukash-na-sude-po-berkutu-raskryla-familii-ubijts-na-majdane.html.

6 *Interfax-Ukraine*, "Full Text of Geneva Agreement on Ukraine."

7 "Lavrov: Russia, US, EU, Ukraine Agree on De-escalation Roadmap," *RT International*, April 17, 2014, https://www.rt.com/news/geneva-document-ukraine-deescalation-224/.

8 Daryna Shevchenko, "Poroshenko Pledges to Step Up Anti-Terrorism Operation," *Kyiv Post*, May 26, 2014, https://www.kyivpost.com/article/content/may-25-presidential-election/poroshenko-pledges-to-step-up-anti-terrorism-operation-bring-success-within-hours-not-months-349441.html.

met with a series of disastrous defeats. After the first, at Ilovaisk in August 2014, President Poroshenko was forced to accept the First Minsk Accords. After the second, at Debaltsevo in February 2015, he was forced to sign the Second Minsk Accords.

Both of these accords continue to assume that the conflict in eastern Ukraine is mostly an internal affair. The essential difference between them lies in their degree of detail. The Second Minsk Accords (Minsk-2) provided a comprehensive framework and specific deadlines for the reintegration of Donbass into Ukraine that followed the logic of the Geneva Agreements: the first three points dealt with the separation of forces; the remaining ten points were confidence-building measures designed to lead to the reintegration of the region into Ukraine. Its most significant points are:

– Point 5, which called for the pardon and amnesty of those engaged in the conflict. The Ukraine parliament did pass such an amnesty law, but applied it only to Ukrainian soldiers and volunteer fighters.
– Points 7 and 8, which called for restoring economic and financial ties with Kiev. Ukraine subsequently shut down all banking and social services in the region, suspended local pension payments, restricted rail and cell phone service, and instituted a blockade of water and electricity.
– And Point 9, which stipulated that control of the border would be transferred to Kiev *after* local elections and a comprehensive political settlement. A comprehensive political settlement was defined as the adoption of constitutional amendments on decentralization that included a local police force, and the right to use the local language (Russian).[9]

Minsk-2 committed both the government in Kiev and the rebels in Donbass to direct negotiations aimed at institutionalizing cultural pluralism in Ukraine. When the deadlines established in Minsk-2 expired, Ukraine extended the agreement. To gain enough support in parliament to do so, however, the Rada simultaneously adopted a law on the restoration of state sovereignty (Law 7163). It laid out a strategy substantially at odds with the Minsk Accords. Under this law, Ukrainian military actions in eastern Ukraine were no longer merely an anti-terrorist operation, but were now a "military operation with the aim of counteracting Russian aggression."[10] Martial law was imposed throughout the region, and the regional

---

9 "Package of Measures for the Implementation of the Minsk Agreements," *OSCE.org*, February 12, 2015, https://www.osce.org/cio/140156.
10 "Pro osoblyvosti derzhavnoy polityky iz zabezpechennya derzhavnoho suverenitetu Ukrainy na tymchasovo okupovanykh terytoriyakh u Donetskii ta Luganskii oblastyakh," [On the Specifics of State Policy to Ensure the State Sovereignty of Ukraine in the Temporarily Occupied Ter-

military commander tasked with supervising governmental, commercial, as well as military activity.

Law 7163 never mentions the Minsk Accords. This is not an oversight. The new law enshrined Kiev's new demand that control of the border be transferred to Ukraine *before* local elections, rather than after them, as stipulated in Point 9 of Minsk-2. This made the implementation of Minsk-2 impossible under Ukrainian law. Moreover, since the government was committed to total Ukrainianization, the provisions in Minsk-2 that required for constitutional changes to ensure local cultural autonomy could also never be implemented.[11]

None of this, however, deterred France and Germany from providing various "roadmaps" for implementing the Second Minsk Accords. In chronological order, they are the Morel Plan, the Sajdik Initiative, the Steinmeier Formula, and the Clusters Approach.

The Morel Plan. Named after French diplomat Pierre Morel, the Morel Plan called for Ukraine to establish a firm date by which to pass a law on local elections in the rebel-held areas of Donbass. These elections would then have to be held within eighty days. Rebel leaders would be given amnesty, and allowed to run for local office. In return, they would cancel their own election plans, and agree to hold elections under Ukrainian law.[12] Germany, Russia, and France agreed to the Morel Plan; Ukraine did not.

The Sajdik Initiative. Named after Austrian diplomat Martin Sajdik, the Saijdik Initiative created a United Nations Special Representative in charge of the military and police components of the Minsk Accords, as well as a European Union Special Representative for the economic development. The UN Special Representative would be responsible for the integration of the entire Donetsk and Lugansk region, and be supported by roughly 20,000 peacekeepers. According to Sajdik, his central idea was to ensure that the population of Donbass ac-

---

ritories in the Donetsk and Lugansk Regions] *Golos Ukrainy*, February 23, 2018, http://www.go-los.com.ua/article/300158.

11 "Poroshenko poobeshchal, chto na ukrainskom yazyke zagovorit vsya Ukraina," [Poroshenko Promises that All of Ukraine Will Speak Ukrainian] *RitmEurasia*, November 10, 2017, https://www.ritmeurasia.org/news–2017–11–10–poroshenko-poobeschal-chto-na-ukrainskom-jazyke-zagovorit-vsja-ukraina-33434.

12 Leonid Bershidsky, "Ukraine Has No Choice but to Live with Putin," *Bloomberg*, October 5, 2015, https://www.bloomberg.com/opinion/articles/2015–10–05/ukraine-has-no-choice-but-to-live-with-putin; Paul Robinson, "Holding Kiev to Account," *Irrussianality*, October 7, 2015, https://irrussianality.wordpress.com/2015/10/06/holding-kiev-to-account/.

tually received the rights prescribed in Minsk-2.[13] Germany, Russia, and France agreed to the Morel Plan; Ukraine did not.

The Steinmeier Formula. Named after former German foreign minister and later president Frank-Walter Steinmeier, this plan proposed a novel procedure for holding elections in Donbass. Instead of passing the special status and amnesty laws *before* the elections, they would enter into force provisionally on the day of the elections, and become permanent after the OSCE had ratified the election results.[14] The central idea here was that, with authorities in Donbass now legitimated through elections, Kiev could begin negotiating with them directly. Again, Germany, Russia, and France agreed to the Steinmeier Formula; Ukraine did not.[15]

The Clusters Approach. This last effort to revive the Minsk process was proposed jointly by the heads of the French and German working groups in the Trilateral Contact Group (TCG). The central idea was for each side to agree on a sequence for implementing broad "clusters," then pass this sequence on to the TCG, which would work out a roadmap with hard deadlines for their implementation. There were two categories of clusters: "Security/Humanitarian" and "Political/Economic." French and German negotiators provided the framework of what should be discussed within each cluster. These would then be reviewed by Ukrainian and Russian negotiators (since Ukraine refused any direct negotiations with Donbass representatives), until they reached agreement. The Clusters Approach got as far as initial drafts in early 2021. Ukraine's draft does not mention any special status for the regions, or any "legislation for Donbass as func-

---

13 Christian Wehrschütz, "Exklusiv-Interview: Sondergesandter Sajdik," [Exclusive Interview: Special Envoy Sajdik] *Kleinezeitung.at*, January 24, 2019, https://www.kleinezeitung.at/politik/aussenpolitik/5567894/.
14 Evgenii Pilipenko, "Putin vspomnil ob osobom statuse Donbassa i amnistii dlya boevikov," [Putin Remembers About the Special Status of Donbass and Amnesty for Militants] *Liga*, August 20, 2019, https://news.liga.net/politics/news/putin-vspomnil-ob-osobom-statuse-donbassa-i-amnistii-dlya-boevikov; "Germany Detailed 'Steinmeier Formula' for ORDLO Elections," *LB.ua*, December 15, 2016, https://en.lb.ua/news/2016/12/15/2617_germany_detailed_steinmeier.html.
15 "Kuchma ne podpisal 'formulu Shtainmaiera,'" [Kuchma Did Not Sign the "Steinmeier Formula"] *Ukraina.ru*, September 18, 2019, https://ukraina.ru/news/20190918/1025039489.html; Vasily Stoyakin, "'Formula Zelenskogo' ot 'diplomata s Maidana' Bogdana Yaromenko," ["The Zelensky Formula" According to "the Maidan's Diplomat" Bogdan Yaryomenko] *Ukraina.ru*, September 24, 2019, https://ukraina.ru/exclusive/20190924/1025089754.html. According to Yaryomenko, the chairman of the Rada's committee on foreign affairs, Ukraine's opposition to the Steinmeier Formula boils down to three points: first, Ukraine refuses to make any changes to its constitution; second, any political initiatives can be undertaken only *after* security guarantees are in place; third, local elections must take place across the entire country and under one set of rules.

tioning on a permanent basis" – the euphemism Kiev uses to refer to constitutional changes. Instead, the Ukrainian draft listed legislation that the Rada might be willing to consider. These included laws on local self-government in the rebel territories, "the peculiarities of local elections," amnesty, the creation of a Special Economic Zone in the rebel regions, and certain amendments to the Ukrainian Constitution to enhance decentralization. At the group's last meeting in March 2021, Russia let it be known that the Donbass representatives were awaiting further details about how such legislation would take the specifics of the Donbass region into account.[16]

6.1.2 Why Minsk-2 Failed

From the outset, Ukraine's strategy was to prevent the implementation of Minsk-2. In an interview with Radio Liberty, retired Ukrainian Foreign Minister Pavlo Klimkin acknowledged that Ukraine's sole objective in signing Minsk-2 was to rebuild the Ukrainian army and strengthen the international coalition against Russia. "Read literally," he says "the Minsk Accords are impossible to implement. That was understood from the very first day."[17] Past and present Ukrainian negotiators have all made the same point, as did President Zelensky's Chief of Staff, Andrei Yermak, in February 2021.[18] As the Secretary of the National Security and Defense Council (NSDC), Oleksiy Danilov put it, Ukraine cannot negotiate

---

16 "Klasterov khvatit na vsekh," [There Are Enough Clusters for Everyone] *Novosti Donbassa*, March 24, 2021, http://novosti.dn.ua/article/7770-klasterov-hvatit-na-vseh-v-moskve-obnarodovali-soderzhanie-novyh-predlozhenij-ukrainy-rossii.
17 Oleksandr Lashchenko, "Klimkin: Shkoduyu, shcho Ukraina ne rozirvala dypvidnosyny z Rosiieyu," [Klimkin: I Regret that Ukraine Did Not Sever Diplomatic Ties with Russia] *Radio Svoboda*, October 4, 2020, https://www.radiosvoboda.org/a/klimkin-shkoduyu-shcho-ukrayina-ne-rozirvala-dypvidnosyny-z-rosiyeyu/30871035.html.
18 "Minsk razonravilsya ukrainskim peregovorshchikam po Donbassu," [Minsk Has Fallen Out of Favor with Ukrainian Negotiators on Donbass] *Timer-Odessa*, April 6, 2021, https://perma.cc/2PK2-DX5 A; Anatoliy Grytsenko, "Minsk Ceasefire Only Anaesthesia, Not Treatment of the Illness," *European Leadership Network*, January 14, 2015, https://www.europeanleadershipnetwork.org/commentary/minsk-ceasefire-only-anaesthesia-not-treatment-of-the-illness/; "Ne demarsh, a isterika," [Not a Demarche, but Hysteria] *Regnum.ru*, March 16, 2021, https://regnum-ru.turbopages.org/regnum.ru/s/news/3216711.html; "Ponimayut otvet s pyatogo raza i khamyat," [They Understand the Answer Only the Fifth Time and Are Rude] *DonPress*, March 3, 2021, https://perma.cc/TQ5D-VW8 J; "Ermak: Minskie soglasheniya vypolnit nevozmozhno, nuzhno vnosit korrektivy," [Yermak: It Is Impossible to Fulfill the Minsk Agreements, We Need to Make Adjustments] *Ukrainska pravda*, February 13, 2021, https://www.pravda.com.ua/rus/news/2021/02/13/7283333/.

with Donbass because "there is no such thing as Donbass ... it is a definition imposed on us by the Russian Federation."[19]

It was believed that this strategy of non-negotiation, which was supported by the United States and its European allies, would eventually force Russia to leave Donbass.[20] Isolated from its main supporter, the rebels would then have no choice but to capitulate on Kiev's terms. If this strategy had worked in Donbass, then it could presumably have been used to gain back Crimea as well. But, instead of surrendering in the face of Western sanctions, Russia increased its aid to the region and raised the stakes by offering Donbass residents Russian passports. By May 2021, more than a third of Donbass residents had acquired Russian passports.[21]

Another problem with Kiev's strategy is that the economic blockade it has imposed on Donbass has further alienated the local population. This disaffection has even been noted by Western researchers, who found that, whereas in 2019 a majority still wanted to be rejoin Ukraine, by 2021, only 12 percent still wanted to be part of Ukraine, while over half now wanted to join Russia.[22]

But while, technically, the failure of Minsk-2 can be traced to Ukraine's unwillingness to negotiate with the rebels, more broadly it stems from Kiev's em-

---

19 "Sekretar sovnatsbeza Ukrainy isklyuchil sushchestvovanie Donbassa," [Secretary of the Security Council of Ukraine Rules out the Existence of Donbass] *Regnum.ru*, March 24, 2021, https://regnum-ru.turbopages.org/regnum.ru/s/news/3224141.html.
20 Kurt Volker, "What Does a Successful Biden-Putin Summit Look Like?," *Center for European Policy Analysis*, June 2, 2021, https://cepa.org/what-does-a-successful-biden-putin-summit-look-like-not-what-you-think/. Volker, the US Special Representative for Ukraine until September 2019, describes America's ideal policy toward Russia as "one of a lack of agreements altogether. Success is confrontation."
21 Alyona Shevchenko, "V MID RF vystupili s zayavleniem o vydache Rossiiskikh pasportov v ORDLO," [The Ministry of Foreign Affairs of the Russian Federation Issued a Statement on the Issuance of Russian Passports in ORDLO] *UA News*, June 26, 2021, https://news.online.ua/v-mid-rf-vystupili-s-zayavleniem-o-vydache-rossiyskih-pasportov-v-ordlo_n834166/.
22 John O'Loughlin, Gwendolyn Sasse, Gerard Toal, and Kristin M. Bakke, "A New Survey of the Ukraine-Russia Conflict Finds Deeply Divided Views in the Contested Donbas Region," *The Washington Post*, February 12, 2021, https://www.washingtonpost.com/politics/2021/02/12/new-survey-ukraine-russia-conflict-finds-deeply-divided-views-contested-donbas-region/; "Residents in Breakaway Ukrainian Donbass Regions Have More Trust in Government than Those Living under Kiev's Rule," *RT International*, February 19, 2021, https://www.rt.com/russia/515965-donbass-more-trust-government-kiev/. A significant change is that 26 percent of those surveyed in rebel held areas said they trusted their officials, compared to less than 10 percent of those living in the areas controlled by Kiev. Fewer than 20 percent of DNR/LNR residents described themselves as "actively distrustful" of their government, compared with 45 percent across the border in Ukrainian controlled territory.

brace of Ukrainian nationalism, which has simply erased the people of Donbass from Ukraine's post-Maidan identity. Popular writer Elena Styazhkina, who is herself originally from Donbass, illustrates this by asking her Kievan audience to imagine Ukraine as a deity: "Can a foreign god be accepted as one's own? Not a compassionate god, no ... First the gallows, then the schools. That is how a new god comes here [to Donbass]."[23]

This left Ukraine with just two options: the military conquest of Donbass, or a frozen conflict. Each option had its supporters in Ukraine. The military conquest option was popularly referred to as "the Croatian scenario," after the eight-day blitzkrieg of August 1995 in which the Croatian army overran the separatist region of *Serbska kraijina*.[24] It was endorsed by such high-ranking Ukrainian officials as Volodymyr Hroysman (then prime minister), the former head and deputy head of the NSDC, the governors of both Donetsk and Lugansk, and the former Ukrainian defense minister.[25] It was, however, pointedly not endorsed by the Commander-in-Chief of the Ukrainian Armed Forces, Ruslan

23 "Vystup roku na TEDxKyiv: Olena Styazhkina pro Donbas, bogiv, shibentsyu i vyiny," [TEDx-Kyiv Talk of the Year: Olena Styazhkina about Donbass, Gods, the Gallows, and War] *Ukrainska pravda*, November 3, 2014, https://life.pravda.com.ua/society/2014/11/3/183223/.

24 "Po primeru Khorvatii," [Following the Example of Croatia] *Sudebno-yuridicheskaya gazeta*, August 20, 2018, https://sud.ua/ru/news/ukraine/123708-po-primeru-khorvatii-diplomat-rasskazal-chto-nuzhno-sdelat-na-donbasse.

25 "Voina neizbezhna," [War Is Inevitable] *Novorossiya*, December 12, 2021, https://tinyurl.com/y6lbhn88; Rodion Vlasov, "Est tolko odin put vernut Donbass," [There Is Only One Way to Return Donbass] *NBNews*, October 2, 2020, https://nbnews.com.ua/politika/2020/10/02/est-tolko-odin-put-vernut-donbass-moskal-predlozhil-radikalnyi-plan/; "V SNBO nazvali usloviya dlya silovogo osvobozhdeniya Donbassa," [The National Security and Defense Council Defines the Conditions for the Forcible Liberation of Donbass] *RBK-Ukraina*, January 20, 2020, https://www.rbc.ua/rus/news/snbo-nazvali-usloviya-silovogo-osvobozhdeniya-1579517895.html; "Turchinov soobshchil o gotovnosti Kieva k blitskrigu protiv DNR i LNR," [Turchynov Says Kiev is Ready for a Blitzkrieg against the DPR and LPR] *Ukraina.ru*, December 16, 2016, https://ukraina.ru/news/20161216/1018022399.html; "Ukrainskie vlasti ozvuchili tri stsenariya vosstanovleniya kontrolya nad Donbassom," [Ukrainian Authorities Have Voiced Three Scenarios for Regaining Control over Donbass] *Ukraina.ru*, May 1, 2018, https://ukraina.ru/news/20180501/1020290080.html; Fyodor Koloskov, "Kak Ukraina Sobiraetsya 'osvobozhdat' Donbass," [How Ukraine Is Going to "Liberate" Donbass] *Ritm Eurasia*, January 30, 2017, https://www.ritmeurasia.org/news-2017-01-30-kak-ukraina-sobiraetsja-osvobozhdat-donbass-28100; "Zhebrivsky zayavil, chto Donbass mozhno osvobodit za chetyre dnya," [Zhebrivsky Says Donbass Can Be Liberated in Four Days] *MIG News*, June 23, 2017, https://m.mignews.com.ua/politics/18374779.html; "Groysman: reintegratsiya Donbassa dolzhna prokhodit po khorvatskomu stsenariyu," [Groysman: Reintegration of Donbass Should Take Place According to the Croatian Scenario] *RIA Novosti*, June 15, 2017, https://ria.ru/20170615/1496614916.html.

Khomchak who, nevertheless, said that the army would follow any orders it was given.[26]

The second option of a frozen conflict has been endorsed by former Ukrainian foreign minister, Pavlo Klimkin, and his successor, Dmytro Kuleba. As the latter put it:

> Even after we return these territories de jure and de facto, Russia will be the same, she will not go anywhere. Accordingly, we must either prepare ourselves for perpetual war, physical, military war; or we must prepare ourselves for perpetual political, economic, and cultural confrontation. I certainly choose the latter. That is to say, the global conflict between Russia and Ukraine is not going anywhere.[27]

Despite its inherent risks, perpetual confrontation with Russia was ultimately deemed beneficial for Ukraine because it would ensure long-term Western assistance, culminating in EU and NATO membership for Ukraine.

6.1.3 Why All Foreign Roads Led to a Frozen Conflict

The ultimate failure of Minsk-2, however, cannot be attributed solely to Ukraine; the West contributed significantly as well. By treating Ukraine, first and foremost, as a means of containing Russia, the West chose to ignore the obvious divisions within Ukrainian society, which made any true solution to the crisis impossible. Broadly speaking, Western approaches on how to resolve the conflict in Ukraine fall into one of two categories: Hardline or Pragmatic.

For Hardliners, the issue at stake is much bigger than Ukraine; it is that Russia has broken the rules of European security, and is now constructing "an alternate reality." According to ambassadors Steven Pifer, Strobe Talbott, Alexander Vershbow, and former NATO General Secretary Anders Fogh Rasmussen, Moscow wants to sow chaos and instability in Ukraine because it fears that a suc-

---

26 "VSU gotovy k nastupliniyu na Donbasse, no budut posledstviya," [The Armed Forces of Ukraine Are Ready for an Offensive in the Donbass, but There Will Be Consequences] *Strana.ua*, March 30, 2021, https://strana.one/news/325420-khomchak-zajavil-chto-vsu-hotovy-k-nastupleniju-na-donbasse.html; "Gotovim voiska," [We Are Preparing the Troops] *DonPress*, February 22, 2021, https://donpress.com/news/22–02–2021-gotovim-voyska-homchak-zayavil-o-podgotovke-vsu-k-boyam-v-gorodskoy-mestnosti.
27 Konstantin Kevorkyan, "Nastupayut v boevom besporyadke," [Advancing in Combat Disarray] *Ukraina.ru*, October 9, 2020, https://ukraina.ru/opinion/20201009/1029194827.html; Vadim Moskalenko, "MID Ukrainy obyavil Rossiyu 'vechnym vragom,'" [Ukrainian Foreign Ministry Declares Russia an "Eternal Enemy"] *Polit Navigator*, September 9, 2020, https://perma.cc/CME6-WTAA.

cessful, pro-Western Ukraine will be popular with Russian citizens.[28] If the West does not push back hard against Russian actions now, it will face even greater challenges in the future.

The Hardline approach is, by its own admission, contemptuous of diplomacy. There is simply nothing to negotiate; Russia must surrender, fully withdraw from Ukraine, and give up the idea that it has any interests in that country. Failure to do so must bring ever increasing pressure to bear.[29] This policy might seem to risk confrontation, but Hardliners see little danger in this, since they believe that Russia is a country in decline. Since it desperately needs Western capital, technology, and contacts, it will have no choice but to capitulate.[30]

By contrast, Pragmatists, like ambassadors Jack F. Matlock, Jr. and Tony Brenton, professors Graham Allison and Henry Kissinger, and former Senator Bill Bradley, believe that the Hardline approach is destined to fail. Even before the Minsk Accords, therefore, they encouraged direct negotiations with Russia as a means of achieving a comprehensive post-Cold War settlement. Some, like professor John J. Mearsheimer, and the late Russia experts George F. Kennan and Stephen F. Cohen, even blamed the West for failing to pursue such a settlement after the Cold War.[31]

For this group the "obvious" formula for peace is greater regional autonomy within a Ukraine that belongs neither to Europe nor to Russia.[32] Critics argue that their proposals are so much in harmony with Moscow's, that they are sometimes made jointly. An example is the Boisto Agenda of August 2014, which was conceived by Thomas Graham, former senior director for Russia on the National Security Council staff, and Alexander Dynkin, former advisor to the prime minister

---

28 Clifford G. Gaddy, Fiona Hill, Steven Pifer, Jeremy Shapiro, and Lilia Shevtsova, "Around the Halls: Has the Ruble Gone to Rubble?," *Brookings*, December 17, 2014, https://www.brookings.edu/blog/up-front/2014/12/17/around-the-halls-has-the-ruble-gone-to-rubble/.

29 Alexander Mercouris, "UN Deadlock on Ukraine Peacekeepers," *The Duran*, September 21, 2017, https://theduran.com/un-deadlock-ukraine-peacekeepers/; Alexander Vershbow, "How to Bring Peace to the Donbas," *Atlantic Council*, January 5, 2018, https://www.atlanticcouncil.org/blogs/ukrainealert/how-to-bring-peace-to-the-donbas-yes-it-s-possible/; "George Soros: A Winning Strategy for Ukraine," *Jewish Business News*, June 19, 2015, https://jewishbusinessnews.com/2015/06/19/george-soros-a-winning-strategy-for-ukraine/.

30 Joseph S. Nye Jr., "A Western Strategy for a Declining Russia," *Project Syndicate*, September 3, 2014, https://www.project-syndicate.org/commentary/joseph-s–nye-wants-to-deter-russia-without-isolating-it.

31 Thomas L. Friedman, "Now a Word from X," *The New York Times*, May 2, 1998, https://www.nytimes.com/1998/05/02/opinion/foreign-affairs-now-a-word-from-x.html.

32 Leslie H. Gelb, "How to Solve the Ukraine," *The Daily Beast*, March 9, 2014, https://www.thedailybeast.com/articles/2014/03/09/leslie-h-gelb-cut-the-baloney-on-ukraine.

of Russia. It identified the key issues as: (1) an enduring ceasefire; (2) humanitarian and legal issues; (3) preserving Ukraine's economic ties with Russia and reviving its energy infrastructure; (4) protection for the Russian language and access to Russian media and television; and (5) a neutral, non-bloc status for Ukraine. The issue of Crimea was set aside for the future.[33]

The Boisto Agenda was such a clear throwback to a bipolar, Cold War view of the world that it did not even bother to include Ukrainians in its deliberations.[34] It therefore quickly became hostage to domestic interests and foreign policy debates far removed from Ukraine itself.[35] Even before Russia's invasion of Ukraine in 2022, thanks to the media prominence given to President Donald Trump's alleged collusion with Russia, the Hardliners were able to steer public discourse away from the issue of how to achieve peace in Ukraine, to how to punish Russia. If Hardliners failed because they offered nothing in exchange for Russian good behavior, Pragmatists failed because they were seen as rewarding Russia for breaking the rules.

Meanwhile, the actual wellbeing of Ukrainians themselves was essentially irrelevant to both Hardliners and Pragmatists, as they sought to promote their own visions of American security. This explains the dogged persistence of some rather bizarre contradictions in US foreign policy toward Ukraine. One is that, although sanctions have never once succeeded in changing Russian policy, it is argued that even more sanctions will succeed in doing so. Another is the portrayal of Western-led reforms in Ukraine as singularly successful, when every survey shows that Ukrainians themselves believe the exact opposite.[36]

---

33 Uri Friedman, "A 24-Step Plan to Resolve the Ukraine Crisis," *The Atlantic*, August 26, 2014, https://www.theatlantic.com/international/archive/2014/08/a-24-step-plan-to-resolve-the-ukraine-crisis/379121/.

34 Robert Legvold, "Facing Reality in Ukraine," *The National Interest*, September 16, 2014, https://nationalinterest.org/feature/facing-reality-ukraine-11289.

35 "Frattini: s Ukrainoi sdelali to zhe, chto i s Gruziei," [Frattini: They Did the Same with Ukraine That They Did with Georgia] *Vesti*, March 7, 2015, https://www.vesti.ru/article/1753965. Former Italian Foreign Minister Franco Frattini is a notable exception. While in office he criticized the EU's Eastern Partnership Agreement as anti-Russian and argued in favor of Ukrainian federalism and regional autonomy for the East.

36 "Zahalnoukrainske sotsiolohichne opituvannya naselennya Ukrainy," [All-Ukraine Sociological Survey of the Population of Ukraine] *Social Monitoring Center*, December 21, 2021, https://smc.org.ua/zagalnoukrayinske-sotsiologichne-opytuvannya-naselennya-ukrayiny-3551/; "Dynamyka sotsialno-politichnykh nastroiv ta otsinok naselennya Ukrainy traven 2021 roku," [Trends in Socio-political Sentiments and Assessments of the Population of Ukraine in May 2021] *Social Monitoring Center*, June 15, 2021, https://smc.org.ua/dynamika-sotsialno-politychnyh-nastroyiv-ta-otsinok-naselennya-ukrayiny-traven-2021-roku-2–2611/.

Game theorists would describe the current situation of perpetual conflict between Russia and the West, bolstered by perpetual instability with Ukraine, as Pareto Optimal, because it appeals to the widest variety of conflict participants: Western, Russian, and Ukrainian Hardliners all derive significant benefits from this conflict, whereas Pragmatists are marginalized. Under these conditions, freezing the conflict, rather than resolving it, becomes the most attractive option.

There are, however, a few problems with prolonged frozen conflict. One is that, according to game theorists, the most likely outcomes for un-freezing this particular frozen conflict is that the West gradually removes its sanctions without any change in Russian behavior, while Russia continues to bloc Ukraine's entry into NATO.[37] It would also be quite disastrous for Ukraine's prospects of developing a harmonious society, since it would push the underlying issues that led to the present conflict even further underground, where they will have time to fester. A third possibility, which very few analysts took seriously before February 24, 2022, is that Russia itself would be dissatisfied with the status quo, and decide to change it.

6.2 Domestic Peace Proposals

All foreign peace plans for Ukraine share one common flaw – a dismissive approach to the country's cultural, religious, and historical differences. They are either ignored entirely, or dismissed as being so trivial that they can be easily managed by a deft combination of diplomatic coercion and economic incentives.

The issue of language rights is rather typical in this regard. Most people in the West have difficulty understanding why one's choice of language should be such a divisive issue, when there are so many multilingual countries in Europe. The answer to this is perfectly obvious to any Ukrainian nationalist, however: allowing Ukrainians to use Russian is, in and of itself, a threat to Ukrainian identity, and therefore a threat to national security.

"The dream," as the government's first language ombudsman, Tatyana Monakhova, once explained, "was always to cultivate, build or construct a powerful homogeneous Ukrainian monolith – a society of the like-minded, who speak the state language, having no disagreements on major issues of state. Monoliths are

---

37 Leonid Bershidsky, "Gaming the Ukraine Crisis," *Bloomberg*, May 13, 2015, https://www.bloomberg.com/opinion/articles/2015 – 05 – 12/gaming-the-ukraine-crisis.

created using both whips and pastries."[38] Her successor, Taras Kremin, has even likened his task to that of Moses.[39] For Ukrainian nationalists the "obvious" solution proposed by well-meaning foreigners – healing the country by expanding political participation – is precisely what led the country to the present impasse.[40]

One way out could be to focus more attention on the domestic components to the conflict, and on the need for a transformation of the attitudes of Ukrainians on both sides of this conflict. Political scientist Jesse Driscoll, and Ukraine analyst for The Crisis Group, Katharine Quinn-Judge, have both suggested the Western peace efforts pay far too little attention to the need for a fundamental change in attitude in the Kiev government toward the people of Donbass.[41]

Unlike Western peace proposals, the need for a profound shift in social attitudes, for a social *catharsis* that would allow Galician and Maloross Ukrainians to engage in a fruitful dialogue with each other, has been a prominent motif of Ukrainian peace activists, whose proposals we will now examine.

---

38 Tatyana Monakhova, "Posle Evromaidana," [After the Euromaidan] *Novosti Donbassa*, January 11, 2019, https://novosti.dn.ua/article/7216-posle-evromaydana-nastupyla-ly-pora-bez-seksyzma-ehydzhyzma-y-gomofobyy.

39 Galina Strus, "Kremin rasskazal o puti k gospodstvu ukrainskogo yazyka," [Kremin Describes the Path to the Dominance of the Ukrainian Language] *Politeka.net*, July 14, 2021, https://perma.cc/C2 J8-BUMP.

40 "Yushchenko pro Krym i Donbas," [Yushchenko on Crimea and Donbass] *Ukrainska pravda*, December 26, 2014, https://www.pravda.com.ua/news/2014/12/26/7053324/; "Vid referendumu my nikudy ne dinemosya, Andrukhovych pro Donbas," [We Cannot Escape a Referendum, Andrukhovych on Donbas] *Radio Liberty*, April 21, 2016, https://www.radiosvoboda.org/a/27689191.html; "Byvshyi prezident Ukrainy Vyktor Yushchenko nazval zhytelei strany kvazinatsyei," [Former President of Ukraine Viktor Yushchenko Calls the Inhabitants of the Country a Quasi-Nation] August 28, 2021, *Argumenty i fakty*, August 28, 2021, https://argumenti-ru.turbopages.org/argumenti.ru/s/world/2021/08/736023; Konstantin Kevorkyan, "Smelost ostavatsia soboi," [Courage to Be Yourself] *Ukraina.ru*, July 16, 2020, https://ukraina.ru/opinion/20200716/1028270703.html; Georgi Luchnikov, "Gotovy k radikalnym deistviyam," [Ready for Radical Action] *Ukraina.ru*, September 17, 2019, https://ukraina.ru/exclusive/20190917/1025010770.html "Tuka: V Kyeve 75% lyudei s vatoy v golove," [Tuka: 75% of People in Kiev Have Cotton in Their Heads] *Ukraina.ru*, October 7, 2015, https://ukraina.ru/news/20151007/1014481939.html; Konstantin Kevorkyan, "Chrezmerno khitro sdelannye," [Made Overly Crafty] *Ukraina.ru*, February 10, 2021, https://ukraina.ru/opinion/20210210/1030508727.html.

41 Katharine Quinn-Judge, "To Reunite Ukraine, Kyiv Must Overcome Its Own Prejudices," *Crisis Group*, March 20, 2018, https://www.crisisgroup.org/europe-central-asia/eastern-europe/ukraine/reunite-ukraine-kyiv-must-overcome-its-own-prejudices; Jesse Driscoll, "Ukraine's Civil War: Would Accepting This Terminology Help Resolve the Conflict?," *Ponars Eurasia*, February 2019, https://www.ponarseurasia.org/wp-content/uploads/attachments/Pepm572_Driscoll_Feb2019_2-1.pdf.

6.2.1 The Medvedchuk and Novinsky Plans

Viktor Medvedchuk was chief of staff for Ukrainian President Leonid Kuchma. In 2015 he was asked by President Petro Poroshenko to serve as an intermediary in the release of Ukrainian soldiers held by the rebels. He was able to negotiate the release of over 400 Ukrainian soldiers, including, most notably, Nadezhda Savchenko, but was fired by President Zelensky.[42] Medvedchuk's diplomatic success was no doubt facilitated by his personal connections with Russian President Vladimir Putin, who is godfather to his second daughter, Darya.

His peace plan focuses on implementing the political aspect of Minsk through direct negotiations with the rebels. These negotiations, he says, should be based on three principles. First, the need to "return people, not territory." Donbass residents must be made to feel safe and welcome in Ukraine.[43] Second, the format should be Kiev-Donetsk-Lugansk-Moscow because "this is an internal conflict of Ukraine ... [but] the Russian Federation has great influence over the current representatives of Donetsk and in Lugansk."[44] Third, there must be full compatibility with the Minsk-2 Accords. Guided by these three principles, Medvedchuk proposed a series of legislative initiatives to economically support Donbass and Crimea, and assist them in establishing a type of autonomy that both the regions and the Ukrainian state can live with.

Medvedchuk calls his strategy "restoring Donbass to Ukraine, and Ukraine to Donbass." He insists that it does not mean transforming Ukraine into a federation (although Medvedchuk is on record as favoring federalism), because the Ukrainian Constitution already provides for the autonomous status of Crimea. He feels that regional special status, however, should also include such things as expanded regional government, a local parliament, and free economic zones.[45]

---

42 Viktor Medvedchuk, "Vernut Donbass v Ukrainu i Ukrainu na Donbass," [Return Donbass to Ukraine and Ukraine to Donbass] *Ukrainsky Vybor*, January 12, 2017, https://perma.cc/ ZUJ6 – 5T3N.

43 Ignasio Ortega, "Plan Medvedchuka," [The Medvedchuk Plan] *Ukrainsky vybor*, April 11, 2019, https://perma.cc/X8YW-YH54.

44 Viktor Medvedchuk, "Presentation of Peace Plan of Settlement of Donbas Conflict in European Council," *112 Ukraine*, July 18, 2019, https://112.international/politics/presentation-of-peace-plan-of-settlement-of-donbas-conflict-in-european-council-full-text-41848.html.

45 "Plan–kontseptsiya uregulirovaniya krizisa na yugo–vostoke Ukrainy," [A Concept-Plan for the Settlement of the Crisis in the Southeast of Ukraine] *Podrobnosti.ua*, January 30, 2019, https://podrobnosti.ua/2280981-plan-kontseptsija-uregulirovanija-krizisa-na-jugo-vostoke-ukrai-ny.html; Ignasio Ortega, "Plan Medvedchuka"; "U "Oppozitsionnoi platformy – Za zhizn est chetkaya programma, kak ustanovit mir i spasti ekonomiku," [The Opposition Platform – For

After being dismissed by President Zelensky, Medvedchuk was elected to the Ukrainian parliament. His party, the Opposition Bloc-For Life, officially adopted his peace plan in January 2019. Although his plan received considerable attention in Ukraine and in Europe for a while, it disappeared from public view in February 2021, when Medvedchuk's assets were seized by order of President Zelensky and he was placed under house arrest.[46] His party's political activities were suspended by President Zelensky on March 20, 2022, and officially disbanded by the government on May 12, 2022.[47]

Vadim Novinsky is another leading member of the Opposition Bloc, as well as one of Ukraine's wealthiest businessmen. At the end of 2018 he launched a "Ukrainian Formula for Peace" around the principles of Humanity – Dialogue – and Conciliarity (*sobornost*).

Ukrainians, he says, need to learn to see each other as co-citizens, rather than as enemies. To achieve this, the Ukrainian media should conduct an "information campaign for peace." It is also vital that the Ukrainian Orthodox Church (MP) become engaged in the peace process, he says, since it is currently the only public institution officially represented in all regions of Ukraine, including both Donbass and Crimea.

To foster dialogue, members of the Rada should meet regularly with representatives of the regional assemblies of occupied Donbass. Together, they should come up with common legislative initiatives for restoring freedom of movement across the demarcation line, revitalizing the economy, and restoring mutual trust. To facilitate such a dialogue, he suggests that members of the Parliamentary Assembly of the Council of Europe be invited to serve as mediators.

Finally, the spirit of reconciliation should be promoted through a permanently functioning "Forum for Donbass." Its task would be to promote "the co-involvement of citizens in a unifying process." While diplomats and politicians

---

Life Has a Clear Program on How to Establish Peace and Save the Economy] *Ukrainsky vybor*, November 12, 2018, https://perma.cc/WP8M-TRYX.

46 "Ukrainian President Zelenskiy Sanctions Pro-Russia Rival Medvedchuk's TV Stations," *Intellinews*, February 3, 2021, https://www.intellinews.com/ukrainian-president-zelenskiy-sanctions-pro-russia-rival-medvedchuk-s-tv-stations-201955/.

47 "Zelensky Bans Main Ukrainian Opposition Party," *RT.com*, March 20, 2022, https://www.rt.com/russia/552321-ukraine-zelensky-opposition-parties/; Roman Kravets and Valentina Romanenko, "OPZZh u Verkhovniy Radi perestala isnuvaty," [Opposition Platform – For Life in the Verkhovna Rada Ceases to Exist] *Ukrainska pravda*, May 12, 2020, https://www.pravda.com.ua/news/2022/05/12/7345720/.

will be needed to set up this forum, over time, he feels it should be led by business people, who must become the new peacemakers.[48]

Novinsky agrees with Medvedchuk that Ukraine is undergoing a civil war, but he too feels that Russia must be a part of this dialogue because "it is our neighbor and is not going anywhere." Unlike Medvedchuk, however, Novinsky believes that the Minsk process has failed and should be replaced.[49] Both the Novinsky and Medvedchuk plans assume that the conflict in Ukraine is a domestic conflict over local autonomy, but that the EU can serve as a valuable intermediary because it has dealt with similar conflicts among its own members. This approach became politically untenable after the Russian invasion of February 2022.

Another peace initiative based on the principle of reconciliation, but not affiliated with any political party, is the "July 16th Initiative – For a Common Future." It was launched in 2020 by several Ukrainian political analysts and former politicians. It calls for the formation of common values and interests; economic modernization while preserving a welfare state; strengthening statehood through honesty and justice; promoting peace through reintegration; and a new, Ukraine-centered foreign policy.[50] Despite a number of prominent signatories, it received very little media attention in Ukraine, Russia, or the West.

A final initiative worth mentioning is "People for Peace," launched in September 2020 at a public forum at Svyatogorsk monastery in Ukraine.[51] It is noteworthy because it was sponsored by the Ukrainian Orthodox Church (MP), which, despite government restrictions, retains an unparalleled ability to bring hundreds of thousand of people onto the streets during its annual religious marches.[52] These impressive numbers, however, do not translate into political in-

---

48 "Ot 'formuly Shtainmaiera' k ukrainskoi formule mira," [From the "Steinmeier Formula" to a Ukrainian Formula for Peace] *Fakty.ua*, October 24, 2019, https://politics.fakty.ua/322157-ot-formuly-shtajnmajera-k-ukrainskoj-formule-mira.
49 Nadiya Sukha, "Partiya yakoho myru."
50 "Radi obshchego budushchego," [For a Common Future] *Interfax-Ukraine*, July 16, 2020, https://interfax.com.ua/news/press-release/675075.html.
51 Oleg Izmaylov, "Pravoslavnaya tserkov perekhvatyvaet initsiativu u politikov ustanovleniya prochnogo mira v Donbasse," [The Orthodox Church Seizes the Initiative from Politicians to Establish a Lasting Peace in the Donbass] *Ukraina.ru*, September 21, 2020, https://ukraina.ru/exclusive/20200921/1028982900.html.
52 Antonina Solovyova, "Krestnyi khod posetili okolo 350 tys. veruyushchikh," [The Church Procession Was Attended by about 350 Thousand Believers] *Ukrainski novini*, July 27, 2021, https://ukranews.com/news/791234-bolee-350-tys-veruyushhih-prinyali-uchastie-v-krestnom-hode; Vasily Stoyakin, "Krestnyi khod pobeditelei," [Procession of Victors] *Ukraina.ru*, July 29, 2019, https://ukraina.ru/exclusive/20190729/1024439106.html; "Na Krestnyi khod vyshli 250 ty-

fluence, since the UOC (MP) tends to be more politically apathetic than the Orthodox Church of Ukraine (OCU). This has resulted in the paradox that, while gathering much smaller numbers for religious functions, the OCU presents a much more politically articulate voice, and is in a far better position to influence the country's political leadership.[53]

6.2.2 Sivokho's National Platform for Reconciliation and Unity

By far the best known domestic peace initiative was spawned with the approval of President Zelensky himself. The fact that he was forced to distance himself from it tells us much about the forces that oppose a lasting peace in Ukraine.

In October 2019, Sergei Sivokho, the creative producer on *Kvartal 95*, Zelensky's signature comedy show, was appointed a consultant to the NSDC. His pur-

---

syach veruyushchikh," [250 Thousand Believers Came to the Church Procession] *Korrespondent*, July 27, 2018, https://korrespondent.net/ukraine/3994634-na-krestnyi-khod-vyshly-250-tysiach-veruuischykh-upts; Mikhail Mishchishin, "Pravoslavie yavlyaetsya neotemlemoy i, pokhozhe, chto glavnoi chastyu Ukrainy," [Orthodoxy Is an Integral and, It Seems, Main Part of Ukraine] *Soyuz pravoslavnykh zhurnalistov*, July 28, 2018, https://spzh.news/ru/socseti/55086-pravosla-vije-javlyajetsya-neotemlemoj-i-pohozhe-chto-glavnoj-chastyju-ukrainy.

53 Mytropolyt Epifaniy, "Derzhavnyi prapor stav lakmusovym papirtsem na ukrainskist," [The State Flag Has Become a Litmus Test for the Ukrainianness] *Ukrinform*, n.d., https://www.ukrin-form.ua/rubric-society/3086380-derzavnij-prapor-stav-lakmusovim-papircem-na-ukrain-skist.html; Ivan Farion, "Derzhavna mova znovu poperek horla ukrainofobam," [Ukrainophobes Are Sick of the State Language Again] *Vysokyi zamok*, December 23, 2020, https://wz.lviv.ua/uk-raine/426637-derzhavna-mova-znovu-poperek-horla-ukrainofobam; "Treba shukaty spilnu ideo-lohiyu," [We Need to Look for a Common Ideology] *Volynski novyny*, December 14, 2020, https://www.volynnews.com/news/all/treba-shukaty-spilnu-ideolohiiu-vladyka-mykhayil-pro-fi-lareta-tomos-ta-moskovskyy-patriarkhat/; "Zvernennya Svyashchennoho Synodu Pravoslavnoï Tserkvy Ukrainy z pryvodu eskalatsyi rosiiskoï ahresii proty Ukrainy," [Address of the Holy Synod of the Orthodox Church of Ukraine on the Escalation of Russian Aggression against Ukraine] *PTsU*, April 19, 2021, https://www.pomisna.info/uk/vsi-novyny/zvernennya-svyashhenno-go-synodu-pravoslavnoyi-tserkvy-ukrainy-z-pryvodu-eskalatsiyi-rosijskoyi-agresiyi-proty-uk-rayiny-ukr-ros/; "'Pochemu ya ne snaiper, pochemu ne strelyayu,'" [Why I Am Not a Sniper, Why I Am Not Shooting] *Strana.ua*, July 27, 2020, https://strana.one/news/281005-ierarkh-ptsu-afana-sij-shkurupij-prokommentiroval-shah-zelenskoho-k-peremiriju-na-donbasse.html; Lucian N. Leustean and Vsevolod Samokhvalov, "The Ukrainian National Church, Religious Diplomacy, and the Conflict in Donbas," *Journal of Orthodox Christian Studies* 2, no. 2 (2019): 199–224, https://doi.org/10.1353/joc.2019.0023.

view, as he describes it, was to give advice on humanitarian policy.[54] Sivokho felt
that it was time to approach the issue of peace from a radically different perspective, by putting an end to what he termed "the war inside our own heads."[55] His
words instantly aroused the anger of Ukrainian nationalists, who were further
outraged by his assertion that "the time has come to correct mistakes, to forgive
and to ask for forgiveness ... to talk to the people living in the uncontrolled territories."[56]

According to Sivokho,

> More terrible than the coronavirus is the virus of hatred. It is important to change not only
> the attitude of the state to its citizens, but the attitude of people to each other ... We need
> new unifying principles and traditions. What my team is doing is trying to incline people to
> mutual understanding ... because the peace that we are all seeking begins in the hearts and
> minds of every Ukrainian.[57]

At first Sivokho's optimism seemed to be echoed by President Zelensky. During
the 2020 Munich Security Conference, and then later that year at the Forum on
Unity in Mariupol, Zelensky called for "a massive national dialogue" in which
people could discuss Ukraine's future face-to-face.[58] To this end, the creation
of a National Platform for Reconciliation and Unity was announced in Mariupol,
and formally presented to the public on March 12, 2020. That presentation lasted
only twenty minutes, however, because a gang of about seventy young people
from the National Corps (Azov) stormed into the hall shouting "traitor" and

---

54 "Serhyi Syvokho Reveals His Responsibilities at Post of Advisor of National Security Secretary," *112 Ukraine*, October 22, 2019, https://censor.net/en/news/3155154/serhiy_sivokho_reveal-
s_his_responsibilities_at_post_of_advisor_of_national_security_secretary.
55 Elena Poskannaya, "Sivokho: zhitelyam Donetskoi oblasti nikogda ne predlagali novykh politikov," [Sivokho: The Residents of Donetsk Region Have Never Been Offered New Politicians]
Gordon.ua, July 12, 2019, https://gordonua.com/publications/sivoho-zhitelyam-doneckoy-oblas
ti-nikogda-ne-predlagali-novyh-politikov-vsegda-byli-kandidaty-kem-to-postavlennye-kem-to-ku
plennye-i-lyudi-znali-kem-1105079.html.
56 "Sivokho prizval Ukrainu poprosit proshcheniya u Donbassa," [Sivokho Urges Ukraine to
Ask for Forgiveness from Donbass] *Novorossiya*, November 20, 2019, https://novorosinform.
org/sivoho-prizval-ukrainu-poprosit-prosheniya-u-donbassa-31504.html.
57 Dina Vishnevsky, "Sergei Sivokho: 'Stranu nuzhno spasat!,'" [Sergei Sivokho: "The Country
Needs to Be Saved!"] *KP v Ukraine*, February 24, 2020, https://kp.ua/politics/660562-serhei-sy
vokho-stranu-nuzhno-spasat.
58 Natalia Lebed, "Plokhoi mir ili khoroshaya voina," [A Bad Peace or a Good War] *112ua.tv*,
February 21, 2020, https://112ua.tv/statji/plohoy-mir-ili-horoshaya-voyna-chto-neset-platforma-
primireniya-ot-sivohi-526515.html.

threw Sivokho to the ground.[59] Two weeks later he was fired from his advisory position at the NSDC.

It may seem odd that talk of reconciliation and dialogue could arouse so much anger, until one realizes that what Sivokho is actually asking for is a fundamental shift in Ukrainian political thinking. He is suggesting that Ukrainians should recognize that they too bear a measure of responsibility for conflict in Donbass, and specifically for de-humanizing its residents. These policies, he says, did not begin in 2014, when the fighting started, but at least a decade earlier.[60] Over the past eight years, official government hostility toward the people of Donbass has only made matters worse. As proof, he cites internal polling done by the Ukrainian government, that shows that only 10 percent of Donbass residents today want to return to Ukraine.[61]

Since being fired, Sivokho has become even more critical of government policy, though never of his friend Zelensky. He has called for changes to the current language laws that severely restrict the public use of Russian.[62] He has said that the government's refusal to implement the Minsk Accords has forced Ukraine into "a dark and isolated corner," and praised rebel leaders for offering free medical and educational services to people coming over the demarcation line, from

59 Olesya Medvedeva, "Sergei Sivokho: 'Otnoshenie komandy prezidenta k Donbassu menyaetsya,'" [Sergei Sivokho: "The Attitude of the President's Team towards Donbass Is Changing"] *Strana.ua*, July 5, 2020, https://strana.one/articles/interview/276900-sivokho-v-intervju-olese-medvedevoj-rasskazal-pochemu-buksuet-mirnyj-protsess-na-donbasse.html; "Takaya vot 'platforma' natsionalnogo primireniya," [Such Is the "Platform" For National Reconciliation] *Gordon.ua*, March 12, 2020, https://gordonua.com/news/politics/takaya-vot-platforma-nacionalnogo-primireniya-s-tolkotney-i-oskorbleniyami-socseti-obsuzhdayut-konflikt-sivoho-s-nacionalistami-1490832.html.
60 Anton Savichev, "Mir na Donbasse i platforma edinstva," [Peace in Donbass and the Unity Platform] *Vesti*, November 16, 2020, https://vesti.ua/politika/sergej-sivoho-ukraina-sejchas-vedet-peregovory-slovno-v-shage-ot-pobedy; Anna Revyakina, "Sergei Sivokho o tom, chto meshaet Ukraine vernut Donbass," [Sergei Sivokho on What Prevents Ukraine from Returning Donbass] *Ukraina.ru*, February 24, 2021, https://ukraina.ru/interview/20210224/1030644960.html.
61 "Sivokho s boem prezentoval platformu primireniya," [Sivokho Presented His Reconciliation Platform in Battle Mode] *Korrespondent*, March 12, 2020, https://korrespondent.net/ukraine/4203426-syvokho-s-boem-prezentoval-platformu-prymyrenyia; Anna Revyakina, "Sergei Sivokho o tom, chto meshaet Ukraine vernut Donbass."
62 Alesya Batsman, "Sivokho: V kakom statuse ya voploshchayu mirnye initsiativy prezidenta?," [Sivokho: In What Capacity Am I Carrying Out the President's Peace Initiatives?] *Gordon.ua*, May 15, 2020, https://gordonua.com/publications/sivoho-v-kakom-statuse-ya-voploshchayu-mirnye-iniciativy-prezidenta-v-statuse-sergeya-sivoho-1498867.html.

Ukraine.[63] He even revealed that the rebels had made a formal proposal to Kiev to return all nationalized companies to their Ukrainian owners, and to make Donbass's "special status" valid only until 2050, but that the Ukrainian government had refused to even discuss these ideas.[64]

Despite many setbacks and threats, over time the National Platform managed to gain new allies – more than seventy civic organizations coordinated their activities under the umbrella of the National Forum.[65] Sivokho was able to set up "peace hubs": – safe spaces for dialogue modeled on those in Cyprus, former Yugoslavia, and Northern Ireland.[66] He also encouraged social media interaction among doctors, students, and tried to organize sporting events and talent shows across the demarcation line.[67] Since the Russian invasion of 2022, Sivokho and the National Platform have vanished from public discourse.

---

63 "Sivokho tknul Ukrainu nosom v politiku LDNR," [Sivokho Poked Ukraine's Nose into the Politics of the Donetsk People's Republic] *Donetskaya Narodnaya Respublika*, February 24, 2021, https://dnr24.su/dnr/31859-sivoho-tknul-ukrainu-nosom-v-politiku-ldnr.html; Taras Kozub, "Intervyu s Sergeem Sivokho – o Donbasse i yazyke," [Interview with Sergei Sivokho – about Donbass and Language] *Vesti*, September 20, 2021, https://vesti.ua/strana/sergej-sivoho-u-nas-svoj-vokabulyar-za-nego-nam-nachalo-priletat; Vadim Golovko, "Sivokho o peregovorakh Kieva s Donbassom i novykh predstavitelyakh ot ORDLO," [Sivokho about Kiev's Negotiations with Donbass and New Representatives from ORDLO] *Dialog.ua*, June 9, 2020, https://www.dialog.ua/ukraine/209099_1591700197.

64 Anton Savichev, "Mir na Donbasse i platforma edinstva"; "Yermolaev pro zustrich Zelenskoho z Baidenom ta povernennya Donbasu," [Yermolaev on Zelensky's Meeting with Biden and Return of Donbass] https://www.youtube.com/watch?v=hLprMiaS-bo. Yermolaev says that these proposals were made in October 2020.

65 Olesya Medvedeva, "Sergei Sivokho: Prezident ne dolzhen boyatsya vypolnyat svoi obeshchaniya po miru na Donbasse," [Sergei Sivokho: The President Should Not Be Afraid to Fulfill His Promises for Peace in Donbas] *Strana.ua*, July 5, 2020, https://strana.one/articles/interview/276900-sivokho-v-intervju-olese-medvedevoj-rasskazal-pochemu-buksuet-mirnyj-protsess-na-donbasse.html.

66 Olesya Medvedeva, "Sergei Sivokho: 'Otnoshenie komandy prezidenta k Donbassu menyaetsya'"; Alesya Batsman, "Sivokho: V kakom statuse ya voploshchayu mirnye initsiativy prezidenta?"

67 *Korrespondent*, "Sivokho s boem prezentoval platformu primireniya"; Anton Pechenkin, "Sivokho rasskazal, kto stoit za atakoi natsionalistov," [Sivokho Tells Who Is behind the Attack of the Nationalists] *Vesti*, March 12, 2020, https://vesti.ua/politika/mirnyj-protsess-neizbezhen-i-eto-tolko-nachalo-intervyu-sivoho-vesti-ua; Taras Kozub, "Sergei Sivokho – o platforme primireniya i otnosheniyakh s OP," [Sergei Sivokho on the Reconciliation Platform and Relations with the Office of the President] *Vesti*, March 19, 2020, https://vesti.ua/strana/sergej-sivoho-u-nas-s-ermakom-odin-vokabulyar; Aleksandr Terekhov-Kruglyĭ, "Sivokho: O primirenii na Donbasse i o budushchem KVN v Ukraine," [Sivokho: About Reconciliation in Donbass and the Future of KVN (a popular Russian and Soviet game show – NP) in Ukraine] Ukraina.ru, May 27, 2020, https://ukraina.ru/interview/20200527/1027816725.html.

6.2.3 The Reznikov Plan: Re-Occupation, Not Reconciliation

In July 2021, thirty-three parliamentarians associated with Sivokho's National Forum set up a new deputies group in support of what they called "a more humane strategy of reunification."[68] They sought to block, unsuccessfully, the adoption of the government-backed law "On the Principles of State Policy During the Transition Period," authored by Oleksiy Reznikov, then Vice-Premier and Minister for Reintegration of the Occupied Territories, and now Defense Minister of Ukraine.[69]

The Reznikov Plan treats the reintegration of Donbass and Ukraine as a security threat, and therefore gives priority to preserving domestic stability during the reintegration period.[70] According to this plan, during the post-conflict phase, Ukrainian is to be imposed immediately as the sole language in all official and public discourse. All public servants are to undergo lustration, and anyone found to have undermined the national security of Ukraine, either through action or inaction, can never hold public office again (Art. 10, pt. 1). There is to be no general amnesty or special status for these regions, and Crimea's autonomous status in the Ukrainian Constitution is to be rescinded.[71]

As for the local economy, use of the Russian ruble will be prohibited (Art. 25), resulting in the *de facto* nationalization of all economic assets in both Crimea and Donbass. The enormous backlog of pensions and social payments owed to Donbass residents is to be "restructured" (Art. 21) and paid out over an unspecified amount of time. The previously stipulated designation of these territories as "regions of priority development" is to be folded into the government's overall strategic development program for the region through 2030.[72]

---

68 "Izbityi natsistami Sivokho vzyalsya za staroe," [Beaten Up by the Nazis, Sivokho Is Back at It] *Ukraina.ru*, July 16, 2021, https://ukraina.ru/news/20210716/1031858276.html.

69 "Pro zasady derzhanvoi polityky perekhidnoho period," [On the Principles of State Policy during the Transition Period] Ministry for Question of Reintegration of Temporarily Occupied Territories of Ukraine, June 2021, https://www.minre.gov.ua/sites/default/files/1._zakono-proyekt_pro_zasady_dppp.pdf.

70 Olga Chekis, "Reintegratsiya Donbassa," [The Reintegration of Donbass] *Zerkalo nedeli*, July 1, 2021, https://zn.ua/POLITICS/reintehratsija-donbassa-kak-i-kohda-nachinat-podhotovku-k-bezopasnym-vyboram.html.

71 Pyotr Safonov, "Tam vsyo protivorechit Minskim soglasheniyam," [Everything There Contradicts the Minsk Accords] *Ukraina.ru*, August 23, 2021, https://ukraina.ru/exclusive/20210823/1032104356.html. The January version allowed the transition to Ukrainian to occur over a two-year period, but this grace period was removed in the final version.

72 Pyotr Safonov, "'Tam vsyo protivorechit Minskim soglasheniyam.'"

The Reznikov Plan devotes considerable attention to the politics of memory. The liberation of each town is to be celebrated locally, and a new national holiday established to commemorate the victims of Russian aggression. In addition, a national "Museum of Overcoming Russia's Aggression against Ukraine" is to be built in Kiev, with branches in Donetsk, Lugansk, Simferopol, and Sevastopol (Art. 22).

Finally, the government intends to set up a National Center for the Development of Peace, whose task will be to gather information about the human rights violations committed by the occupation forces. Access to information about other human rights violations will be restricted (Art. 14, pt. 3), even though Ukraine's former chief military prosecutor, Anatoliy Matios, has already documented many such violations by Ukrainian volunteer battalions.[73] Such a carefully crafted memorial policy suggests that the government's primary objective is not, as it declares, "a lasting peace," but rather to recast local memory of the rebellion as part of Ukraine's eternal struggle against Russia.

Sivokho complained bitterly that the Reznikov Plan, which was approved by the Cabinet of Ministers on August 4, 2021, treats the Ukrainians in Donbass and Crimea as conquered people.[74] While it pledges that the transition will involve "the construction of stable peace, including among other things a national dialogue and other dialogue processes," everything in it, he says, suggests otherwise.[75]

---

73 "Pytki v SBU," [Torture in the SBU] *Korrespondent*, August 30, 2016, https://korrespondent.net/ukraine/3738354-pytky-v-sbu-novyi-vytok-skandala; "Neveroyatnye protokoly pytok v 'Tornado,'" [Incredible "Tornado" Torture Protocols] *Polit Forums*, June 22, 2015, https://perma.cc/G8 V5–9AEP; Fyodor Koloskov, "Voennye prestupleniya karatelei v Donbasse," *RitmEurasia*, March 17, 2020, https://www.ritmeurasia.org/news–2020–03–17–voennye-prestuplenija-karatelej-v-donbasse-skolko-verevochke-ni-vitsja-47996; "Ukraine: Authorities Must Commit to a Thorough Investigation after 13 People Released from Secret Detention," *Amnesty International*, August 29, 2016, https://perma.cc/7HHY-X2HM; Konstantin Kevorkyan, "Vyrozhdenie i begstvo kak povod natsionalnoy gordosti ukraintsa," [Degeneration and Flight as Reasons for Ukrainian National Pride] *Ukraina.ru*, November 1, 2018, https://ukraina.ru/opinion/20181101/1021613547.html. According to Matios, every second Ukrainian soldier suffers from mental trauma as a result of the conflict, and requires professional psychiatric treatment.
74 "Sivokho predlozhil alternativny plan reintegratsii Donbassa," [Sivokho Proposed an Alternative Plan for the Reintegration of Donbass] *Versii*, August 31, 2021, https://versii.com/news/sivoho-predlozhil-alternativnyj-plan-reintegracii-donbassa/.
75 Pyotr Safonov, "Tam vsyo protivorechit Minskim soglasheniyam." In earlier drafts national dialogue was defined as "a mechanism of public negotiation, designed to expand the range of participants involved in overcoming the consequences of the armed aggression of the Russian Federation against Ukraine, constituting both official events and informal functions involving representatives of civic groups." In the final version this was removed.

Rather than getting animosities to subside, the Reznikov Plan, should it be implemented, is likely to ensure that they are passed on to the next generation. The rebels themselves may be long gone, but like Banquo's Ghost, they will haunt Ukraine's future, an impertinent reminder of the Ukrainians that nationalism tried to erase.

6.2.4 Common Flaws of the Peace Process

Western analysts commonly assume that domestic reforms and the restoration of the lost territories are converging objectives. For many in Kiev, however, they are mutually exclusive: the more reformist the government, the less it wants to be bogged down by the cultural and political ballast ostensibly carried by Donbass and Crimea.[76] This is one reason why the Ukrainian government has shown so little interest in implementing the Minsk-2 Accords, and why its latest proposals – to deprive Donbass residents of their political and civil rights for at least twenty-five years, and to deport hundreds of thousands of Crimeans who have taken Russian citizenship – have gone in precisely the opposite direction.[77]

On the other hand, the common flaw of indigenous peace efforts is that they fail to appreciate just how much nationalism has contributed to the current stalemate within Ukrainian society. Even those who, like Sivokho and Medvedchuk, call for "restoring Donbass to Ukraine, and Ukraine to Donbass," rarely challenge Ukrainian nationalism directly. This is because, for many Ukrainians, it has become synonymous with patriotism, a confusion that has prevented the development of a healthy and pluralistic civil society.

---

76 Yuri Lutsenko, "Formula 'avtonomiya zamist vtorgnennya' smertelno nebezpechna dlya Ukrainy," [The Formula "Autonomy Instead of Invasion" Is Deadly for Ukraine] *Ukrainska pravda*, December 10, 2021, https://blogs.pravda.com.ua/authors/lucenko/61b332fdabc75/; Georgy Luchnokov, "Gotovy k radikalnym deistviyam"; "Zhebrivsky naznachil mestny vybory v chasti Donbassa 29 noyabrya," [Zhebrovsky Called Local Elections in the Donbass on November 29] *Zerkalo nedeli*, August 19, 2015, https://zn.ua/POLITICS/zhebrivskiy-naznachil-mestnye-vybory-na-chasti-donbassa-na-29-noyabrya-186076_.html "Tuka: V Kieve 75% lyudei s vatoi v golove.
77 Pavlo Vuiets and Stanislav Gruzdev, " Oleksiy Reznikov: Bezpechna reintehratsiya Donbasu zaime minimum 25 rokiv," [Oleksiy Reznikov: The Safe Reintegration of Donbass Will Take at Least 25 Years] *Glavkom*, July 11, 2020, https://perma.cc/Z5P3-PVQJ; Valeriya Kondratova and Boris Davidenko, "Aleksei Reznikov: Mir menyaetsya," [Oleksiy Reznikov: The World Is Changing] *Liga.net*, September 2, 2021, https://perma.cc/HD2K-LZQL; Marina Yakovenko, "Reintegratsiya Donbassa," [The Reintegration of Donbass] *Vesti*, September 9, 2020, https://vesti.ua/politika/tam-zhivut-prestupniki-pochemu-vlasti-slivayut-vozvrashhenie-donbassa.

6.3 How Cleft Societies Can Be Made Whole

To summarize what has been discussed so far, Ukraine's failure to obtain its independence in the aftermath of both World Wars led to nationalism becoming the driving political motif of Ukraine's exiled political elites. Ukrainian nationalists managed to survive their wartime alliance with Nazi Germany by positioning themselves as allies of the West in the new Cold War against the Soviet Union. After the collapse of the USSR, they re-established themselves as regional actors in western Ukraine, and from this Galician base sought to commandeer the direction of Ukrainian politics.

Despite being a political minority within Ukraine, Galician-inspired Ukrainian nationalists have been encouraged by the West, because they can always be relied on to oppose closer ties with Russia. This, however, has deepened the split along the country's linguistic, religious, and cultural fault lines.

The Maidan Revolt of 2014 offered a unique opportunity to deal a crushing blow to Maloross Ukrainian identity by establishing a Galician nationalist-oriented regime in Kiev. Although this regime initially had to rely on the military support of the Far Right, many pro-Maidan liberals saw this as a price worth paying to achieve final and complete independence from Russia. This marriage of convenience also suited the interests of Ukrainian nationalists, who saw their own political influence greatly magnified, as they prepared to play the long game for social and political dominance in Ukraine.

To restore social harmony, both Maloross and Galician Ukrainians will have to acknowledged each other's fear, and feel free to tell their own side of the Ukrainian story.

There is, simply, no way to resolve this crisis without confronting this trauma. Ukrainians need to recognize each other's fears, as well as the mutual pain that they have caused each other. Reconciliation will require that they do three things: (1) reject hatred and embrace all Ukrainians as true Ukrainians, regardless of their culture, religion, language, or ethnicity; (2) reconstitute social discourse, to allow for dialogue between Galicia and Maloross Ukraine; and (3) replace nationalism with a civic patriotism that accentuates the values that unite Ukrainians, rather than divide them. Let us look at some ways this might be accomplished.

6.3.1 Rejecting Rage; Embracing Catharsis

Legendary Ukrainian film director Alexander Dovzhenko had a keen eye for scenarios. His diary contains an idea for the film "Ukraine in Flames," which he was working on in 1943. He imagines a concentration camp guard and an inmate, both Ukrainians, striking up a conversation across the barbed wire that separates them, a conversation made "all the more terrible" he writes, "because of its fervent hatred."[78] In the final scene they seize each other through the barbed wire, the guard trying to choke the prisoner, the prisoner refusing to let go for fear of being shot.

Dovzhenko wonders what they might have talked about:

> about the authorities, about socialism, about collective farms, about Hitler, about history. About Bohdan [Khmelnitsky], about Mazepa, about everything – a symbolic eternal picture, a centuries old duel of two Ukrainians hardened by their long, hard, thorny road. About Siberia. Perhaps the guard was a Galician, a leader of his local village, or perhaps he was just a simple peasant. Their conversation is shown up close, then from a distance: the head and barbed wire, the head and barbed wire and blood. Eyes and teeth glinting in the darkness, the wire of thorns surrounding their temples gouging into their foreheads, blood dripping with pain and hatred and passion ... That is how they found them the next morning, dead in each other's arms, in the twisted embrace of the barbed wire.

For writer Myroslava Berdnyk, this fragment from Dovzhenko's diary encapsulates the hatred that some Ukrainians pass on from one generation to the next.[79] The only way to escape it, says political commentator Andrei Yermolaev, is to undergo a *catharsis* that expunges fear, and lets people see the humanity of their antagonists. Without such a *catharsis* there can be no dialogue about the future, since there is no future that either side can see in which both sides coexist.[80]

In her book, *Enraged: Why Violent Times Need Ancient Greek Myths*, Emily Katz Anhalt shows how classical Greek tragedy helped to contain and redirect individual anger into empathy.[81] Rage, as classicist Mary Beard reminds us, is

---

78 "Dnevnikovye zapisi Aleksandra Dovzhenko obyasnyayut segodnya grazhdanskuyu voynu Na Ukraine," [Alexander Dovzhenko's Diary Entries Explain Today's Civil War in Ukraine] *Livejournal*, September 16, 2020, https://perma.cc/XU34-DCY9. The film's distribution in the USSR was prohibited for not mentioning the leading role of the Communist Party in the resistance, and for its sympathetic portrayal of collaboration with the enemy.

79 *Livejournal*, "Dnevnikovye zapisi Aleksandra Dovzhenko obyasnyayut segodnya grazhdanskuyu voinu na Ukraine."

80 Ekaterina Chesnokova, "Esli Kiev ne proidet svoi katarsis, Donbass uidet k RF i Belorussii – Yermolaev," [If Kiev Does Not Pass Its Catharsis, Donbass Will Go to the Russian Federation and Belarus – Yermolaev] *Ukraina.ru*, December 18, 2019, https://ukraina.ru/news/20191218/1026067559.html; "Ukraina: starye granitsy, novaya strana," [Ukraine: Old Borders, New Country] *Topinform*, June 17, 2017, https://www.youtube.com/watch?v=lohHxTMnJo0 (at 02:16:32).

81 Emily Katz Anhalt, *Enraged: Why Violent Times Need Ancient Greek Myths* (New Haven, CT: Yale University Press, 2017), 99.

the first word in the history of Western literature.[82] It is also the driving force in many Greek tragedies: from Ajax's fury at being passed over for Achilles's armor, to the violence of Hecuba's "justice," blinding Polymestor and murdering his children. And yet, in Sophocles's and Euripides's telling of these tales, we are also shown the enemy's point of view, in order to cultivate the audience's empathy and self-reflection.

These are essential qualities for conflict resolution because they encourage human agency – the idea that human beings, not the gods, are ultimately accountable for the decisions they make. Thus, even when two great warriors like Diomedes and Glaucon meet on the field of battle, Homer, in *The Iliad*, reminds us that their fates are not yet sealed. They wind up refusing to fight each other because their grandfathers had once exchanged guest-gifts. Homer is telling his audience that, even in the midst of battle, individuals can engage in dialogue and choose to avoid violence.

Rage often masquerades as justice, but is really its opposite. Instead of solace and peace, it brings only further rage and retribution. Achilles's insatiable rage was finally spent when he learned how to feel compassion for Hector's father. It was by learning how to manage their rage, and replace vengeance with empathy, says Anhalt, that the ancient Greeks moved "from tribalism to civil society."[83]

Anhalt's approach complements my earlier critique of the tragic realists – Morgenthau, Niebuhr, and Arendt – who gave up too quickly on the therapeutic potential of tragedy, because they deemed the human condition unchangeable. But, while an individual's choice of what actions to take remains their own, it often depends upon the stories we tell ourselves about who we are. This is where tragedy's moral message begins to have broader social significance, forcing us to "recognize our own needs in the needs of others."[84]

Having reminded us of the centrality of tragedy to Greek life, and the subtle ways in which it raised important political and moral issues, however, Anhalt also suggests that classical Greek tragedy initiated "a movement toward individual autonomy and universal human rights."[85] By attributing too much to classical Greek tragedy, she winds up overlooking the more limited role for which it is optimally suited – conflict resolution. Before a conflict can be resolved, the tragic

---

82 Mary Beard, "What the Greek Myths Teach Us about Anger in Troubled Times," *New York Times*, September 7, 2017, https://www.nytimes.com/2017/09/07/books/review/emily-katz-anhalt-enraged.html.
83 Emily Katz Anhalt, *Enraged*, 3, 112.
84 Emily Katz Anhalt, *Enraged*, 112.
85 Emily Katz Anhalt, *Enraged*, 6.

cycle fueled by vengeance must end. Building empathy for one's enemies, through tragedy, serves this very purpose, which obviously promotes social stability. Whether it also leads to universal human rights is far less obvious.

Thus, while tragedy is not a cure-all for violence, its message of empathy, dialogue, and compassion remains worth affirming. The main thing that social analysts should take away from classical Greek tragedy is the importance of benign social messaging, and of spreading the message of compassion effectively to all groups of society. Institutions *per se* are not enough to resolve conflict. Without a true change of heart, social transformation cannot take root. Put another way, there can be no conflict resolution without *catharsis*.

6.3.2 Building Shared Values through Dialogue

Classical Greek tragedy teaches that the pursuit of total victory in a conflict invariably breeds renewed conflict. To break this cycle, the participants must recognize that they each see only a part of the truth, and then allow themselves to appreciate the other parts of the truth, seen by their opponents. Without this, any victory will only turn to ashes.

Nothing illustrates this better than the intensity with which the opposing sides in Ukraine cling to their mutually exclusive views of what constitutes justice. If Ukrainian history is indeed a repeating cycle of mutual grievances, then perhaps the way out lies in recognizing that it is this very effort to "fix" Ukraine, that is perpetuating the tragic cycle.

Dialogue is the key to restoring community because, unlike conversation, discussion, or debate, dialogue is fundamentally concerned with sustaining the relationship of the participants. It is, in William Isaacs's words, a conversation with a center, not sides.[86] Its objective is not momentary consensus, but a complete self-transformation that creates a new relationship among the antagonists. Classical Greek tragedy is thus, quintessentially, a series of dialogues in which we expose our own tragic flaws to ourselves.

Today, many people, even diplomats, seem to think that dialogue means nothing more than communicating one's wishes to another party. But a prison warden does that to his inmates. One of the most ancient meanings of the

---

86 William Isaacs, *Dialogue and the Art of Thinking Together: A Pioneering Approach to Communicating in Business and in Life*, 1st ed (New York: Currency, 1999), quoted in "What Is Dialogue? | Difficult Dialogues," Clark University, https://www2.clarku.edu/difficultdialogues/learn/index.cfm.

word *logos* is "to gather together," which some scholars render as "relationship." In this vein, the opening words of the Gospel of St. John reveal this insight: "In the beginning was the Relationship ...."[87] Perhaps it is for this very reason that Archdeacon John Chryssavgis describes dialogue as sacred:

> If we are true to ourselves and honest with those with whom we are in dialogue; if we are not simply in dialogue in order to impose our own will and our own way; if we approach the other in dialogue in truth and in love, then we leave ourselves susceptible to transformation. Dialogue renders us more vulnerable, more receptive to divine grace and actual growth.[88]

Back in May 2014, the Supreme Rada seemed to grasp the need for such self-transformation, when it adopted a "Memorandum on Mutual Understanding and Peace."[89] It called on Ukrainians to "extend a hand to each other, to reject radical actions, hatred, and to restore, together, common efforts in defense, development, and the establishment of a democratic, sovereign and united Ukraine, in which people of all nationalities, political beliefs, and faiths can live in friendship." To achieve this, the memorandum called for "a national dialogue within the framework of roundtable of national unity." Alas, this idea was never implemented. Instead, President Poroshenko banked on nationalism, which seemed to offer a speedier, albeit more violent, remedy. Had a national dialogue been attempted, perhaps Ukraine's history would have been different.

Sivokho has suggested another way to begin such a dialogue, by rebuilding professional contacts among Ukrainians in different parts of the country. He points to the example of the Moldovan soccer team "Sheriff." Even though its home stadium is in Tiraspol, the capitol of the rebel region of Transdnistria, it competes in the Moldovan championship league and in UEFA, with the blessing of Moldovan authorities. This willingness of Moldovan authorities to encourage trade, sports, and cultural ties with its own rebel region has encouraged Moldovans on both sides to treat each other more humanely, and to envision the possibility of reintegration.[90]

---

87 William Isaacs, *Dialogue and the Art of Thinking Together.*
88 Sean Gallagher, "Catholic Archbishop, Orthodox Leader See Significance in Havana Meeting," *Catholic Philly,* February 23, 2016, https://catholicphilly.com/2016/02/news/national-news/catholic-archbishop-orthodox-leader-see-significance-in-havana-meeting/.
89 "Pro memorandum porozuminnya i myru," [On the Memorandum of Understanding and Peace] *Ofitsiinyi vebportal parlamentu Ukraïny,* May 20, 2014, https://zakon.rada.gov.ua/go/1280–18.
90 Dmitriy Zakharov, "Ekspert nazval dva stsenariya prekrashcheniya voiny v Donbasse," [An Expert Names Two Scenarios for Ending the War in Donbass] *Zerkalo nedeli,* January 14,

Therefore, instead of prohibiting contacts between local government officials across the contact line, Sivokho says, the Ukrainian government should encourage them to talk to each other. "Imagine," he says, "they would now rejoice and sorrow together. If they were only allowed to return there, they would restore their villages on their own, from both sides. What a fantastic example that would be!"[91]

6.3.3 Moving beyond Nationalism

Compassion and *catharsis* are fundamental to the reconstitution of discourse among estranged social groups. As the authors of the "July 16th Initiative" put it:

> We need an inclusive national dialogue in order to determine a Ukrainian future that is comfortable for all. We need an integral state policy of national consensus … There is a place in Ukrainian history for the UNR as well as the Ukrainian SSR. We must embrace all the diversity of our history, along with all the diversity of our era … We need an inclusive national dialogue, national reconciliation and solidarity based on these principles. We need a victory that will not be a defeat of the other.[92]

A society that embraces its culturally diverse communities is inherently more stable than one that seeks to eradicate them. Reconstituting the basic grammar of a national community therefore means replacing the divisive discourse of ethnic nationalism with the unifying language of civic patriotism. Only by viewing all

---

2020, https://zn.ua/POLITICS/ekspert-nazval-dva-scenariya-prekrascheniya-voyny-v-donbasse-235849_.html; Denis Rudometov, "Oleg Nyomensky: Ukraine udobno kormit Rossiyu nadezhdami na to, chto Minskie soglasheniya budut vypolneny," [Oleg Nyomensky: It Is Convenient for Ukraine to Feed Russia with Hopes that the Minsk Agreements Will Be Implemented] *Ukraina.ru*, June 23, 2020, https://ukraina.ru/interview/20200623/1028061194.html; Fred Weir, "'Moldova Miracle' Offers Hope for Russia-West Progress in Ukraine," *Christian Science Monitor*, August 17, 2017, https://www.csmonitor.com/World/Europe/2019/0717/Moldova-shows-Russia-and-the-West-can-work-together.-Can-they-do-it-again; Konstantin Volkov, "Prezident Moldavii vystupil protiv zapreta retranslyatsii lyubykh SMI," [The President of Moldova Speaks Out against Banning the Retransmission of Any Media] *Rossiĭskaya gazeta*, January 17, 2017, https://rg.ru/2017/01/17/prezident-moldavii-vystupil-protiv-zapreta-retransliacii-liubyh-smi.html; Andrei Mospanov, "Na Dnestre – 25 let mira," [25 Years of Peace on the Dniester] *Ritm Eurasia*, August 2, 2017, https://www.ritmeurasia.org/news–2017–08–02–na-dnestre-25-let-mira.-hotja-zhelajuschih-razmorozit-konflikt-ne-perevoditsja-31633.

91 Taras Kozub, "Intervyu s Sergeem Sivokho – o Donbasse i yazyke."

92 *Interfax-Ukraine*, "Radi obshchego budushchego."

Ukrainians as a legitimate part of the nation can binding ties of loyalty to the national community be forged.

This raises the issue of what to do about Ukrainian nationalism, especially the type that consciously seeks to forge national unity through the suppression of cultural and religious diversity. Political realists like Morgenthau, Arendt, and Niebuhr all saw nationalism as a tragic flaw of modern societies, and foretold the tragic consequences of giving in to nationalism. Their criticism, however, amounted to little more than social commentary, because of the absence today of any viable instrument for administering social therapy. In Athens this was done through the *Dionysia*, the annual festivals in which citizens participated in a ritual of collective social reflection that was sanctioned by both civil and religious authorities. The obligatory participation of citizens in these dramatic presentations, and in the subsequent public debates about them, gave cohesion and flexibility to the Athenian republic.

When society is under social, economic, and political stress, nationalism understandably develops a broad following. It provides a quick fix, but just like addicts seeking a quick high, its followers usually fail to consider its long-term effects. Nationalism is a false cure, because the harm it does by dividing society into loyalists and traitors, is far greater than the brief surge it gives to national unity. What is needed instead are social mechanisms that can bridle the social rage that feeds nationalism, that can teach compassion and forgiveness, and that can promote social harmony. Fortunately, such mechanisms are already in common use in many countries afflicted by social trauma – I am referring to Truth and Reconciliation Commissions.

6.4 Truth and Reconciliation: A Model for Ukraine?

There is broad agreement that Ukraine needs a new model of social development, one capable of bringing society together. Many would also say that the weakness of Ukraine's political institutions has been a major obstacle to achieving unity, since they have proved incapable of restraining either rapacious oligarchs, or virulent nationalism. As a result, almost by default, Ukrainian elites wind up chasing the same old get-rich-quick schemes, failing to incorporate Ukraine's cultural diversity into its system of government, and sowing the seed of future discord.

Social healing will require that individuals reaffirm their shared values, and Greek tragedy goes to the very heart of this task. Unlike modern societies, the Greeks did not assume that the polity would magically arrive at the proper balance between individual and social needs through a system of checks and balances. Rather, they believed that the achievement and preservation of social harmony required constant instruction in repentance, *catharsis*, and compassion. The public rituals of the Dionysian festivals served this very purpose.

Today, Truth and Reconciliation Commissions (TRC) deal with issues of social reconciliation and deep social trauma in ways that are very reminiscent of the *Dionysia*. Among the four dozen Commissions that have been set up since the first one in Uganda in 1974, the approaches taken by TRCs in South Africa, Guatemala, and Spain strike me as especially relevant for Ukraine. South Africa, because of the church's role in transforming a situation fraught with the potential for violent retribution into one of forgiveness. Guatemala, for its ability to begin a national historical discussion, despite the government's reluctance to do so. And Spain, because, despite thirty years of silence about atrocities of the regime of dictator Francisco Franco, Spanish civil society eventually succeeded in giving birth to democratic institutions.

6.4.1 South Africa's Truth and Reconciliation Commission

Following the end of apartheid in 1991, and the transition of political power from the National Party to the African National Congress, the new government set up a Truth and Reconciliation Commission (TRC) that functioned for seven years. The 1995 Promotion of National Unity and Reconciliation Act was designed to offer perpetrators individual amnesty in exchange for full and voluntary disclosure of their crimes. The South African Truth and Reconciliation process was a public storytelling, a way to forge a shared memory among victims, perpetrators, and bystanders, who had previously merely ignored each other.[93]

The TRC chose to focus not on punishment, or even moral judgment, but on mutual forgiveness and reconciliation. This was due to the preponderant influence of clergy, and in particular of Archbishop Desmond Tutu. Hearings were reminiscent of church services, with Archbishop Tutu formally dressed in his purple clerical robes. On the first day of the televised hearings, Archbishop

---

93 H. Richard Niebuhr, *The Meaning of Revelation* (Louisville, KY: Westminster John Knox Press, 2006). Niebuhr writes: "Where common memory is lacking, where people do not share in the same past, there can be no real community, and where community is to be formed, common memory must be created."

Tutu appealed to the different communities of faith to support the work of the Commission with "fervent prayer and intercession."[94]

The South African TRC took the view that, in a sinful world, no one's hands are ever entirely clean. As a result, both sides – oppressors and oppressed – shared responsibility, and each should acknowledge its faults. No moral distinction was made between the violence used to maintain an unjust system, and the violence used to oppose it. In this way the TRC sought to overcome two objections. First, that by focusing on select perpetrators, the majority, who tacitly supported apartheid, would not be forced to confront their complicity. Second, that if perpetrators did not come forward, an essential part of the narrative would remain untold. By assuming guilt on the part of all, it was hoped that righteousness and vengeance would be curbed, and forgiveness encouraged.

The actual process, of course, went far beyond just storytelling. The final report of the South Africa Commission listed eight major recommendations for the South African people:

1. Accept our own need for healing;
2. Reach out to fellow South Africans in a spirit of tolerance and understanding;
3. Work actively to build bridges across the divisions of language, faith, and history;
4. Strive constantly, in the process of transformation, to be sensitive to the needs of those groups which have been particularly disadvantaged in the past, specifically women and children;
5. Encourage a culture of debate so that, together, we can resolve the pressing issues of our time;
6. Initiate programs of action in our own spheres of interest and influence, whether it be education, religion, business, labor, arts, or politics, so that the process of reconciliation can be implemented from a grassroots level;
7. Address the reality of ongoing racial discrimination and work towards a non-racial society;
8. Call upon leaders in local, provincial, and national government to place the goal of reconciliation and unity at the top of their respective agendas.[95]

---

94 Lyn S. Graybill, "South Africa's Truth and Reconciliation Commission: Ethical and Theological Perspectives," *Ethics & International Affairs* 12 (March 1998): 48, https://doi.org/10.1111/j.1747–7093.1998.tb00037.x.

95 "Truth and Reconciliation Commission of South Africa Report," *South African Broadcasting Corporation* 5 (October 29, 1998), 304, https://sabctrc.saha.org.za/originals/finalreport/volume5/volume5.pdf.

By all accounts, the TRC's greatest achievement was establishing a public record of the nation's shared pain. For the Xhosa, in particular, the TRC process promoted reconciliation. By contrast, Dutch and English-speaking South Africans, while agreeing that it had revealed the painful truth, felt it had been less successful in promoting reconciliation and political stability.[96] The fact that the Commission regarded justice as less important than Christian mercy, also became one of the charges against it; specifically that it had not done enough to change the attitudes of the white population, since the major actors of the apartheid regime were never forced to acknowledge their guilt.

Despite these flaws, however, it is hard to disagree with Archbishop Tutu's final assessment that the process offered "the possibility of continuing survival for all of us," in contrast to what he called "justice with ashes."[97]

6.4.2 Guatemala's Historical Clarification Commission

The Guatemalan Historical Clarification Commission (CEH) lies at the other extreme of TRC processes. One unusual feature of the CEH is that it was developed as part of the June 1994 peace accord between the government and the Guatemalan rebels. Unlike the much larger South African TRC, the CEH consisted of just three persons: one appointed by the government, one by the rebels, and a third by the United Nations, who chaired the Commission. This was German legal scholar and human rights expert, Christian Tomuschat.

In February 1999, the CEH presented a twelve-volume report that chronicled the origins, characteristics, and consequences of the thirty-six-year civil war in Guatemala, and gave specific recommendations on how to promote peace and national harmony in Guatemala. These included:
- Take measures to preserve the memory of the victims;
- Those responsible for the crimes should assume responsibility;
- Restore material possessions and economic compensation;
- Conduct investigations into all known forced disappearances;
- Create an immediate exhumation policy of all victims' remains;
- Foster mutual respect and observance of human rights;

---

96 Jay A. Vora and Erika Vora, "The Effectiveness of South Africa's Truth and Reconciliation Commission: Perceptions of Xhosa, Afrikaner, and English South Africans," *Journal of Black Studies* 34, no. 3 (2004): 308, http://www.jstor.org/stable/3180939.
97 Lyn S. Graybill, "South Africa's Truth and Reconciliation Commission."

– Strengthen the democratic process (judicial and military reform).[98]

Among the many different TRC formats, Guatemala's is often considered one of the weakest, since the CEH did not have the power to subpoena witnesses or records, could not name perpetrators, and did not hold public hearings. It was also preceded by a blanket amnesty that offered immunity for all but the most heinous human rights crimes. On the other hand, since the Commission could not "individualize responsibilities," it was able to focus on delineating institutional responsibility and detailing the modus operandi of these institutions.

One of its most important findings was that government violence against the Mayan population during the 1980s constituted genocide. As a result, in 2013 former Guatemalan dictator Efrain Rios Montt was tried for crimes against humanity and sentenced to eighty years in prison. His sentence, however, was later overturned by the Guatemalan Constitutional Court, and he died before his retrial could be completed.[99]

Despite the military's opposition, the report was widely disseminated inside Guatemala. In 2002 there was even a *radionovela* (radio soap opera) made about it and broadcast in the regions of the country that had been most severely affected by the war. A human rights component was later added to the national curriculum, which included "a public history of the violence and opening up space for further discussion about the past."[100] In 2003, twenty years after the majority of human rights violations had occurred, the Guatemalan government set up a National Reparations Program.

The Guatemalan example reveals that, despite weak institutional support, with the passage of time, and an educational system focused on promoting a common historical vision and dialogue – two core elements of the TRC process – society's wounds can begin to heal. Critics of the Guatemalan process argue that by encouraging a modus vivendi in which the conflicting parties coexisted, but never truly reconciled, the process abandoned justice altogether and encour-

---

98 "Report of the Commission for Historical Clarification: Conclusions and Recommendations," https://www.ca1.uscourts.gov/sites/ca1/files/citations/Guatemala%20Memory%20of%20Silence %20Report%20of%20the%20Commission%20for%20Historical%20Clarification%20Conclusions%20and%20Recommendations.pdf.
99 "Truth Commission: Guatemala," *United States Institute of Peace*, February 1, 1997, https://www.usip.org/publications/1997/02/truth-commission-guatemala.
100 Elizabeth Oglesby, "History Education and Reconciliation in Guatemala," *Carnegie Council*, September 1, 2004, https://www.carnegiecouncil.org/publications/articles_papers_reports/4996/_res/id=Attachments/index=0/4996_Elizabeth_Oglesby_Working_Paper.pdf.

aged political apathy.[101] Such arguments overlook the fact that sometimes the goals of peace and justice can be in direct conflict, and may need to be pursued sequentially, rather than simultaneously. Such was Spain's experience.

6.4.3 Spain: A Conspiracy of Silence in the Public Interest

Like Ukraine, the Spanish Civil War was an internationalized conflict. Franco's fascist movement, however, survived and continued to rule Spain until 1975. Following Franco's death, fear that the bloody civil war might resume led a pact among political parties to, literally, forget the past – *Pacto de Olvido*. The intent of this pact was to offer protection "to everybody from everybody," at least during the transition period.[102]

To prevent the past from being used as a political weapon by either side, Spaniards were asked to accept the moral equivalence of both sides in the Civil War. Spain's 1977 Amnesty Law freed political prisoners, permitted the return of exiles, and provided a sweeping amnesty for any crimes committed during the Civil War, or during the entire Franco era. By wiping the historical slate clean, the government was able to establish the transition to democracy as the clear priority of the first post-Franco generation of Spanish politicians.

Along with the new monuments and joint commemorations for victims on both sides of the Civil War, the government also adopted the slogan "*todos fuimos culpables*" (we all were guilty). The new national education curriculum required teachers to discuss the negative effects of the Civil War and dictatorship. Spanish history was firmly placed within the context of European history, and, for the first time, the autonomous regions of Galicia, Catalonia, and the Basque lands were given the opportunity to determine 35 to 40 percent of the educational curriculum for themselves.

From 2002 and 2005, the regional governments from Asturias, Catalonia, Extremadura, the Basque Country, Navarra, and Andalusia decided to fund the exhumation and reburial of victims of the Civil War from their own budgets. In 2007, as increasing evidence of Franco's human rights violations was uncovered,

---

101 Kora Andrieu, "Reconciliation," *Oxford Bibliographies Online* (Oxford University Press, February 26, 2013), https://doi.org/10.1093/obo/9780199743292–0148.
102 Omar G. Encarnación, "Reconciliation after Democratization: Coping with the Past in Spain," *Political Science Quarterly* 123, no. 3 (2008): 438, http://www.jstor.org/stable/20203049.

the Spanish parliament passed a Historical Memory Act to provide individual reparations.[103]

Under the conservative government of Mariano Rajoy (2011–2018), some of these reforms were scaled back in order to emphasize Spanish national identity, but progress toward a more pluricultural Spanish identity later resumed. At the end of 2018, the Spanish Justice Ministry announced that the government would establish a Truth Commission to investigate human rights of the Civil War and Franco eras, and in 2020 the government adopted the Democratic Memory Law, which further repealed the criminal convictions of members of the political opposition to Franco, expanded funding for the exhumation and reburial of victims, and systematically removed all Franco-era symbols. The last statue of Franco in Spain was removed in February 2021.[104]

The Spanish elite's choice to "forget the past for the sake of the present," has been criticized in Spain and without.[105] The United Nations repeatedly called on the Spanish government to repeal the 1997 Amnesty Act and prosecute members of the previous regime for war crimes.[106] But there are also those who suggest that the country's relatively smooth transition from dictatorship to democracy owes a great deal to this strategy of forgetting, which is the same strategy that Aeschylus recommended in his *Oresteia* trilogy more than 2,400 years ago.[107] They describe it not as forgetting about justice, but rather of deferring justice until society as a whole has healed sufficiently to revisit its old wounds.[108]

---

103 Ackar Kadribasic, "Transitional Justice in Democratization Processes: The Case of Spain from an International Point of View," *International Journal of Rule of Law, Transitional Justice and Human Rights* 1 (December 2010): 126, https://tinyurl.com/2pkyk95u.

104 "Last Statue of General Franco Removed in Spain," *Madrid Metropolitan*, February 24, 2021, https://www.madridmetropolitan.com/last-statue-of-dictator-franco-removed-in-spain/.

105 Madeleine Davis, "Is Spain Recovering Its Memory? Breaking the 'Pacto del Olvido,'" *Human Rights Quarterly* 27, no. 3 (2005): 858, http://www.jstor.org/stable/20069813; "Proposal for Spain to Reckon with Its Past during Franco Era, Welcomed by UN Rights Experts," *United Nations News*, July 25, 2018, https://news.un.org/en/story/2018/07/1015522.

106 "UN Expert Urges Spain to Probe Alleged Atrocities during 1930's Civil War," *United Nations News*, February 5, 2014, https://news.un.org/en/story/2014/02/461222-un-expert-urges-spain-probe-alleged-atrocities-during-1930s-civil-war.

107 Friedrich Nietzsche seems to echo this sentiment when he writes: "Life in any true sense is absolutely impossible without forgetfulness. Or, to put my conclusion better, there is a degree of sleeplessness, of rumination, of 'historical sense,' that injures and finally destroys the living thing, be it a man or a people or a system of culture." Friedrich Nietzsche, *The Use and Abuse of History* (New York: Cosimo Classics, 2010), 7.

108 Carolyn Boyd, David A. Crocker, and Elizabeth A. Cole, "Democratic Development and Reckoning with the Past: The Case of Spain in Comparative Context," *Carnegie Council for Ethics*

6.4.4 Can Transitional Justice Work in Ukraine?

Truth and Reconciliation Commissions are a vital part of transitional justice, which is described as "justice adapted to societies transforming themselves after a period of pervasive human rights abuse."[109] The attempt to simultaneously promote "recognition for victims and promotion of possibilities for peace, reconciliation and democracy," however, can lead to sharp disagreements between those who would prioritize the need for justice, and those who would give priority to forgiveness.

According to David Crocker, of the three kinds of reconciliation that transitional justice encourages, the thinnest is the cessation of conflict and non-lethal coexistence.[110] Slightly better is democratic reciprocity – the ability to debate most difficult issues in order to have policies most citizens can accept – while the thickest form of reconciliation, the one that in my view corresponds most closely to what the Greeks sought to accomplish through tragedy, is restoring society to the original ideal of social harmony. Archbishop Tutu saw this as akin to the African concept of *ubuntu*, which combines compassion with an appreciation of the humanity of others.[111]

Notably missing from these definitions of transitional justice is the nation, because true justice is an act of individual forgiveness, not something that governments can dictate. The importance of this distinction becomes apparent when looking at the Ukrainian government's efforts to legislate transitional justice, which describe it as allowing for the suspension of civil rights in parts of Donbass and Crimea after they rejoin Ukraine.[112]

---

in *International Affairs*, June 25, 2003, https://www.carnegiecouncil.org/publications/articles_-papers_reports/957.

109 "What Is Transitional Justice?," *International Center for Transitional Justice*, February 22, 2011, https://tinyurl.com/y35kslwh.

110 Carolyn Boyd, David A. Crocker, and Elizabeth A. Cole, "Democratic Development and Reckoning with the Past: The Case of Spain in Comparative Context." Despite their generally positive assessments of modern Spain, Crocker and Boyd disagree strongly over one particular symbol – García Lorca's statue in the Plaza de Victoria. Crocker argues that it is "still an emblem of the contested past: each day, the Left puts a red kerchief on the neck of the statue, and someone from the Right comes later to take it off." Boyd, on the other hand, contends that "Lorca has been fully incorporated into the Spanish cannon for a long time, at least since the death of Franco, if not before."

111 Dirk J. Louw, "Ubuntu: An African Assessment of the Religious Other," *Paideia*, n.d., http://www.bu.edu/wcp/Papers/Afri/AfriLouw.htm.

112 Taras Kozub, "Kiev gotovit spetssudy i bolshuyu amnistiyu dlya Donbassa," [Kiev Is Preparing Special Courts and a Big Amnesty for Donbass] *Vesti*, November 21, 2017, https://vesti.ua/po-

Just how far this is from transitional justice can be seen in the widely discussed "Law on Forgiveness," proposed in 2018 by former MP and lawyer Andrei Senchenko, and endorsed by Ukraine's first president, Leonid Kravchuk. Senchenko seeks to address the problem that, under Ukrainian law, every inhabitant of Crimea and Donbass is automatically considered a collaborator. The solution he proposes is to require all inhabitants of Donbass and Crimea to ask forgiveness of Ukraine.[113]

Senchenko stresses that this is not amnesty, but rather an appeal for clemency for crimes against the state. For minor offenses, they may submit a petition of forgiveness to the courts and serve an alternative sentence, rather than jailtime.[114] He estimates that, after every possible leniency is shown, half a million people – 400,000 in Donbass and 100,000 in Crimea – will need to apply for forgiveness. This does not include those who have taken Russian citizenship – already a much larger number – who will presumably have to be deported.[115] In the final version of the law, local residents will have six months after the end of the occupation to apply for forgiveness. Those who do not, and thereby fail

---

litika/266180-kiev-hotovit-donbassu-bolshuju-amnistiju. Both Ukraine's former Ombudsman, Valeriya Lutkovskaya and her assistant Mikhail Chaplyga, also refer to Donetsk officials being investigated by reconciliation commissions as "transitional justice."

113 Ivan Kapsamun, Dmitry Plakhta, and Olesya Shutkevich, "My popali v nerv," [We Hit a Nerve] *Den*, March 12, 2018, //m.day.kyiv.ua/ru/article/podrobnosti/my-popali-v-nerv; "Proekt zakona Ukrainy ob otvetstvennosti," [Draft Law of Ukraine on Liability] *Sila prava*, September 9, 2020, https://sila-prava.org/ru/news-ru/39993738/. The formula proposed to petition the state for forgiveness is: "I, a citizen of Ukraine (full name), during the period of armed aggression of the Russian Federation against our country, committed in the interests of the aggressor state, to the detriment of the interests of Ukraine, a criminal offense(s), the circumstances of which are set forth by me in the statement on the committed criminal offense(s), provided by me together with this request for forgiveness. I admit my guilt, sincerely repent and ask the Ukrainian people and the state for forgiveness for the crime(s) I committed. I ask you to apply to me the procedure of forgiveness and the alternative main punishment provided for by the Law of Ukraine 'On Responsibility.'"

114 "Proekt zakona Ukrainy ob otvetstvennosti." Proposed alternatives include: the denial of government employment, prohibitions on running for public office, teaching, or voting for five to ten years.

115 Yulia Bezpechnaya, "Ne lyublyu slovo 'deportatsiya,'" [I Don't Like the Word "Deportation"] *Segodnya.ua*, March 28, 2021, https://www.segodnya.ua/regions/krym/ne-lyublyu-slovo-deportaciya-reznikov-rasskazal-chto-budet-s-pereehavshimi-v-krym-rossiyanami-1515289.html; Dmitriy Ponomarenko, "Ukraina mozhet vygnat vsekh rossiyan iz Kryma posle deokkupatsii poluostrova, – Reznikov," [Ukraine Could Expel All Russians from Crimea after De-occupying the Peninsula – Reznikov] *Ukranews*, July 9, 2021, https://archive.ph/Mjrnb.

to acknowledge their crimes, should expect to be prosecuted to the full extent of the law.[116]

The objective of this legislation, according to Senchenko, is to achieve justice for the state. Another objective is to protect Ukraine by "cleansing" it of the "virus of separatism." That is why the individual must ask forgiveness, first and foremost, of the state. A third benefit of this law, says Senchenko, is that it would prevent the implementation of the Minsk Accords.[117]

Of the three pillars of transitional justice – legal justice, restorative justice, and social justice – Senchenko adopts only the first.[118] There is no effort in his legislation to achieve reconciliation, since the only real victim is the Ukrainian state. Everyone who stayed at home and continued to live under occupation is presumed to have collaborated with the aggressor in some form or other, and therefore deserves some form of punishment. This is precisely the sort of retribution that transitional justice seeks to avoid.[119]

Senchenko's legislation was submitted to the Rada in its final form in 2020, but by that time had already been superseded by the Law on Reintegration, which maintained the same logic of treating Ukrainians in the occupied territories as collaborators. This again highlights the crucial role that Ukrainian nationalism plays in preventing reconciliation. For nationalists, social harmony can only come about if those who have sinned against the Ukrainian state ask for its forgiveness.

---

116 "Proekt zakona Ukrainy ob otvetstvennosti." Articles 7 and 22. In the final version of this law, its purpose is designated more accurately by renaming it "The Law on Responsibility."
117 Andriy Senchenko, "Arestovicha ne sprosili!," [Arestovich Was Not Asked!] *Facebook*, June 8, 2021, https://www.facebook.com/andriy.senchenko/posts/2611117692522693; "Prostit Donbass," [To Forgive Donbas] *Avdeevka City*, April 9, 2018, http://avdeevka.city/news/view/prostit-donbass-e-ksperty-razmyshlyayut-o-novom-zakonoproekte.
118 Kora Andrieu, "Transitional Justice: A New Discipline in Human Rights," *Mass Violence & Resistance*, Sciences Po, January 18, 2010, https://www.sciencespo.fr/mass-violence-war-massacre-resistance/en/document/transitional-justice-new-discipline-human-rights-0.html. "OHCHR | Rule of Law – Transitional Justice," United Nations Office of Human Rights, November 9, 2021, https://www.ohchr.org/en/issues/ruleoflaw/pages/transitionaljustice.aspx; "Proekt Zakona Ukrainy ob Otvetstvennosti." The UN backgrounder on transitional justice specifically points out that transitional justice must always be conducted in conformity with international legal standards and obligations, not in the form of special legislation that sets a certain population apart and restricts their rights. The final version of Senchenko's legislation explicitly rejects this, stating that "there is not a single country in the world that, having passed through an armed conflict, existing legislation sufficed for the post-war settlement. In every instance, special laws were written 'from a blank slate.'"
119 "What Is Transitional Justice?," *UN.org*, February 20, 2008, https://www.un.org/peacebuilding/sites/www.un.org.peacebuilding/files/documents/26_02_2008_background_note.pdf.

The rebels, meanwhile, insist that the Ukrainian state abandoned them. These two points of view are so far apart that only a profound change of heart, supported by concrete actions, can bring them closer. This is where tragedy can play an important role in social healing. In Greek society, tragedy was used to purge mutual hatred (*catharsis*), so that confrontation could give way to a dialogue based on compassion and forgiveness. Only such a dialogue can restore true justice and social harmony.

What might such a *catharsis* look like in Ukraine? The Truth and Reconciliation process suggests that it should include two broad initiatives: public messaging aimed at healing the cultural rift in society, and confidence-building measures aimed at restoring trust in government.

To address low confidence in Ukrainian institutions and the rule of law, the government might consider inviting the residents of the occupied territories to help form the political institutions under which they are expected to live. Working within the framework of the Ukrainian Constitution, residents could be encouraged to take the lead in establishing their own local governments, to avoid the impression that they are being imposed on them against their will. At the same time, to strengthen local allegiance to national institutions, these regions must also have a voice in the national parliament. Current government proposals to limit their political and civil rights until they have been properly re-educated can only undermine local confidence in Ukrainian institutions and laws.

Second, to counteract the widespread demonization of Maloross Ukrainians, the government should promote a media discourse that treats all Ukrainian citizens as legitimate members of society, regardless of their language, creed, or culture. Ukrainian officials who repeat the divisive rhetoric of Far Right nationalism are, wittingly or unwittingly, undermining efforts to achieve reintegration, and preventing common bonds of Ukrainian identity from being formed.[120]

Third, to restore harmony to a fractured polity, the government should consider encouraging a culture of civic discourse. The best designed social and political institutions cannot work without a culture of tolerance. This lesson has had to be learned by every country that has ever emerged from civil war, and is specifically mentioned in the concluding reports of the South African and Gua-

---

120 "Natsist Drozdov nazval Donbass 'naikhudshim regionom,' zaselennym 'parnokopytnymi,'" [The Nazi Drozdov Calls Donbass the "Worst Region," Inhabited by "Hoofed Animals"] *Novoros Inform*, October 28, 2021, https://novorosinform.org/nacist-drozdov-nazval-donbass-naihudshim-regionom-zaselennym-parnokopytnymi-32551.html; Mykhailo Dubynyanskyi, "Ukraina velyka i mala," [Ukraine Big and Small] *Ukrainska pravda*, April 10, 2021, https://www.pravda.com.ua/articles/2021/04/10/7289691/.

temalan Truth and Reconciliation Commissions. Social discourse that is based on civic patriotism, could encourage cultural pluralism to become an asset for Ukraine, rather than something to be feared.

Assuaging the security fears of pluricultural countries is not an easy task, but it cannot be ignored in the hope that prosperity will make it go away, as liberals are wont to do, nor can it be suppressed by force, as nationalists suggest. The problem is made more acute by the fact that minority communities will often take aggressive stands, for fear that making cultural concessions to the state will ultimately leave them defenseless. In response, states will often act proactively to remove the threat by suppressing cultural autonomy before it can lead to demands for political autonomy. Ukraine is hardly unusual in this regard. We have seen the same pattern in Georgia, Spain, the United Kingdom, China, and elsewhere. What it also reveals, however, is that such suppression invariably gives rise to the very security threats that the state is trying to avoid.

One way to avoid such a destructive escalation is to embrace the concept of cultural security. Also known as the Copenhagen School of Security Studies, cultural security argues that national security is actually enhanced if the needs of minorities are anticipated and accommodated by the state, rather than suppressed by it. As Barry Buzan and Ole Waever put it, nation-states with diverse populations do better if they "leave room for a concept of politics detached from the state, and for circumstances in which identity politics [is] about maintaining difference rather than finding a collective image."[121] This stands in sharp contrast to efforts, like those of former Ukrainian President Viktor Yushchenko, to emphasize the "utter foreignness" of Maloross Ukraine.[122]

Minsk-2 resulted in a stalemate because Donbass refused to give up all that it had fought for, while Kiev refused to accept Donbass under any terms but unconditional surrender. Resolving this impasse will require confidence-building measures that reconcile *raison d'etat* with individual freedom. Here too, classical Greek tragedy offers some valuable lessons.

In *Antigone*, Sophocles portrays Creon, the ruler of Thebes, as someone who is utterly convinced that he is pursuing the *polis'* best interest by denying a public burial to an enemy of the state. His logic is unimpeachable, but his absolute devotion to *raison d'etat* blinds him to the possibility of dialogue or compromise. He does not understand that true justice requires the triumph of the whole, rather than the triumph of his own, particular view of justice. This ultimately

---

121 Barry Buzan and Ole Waever, "Slippery? Contradictory? Sociologically Untenable? The Copenhagen School Replies," *Review of International Studies* 23 (1997): 248.
122 *Ukrainska pravda*, "Yushchenko pro Krym i Donbas."

leads to his downfall and to Antigone's as well, for she is so obsessed with justice for herself, that she is willing to commit a "holy" crime to achieve it. What Sophocles is hinting at here is that conflicts over values cannot be resolved by force. The real solution lies in recognizing that both sides in a conflict can share noble aspirations, and must be willing to forego their own partial victory for the sake of those ideals.

It is therefore just as important, when building confidence in the national government in Malorossiya, to not simultaneously undermine it in Galicia. Experience suggests that this is possible, if public discourse shifts from what each side has to lose, to how both sides can benefit.

For example, Ukrainian industry, which is located primarily in the east, has suffered the most from being cut off from economic ties with Russia, while western Ukraine has suffered the most from being the country's primary exporter of labor. Neither side benefits from policies that are the product of nationalist ideology, rather than economic rationality.

It would thus make better sense to position Ukraine as a commercial bridge between Eurasia and Europe, rather than as a wall between them. Re-establishing mutually beneficial commercial ties with Russia would not only revitalize the country's industrial production, but also promote healing within Ukraine by encouraging internal rather than external migration.

6.5 Afterword: The Lessons of Tragedy

This chapter was finalized before the February 2022 Russian invasion of Ukraine. That is why it focuses mostly on the failure of the Minsk Accord, which stemmed, in my opinion, from Kiev's unwillingness to accept a pluricultural Ukraine. This reluctance explains why all peace efforts, whether internal or external, whether linked to the Minsk process or not, were doomed to fail. To escape this conundrum, I argued that both Galician and Maloross Ukrainians would need to recognize and discuss each other's most intense fears. Only at the end of such a dialogue would a lasting peace in Ukraine be possible. I saw the Truth and Reconciliation process as a way to facilitate such a dialogue.

Recent events have confirmed some parts of my analysis, while forcing me to re-evaluate other parts. They have confirmed my view of politics as a tragic cycle propelled by mutual fear and the loss of communication. What I failed to appreciate was how little external parties care about resolving the conflict within Ukraine itself, especially if resolving it stands in the way of achieving some grander geopolitical objective.

For the United States that grander objective is maintaining pre-eminence in a world order that so perfectly suits its needs. For Russia that grander objective is breaking the current world order, which leaves it permanently marginalized. Both sides have shown very little interest in seeing the crisis resolved by Ukrainians themselves, since this would only diminish their own political influence within the country.[123] I also underestimated the depth of the Russian elite's anger at the West for containing Russia while simultaneously expanding NATO. To be fair, though, almost no-one anticipated that Russia's frustration would lead to an explosion of violence against Ukraine that could bring the entire world to the brink of war.

And yet, despite the fact that Russia's invasion has put the spotlight on the geopolitical conflict over Ukraine, I remain convinced that it is the domestic conflict within the country that holds the key to bringing the current cycle of tragedy to an end. To understand why, we need to see the present conflict as not one, but three interrelated conflicts.

The first conflict is the result of America's longstanding efforts to detach Ukraine from Russia's sphere of influence. The roots of this geopolitical tug-of-war go back to Zbigniew Brzezinski's thesis that Ukrainian independence can be used as a geopolitical pivot for transforming Russia.[124] Since it was first articulated in 1997, it has become a cornerstone of US foreign policy. As the longtime president of the National Endowment for Democracy, Carl Gershman, put it in 2014, "Ukraine is the biggest prize." If it could be pulled away from Russia, then "Putin may find himself on the losing end not just in the near abroad but within Russia itself."[125]

The second conflict stems from the clash of visions over the nature and extent of Ukrainian sovereignty. In Russia, hostility to Ukrainian sovereignty is fueled by fear that the Far Right, which has grown significantly in social influence since 2014, will transform Ukraine from a friendly neighbor into "anti-Russia."[126]

123 Ted Snider, "Is the US Hindering Much-Needed Diplomatic Efforts?," *Responsible Statecraft*, April 9, 2022, https://responsiblestatecraft.org/2022/04/09/is-the-us-hindering-much-needed-diplomatic-efforts/.
124 Zbigniew Brzezinski, *The Grand Chessboard: American Primacy and Its Geostrategic Imperatives*, 2nd ed. (New York: Basic Books, 2016), 47.
125 Carl Gershman, "Former Soviet States Stand Up to Russia. Will the U.S.?," *Washington Post*, September 26, 2013, https://www.washingtonpost.com/opinions/former-soviet-states-stand-up-to-russia-will-the-us/2013/09/26/b5ad2be4–246a-11e3-b75d-5b7f66349852_story.html.
126 Ilya Barabanov, "Vladimir Putin napisal statyu pro proekt 'anti-Rossiya,'" [Vladimir Putin Wrote an Article about the "Anti-Russia" Project] *BBC*, July 13, 2021, https://www.bbc.com/russian/news-57795642.

In Ukraine, by contrast, hostility toward Russia is fueled by fear that the failure to draw a sharp enough distinction between the two nations will prevent the emergence of a Ukrainian national identity. As former Ukrainian President Viktor Yushchenko put it, "if Russians and Ukrainians are one people, then the Ukrainian people do not exist."[127]

But to my mind the most important conflict is still the conflict within Ukraine, between its Russophile east (Malorossiya) and its Russophobe west (Galicia). This conflict has been going on for at least 150 years, and has erupted in serious military hostilities inside Ukraine four times: during the World Wars I and II, after the 2014 Maidan, and now in 2022. It should be noted that in each instance violence was exacerbated by the intervention of foreign powers seeking to tip the scales within Ukraine to their own advantage. Resolving this internecine conflict would therefore go a long way toward limiting the ability of foreign actors to intervene. This, however, would require a new level of dialogue, compassion, and mutual reconciliation among Ukrainians themselves.

Any hope of such a reconciliation taking place in this generation would seem to have been dashed by Russia's 2022 invasion, which has reignited the civil war in Donbass and thus renewed the cycle of tragedy. In the selfish pursuit of its own national interests, Russia is trying to impose neutrality and *de facto* federalism on Ukraine. It hopes to thereby reverse its setbacks in all three conflicts simultaneously: in the strategic conflict with America, by forcing the United States to acknowledge Russia's "red lines"; in the bilateral conflict with Ukraine, by ending NATO's military plans for the country; and in the domestic conflict, by restoring the balance of interests between eastern and western Ukraine to what they were before 2014.

Russia's use of brute force to get its way has spawned such significant resistance in Maloross Ukraine that many analysts are predicting that Ukraine's longstanding domestic conflicts will now be a thing of the past, that the crucible of war with Russia is forging a united Ukrainian nation. This is not a new argument, indeed, it has been the hope of many Ukrainian government officials, since Ukraine's Interior Minister Arsen Avakov famously asserted, back in June 2014, that war with Russia would have a salutary "cleansing" effect on the nation.[128]

127 "Yak bachat 30 rokiv nezalezhnosti prezidenty," [How the Presidents View 30 Years of Independence] *Ukrainska pravda*, August 26, 2021, https://www.pravda.com.ua/articles/2021/08/26/7304998/.
128 Arsen Avakov, "V eti paru dnei mnogo govoril s nashimi v zone ATO," [In These Past Few Days I Spoke with a Lot of Our People in the ATO] *Facebook*, June 22, 2014, https://www.facebook.com/arsen.avakov.1/posts/657281451028631%20%5b25.

And yet, the fact that hostility toward Russia is currently at an all time high, cannot automatically be taken as an indication that it will always continue to be so. It is worth recalling President John F. Kennedy's wise words in 1963, just a few months after the Cuban missile crisis, that "history teaches us that enmities between nations, as between individuals, do not last forever. However fixed our likes and dislikes may seem, the tide of time and events will often bring surprising changes in the relations between nations and neighbors."[129] Indeed, one need only think of how dramatically attitudes have shifted between England and Ireland, Mexico and the United States, or France and Germany.[130] Perhaps, as a result of this war, there will now be a permanent shift in the mentality of Maloross Ukrainians, but if the past eight years of war are any indication, then a fundamental values re-orientation of Russophile Ukrainians away from Russia seems unlikely.

It is worth noting, for instance, that while positive attitudes toward Putin and the Russian government have fallen sharply since 2014, personal sympathy for average Russians much less so.[131] And even though the Russian language has been effectively forced out of the public sphere, it nevertheless remains the language of choice in schools, publishing, entertainment, and internet usage in

---

129 John F. Kennedy, Commencement Address at American University, Washington, DC, June 10, 1963, JFK Library, https://www.jfklibrary.org/archives/other-resources/john-f-kennedy-speeches/american-university-19630610.

130 Herbert Butterfield, *Writings on Christianity and History* (New York: Oxford University Press, 1979), 54–55. To quote Sir Herbert on the vagaries of history: "In the days of my own childhood, it was still the English against the French, these latter being the traditional enemy. I can remember even now the schoolbook which said that the English owed all their freedom to their kinship with the Germans, for liberty went back to the Teutons in their primeval forests. The Reformation, the emancipation of religion, came from Martin Luther, and Germany in any case had long enjoyed federal government, state rights and even free, independent, self-governing cities, like Hamburg. The antithesis to all this was to be found in the Latin countries. I still remember how it was all spelt out: Italy stood for the Papacy, Spain had had the Inquisition, while France, twice over, if you please, had chosen to live under Napoleonic dictatorships, an evil which, in my young days, had as yet had no parallel in other countries."

131 "Press-relizy i otchety otnoshenie naseleniya Ukrainy k Rossii i naseleniya Rossii k Ukraine," [Press Releases and Reports on the Attitude of the Population of Ukraine towards Russia and the Population of Russia towards Ukraine] *Kiev International Institute of Sociology*, March 2, 2021, https://www.kiis.com.ua/?lang=rus&cat=reports&id=1015&page=2. After reaching an all time low of 30 percent in May 2015, positive attitudes toward Russia prior to 2022 oscillated between 40 and 60 percent. Western Ukraine is the only region where the majority support a complete separation from Russia, although even there 40 percent say they favor friendly relations and open borders with Russia.

every region of the country but historical Galicia.[132] As the pro-Maidan journalist Vitaly Portnikov remarked disconsolately earlier this year: "As long as Ukrainians and Russians cry over the same television shows, the president of Ukraine is definitely Vladimir Putin, not Vladimir Zelensky. At least for a vast number of Ukrainians."[133]

Another conundrum that many Western analysts prefer not to delve into too deeply is what to do with the people in Donbass and Crimea, many of whom no longer want to be part of Ukraine. This is corroborated by numerous Western polls, as well as by internal polling done by the Ukrainian government.[134]

The nightmare scenario facing Ukraine today is that the front line of this new Cold War, the new "Iron Curtain" between Russia and the West, will be established right across its territory, prolonging the conflict within the country indefinitely. How can this nightmare be prevented, particularly now that the sides are engaged in a full-blown military conflict? By removing Ukraine as a source of contention between external actors, thereby restoring both agency and sovereignty to the Ukrainian people.

The most important requirement for restoring agency is establishing social harmony between Galician and Maloross Ukraine. This will require both grassroots initiatives and government policies that promote Maloross culture as a legitimate part of Ukraine's indigenous diversity. The trade-off, which was actually quite effective in preserving national unity before 2004, is well known to anyone familiar with federalism: cultural autonomy, for political loyalty.

As for restoring sovereignty, while there are many ways to resolve the conflict between Russia and the West, most are at the expense of Ukrainian sovereignty.

---

132 Viktoriya Venk, "Zrada pod elochku," [Treason under the Christmas Tree] *Strana.ua*, January 2, 2021, https://strana.one/news/309931-chto-ukraintsy-iskali-v-google-i-smotreli-v-youtube-na-novyj-hod.html; Olena Barsukova, "'Ukraina' zamist 'Ukrayna,'" [UkraIna instead of UkrAina] *Ukrainska pravda*, January 4, 2022, https://life.pravda.com.ua/society/2022/01/4/247047/. The authors of this last report tout the fact that searches for "Ukraine" in Ukrainian have risen from 7 percent to 13 percent since 2013, which shows just how far Ukrainianization has yet to go.
133 "V Kieve zayavili, chto bolshinstvo Ukraintsev schitaet Putina prezidentom," [In Kiev, They Say that the Majority of Ukrainians Consider Putin Their President] *Regnum*, January 1, 2022, https://regnum-ru.turbopages.org/regnum.ru/s/news/3467722.html.
134 Alesya Batsman, "Sivokho: V kakom statuse ya voploshchayu mirnye initsiativy prezidenta?"; Vladimir Gladkov, "V Kieve poboyalis publikovat rezultaty zapadnogo sotsoprosa v Krymu," [Kiev Afraid to Publish the Results of a Western Opinion Poll in Crimea] *PolitNavigator*, September 7, 2021, https://www.politnavigator.net/v-kieve-poboyalis-publikovat-rezultaty-zapadnogo-socoprosa-v-krymu.html. Unpublished polls conducted in June 2021, and later leaked to the press, indicate that more than three-quarters of Crimeans feel that their life under Russian rule has become better, while 79 percent believe that Russia is making the right decisions for the peninsula.

The best way to strengthen Ukraine's actual independence would be for it to develop greater immunity to all foreign influence, both Russian and Western. Again, this would require Maloross and Galician Ukrainians to forge a common vision of the future, by engaging in a process of national reconciliation.

Forging such a common vision of the future, however, means repudiating integral nationalism. Only then could a patriotism that defines Ukraine as primarily a civic community emerge. In a civic Ukraine, Galician nationalists would have to give up their 1930s view that national security demands total cultural homogeneity, while Russophile Ukrainians would have to prioritize their allegiance to the Ukrainian state, which would accept them as they are. Both tasks rely on empathy to allay the fears of the other side, and allow true dialogue between them to begin.

Such a dialogue, aimed at forging a non-exclusive, civic concept of Ukrainian identity, could begin under the auspices of a Ukrainian Truth and Reconciliation Commission. By giving voice to the grievances of all those who fought, regardless of which side they were on, it could become the modern day equivalent of the Dionysian festivals of ancient Greece. It would offer riveting emotional testimony, through highly choreographed and dramatized public spectacles, leading the public to *catharsis* – a purging of the soul that restores a healthy perspective by removing hatred. This may seem like a tall order for Ukraine, but we should not forget that such commissions already have a track record of social healing in more than forty-seven countries once engulfed by hatred and conflict.[135]

One important element of virtually all TRCs is the propagation of liberal values and human rights. Experience suggests that the best way to popularize such values is not to have foreign elites impose Western models of thinking and governance, but rather to make people more aware of their own liberal traditions, why they developed, and how they might be used to respond to current challenges.

Despite a nineteenth-century liberal tradition that includes such illustrious names as Mykhailo Drahomanov, Maksim Kovalevsky, Bohdan Kistiakovsky, Mykhailo Tuhan-Baranovsky, Mykola Vasylenko, and Volodymyr Vernadsky, Ukrainian liberalism today has been totally eclipsed by Ukrainian nationalism, which sees not enough that is distinctively Ukrainian in it.[136] This is only partly correct.

---

135 Ruben Carranza, "Plunder and Pain: Should Transitional Justice Engage with Corruption and Economic Crimes?" *International Journal of Transitional Justice* 2, no. 3 (December 2008): 315, https://doi.org/10.1093/ijtj/ijn023.

136 Myroslav Popovych, "Is Liberalism Un-Ukrainian?," *Den*, October 31, 2000, https://day.kyiv.ua/en/article/close/liberalism-un-ukrainian; Karina V. Korostelina, "Mapping National Identi-

The liberal intellectual tradition that arose in the late Russian Empire was indeed a heritage shared by both Russians and Ukrainians alike, but this is precisely why it would be invaluable for establishing both a patriotic civic consensus, and for forging new ties with both Russia and Europe on the basis of shared values.

Of course, not all aspects of the Truth and Reconciliation process are appropriate for all situations. What worked for Spain or Guatemala might not work for Ukraine. Nevertheless, all successful models seem to have one thing in common – they begin with an interim, often imperfect, peace settlement that satisfies no one. This lull in hostilities creates an opportunity for cooler heads to emerge who, over time, forge longer-term solutions.[137] That is because forgiveness and compassion require a calm social space, where hatred can give way to dialogue, and the healing of society begin. As Archbishop Desmond Tutu put it, when it is

---

ty Narratives in Ukraine," *Nationalities Papers* 41, no. 2 (March 2013), https://doi.org/10.1080/ 00905992.2012.747498, 312. Korostelina notes that "the intellectual landscape of Ukraine is deficient in liberal civic ideologies that define society as a community of equal citizens independently of their ethnicity, language, or religion."

137 "UNTAES," United Nations Department of Public Information, accessed January 9, 2022, https://peacekeeping.un.org/en/mission/past/untaes.htm; "UNMIS," United Nations Mission in Sudan, accessed January 9, 2022, https://unmis.unmissions.org/; Stefan Wolff and Annemarie Peen Rodt, "Self-Determination after Kosovo," *Europe-Asia Studies* 65, no. 5 (2013): 799–822, https://doi.org/10.1080/09668136.2013.792450; "The Belfast Agreement/Good Friday Agreement 1998," Northern Ireland Assembly, accessed January 9, 2022, https://education.niassembly.gov.uk/post_16/snapshots_of_devolution/gfa; "Key Points of the Bougainville Peace Agreement | Conciliation Resources," *Accord* 12 (September 2002), https://www.c-r.org/accord/papua-new-guinea%E2%80%93bougainville/key-points-bougainville-peace-agreement; "Ballot for the Saarland Referendum (January 13, 1935)," GHDI Image, accessed January 9, 2022, https://germanhistorydocs.ghi-dc.org/sub_image.cfm?image_id=1983; Chris Dye, "Independence Referendums: Ballot for Saarland Referendum 1955," *Independence Referendums*, November 3, 2010, http://independencereferendum.blogspot.com/2010/11/ballot-for-saarland-referendum-1955.html; Stefan Wolff and Tatyana Malyarenko, "How Can Ukraine, Crimea and Russia Secure a Stable Future?," *The Conversation*, March 4, 2014, http://theconversation.com/how-can-ukraine-crimea-and-russia-secure-a-stable-future-23947. Some of these approaches have a mixed track record. In Croatia, in the second half of the 1990s, an UN-administered interim accord facilitated the reintegration of Serb-majority parts of the country, whereas in Sudan and Kosovo new states were created. The Northern Ireland Agreement and the Papua-New Guinea – Bougainville Agreement have the option of future constitutional changes built in. The Saarland, a territory historically disputed between France and Germany, before and after World War II voted to return to Germany, rather than become a part of France, or remain an internationally administered territory.

implemented systematically, forgiveness can become, "thoroughly political. It *is* realpolitik."[138]

The prospects for social healing in Ukraine today are admittedly very slim. Given the passions aroused by Russia's invasion, and the social and political influence that Ukrainian nationalists already exert, what incentive would they have to share power? Not much, unless they believed that the nation's very survival was at stake.

During World War I, Semyon Petlyura, the president of the brief-lived Ukrainian People's Republic, ceded all of western Ukraine to Poland in exchange for Polish support against the Red Army. This triggered Galicia's denunciation of the *Akt Zluki*, Ukraine's first declaration of independence, and resulted in the *de facto* disintegration of Ukraine. Nevertheless, today Petlyura is honored as a national hero in Ukraine.[139]

At the end of World War II, in order to better cast their alliance with Nazi Germany as a struggle for Ukrainian independence, the leaders of the Organization of Ukrainian Nationalists rewrote their charter, removing its most racially offensive and undemocratic portions. Likewise, in 1991, when it seemed that some regions of the country might not vote for independence, the leader of Rukh, Vyacheslav Chornovil, embraced German style federalism as the best option for Ukraine. And in 2015, when faced with military collapse, President Poroshenko agreed to autonomy for parts of Donbass in the Minsk Accords. Could we be looking at a similar situation today? Only time will tell.

One could argue that all that these examples prove is that nationalists cannot be trusted to compromise, that their willingness to do so is purely tactical. But it is also conceivable that, when confronted with the reality that their policies have led to the *de facto* partition of Ukraine, some nationalists might revisit their assumption that cultural, religious, and linguistic monism is the only path to national unity. It might then be possible to persuade some of them – those not fanatically committed to a totalitarian form of nationalism – that by accepting political loyalty in exchange for cultural diversity they would actually be achieving their *summum bonum* – the restoration of political agency and sovereignty to Ukraine.

* * *

---

138 David Goodman, "One of the Most Meaningful Experiences of My Life Was Covering Archbishop Desmond Tutu as He Led South Africa's Truth & Reconciliation Commission in 1996–97," *Facebook*, December 26, 2021, https://m.facebook.com/story.php?story_fbid=10224258681869185&id=1067218835.
139 "Za chto nash zemlyak ubil Simona Petlyuru?," [Why Did Our Countryman Kill Symon Petlyura?] *Timer-Odessa*, February 3, 2016, https://perma.cc/SUL2-EE68.

Ukraine's profound divisions are rooted in mutual grievances that cry out for justice, yet they cannot agree on what justice means. For Galician Ukrainians, justice demands that all Ukrainians be united by a common language, culture, religion, and historical vision, or Ukraine is doomed. For Maloross Ukrainians, justice demands that the cultural, religious, and historical pluralism of Ukraine be recognized, or Ukraine is doomed. It is this very yearning for a perfect justice, one that will bring as a final reckoning with the past, that has been tearing Ukraine apart for decades. Until these incompatible definitions of justice are reconciled, Ukrainian society cannot heal.

The situation may seem hopeless, but a tragic worldview allows us to see glimmers of hope in the broader context of history. Tragic cycles come and go. Tragedy will always be part of the human experience, but because it is linked to the choices that individuals make, individual actions can either shorten or prolong it. The key to breaking the cycle is to move social discourse away from the quest for vengeance (often mislabeled "justice"), to the goal of building a society together with one's former enemies. For this to happen in Ukraine, the government would need to embrace three postulates:

First, that *being a Russophile Ukrainian does not mean being anti-Ukrainian.* Greek tragedy tells us that to achieve social harmony, one must be willing to treat one's enemy with the same honor that one seeks for one's self. This truism is not based on abstract morality, but on the practical calculation that fair and equal treatment is the most binding of all social ties.

Second, that *punishing Russia (or the West, for that matter) does not mean healing Ukraine.* It is an axiom of international politics that no country has ever prospered by making an enemy of a more powerful neighbor. Moreover, countries that obsess over their national identity and security, often wind up losing both.

Third, that *social harmony in Ukraine can only be established by Ukrainians* themselves. External actors have their own agenda, which will rarely, if ever, coincide with the interests of Ukraine. To establish lasting social harmony Ukrainians will have to overcome their fear of their own diversity, and be willing to call upon their entire history and culture, both Galician and Maloross.

But perhaps the most important lesson that the tragic view of politics has to impart is that the pursuit of total victory over one's enemies can only breed renewed conflict. Herein lies a crucial difference between an incomplete revolution, one that is forever in search of perfect justice and is therefore forever doomed to repeat itself, and a revolution that has completed its cycle. Over time, the latter can bring society to a point of healing and rest, because it sees the suffering of those who opposed the revolution as a common tragedy, rather than as a justification for more revolution and more suffering. The tragic cycle of

Ukraine will therefore end when Ukrainians realize that a completed revolution is a revolution of compassion and dignity that views all Ukrainians, regardless of religion, language, or cultural heritage, as indispensable to the Ukrainian nation.

Index

Note: Page numbers in bold indicate tables; page numbers following "n" refer to footnotes.

Act of Ukrainian Sovereignty (1990) 70–71, 75
Act of Unification (Akt Zluki) 54, 55, 272
Aeschylus 4, 9, 26, 30, 32, 125
Agamemnon (play by Aeschylus) 8–9, 24, 25
agnorisis (recognition) 23
agon (struggle) 23
Ajax (play by Sophocles) 5–7
Aksyonov, S. 188, 190, 191
Alford C. F. 22
Allison, G. 233
anagnorisis 30, 136
Andromache (play by Euripides) 9
Andrukhovych, Yu. 201
Anhalt, E. K. 248, 249
Anti-Terrorist Operation (ATO) 1, 210–213, 225–226
Antigone (play by Sophocles) 4–5, 7–8, 264–265
Antonovich, V. 46
"Appeal to Russian Co-citizens" 76
Applebaum, A. 121–122
Arendt, H. 13–14, 17, 17n62, 120, 128, 249, 253
Aristophanes 5
Armstrong, J. 61
Arrowsmith, W. 9
Austro-Hungarian Empire 44, 53
– culture cleansing pattern in Galicia under 164–165
– "Eastern Policy" 49–50
– Galician Ukraine under 48–51
Autonomous Crimean Republic (ACR) 180
"Autonomous Southeastern Ukrainian Republic" 206
Avakov, A. **117**, 175, 189, 267
Azarov, N. 90
Azov battalion 97, 107, 114, 241

Babin, B. 201
Bader, V. 135

Bakharev, K. 187
Bakke, K. 197n73, 198, 230n22
Bandera, S. 36, 60, 62n72, 64n79, 68, 83, 90, 94n19, 98n35, 115, 120
Bax, E. B. 134
Beard, M. 248–249
Berdnyk, M. 248
Berdyaev, N. 57
Beria, L. 66
Biletsky, A. 97
Black Sea Fleet Agreement 82, 175n5, 190–191, 192
Blok, A. 201
Boisto Agenda 233, 234
Bojanowska, E. 165
Bolsheviks 56, 65
Bond, R. 31
Boyd, C. 260n110
Brands, H. 19, 20
Brenton, T. 233
Brotherhood of Saints Cyril and Methodius 45
Brzezinski, Z. 266
Bulatov, D. 99
Burjanadze, N. 196n71
Butterfield, H. 16
Buzan, B. 264

C14 (paramilitary groups) 113
Capture of Miletus (Phrynichus) 11
Carr, E. H. 16
Carter, J. 196n71
catharsis (cleansing) 9, 10, 23–24, 20, 29, 30, 247–250, 252, 254, 263, 270
Catholicism 49
Center for East European and International Studies (ZOiS) 198
Chekhov, A. 44
Chemakin, A. 48n29
Chernovol, T. 211n16
Chesterton, G. K. 132, 134

https://doi.org/10.1515/9783110743371-011

Chornovil, V. 77–78, 272
Christian realism 20
Chryssavgis, J. 251
Chubinsky, P. 45n19
Clusters Approach 228–229
Cohen, S. F. 233
Collective Security Treaty Organization
  (CSTO) 174
Commonwealth of Independent States (CIS)
  85, 147
Communist party elite (nomenklatura) 70, 71,
  72
Communist Party of Soviet Union (CPSU) 71
Communist Party of Ukraine 72–73, 208
Congress of Severodonetsk 206–208
Copenhagen School of Security Studies 264
Cossacks 41, 42–43, 55
Council of the Gentry (Zemsky Sobor) 41–42
COVAX consortium 137
CoviShield vaccine 138, 140
Crimea 174–175, 179, 269
– 1992 Crimean Constitution 182, 193
– ACR 180
– assessing legitimacy of annexation of
  192–201
– de facto nationalization 244
– failure of interim government to respond
  Russia's intervention 188–190
– "Law on Forgiveness" for inhabitants
  261–262
– quest for autonomy 178–186
– referendum to restore Constitution 187–
  188, 191
– regional identity 183
– Russian Black Sea Fleet 192
– Russian military incursion in 186–188
Crimean Autonomous Republic (CAR) 193n66
Critchley, S. 1, 21, 23, 31
"Croatian Scenario" for Donbass 231
Croatian Ustashi case 62–63
Crocker, D. 260, 260n110
Czapliński, D. 41

Danilov, O. 207, 229
D'Estaigne, V.G. 196n71
Declaration of Rights of Nationalities of Uk-
  raine 76n110

Deep and Comprehensive Free Trade Area
  (DCFTA) 145–146
Denikin, A. 47, 55
Dietz, M. 130, 135
Dionysia (festival of Athens) 3–5, 24, 254
Directorate 54, 55
Donbass 174–175, 178, 208–210, 269
– Anti-Terrorist Operation 210–213
– Congress of Severodonetsk 206–208
– DKR 203–204
– Donetsk and Lugansk Referenda 212
– Donetsk Referendum and Lugansk Opinion
  Poll 205
– growth of 201–202
– historical characteristics 202–203
– "Law on Forgiveness" for inhabitants
  261–262
– revolt in 213–220
– rise of Donbass regionalism 204–206
Donetsk-Krivoi Rog Soviet Republic (DKR)
  203–204
Donetsk People's Republic (DPR) 207, 208
Donetsk Regional Soviet 204, 205
Donetsk Strike Committee 204
Dontsov, D. 57, 60, 62n72, 94n19, 105n56,
  175
Dover, K. 31
Dovzhenko, A. 247–248
Drahomanov, M. 45n19, 48, 270
dual citizenship 217n146
Dubinyanski, M. 223
Durnovo, P. N. 37
Dynkin, A. 233–234
Dzyuba, I. 67

Eagleton, T. 13
Eckstein, H. 33
Edel, C. 19, 20
ekstasis 23
energy policy of Ukraine 151, 158–163
Enraged: Why Violent Times Need Ancient
  Greek Myths (Anhalt) 248
episteme 21n78
EU Association Agreement 85, 86, 145–147
Euben, J. P. 10, 22
Eumenides (play by Aeschylus) 9, 125
Euripides 4, 6n19, 9, 10, 10, 21

Far Right in Ukrainian politics 90, 111–114, 266
- electricity supply blockade to Crimea 149
- eternal vigilance 107–108
- expanding influence in Ukrainian politics 119–120
- lack of political and ideological boundaries 113
- modern Ukrainian nationalism 114–115
- organizational and military preparedness 106–107
- political and ideological continuity 115–116
- Poroshenko on Ukrainian Fifth Column 108, **109–110**
- pro-Maidan forces on 217–218
- promoting ideological innovation in government 107
- Revolution of Dignity 119
- Right Sector 94–106
- role of Rukh 112–113
- Svoboda Party 91–94
- Ukrainian Officials on Treasonous Nature of Maloross Ukrainians **116–118**
Federal Agency for Ethnic Affairs 198
Fedotov, G. P. 223
Fedotov, Yu. 193n68
Feldman, A. 122
Ferguson, J. 6n19
Filaret of Kiev 170, 172
First Minsk Accords (Minsk-1) 213, 226
Flynn, M. K. 206n105
foreign debt restructuring of Ukraine 152–153
foreign direct investment (FDI) 154
forgiveness 23, 26, 30, 41, 125, 272
"Forum for Donbass" 238
Franco, F. 258
Franko, I. 45n19, 48
Frattini, F. 234n35
Frost, M. 18
Fukuyama, F. 129

Galicia see Galician Ukraine
Galician-Maloross divide 84
Galician Assembly in western Ukraine 205

Galician nationalist-oriented regime in Kiev 247
Galician Ukraine/Ukrainians 36–37, 118, 120
- under Austro-Hungarian Rule 48–51
- culture cleansing pattern in 164–165
- debate over origins 37–40
- demand for justice 273
- fear of losing identity 125
- Galician-inspired Ukrainian nationalists 247
- Galician ideal 50–51
- impact of 1991 independence 70–73
- Maidan impact 83–89
- need of reconciliation 247
- Orange Revolution impact 79–83
- and OUN 59–64
- requirement for restoring agency in 269
- responses to collapse of Empires 51–57
- restoring faith in social institutions in 125
- and Ukrainianization 65–70
- unrest under Polish Rule 57–59
Gershman, C. 266
"Glazyev Tapes" 217n146
global citizenship 128–129
Gogol, N. 44, 165
Goldhill, S. 5
Gołuchowski, A. R. 50
Gontareva, V. 148, 149n99
Gorbachev, M. 70–71, 77, 179–180
Graham, T. 233
Greek tragedy, classical 125, 224, 249–250, 273
- *Agamemnon* 25
- *Ajax* 6–7
- *Antigone* 7–8
- Athena's strategy for social harmony 29–31
- *Dionysia* as political institution in 3–5
- *Kindly Ones*, The 27–29
- *Libation Bearers* 25–26
- *mimesis* of reality 33–34
- vs. modern political realism 16–21
- impact of modern politics 11–16
- *Oresteia* trilogy 8–11
- political lessons of Oresteia 25
- *Prometheus Bound* 6
- role of modern politics 21–23

– as social therapy 23–24
– study of 2
Grosby, S. 128
Guatemalan Historical Clarification Commission (CEH) 256–258
Gubarev, P. 208, 209, 210
Guzhva, I. 72, 73, 88

Habermas, J. 133, 135
Habsburg Monarchy of Austro-Hungary *see* Austro-Hungarian Empire
Hahn, G. M. 57n55, 63n76, 83n133, 85n140m, 86n144, 89n154, 93n15, 100n38, 102n47
hamartia 10, 20
Hardline approach 232–233
"Heavenly Hundred, The" 88n150, 99
Hecabe (play by Euripides) 21
Hechter, M. 134
Heletey, V. 213
Herodotus 11
Hobson, J. A. 134
Homer 5, 249
Honcharuk, O. 113
Hrabovskyi, S. 66
Hroysman, V. 231
Hrushevsky, M. 39–40, 46–48, 49, 56
Hrytsak, Ya. 127n7
hubris 10, 31
Hughes, J. 202

idiotes 31
Ignatieff, M. 17, 129
Iliad, The (Homer) 5, 249
Ilyin, Yu. 184n33
Innocent, Abbot 38–39
Institute of History of Ukrainian Academy of Sciences 64
Institute of National Memory (INP) 64, 82, 124, 127, 221n154
Interdvizhenie 204
International Court of Justice (ICJ) 193, 194
Internationalism or Russification (Dzyuba) 67
Isaacs, W. 250
Ishchenko, V. 94, 95n22, 113
– comparing Svoboda and Right Sector 94–95

– steps for Ukrainian national revolution 95–96
Ivanishin, V. 114

Johnson, L. 15
Józewski, H. 58
"July 16th Initiative–For a Common Future" 239, 252

Kalachova, H. 153
Karasyov, V. 124
Karlin, A. 183
Katz, E. A. 11
Kedourie, E. 128
Kennan, Jr., G. F. 16, 19, 233
Kennedy, J. F. 268
Kerch Straits incident 176
Kharitonov, A. 209–210
Kharkov 45, 55, 207
Khmelnitsky, B. 37, 40, 41–43, 46, 47, 67
Khomchak, R. 231–232
Khrushchev, N. 66, 68
Khvylevoi, N. 65
Kievan Patriarchate (KP) 82, 170
Kievan Synopsis (Innocent) 39
Kiev International Institute of Sociology (KIIS) 83–84
Kindly Ones, The (Eumenides) (play by Aeschylus) 8, 24, 27–29
Kiselyova, N. 183
Kiselyov, E. 98
Kissinger, H. 37n6, 233
Kistiakovsky, B. 270
Kivalov-Kolesnichenko Law 76, 84
Klein, N. 151
Klichko, V. 92, 101
Klimkin, P. 229, 232
Klusmeyer, D. 20
Koltunovich, A. 161
Konovalets, E. 59, 63n74, 94n19
Konstantinov, V. 193
Korchinsky, D. 185
korenizatiia process 56–57
Kornilov, V. 36, 206
Kostomarov, N. 45, 46
Kotlyarevski, I. 44, 66
Kovalevsky, M. 270

Kralyuk, P. 66, 67
Krasner, S. 80
Kravchenko, S. 138
Kravchuk, L. 36, 70–72, 76, 79, 120, 143, 205, 206n105, 261
Kremin, T. 169, 236
Kuchma, L. xiii, 37, 72, 78, 144, 181, 205–206, 206n105, 207n109, 212n131, 214n135, 228n15, 237
Kudelia, S. 216, 216n145, 217n146
Kuleba, D. 137, 177n13, 197n73, 232
Kwasniewski, A. 80, 196n71

Lane, D. 113
Lavrov, S. 225
"Law on Forgiveness" for inhabitants 261
Lebow, R. N. xiii, 11n35, 13, 15n54n56, 16, 20–24, 33n106, 35n110, 132
legal justice 262
Lenkavsky, S. 91
"Lesser" Rus 51n39
Libation Bearers, The (play by Aeschylus) 8, 24, 25–26
Little Poland see Malopolska
Livingstone, R. W. 30, 32
Lorca, G. 260n110
Lugansk 207
Lukash, E. 89n155, 102n44
Lutsenko, Yu. 117
Lyamets, S. 153

Maidan see Revolution of Dignity
Makhno, N. 202–203, 208
Malopolska 53
Malorossiyan ideal 51
Maloross Ukraine/Ukrainians 36–37, 108, 118, 220
– 1991 independence, impact of 70–73
– cultural identity 163–164
– debate over origins of Rus 37–40
– decrease of political rights of 178
– demand for justice 273
– Far Right, impact of rise of 111–112
– fear of losing identity 125
– identity of Ukraine 50
– Maidan impact 83–89, 178
– need of reconciliation 247
– Orange Revolution impact 79–83
– and OUN 59–64
– and Party of Regions 74–76
– permanent shift mentality in 268
– requirement for restoring agency in 269
– responses to collapse of Empires 51–57
– restoring faith in social institutions in 125
– and Rukh 77–79
– Russian culture for 165
– under Russian Rule 44–48
– Ukraine's industrial base, impact of dismantling 158
– and Ukrainianization 65–70
– Ukrainian Officials on Treasonous Nature of **116–118**
– "utter foreignness" of 264
Marchuk, E. 185
Mariupol 27
Markov, D. A. 49n33
Martial law 226–227
Masterman, C. F. G. 134
Matios, A. 111, 245
Matlock, Jr., J. F. 233
Mazepa, I. 43, 43n18, 49n34, 46, 51, 67
Mearsheimer, J. J. 175n5, 233
Medvedchuk, V. 137, 212, 212n131, 237–238, 246
Medvedev, D. 145
Melnyk, A. 59
Merkel, A. 196n72
Meshkov, Yu. 181
Metropolitan of Kiev 170
Metropolitan Onufriy 172
Mikhailova, O. 127
Mikhnovsky, M. 52n40
Minsk Accords 224, 239
– failure of 265
– Minsk-1, 226
– Minsk-2, 226–229, 264
Mironenko, O. 76n112
Mogiloyv, A. 182
Molotov-Ribbentrop Pact 61
Montt, E. R. 257
Morel, P. 227
Morel Plan 227
Morgenthau, H. J. 13–15, 17, 19, 120, 127, 128, 249, 253

Morris, W. 134
Moscow Patriarchate (MP) 170
Mosiychuk, I. 185
Moskal, G. **116**, 120n111, 221n154, 231n25
Munich Security Conference 241
Murayev, E. 120
Muscovy 40, 47, 164
"Museum of Overcoming Russia's Aggression against Ukraine" 245
Muzhenko, V. 189

Nalyvaichenko, V. 65n79, 83, 105, 189, 211n126
Nasha Ukraina (Yushchenko) 92
Natiocracy (Stsiborskyi) 93
National Center for Development of Peace 245
National Institute for Strategic Research (NISS) 170
nationalism 124–125, 131, 163, 247
– characteristics of state-sponsored 128
– forms of social solidarity 125
– influencing government policies 126–128
– moving beyond 252–253
– natio or birthplace 129–130
– need of global citizenship for 128–129
– problems with 120–123
– tragedy of 14–15
Nationalism (Dontsov) 57
national patriotic education 113–114
National Platform for Reconciliation and Unity 224, 240–243
National Reparations Program 257
National Security and Defense Council (NSDC) 229
National Self-defense battalions 92
National Socialism 128
Nation and Revolution (Yarosh) 105
Nayem, M. 200
Nestor the Chronicler 39
Niebuhr, R. 13, 16. 19, 20, 127, 249, 253
Nietzsche, F. 259n107
North Atlantic Treaty Organization (NATO): Action Plan 81
– membership for Ukraine 175
Northern Ireland Agreement 271n137
Novavax vaccine 138

Novinsky, V. 148, 223, 238–239
Novorossiya 208, 208n114
Nussbaum, M. 135
Nyomensky, O. 67–68

Oakeshott, M. 18
Odessa 45, 50, 57n54, 84, 87n148, 104n54, 107n63, 208n114, 217, 221n154
Oedipus at Colonus (play by Sophocles) 9
O'Loughlin, J. 197n73, 198, 230n22
Omelyan, V. 90, 161–162
Onatsky, E. 62, 64
Opposition Bloc-For Life 238
Opposition Bloc 117
Orange Revolution 79–83, 113, 163, 206 see also Revolution of Dignity
Oresteia trilogy (play by Aeschylus) 8–11, 25, 30
Organization of Ukrainian Nationalists (OUN) 58, 59, 97
– alliance with Axis powers 62
– anti-Russian policy 61
– failures to achieve Ukrainian independence 63–64
– ideology of 60
– integral nationalism of 61
– role in World War II 63
– Stsiborskyi Constitution 61
Organization of Ukrainian Nationalists-Ukrainian Insurgent Army (OUN-UPA) 63, 83, 91
Orlyk Constitution 43n18
Orthodox Church in Ukraine (OCU) 172, 240
Orwell, G. 126, 133
OSCE Special Monitoring Mission 225
OUN-affiliated Center for Study of Liberation Movement 82
Our Soviet Ukraine (Shelest) 67

Pacto de Olvido 258
Papua-New Guinea–Bougainville Agreement 271n137
Party of Regions 74–76, 81, 84, 88, 208, 214n135
Parubiy, A. 87, 92, 97n31, 116, 172n182
Pascual, C. 80
Pashinsky, S. 191, 211n126

Pashkina, T. 155
patriotism 124–125, 224
– advantages of 132–134
– as antidote to nationalism 131
– disadvantages of 135–136
– distinctiveness from nationalism 129
– forms of social solidarity 125
– patria or homeland 129–130, 131
– shift to civic identity 131
Pavlenko, R. 171
Pavlyk, M. 48
peace efforts in Ukraine 223–224
– Boisto Agenda 233–234
– building shared values through dialogue
  250–252
– flaws of peace process 246
– Geneva Agreement 224–225
– Hardline approach 232–233, 235
– Minsk Accords 226–232
– moving beyond nationalism 252–253
– Pragmatic approach 233, 235
– rejecting rage and embracing catharsis
  247–250
peace proposals in Ukraine, domestic 235–
  236
– "July 16th Initiative–For a Common Future"
  239
– Medvedchuk and Novinsky plans 237–239
– National Platform for Reconciliation and
  Unity 240–243
– "People for Peace" initiative 239–240
– Reznikov Plan 244–246
Peloponnesian War, The (Thucydides) 16, 132
"People for Peace" initiative 239–240
People's Democratic Party of Ukraine 48
People's Movement of Ukraine (Rukh) 77–79
peripeteia (wanderings) 23
Persians, The (play by Aeschylus) 5
Petlyura, S. 49n34, 54, 272
Petrushevich, E. 49n33
Phoenician Women (play by Euripides) 4
Phrynichus 11
Pifer, S. 32n102, 232
Pirro, R. C. 13
Plato 12
Podolyak, M. 223
Pogrebinsky, M. 124

Poland 49
Poltava, Battle of 51
Pompeo, M. 194
Ponomaryov, S. V. 209n118
Poole, R. 131
"Popular Movement in Support of Perestroi-
  ka" 77
Poroshenko, P. 65, 75, 90, 108, 117–118,
  144, 148, 159, 176, 212, 213, 237, 272
– abandonment of Geneva Agreement 225–
  226
– banked on nationalism 251
– on Ukrainian Fifth Column 108, **109–110**
Portnikov, V. 73, 269
Portnov, A. 214
Poryakov, S. 99
Poturayev, N. **117, 124**
Power, S. 213–214
Pragmatic approach 233–234
Primachenko, Y. 64
Prodanchuk, N. 138
Progressive Socialist Party of Ukraine 208
Prometheus Bound (play by Aeschylus) 6
Promotion of National Unity and Reconcilia-
  tion Act (1995) 254
Prystaiko, V **116**
Purgin, A. 207
Putin, V. 32n104, 104, 137, 174, 187, 190,
  192, 207, 211, 213, 237, 266, 269
Pyatt, G. 157

Radutsky, M. 137, 140
Rajoy, M. 259
Rasevich, V. 116n93
Rasmussen, A. F. 232
Red Army 55–56, 203
Regional Economic Self-government (REK)
  204–205
Rengger, N. 20
Republic, The (Plato) 12
Reva, A. **117**
Revolutionary Ukrainian Party 52n40
Revolution of Dignity 1, 83–89, 92, 113, 119,
  145, 177, 185, 214 see also Orange Revo-
  lution
– in Maloross Ukraine 178

– role of Right Sector during and after 98–
    106
Reznikov, O. **116**, 141, 200, 244
Reznikov Plan 244–246
Riabchuk, M. xiii-xiv, 127n7
Rice, C. 80
Right Sector *see also* Far Right in Ukrainian
    politics; Svoboda (Freedom Party)
– civic and social organizations creation
    105–106
– creation of volunteer battalions 102–103,
    104–105
– formation of 98n35
– "Heavenly Hundred, The", killing of 99–
    100
– ideological oversight of Ukrainian govern-
    ment 103–104
– Ishchenko's views on 94–96
– maintaining functional autonomy 105
– regional militia units 98
– role in 2014 Maidan 98
– seizure of control of border crossings with
    Crimea 149–150
– social media influence 100–101
– as supra-institutional 105
– vs. Svoboda Party 94–95
– tactical act of Ukrainian media 97
– Yarosh's role 95–96
Robinson, P. 216n142, 217n146, 227n12
Romanov, A. 41
Rukh 91, 112–113
Rus 164
– "Greater" and "Lesser" Rus 51n39
– origins of 37–40
Russian Orthodox Church 170, 171
Russia(n)/Russian Empire: 2014 and 2022 in-
    terventions to Ukraine 178
– banks closing in Ukraine 154
– colonialism 86
– culture for Ukraine 165–169
– as Eternal Enemy by Galician narrative
    222
– as Eternal Partner by Maloross narrative
    222
– geopolitical conflicts 266–267
– Maloross Ukraine under 44–48
– military incursion in Crimea 186–188, 190

– military intervention in Ukraine 224
– objective on world order 266
– story of Ukraine joining in 40–43
– Ukraine's economic relations with 145–
    152
Russian Soviet Federative Socialist Republic
    (RSFSR) 142
"Russian Spring (2014)" 207
Russophile Ukrainians 45n19, 107, 108, 126,
    270

Sajdik Initiative 227–228
Sajdik, M. 227
Sakwa, R. 84n138, 88n153m, 107n61,
    143n75, 145n81, 146n86
Sarkozy, N. 196n71
Sasse, G. 179n16, 191, 198, 230n22
Savchenko, N. 237
Savitsky, P. 57
Schaar, J. H. 135
Schröder, G. 195n71
Schmidt, H. 195n71
Second Minsk Accords (Minsk-2) 226–227
– Clusters Approach 228–229
– failure of 229–232
– Morel Plan 227
– Sajdik Initiative 227–228
– Second Minsk Protocol 213
– Steinmeier Formula 228
Security Service of Ukraine (SBU) 216n140
Semenchenko, S. 118
Senchenko, A. 261, 262
Shcherbitsky, V. 67
Shelest, P. 66–67
Shevchenko, T. 44, 45, 66
Shishatsky, A. 209
Shklyar, V. 201
Shock Doctrine, The (Klein) 151
Shufrich, N. 212, 212n131
Shulgin, V. 46, 47–48, 56
Shumsky, A. 65
Sikorski, R. 196n71
Sikorsky, I. 45n19
Sinovac Biotech 137
Sinovac vaccine 139, 140
Sivokho, S. 240–243, 245, 246, 251–252
Skoropadsky, P. 54, 203

Skrypnik, N. 65, 66, 203
Smena vekh movement 57
Smolin, M. 51n39
Sobolev, Yu. 97
Social Nationalist Party of Ukraine 82
Social-National Party of Ukraine (SNPU) 91, 92
Sophocles 6–7, 9, 264–265
Southeastern Ukrainian Republic 207
Spain, Truth Commission in 258–259
Sputnik V vaccine 137, 138, 139, 141
State Archives of the Security Services of Ukraine (SBU) 83
Stavitsky, E. 147
Steinmeier Formula 228
Steinmeier, F-W. 228
Stepanov, M. 136–137, 139, 140
Strengthening Electoral Administration in Ukraine Project (SEAUP) 81
Stsiborskyi Constitution 61
Stsiborskyi, M. 60
Styazhkina, E. 231
Subtelny, O. 44n13, 61n70, 68n91
Sulnikova, O. 188
Suppliants, The (play by Aeschylus) 4
Suppliant Women (play by Euripides) 9, 10
Surylov, A. 208
surzhyk 74
Svoboda (Freedom Party) 91–94, 106 *see also* Right Sector
– into liberal Euromaidan coalition 98
– political and media influence 96
– vs. Right Sector 94–95
– social media influence 100–101
Syroyid, O. 100

Tagliavini, H. 212n131
Talbott, S. 232
Tamir, Y. 129
tariff rate quotas (TRQs) 157
tekne 21n78
Tenyukh, I. 186n38, 189
Teutonic Wolfsangel 91–92
theaomai (theater in Greek) 4
Thompson, K. W. 16
Thucydides 16, 132
Toal, G. 197n73, 198, 230n22

Tokman, V. 170, 171
Tolochko, P. 174
"Tornado" battalion 103, 120n111
"total Ukrainianization" plan 65, 75
Toth, S. 132–133
tragedy and healing, cycle of **126**
Tragic Vision of Politics, The (Lebow) 16
Trilateral Contact Group (TCG) 228
Trojan Women, The (play by Euripides) 4
Troyan, V. 107
Trump, D. 196n71, 234
Truth and Reconciliation Commissions (TRC) 253–254
– Guatemalan CEH 256–258
– propagation of liberal values and human rights 270
– in South Africa 254–256
– in Spain 258–259
– in transitional justice 260–265
– Ukrainian 270, 271
Tuhan-Baranovsky, M. 270
Tuka, G. **117**, 120n111, 150, 221n154, 236n40
Turchynov, O. 88, 189, 102n44, 188n48, 189, 190n53, 209–213, 231n25
Tutu, D. 254–255, 256, 260, 271–273
Tyahnybok, O. 92, 93, 96, **118**, 184n33
ubuntu concept 260
Ukrainian Autocephalous Orthodox Church (UAOC) 61, 170
Ukrainian Communist Party (UCP) 70, 204
Ukrainian Constitution (1996) 75, 174
"Ukrainian Formula for Peace" 238
"Ukrainian Independent and Conciliar State (*Ukrainskoi Samostiynoi Sobornoi Derzhavy*)" 114
Ukrainian Insurgent Army (UPA) 58, 84
Ukrainianization 58, 65, 220
– electoral divisions in Ukraine 69–70, 69
– national museums for Ukrainian folklore and architecture 67
– official goal of 66
– periodic resurgence of 67–68
– role of Shelest 66
– Soviet Ukrainian consensus 69
Ukrainian Military Organization (UVO) 59, 97
Ukrainian National Self-defense (UNSO) 91, 97

Ukrainian Orthodox Church (UOC (KP)) 170, 171, 172
Ukrainian Orthodox Church (UOC (MP)) 170, 171, 172, 238, 240
Ukrainian People's Republic 52, 53, 54
Ukrainian Revolution: XXI Century (Yarosh) 95
Ukrainian Security Services (SBU) 211n16
Ukrainian Soviet Republic 55–56, 65–70, 179–180, 203
Ukrainian/Ukraine 38–39, 171 see also peace efforts in Ukraine
- benefits of Soviet rule for 67–68
- closing of Russian banks in 154
- complexities in 1991 independence 70–73
- conflicts with Russia 1–2, 33–4, 163–165, 175–176, 235
- consequences of economic nationalism 142–145
- debt repayment schedule **153**
- *de facto* bilingualism 74–75
- difficulty with nationalism 32
- economic relations with Russia and DCFTA 145–152
- electoral divisions in 69–70, 69
- fascism 113
- Fifth Column 108, **109–110, 117**
- foreign debt restructuring 152–153
- Greek-Catholic Church 61
- hostility toward Russia 267–268
- importance of Ukrainian language development 75, **75**
- independence 112
- language speaking in 168
- liberalism 270
- nationalist struggle to vaccinate 136–142
- NATO membership issue 175
- private transfers compared to FDI 155
- problems arise when using conflicts with Russia 176–178
- problems with nationalism 120–123
- receiving Russian citizenship **156**
- religious identity 169
- responsibility of government to restore peace 273
- restoration of political agency and sovereignty to 272
- Russian culture for 165–169
- Russia's military intervention in 224
- social consciousness 32–3
- solution to 220–222
- spiritual totalitarianism 60, 93
- State Church for Ukrainian Nation 170–172
- story of joining in Russian Empire 40–43
- strategic de-industrialization of 157–158
- struggling to combine economic and security integration 174
- suicide economics and energy policy of 151, 158–163
- tragic nature of internal crisis 31–2
- transitional justice 260–265
- TRC 270, 271
- worker exodus and population loss in 154–156
Ukrainka, L. 66
Umerov, I. 200
Umland, A. 216–217
Union for Liberation of Ukraine 49
United Nations Development Program (UNDP) 183
United States (US) 230, 267
- American exceptionalism 121
- civic nationalism 129
- objective on world order 266
Universal of National Unity 81, 82
V
Vasylenko, M. 270
Venediktova, I. 88n150
Vernadsky, V. 45n19, 270
Vershbow, A. 232
Vinnichenko, V. 54, 56
Viroli, M. 121n116, 128n14, 131, 135
Vladislav IV 41
Volga, V. 90
Volker, K. 230n20
Volyn Program 58–59
Vovk, V. 90
Vyatrovych, V. 83, 84, 221n154
Vydrin, D. 1
Vynnychenko, V. 36
Waever, O. 264
Watson, J. H. A. 16

Western Ukrainian People's Republic (ZUNR)
53 – 55
White Russians in west 38 – 39
Wiles, P. 151
Williams, R. 13, 31, 126
Women of Troy (Euripides) 9 – 10
Yahun, V. **118**
Yanukovych, V. 81, 84 – 85, 98, 144, 184n33,
186, 187, 206, 207
– refusal to sign Association Agreement
85 – 86
– resignation from presidential power 88,
106
– strategy of playing off EU and Russia
146 – 147
Yarosh, D. 94n19, 95, 99n36, 102n45, 103 –
105, 111n79, 114n90, 115, 210, 211n126
Yaryomenko, B. 228n15

Yatsenyuk, A. 88, 92, 96n28
Yeltsin, B. 71
Yermak, A. 176, 229
Yermolaev, A. 111n77, 125, 207, 243n64, 248
Yushchenko, V. 37, 74, 75, 76n112, 81 – 83,
92, **118**, 144, 164, 168, 174, 201, 207,
267

Zakharchenko, A. 208
Zaporozhian Cossack Assembly 40
Zdioruk, S. 170, 171
Zelensky, V. 75, 90, 111, 144, 162, 172, 237,
238, 241, 269
Zhebrivsky, P. 108n65, 112n82, **118**, 150,
176n8, 231n25, 246n76
Zubyuk, P. 174
Zurabov, M. 212n131